TO KILL A PEOPLE

Genocide in the Twentieth Century

JOHN COX

New York   Oxford
OXFORD UNIVERSITY PRESS

Oxford University Press is a department of the University of Oxford.
It furthers the University's objective of excellence in research,
scholarship, and education by publishing worldwide.

Oxford   New York
Auckland ' Cape Town   Dar es Salaam   Hong Kong   Karachi
Kuala Lumpur   Madrid   Melbourne   Mexico City   Nairobi
New Delhi   Shanghai   Taipei   Toronto

With offices in
Argentina   Austria   Brazil   Chile   Czech Republic   France   Greece
Guatemala   Hungary   Italy   Japan   Poland   Portugal   Singapore
South Korea   Switzerland   Thailand   Turkey   Ukraine   Vietnam

For titles covered by Section 112 of the US Higher Education
Opportunity Act, please visit www.oup.com/us/he for the
latest information about pricing and alternate formats.

Published by Oxford University Press
198 Madison Avenue, New York, New York 10016
http://www.oup.com

Library of Congress Cataloging-in-Publication Data

Cox, John M., 1963- author.
    To kill a people : genocide in the twentieth century / John Cox.
        pages cm
    Includes bibliographical references and index.
    ISBN 978-0-19-023647-2 (pbk.)
    1. Genocide--History--20th century. I. Title.
    HV6322.7.C69 2017
    364.15'10904--dc23

                                    2015027825

CONTENTS

LIST OF MAPS

LIST OF FIGURES

ACKNOWLEDGMENTS

I'll start in an unusual fashion: by apologizing to the many colleagues, friends, and students I am surely forgetting. Any decent book is to some degree a collective effort, and I am fortunate to have profited from the selfless assistance of many, many people. I am deeply grateful for the generous support and feedback of several of the world's top genocide experts. Drs. Uğur Ümit Üngör and Ronald Grigor Suny took the time to read the Armenian chapter and spare me some embarrassment; Christopher Browning and Ed Westermann helped me sharpen my analysis, and detected a handful of errors, in the Holocaust chapter; Craig Etcheson as well as Ben Kiernan performed similar services for the chapter on Cambodia; and my colleague Beth Whitaker shared her considerable expertise on Rwanda and east Africa. Adam Jones somehow found the time, between writing his twentieth or thirtieth book, to carefully read the entire manuscript and was also gracious in offering some of his masterful photographs. Thomas Pegelow-Kaplan helped likewise, sans photos, as did David Crowe. For any factual or interpretative errors that slipped through, please blame me alone.

I appreciate the generosity and professionalism of the research staffs at the Institute for War, Holocaust, and Genocide Studies (NIOD) in Amsterdam; Kigali's genocide center; the Wiener Library for the Study of the Holocaust and Genocide in London; and especially the Jack, Joseph, and Morton Mandel Center for Advanced Holocaust Studies at the Holocaust museum (USHMM) in Washington. This book also benefitted enormously from fellowships and symposia at the USHMM in the summers of 2012 and 2013, and from feedback I received at conferences of the International Network of Genocide Scholars, the Holocaust Educational Foundation of Northwestern, the World History Association, and the University of Zaragoza. I have also found inspiration as well as valuable ideas each summer at the annual Holocaust symposia at Appalachian State University. And thanks again, Rennie Brantz—the founder of ASU's Holocaust Studies Center—for setting me on this path lo' those many years ago.

Nicola Foote provided some astute insights to help refine my passages on Latin America, as well as helping me reconsider a fundamental topic: the relationships of various atrocities to one another. And, once again, Nicola: I'm sorry! (Inside joke.) My longtime friends and *compañeros* Will Cox and Tim Austin, as well as my UNC Charlotte colleagues Ritika Prasad, Jill Massino, and Oscar de la Torre, also deserve big "shout-outs" and *abrazos* for sharing their thoughts and for their support.

Charles Cavaliere, my editor at Oxford University Press, helped refine my prose and has been a great friend and ally for several years. I will be fortunate indeed to work with such an outstanding editor in the future. The other members of OUP's staff, as well as project manager Lori Bradshaw and copyeditor Leslie Anglin, also deserve the highest praise, as well as large pay raises. A few typos and errors always survive countless edits; some will perhaps survive, alongside the cockroaches, the destruction of the earth in a few years. This book followed a circuitous path to publication, and from the start Alfred Andrea has been immensely helpful and supportive, as well as wise and skillful in his editorial assistance. Your generous spirit and infectious *joie de vivre*, Al, sustained me through difficult times!

"Every historical question is a moral question," Yehuda Bauer remarked at a lecture in Chapel Hill many years ago. A work like this *should* be infused with this understanding, and with humanism as well as moral indignation. My father and mother, Richard Cox and Mary Alicia Cox, are largely responsible for imbuing me with a desire to contribute to a better world and for alerting me, from a very early age, to the evils of racism and bigotry. Not a small feat, in the southern United States during that time. Thanks also to the many wonderful students I have taught—and learned from—at Florida Gulf Coast University and at the University of North Carolina Charlotte while composing this book. Finally, let me express my eternal gratitude to my partner and soulmate, Louise Clark: A sustained study of humankind's follies and crimes can bring one low, but you always help me see the many beautiful and noble things in this world.

John Cox
Charlotte, North Carolina
January 2016

ABOUT THE AUTHOR

John Cox is an associate professor at the University of North Carolina Charlotte, where he directs the university's Center for Holocaust, Genocide & Human Rights Studies. He previously founded and directed a genocide studies center at Florida Gulf Coast University. Dr. Cox earned his PhD in history at the University of North Carolina at Chapel Hill in 2005. His first book, *Circles of Resistance: Jewish, Leftist, and Youth Dissidence in Nazi Germany*, was published in 2009. Dr. Cox serves on the steering committee of Historians Against the War and has written and lectured extensively on genocide, war crimes, resistance, and human rights. His current projects examine resistance inside Buchenwald concentration camp; the role of Jewish fighters in the Spanish Civil War; and resistance to genocidal and other authoritarian (regimes, period).

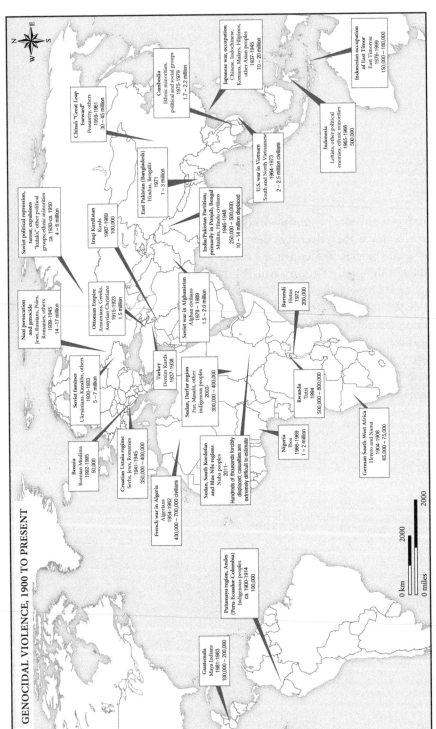

GENOCIDAL VIOLENCE, 1900 TO PRESENT

Soviet political repression, terror, expulsions
"kulaks," other political groups; ethnic minorities
ca. 1930-ca. 1950
4 – 6 million

China's "Great Leap Forward"
Peasantry, others
1959-1961
30 – 45 million

Cambodia
Ethnic minorities,
political and social groups
1975-1979
1.7 – 2.2 million

Japanese war, occupation
Chinese, Indochinese,
Koreans, Malays, Filipinos,
other Asian peoples
1937-1945
10 – 20 million

Indonesian occupation
of East Timor
East Timorese
1975-1999
150,000 – 180,000

Nazi persecution
and genocide
Jews, Russians, Poles,
Romanies, others
1939-1945
14 –17 million

East Pakistan (Bangladesh)
1971
Hindus, Bengalis
1 – 3 million

Iraqi Kurdistan
Kurds
1987-1989
100,000

U.S. war in Vietnam
South and North Vietnamese
1964-1973
2 – 2.5 million civilians

Indonesia
Leftists, other political
enemies, ethnic minorities
1965-1966
500,000

Soviet famines
Ukrainians, Kazakhs, others
1930-1933
5 – 7 million

Ottoman Empire
Armenians, Greeks,
Assyrian Christians
1915-1923
1.5 million

India/Pakistan Partition;
primarily in Punjab, Bengal
Muslim, Hindu civilians
1946-1948
250,000 – 500,000;
10 – 14 million displaced

Burundi
Hutus
1972
200,000

Bosnia
Bosnian Muslims
1992-1995
50,000

Turkey
Dersim Kurds
1937-1938

Soviet war in Afghanistan
Afghan civilians
1979 – 1989
1.5 – 2.0 million

Rwanda
Tutsi
1994
500,000 – 800,000

Croatian Ustaša regime
Serbs, Jews, Romanies
1941-1945
350,000-400,000

Sudan, Darfur region
Fur, Masalit, other
indigenous peoples
2003-
300,000 – 400,000

Nigeria
Ibos
1966-1969
1 – 2 million

German South-West Africa
Herero and Nama
1904-1908
65,000 – 75,000

French war in Algeria
Algerians
1954-1962
400,000 – 700,000 civilians

Sudan, South Kordofan
and Blue Nile regions
Nuba peoples
2011-
Hundreds of thousands forcibly
displaced; casualties are
extremely difficult to estimate

Putumayo region, Andes
(Peru-Ecuador-Colombia)
Indigenous peoples
ca. 1900-1914
100,000

Guatemala
Maya Indians
1981-1983
100,000 – 200,000

0 km   2000

0 miles   2000

Genocidal Violence, 1900 to the Present

Introduction
GENOCIDE AS A PRACTICE
AND A CONCEPT

ON OCTOBER 2, 1904, General Lothar von Trotha issued this proclamation to the Herero people of German South-West Africa:

> I, the great General of the German soldiers, address this letter to the Herero people. . . . The Herero are no longer German subjects. . . . You Herero people must now leave this land, it belongs to the German. If the populace does not do this I will force them with the cannon. Within the German borders every Herero, with or without a gun, with or without cattle, will be shot. I will no longer accept women and children, I will drive them back to their people or I will let them be shot at. These are my words to the Herero people.[1]

With those words, General von Trotha announced a policy of the murder and destruction of an entire people: in other words, genocide, to use a term that was later coined. At the end of his speech von Trotha turned his gaze toward thirty-five recently captured Herero, write the authors of an important study of this genocide. "On the general's orders, two of their number were dragged toward a makeshift gallows where they became victims" of what another officer "described in his diary as a 'theatrical hanging.'"[2] The following April, von Trotha reiterated this threat, declaring that rebellious Hereros suspected of killing whites "have by law forfeited their lives." Women and children uninvolved in any fighting should be treated likewise, von Trotha affirmed in a letter to the chief of the General staff in

---

[1]"Proklamation General von Trothas an das Volk der Herero," in Jürgen Zimmerer, *Von Windhuk nach Auschwitz? Beiträge zum Verhältnis von Kolonialismus und Holocaust* (Münster: LIT Verlag, 2011), 51–52. Translation by John Cox.
[2]David Olusoga and Casper W. Erichsen, *The Kaiser's Holocaust: Germany's Forgotten Genocide* (London: Faber and Faber, 2010), 150.

Berlin: "I deem it wiser for the entire nation to perish" than to attempt to hold any sick civilians or prisoners.[3]

A latecomer to the "scramble for Africa," which was ruthlessly pursued by Western European powers in the late nineteenth and early twentieth centuries, Germany had secured colonies in scattered regions of the continent. The Germans had gained control of South-West Africa—present-day Namibia—in 1884. As elsewhere, European rule provoked resistance, and in 1904 the Herero people revolted against the colonial authorities. The German administration and army responded with detentions in concentration camps, hangings, and shootings; and finally, by driving the remnants of the Herero into the parched Kalahari Desert, where most of the survivors then perished. By 1910, about 80 percent of the Herero people had been killed, while another 5 to 10 percent were driven into exile. The death toll was approximately 65,000 Herero plus roughly half the pre-genocide Nama population of 20,000.[4] This genocide marked the first use by the Germans of the term *Konzentrationslager* (concentration camp) and included the first "death camp"—designed specifically for mass killing; the concepts of "living space" (*Lebensraum*) and "war of annihilation," which guided the Holocaust, were introduced; and some individuals who orchestrated the murder of the Herero and Nama were later involved in the Nazi genocide.

This was not the first time European colonizers had unleashed indiscriminate violence upon their colonial subjects. Today, the concentration camp is linked in the public imagination solely to the Nazis. By the end of the first decade of the twentieth century, however, Western powers had already introduced the concentration camp for dissident elements opposing colonial rule in such places as Cuba (the Spaniards), South Africa (British authorities), the Philippines (US forces), and Germany's colony of South-West Africa. British and French airplanes also rained bombs upon "rebellious tribes" and helpless civilians in North Africa and the Middle East. But the German assault on the Herero and Nama heralded a more merciless response to colonial unrest and brought into the twentieth century an age-old ambition: to destroy an entire people. This ambition, coupled with modern technology and organization, created the "century of genocide" that this book chronicles.

A few short years later, the decaying Ottoman Empire attempted to destroy its Armenian population, the topic of Chapter 1. The architects of history's most notorious genocide—the Nazi Holocaust—borrowed tactics and strategies from the Herero and Armenian genocides. Post–World War II revelations of the extent and

---

[3]Manus I. Midlarsky, *The Killing Trap: Genocide in the Twentieth Century* (New York: Cambridge University Press, 2005), 32. In a November 1904 letter, von Trotha declared his intention to unleash "extreme terror and cruelty" in order to destroy "the rebellious tribes in rivers of blood." Quoted in Horst Dreschler, *Südwestafrika unter deutscher Kolonialherrschaft: Der Kampf der Herero und Nama gegen den deutschen Imperialismus (1884–1915)* (Berlin: Akademie-Verlag, 1984), 156. In 1933 Nazi authorities named a street in Munich, birthplace of their party, in Von Trotha's honor. It kept that name until 2006, when Munich's city government changed the name to "Herero Street."

[4]Olusoga and Erichsen, 228–230.

Hendrik Witbooi
Hendrik Witbooi (1830–1905) was a masterful political and military leader of the Nama people in German South-West Africa. After initially siding with the Germans, who employed a classic "divide and rule" policy in hopes of preventing Herero-Nama unity, Witbooi responded to an appeal from the Herero to rise against the colonizers. He organized a Nama uprising that began the day after General Von Trotha's infamous "annihilation order." Witbooi was killed in battle in October 1905.

barbarity of the Nazi regime's crimes provoked universal outrage and sincere but ineffectual calls for vigilance against the repetition of such horrors. This has not prevented genocidal outbreaks since World War II from South and Central America to Africa and the Middle East and to South and Southeast Asia. Genocide was not invented at the dawn of the "century of genocide," though: The genocidal impulse can be traced back to antiquity. The Nazi Holocaust shocked the world with its cruelty, scope, and zealous organization, but we have come to understand that this was merely the most notorious—and by no means the final—chapter in a long, dismal history.

To Kill a People does not presume to offer a thorough overview of twentieth-century genocide and mass killing. The following chapters explore four case studies—the Armenian genocide, the Holocaust, and the genocides in Cambodia and Rwanda—that provide some chronological and geographic breadth but that also allow us to find similarities and differences that have wider applicability. In selecting the genocides for this book, there were unfortunately far too many to choose from. As Holocaust historian Yehuda Bauer once noted, "The horror of the Holocaust is not that it deviated from human norms; the horror is that it didn't."[5]

DEFINING GENOCIDE

In a 1944 book, Raphael Lemkin, a Polish-Jewish jurist, introduced the term "genocide"—combining the Greek *genos* (and Latin *gens*) for "race" or "family" and the suffix "-cide" for "killing." But for Lemkin—who himself could well have fallen victim to the Nazi genocide had he not fled Poland shortly after the German invasion of 1939—genocide was not simply physical extermination, but rather the calculated destruction of a group's ability to maintain its identity and its collective existence: "A coordinated plan," he wrote, "aiming at the destruction of essential foundations of the life of national groups."[6] In contrast to the more restrictive approaches adopted by others in later years, he recognized and warned against efforts to destroy the cultural fabric and continuity of particular groups. Lemkin singled out, for example, the Nazis' burning of a Talmudic library in Lublin in 1941 as "indication of an intent to obliterate" the Jews' culture and thereby undermine their ability to survive as a people.[7]

Since the early 1930s, Lemkin had appealed to international opinion to recognize and take action against "barbarity" and cultural "vandalism," terms he used before coining "genocide." In the 1930s he had raised his concerns at law conferences throughout Europe, most notably a 1933 international law conference

---

[5]Yehuda Bauer, *Rethinking the Holocaust* (New Haven, CT: Yale University Press, 2002), 42.
[6]Raphael Lemkin, *Axis Rule in Occupied Europe* (Clark, NJ: The Lawbook Exchange, 2008), i. The first edition of his book was published by the Carnegie Endowment for International Peace in November 1944. Lemkin coined the term while writing the book's preface one year earlier.
[7]Ibid., 85.

Raphael Lemkin

Raphael Lemkin (L) with Ricardo Alfaro, chairman of the legal committee of the U.N. General Assembly (and former Panamanian president) on December 9, 1948—the day that the UN adopted the genocide resolution for which Lemkin campaigned so vigorously. Lemkin's work would continue: He consumed the remaining eleven years of his life trying to convince individual governments to ratify the genocide treaty. (Technically, the process of ratification ended in 1951, and since then individual countries may sign or "accede" to it.)

organized by the League of Nations in Madrid. After the end of the war in 1945, Lemkin continued his restless campaign to criminalize and prevent genocide. His new term was widely adopted within a few years and was cited in the Nuremberg indictments of Nazi war criminals. Largely at Lemkin's instigation, in 1948 the United Nations (UN) held the Convention on the Prevention and Punishment of the Crime of Genocide, which formulated the most widely cited and influential definition to date:

> Any of the following acts committed with intent to destroy, in whole or in part, a national, ethnical [sic], racial or religious group, as such: (a) Killing members of the group; (b) Causing serious bodily or mental harm to members of the group; (c) Deliberately inflicting on the group conditions of life calculated to bring about its physical destruction in whole or in part; (d) Imposing measures intended to

prevent births within the group; (e) Forcibly transferring children of the group to another group.[8]

Borrowing from Lemkin, this definition is very carefully phrased, each component significant. But while the UN definition is the only definition that carries the force of international law, it is imperfect, as its own framers acknowledged at the time. The exclusion of political, social, sexual, or economic groups from the list of categories is a glaring weakness, made even more troubling by the knowledge that Soviet diplomats, whose government had targeted people for presumably belonging to ill-defined political and social groups, were instrumental in preventing those categories from being included.[9] The Soviets were not alone in shunting aside some of Lemkin's more universal, inclusive concepts. South Africa, Brazil, and other undemocratic states were also opposed to Lemkin's warnings against attacks on cultural traditions and institutions, which implied the protection of minorities.[10]

Even after his apparent success at the UN Convention in 1948, Lemkin continued his lonesome struggle, now focused on convincing individual countries to adopt the Genocide Convention. The refusal of the US Congress to adopt the Convention was one of his bitterest disappointments. In August 1959 Lemkin collapsed and died from a heart attack in the Manhattan office building of a public relations firm, "his blazer leaking papers at the seams. His one-room apartment . . . was left overflowing with memos prepared for foreign ministers" and piles of other documents and books related to his work. *The New York Times* eulogized him by noting that "diplomats of this and other nations" who dreaded the sight of "the slightly stooped figure" of Dr. Lemkin—knowing he would corner them and beseech them to join his campaign—"need not be uneasy anymore. They will not have to think up explanations for their failure to ratify the genocide convention for which Dr. Lemkin worked so patiently and unselfishly for a decade and a half."[11]

In recent years—especially since the advent of genocide studies in the 1980s and 1990s—numerous scholars, human rights activists, and legal experts have criticized

---

[8]Article II of United Nations Resolution 260, adopted December 9, 1948; the full text, in the original French and English, is available here: http://www.un.org/documents/ga/res/3/ares3.htm (accessed May 3, 2013).

[9]Norman Naimark, *Stalin's Genocides* (Princeton, NJ: Princeton University Press, 2010), 20–23. "Argentina, Brazil, the Dominican Republic, Iran, and South Africa," reported Naimark, "were worried that they could be accused of genocide if they fought against domestic political insurgencies by revolutionary groups. Thus the Soviets and their right-wing political opponents joined forces in the United Nations on the genocide issue." Naimark, 22.

[10]Mark Levene, *The Meaning of Genocide*, Vol. 1, *Genocide in the Age of the Nation State* (London: I.B. Taurus, 2008), 44. A Brazilian delegate, whose government repressed numerous indigenous groups, stated his concern that minorities could use such language as "an excuse for opposing perfectly normal assimilation." William A. Schabas, *Genocide in International Law* (New York: Cambridge University Press, 2000), 184, quoted in Levene, 45.

[11]Samantha Power, *A Problem from Hell: America and the Age of Genocide* (New York: Harper Perennial, 2003), 78. See Power, 17–78, for a fuller description of Lemkin's single-minded, quarter-century-long campaign. Also see Raphael Lemkin, *Totally Unofficial: The Autobiography of Raphael Lemkin* (New Haven, CT: Yale University Press, 2013), edited by Donna-Lee Frieze.

or, in other cases, enhanced this definition, but so far no adequate alternative has won wide acceptance. Dutch scholar Pieter Drost offered a simple but clear definition in 1959: "Genocide is the deliberate destruction of [the] physical life of individual human beings by reason of their membership of any human collectivity as such." This is closer to Lemkin's spirit as well as to a 1946 UN draft, which defined genocide as "the denial of the right of existence of entire human groups."[12] "Human groups" is, in my view, preferable to the excessive concern with categorization that often attends these debates. (And most humans, after all, have multiple, overlapping, complex identities and would resist having their self-identity reduced to a single element, such as their religion or nationality.)

Many definitions formulated by scholars since Drost have enhanced our understanding and pointed toward other avenues of research, but none has been fully satisfactory. In 1982, Jack Nusan Porter, a Ukrainian-born US sociologist, defined genocide as "the deliberate destruction, in whole or in part, by a government or its agents, of a racial, sexual, religious, tribal or political minority. It can involve not only mass murder, but also starvation, forced deportation, and political, economic and biological subjugation." Insisting that a victimized group must be a "minority," though, is problematic: In Burundi in 1972, for example, the majority Hutu population was targeted by a Tutsi-led government for genocidal massacres that killed 200,000 people. In Bosnia-Herzegovina in the 1990s, the principal victims of genocidal campaigns were the Bosnian Muslims (also termed "Bosniaks"), who constituted roughly three-sevenths of the population, a larger proportion than either of the other two major demographic groups.

Other definitions have stressed "innocence" and "vulnerability." In an important 1976 book, for example, American sociologist Irving Louis Horowitz wrote, "[Genocide is] a structural and systematic destruction of innocent people by a state bureaucratic apparatus. . . . Genocide represents a systematic effort over time to liquidate a national population, usually a minority . . . [and] functions as a fundamental political policy to assure conformity and participation of the citizenry." Israel Charny, an Israeli pioneer of genocide studies, stressed that genocide entailed the "mass killing" of peoples "under conditions of the essential defencelessness of the victim." The 1994 Rwandan genocide (Chapter 4) highlights the problem with this emphasis. An invasion organized by a Tutsi-led army from abroad was among the factors that precipitated the genocide of hundreds of thousands of Rwandan Tutsi, and a closer examination of other genocides—such as those of the Herero and the Armenians—also finds that the exterminations often occurred in the context of rebellion or insurgency. This in no way mitigates the guilt of the perpetrators, and students of history should not shy away from these sorts of moral complexities.

Steven Katz, a philosopher known principally for his writing on Jewish intellectual traditions, as well as on the Holocaust, sees genocide as "the *actualization*

---

[12]December 1946, Resolution 96(I): http://daccess-dds-ny.un.org/doc/RESOLUTION/GEN/NR0/033/47/IMG/NR003347.pdf?OpenElement (accessed June 30, 2012).

[emphasis added] of the intent, however successfully carried out, to murder in its totality any national, ethnic, racial, religious, political, social, gender or economic group, as these groups are defined by the perpetrator, by whatever means."[13] Katz has been justly criticized for arguing that the Jewish catastrophe was utterly unique, and his emphasis on the "actualization," as well as the "totality" of the attempt, makes his definition overly exclusive. Even the architects of the Rwandan genocide—one of history's most brutal and thorough—did not aim to murder *all* Tutsi, which would require going well beyond the nation's borders. The Nazis' pursuit of small, unarmed, utterly harmless Jewish populations in all corners of Germany and German-occupied territory is indeed among the Holocaust's distinctive features; it could also be said, though, that the high proportion of civilian murderers—higher than in others— marks the Rwandan genocide as "uniquely horrible." Katz, among others, attempts to use the Nazi Holocaust as a yardstick or standard by which to measure other mass atrocities, and by doing so to deny them the status of "genocide."

Helen Fein and Adam Jones have offered two conceptions of "genocide" that are closest to my own. In a 1990 book, Fein saw genocide as "a series of purposeful actions by a perpetrator(s) to destroy a collectivity." She added some clarifications (see footnote), but this first phrase is particularly effective and clear, and confronts the "intent" issue through her more subtle understanding of "purposeful actions."[14] More recently, Jones expanded upon earlier definitions by Katz and others, and crafted this inclusive but concise phrasing: "the actualization of the intent," by whatever means and "however successfully carried out, to murder *in whole or in substantial part* [emphasis in the original] any national, ethnic, racial, religious, political, social, gender or economic group, as these groups are defined by the perpetrator."[15] Jones's "in substantial part" is a significant improvement upon definitions that would exclude any cases that did not end in near-total annihilation, which is a rare occurrence (see footnote 36).

OTHER DISPUTES OVER TERMINOLOGY AND DEFINITIONS

The UN Convention's inclusion of "intent" has come under special scrutiny by scholars and others. The emphasis on "intent" suggests an excessively legalistic approach—and, in reality, it is often very difficult to ascertain the intentions of regimes or armies that commit mass atrocities. Even in the most extreme case

[13]Charny, Drost, Horowitz, Katz, and Porter definitions from Adam Jones, *Genocide: A Comprehensive Introduction* (New York: Routledge, 2010), 15–18.
[14]Helen Fein, *Genocide: A Sociological Perspective* (London: Sage Publications, 1990). Fein continued that this series of actions included "mass or selective murders of group members and suppressing the biological and social reproduction of the collectivity. This can be accomplished through the imposed proscription or restriction of reproduction of group members, increasing infant mortality, and breaking the linkage between reproduction and socialization of children in the family or group of origin. The perpetrator may represent the state of the victim, another state, or another collectivity." Quoted in Jones, *Genocide*, 18.
[15]Adam Jones, "Gendercide and Genocide," *Journal of Genocide Research* 2, no. 2 (June 2000), 199.

examined in this book—the Nazi Holocaust—the architects of that atrocity camouflaged their actions and goals, precisely to obscure their intentions. Too much emphasis on "intent"—rather than outcomes—can make it easier for criminal states to sidestep the legal and moral price attached to responsibility for genocide. The International Law Commission (established by the UN in 1948 at the time of the Convention on the Prevention and Punishment of the Crime of Genocide) holds that "a general awareness of the *probable* consequences" of destructive acts "is not sufficient" to assign guilt for genocide.[16]

Today many genocide scholars and others challenge this overly legalistic approach. Further, the very concept of "intention" is more complex than it appears on the surface. In US law, for example, criminal intent can be ascribed if an individual "contemplates any result, as likely to follow from a deliberate act of his own."[17] It can be argued that when mass suffering and death result from criminal indifference, or are nearly inevitable and should have been anticipated by a conquering or occupying power, then that power is no less guilty of genocide, if other elements of the standard definitions are met. Genocide scholar Dirk Moses pointed out that in nineteenth-century English law, a person was assumed to have intended the "'natural consequences' of his or her actions" if the result was "reasonably foreseeable."[18] "Too great a focus on what was or what might have been going on in the minds of the perpetrators," astutely argues sociologist Christopher Powell, "distracts us from the tangible consequences, and the preventable causes, of atrocity."[19]

Another oft-criticized weakness of the 1948 UN definition, as mentioned earlier, is its failure to include social, economic, or political groups in its list of potential victims. (It includes only "national, ethnical [sic], racial or religious group[s].") "In the contemporary world, political differences are at the very least as significant a basis for massacre and annihilation as racial, national, ethnic or religious differences" argued Leo Kuper, a South African–born sociologist who helped pioneered genocide studies.[20] It is also entirely possible that, in the near future, groups could be targeted for genocide based on their gender identity or sexual orientation—or that a group could be singled out for some other characteristic that we cannot yet imagine.[21]

---

[16]Ben Kiernan, *Blood and Soil: A World History of Genocide and Extermination from Sparta to Darfur* (New Haven, CT: Yale University Press, 2007), 17.

[17]Norbert Finzsch, "If it looks like a duck, if it walks like a duck, if it quacks like a duck," *Journal of Genocide Research* 10, no. 1 (March 2008), 120.

[18]Dirk A. Moses, "Genocide and Settler Society in Australian History," in Moses, ed., *Genocide and Settler Society: Frontier Violence and Stolen Indigenous Children in Australian History* (New York: Berghahn, 2005), 28.

[19]Christopher Powell, *Barbaric Civilization: A Critical Sociology of Genocide* (Kingston, Ontario: McGill-Queen's University Press, 2011), 64.

[20]Leo Kuper, *Genocide: Its Political Use in the Twentieth Century* (New Haven, CT: Yale University Press, 1981), 39.

[21]In the early twenty-first century, homosexuals suffer harsh, government-sanctioned persecution in Iran, Uganda, Mauritania, and elsewhere—far short of genocide, but an indication that under certain conditions it is conceivable that a government could attempt a systematic extermination of homosexuals, in particular gay men.

A fundamental tension underlies all these debates: Should we define genocide broadly and inclusively, or narrowly and exclusively? The former runs the risk of stripping the term of its power—and, after all, "atrocity," "war crime," and "crime against humanity" should be sufficiently strong terms to characterize certain actions that are not necessarily genocidal. On the other hand, the tendency to define genocide too narrowly can generate an unseemly competition for victimhood, driven by a misguided belief that "the suffering of my group will be lost if we talk about too many other groups." For these reasons, I favor the formulation offered by the tribunal that was convened after the Rwandan genocide that "any stable and permanent group" is in fact to be accorded protection under the Convention, an approach that, according to leading genocide scholar Adam Jones, "is likely to become the norm in future judgments."[22]

A fundamental problem with this debate over definitions is that it can lead to paralysis, especially when this debate is conducted in the dishonest arenas of international diplomacy, where hypocrisy and self-interest reign. The Sudanese government and a group of militias it supports have engaged in widespread massacres and the dispersal of targeted peoples in the Darfur region since 2003. Whether this constitutes genocide—an issue that is debated by reputable, humane

Indian massacre of settlers
This 19th-century sketching by an English settler depicted the supposed bloodthirstiness of the Indians. Indigenous people did indeed resist and sometimes attack the encroachers, but these sorts of highly fanciful renderings perpetuated an image of peaceful, innocent whites beset by murderous savages—an image sustained today by sports nicknames and mascots that evoke the eternal Indian "warrior." A common dynamic in genocidal violence is that "barbaric actions are justified for fear of being subjected to barbaric actions," as historian Dan Stone noted.

---

[22]Jones, *Genocide*, 13.

scholars—does not diminish the scale of the atrocities or the urgent need for international action, yet diplomats and lawmakers have whiled away precious time in fruitless linguistic debates, rather than taking steps to alleviate the suffering in Darfur. "Since my return" from Darfur, an aid worker lamented, "my heart has sunk as arguments intensified about whether the Darfur situation should be defined as genocide or ethnic cleansing. . . . What's happening in Darfur is the wholesale slaughter and rape of unimaginable numbers of human beings . . . Definitions should be left to the dictionary—now is the time for action."[23]

THIS BOOK'S DEFINITION

In this spirit, I argue against rigid definitions and support the trend toward a continual reexamination of existing terminology. For the purposes of this book, I will follow in the recent tradition of inclusiveness, while recognizing that many atrocities defy precise characterization.

The title of this book (*To Kill a People*) condenses the working definition of genocide that guides the following chapters. Genocide is the attempt to destroy any *recognized, stable, and permanent group* as it is defined by the perpetrator; it is a concerted effort to eliminate its individual members and to destroy the group's ability to maintain its social and cultural cohesion and, thus, its existence as a group. The perpetrators' genocidal intent can be uncovered by examining policies, actions, and outcomes. Also the following should be considered:

- Genocides are perpetrated through some combination of the measures listed in the 1948 UN Convention: physical violence, including deportations and "ethnic cleansing"; imposing conditions that bring about the decimation of the group; and "forcibly transferring children of the group to another group."

- Genocide almost always develops out of violent conflict or as part of a process of demographic or political reordering, and thus it should be viewed as part of those processes, rather than as a completely separate phenomenon. In the course of military and political conflict, "leaders and their subordinates perceive and respond to supposed threats and changing conditions."[24]

- Because no group will passively accept its destruction, genocide cannot be attempted without large-scale violence.

---

[23]Luke Glanville, "Is Genocide Still a Powerful Word?," *Journal of Genocide Research* 11, no. 4 (December 2009), 474. Glanville was quoting from an article by Bob MacPherson, "Stop the Slaughter," *Washington Post*, August 8, 2004. After the Yugoslav wars of the 1990s, which popularized the term "ethnic cleansing," many experts consider ethnic cleansing to be synonymous with genocide, as it is conducted for genocidal purposes. Therefore, it is especially unhelpful to waste time debating whether Sudanese actions in Darfur, or atrocities elsewhere, constitute "ethnic cleansing" or "genocide," as if a large gulf exists between the two. [24]Ernesto Verdeja, "The Political Science of Genocide: Outlines of an Emerging Research Agenda," *Patterns of Prejudice* 10, no. 2 (June 2012), 310.

High numbers of deaths, though, should not be the defining factor; if they were, we would find ourselves in an unseemly and absurd search for a number to serve as a standard (perhaps 99,999 deaths does not qualify as a genocide, but 100,000 does?). More important is the guiding philosophy or aims.

The following chapters will consistently acknowledge that nongenocidal atrocities can be as bad or worse for the victims as those deemed "genocidal," while recognizing that genocide—by seeking not only the physical elimination of large numbers of human beings, but, more permanently, the eradication of the means of sustaining a culture or ethnicity—is a uniquely sinister, irreparable crime. At the same time, logic and compassion dictate that any examination of genocide includes instances of mass killing that fall short of our working definition of genocide. Genocide shares many characteristics and dynamics with nongenocidal mass murder, another reason we should not rigidly delineate the two. And to the family, witness, or survivor of a brutal massacre in a village in Sierra Leone or Afghanistan or El Salvador, it would not be the least bit comforting to learn that someone far away determined that the killing was "merely" a human rights abuse or war crime rather than "genocide."

GENOCIDE IN THE ANCIENT AND MEDIEVAL WORLDS

Although the Old Testament cannot be taken as historically precise, it is highly instructive that this text, which is so deeply embedded in the Western tradition, issues more than one blood-curdling call for genocidal destruction. "But as regards the towns of those peoples [the Canaanites] which Yahweh your God gives you as your own inheritance; you must not spare the life of any living thing," commands the God of the Israelites (Deuteronomy 20: 16–17). See also Joshua, Chapters 8–10, and Samuel, Chapter 15, in which God commands, "kill man and woman, babe and suckling, ox and sheep, camel and donkey."[25]

Despite the paucity and unreliability of sources, we know that ancient history included several instances of the attempted eradication of entire populations. In present-day Iraq, the Neo-Assyrian Empire (also known as the Second Assyrian Empire) wreaked utter devastation on the ancient civilization of Elam, in retaliation for a rebellion, in the mid-seventh century BCE. Late in the fifth century BCE, Thucydides reported in chilling and terse language that—to punish the people of Melos for their insistence on remaining neutral in the Peloponnesian War—Athens executed all the island's military-age men and then sold the women and children into slavery, while colonizing Melos with Athenians.[26]

---

[25] *Jerusalem Bible*, 1966. I agree with psychologist Steven Pinker's point that regardless of their historical precision, the Old Testament's historical accounts "offer a window into the lives and values of Near Eastern civilizations in the mid-1st millennium BCE" and demonstrate that its peoples "thought [genocide] was a good idea" whether or not they practiced it. Pinker, *The Better Angels of Our Nature: The Decline of Violence in History and Its Causes* (London: Allen Lane, 2011), 11.
[26] Thucydides, *The Peloponnesian War* (Indianapolis: Hackett, 1998), 300–301.

The Battle of Ascalon
The Battle of Ascalon, August 1099, at the end of the First Crusade. Upon capturing Jerusalem one month earlier, Christian Crusaders carried out indiscriminate massacres of its residents. The Crusaders were motivated not only by religious zealotry, but a belief in the inferiority and demonic nature of their Muslim (as well as Jewish) victims. Engraving by C.W. Sharpe, based on a painting of the same title by Gustave Doré, a famous 19th-century illustrator.

Some scholars assert that Rome's destruction of the North African city-state of Carthage at the end of the Third Punic War (149–146 BCE) also represents a precedent for modern genocide. Roman troops killed between 40 and 70 percent of the population (the survivors were enslaved) and were guided by orders that meet certain modern standards of genocide. The large majority of those slain, though, were killed as military foes, rather than as civilian members of a targeted group, and the destruction of Carthage gave rise to legends that are today rejected by historians of the ancient world (e.g., that the Romans sowed the city's fields with salt to render them infertile). Nonetheless, the bloodthirsty declarations of the Roman leader Cato, who in the years before the Third Punic War concluded his speeches before the Senate—regardless of topic—with the exclamation "Carthage must be destroyed," expressed a desire to erase the foundations of Carthaginian civilization.[27]

During the First Crusade (1096–1099) and the succeeding crusades, fanatical Christians inflicted horrendous cruelties upon their Muslim (and sometimes Jewish and even Eastern Christian) victims, and in some cases sought—although

---

[27]David Crowe, *War Crimes, Genocide, and Justice: A Global History* (New York: Palgrave Macmillan, 2014), 14. The phrase attributed to Cato is "*Ceretum censeo delendan esse Carthanginem*"—"Besides, I think that Carthage must be destroyed."

without success—to empty entire cities, such as Jerusalem and Antioch, of their non-Christian inhabitants. Muslim warriors sometimes responded in kind, as during the bloody conquest of Acre in 1291 by the Mamluks, a powerful Muslim sultanate based in Egypt. To the east, a devastating new imperial power arose: the Mongol armies of Chinggis Khan (ca. 1162–1227), which destroyed vast swathes of territory in their rampages across Central Asia and beyond. As their armies advanced across Eurasia, the Mongols' plunder and mass murder assumed genocidal proportions and characteristics.

Other mass atrocities abounded in the late Middle Ages, from Ireland to East Asia. But it is in the Americas that we find mass destruction on a scale and thoroughness that presage that of the modern era.

DESTRUCTION OF THE NATIVE PEOPLES OF THE AMERICAS

Columbus's arrival in the "New World" in 1492 marked the beginning of history's most prolonged and extensive demographic disaster. The first victims were the indigenous peoples of Hispaniola, where Columbus and his men landed, mistakenly believing they had found the Indies (a belief that Columbus stubbornly clung to for the rest of his life).[28] A lust for gold and lucrative spices and dreams of power, alongside beliefs regarding an obligation to save the souls of the natives, induced Columbus's legions to enslave, torture, and murder thousands of native people, while many more perished from new diseases borne by the European invaders.

After five hundred years, scholars have yet to agree on population estimates for the pre-Columbian Americas, making it very difficult to quantify the demographic disaster that befell the indigenous peoples. Keeping in mind that all these figures are disputed (and are often hostage to political agendas), the most reliable, widely agreed-upon estimates indicate that the Americas were home to roughly 50 million people in 1492, about 5 million of them living north of Mexico.[29] By 1570, the native population throughout the hemisphere had declined to about 14 million; in North America, the indigenous population declined to roughly 250,000 by the end of the nineteenth century.

---

[28]Hispaniola's Taino people were nearly completely eradicated within two generations. See Irving Rouse, *The Tainos: Rise and Decline of the People Who Greeted Columbus* (New Haven, CT: Yale University Press, 1992). "Columbus encountered Tainos throughout most of the West Indies," Rouse noted (ibid., 5) and Taino populations in Puerto Rico, Jamaica, and elsewhere were also decimated. Today there is a growing group of people who self-identify as Taino (usually spelled Taíno now), but this is very recent, and they acknowledge that "biologically" they would be only a small percentage Taino. Their ancestors are primarily African and partially European. In using the name, they are claiming a cultural tradition rather than direct lineage to the pre-Columbian Taino. Dr. Nicola Foote, email to John Cox, August 4, 2013.

[29]Thomas Benjamin, *The Atlantic World: Europeans, Africans, Indians and Their Shared History, 1400–1900* (Cambridge, UK: Cambridge University Press, 2009), 321, and Alan Taylor, *American Colonies* (New York: Penguin, 2001), 40.

THE SPANISH CONQUEST OF THE AMERICAS TO 1550

Spanish
Portuguese
Mexica Empire (at time of conquest)
Inca Empire (at time of conquest)
⚒ Mining

The Spanish Conquest of the Americas to 1550

But was this genocide? What were the goals of the conquerors and the colonial administrations? This is a contentious, complex question—not least of all because the demographic catastrophe unfolded over such a long period of time, in greatly varying circumstances, and under the auspices of several different sets of authorities (Spanish, Portuguese, Dutch, French, English, and finally, American). Disease was principally responsible for the enormous toll. The infamous conquistador Hernando de Soto and his soldiers roamed the southeast of today's United States in the 1540s, torturing, enslaving, and killing countless Indians. But as one writer documents, "the worst thing he did . . . was entirely without malice—he brought pigs."[30]

---

[30]Charles C. Mann, *1491: New Revelations of the Americas Before Columbus* (New York: Knopf, 2005), 97.

In de Soto's wake, the Caddo Indian population declined by 95 percent over the next few generations due to smallpox, measles, and other diseases.[31]

Such devastating epidemics were not new to humankind. The bubonic plague had swept large parts of Asia, the Middle East, and Europe during the fourteenth century. As many as 20 million Europeans—one-third to one-half of the population—died within two or three years in the middle of the century, and the Black Death claimed an even larger number of Chinese a few years earlier, perhaps one-half of the population.

During the worst decades of the disaster in the Americas—in the sixteenth and seventeenth centuries—both the European colonizers and the natives were ignorant of the causes of diseases and their spread. At that time, the Europeans could not have intentionally disseminated disease if they had wanted to, and their need for Indian labor sometimes outweighed their desire for the Indians to leave the land. In many times and places, though, for example as the United States expanded westward, the disappearance of the Indians harmonized with government policy or aims. US officials were "strongly disinclined to take active measures against the spread of epidemics among the Indians" in the early years of the new American republic, according to two experts. In some cases in the late 1700s, African slaves were inoculated against smallpox, while Indians were left to their fate.[32] And as sociologist and genocide researcher Christopher Powell has argued, genocidal policy or acts often emerge—even if not the top priority of the perpetrator regime or army—from intentional social or political action. As the genocidal effects become clear, the policy or project continues because of the unimportance (to the authorities) of the survival of the affected group.[33]

Further, throughout those four centuries, up to the late 1800s, governing authorities accelerated the disappearance of the land's indigenous peoples through forced deportations and murder. By the end of the 1800s, the prolonged genocide evolved into what some would term "ethnocide"—that is, "the destruction of a culture rather than a people per se," through such measures as "forced relocation, compulsory transfer of native children . . . to assimilate them into white society." The destructive effects of these policies were compounded by "decimation of indigenous economies" and the "forced imposition of new forms of sociopolitical organization in reservation settings."[34] Throughout the long, precipitous population decline, "epidemic disease in the Americas," unlike in Europe in earlier, "was accompanied by colonialism," as one expert observed—colonialism that brought violence, social crises, and social dislocation that "greatly exacerbated native American mortality."[35]

---

[31]Ibid., 99.

[32]Frank Chalk and Kurt Jonassohn, *The History and Sociology of Genocide* (New Haven, CT: Yale University Press, 1990), 177.

[33]Powell, *Barbaric Civilization*, 224–225. Powell used the fate of the Tasmanians to illustrate this point.

[34]Waller, *Becoming Evil*, 28–29.

[35]Benjamin, *The Atlantic World*, 322.

As one example, the fate of northern California's Yuki Indians illustrates the deadly combination of settler-colonial brutality and government complicity. The US government gained control of the Yuki region in 1847, and a few months later the "Gold Rush" commenced. The area was flooded with profit-seekers and assorted adventurers; with impunity, these settlers robbed and murdered Yuki men and enslaved the women, crimes that were condoned and even encouraged by the state government, which helped organize militias that indulged in genocidal slaughter. From 20,000 people in the 1840s, the Yuki were reduced by 85 to 90 percent within six years, and by 1880 only 168 remained—one of history's few near-total genocides.[36]

The overall character and effect of four centuries of colonization, violence, land theft, ethnic cleansing, and brutal indifference to the lives of Indians—punctuated by multiple individual genocides such as that of the Yuki—can only be characterized as genocidal.

THE "CENTURY OF GENOCIDE"

The twentieth century brought about both the technological means and the radical, all-encompassing political philosophies that made it both possible and desirable (from the perspective of certain governments or political movements) to murder huge numbers of human beings. Racism, a new ideological force that would be an indispensable component of twentieth-century genocide, took hold in Western thought by the early 1800s, and by the end of the century it had become an obsession of European societies, gripping the popular imagination and seeping into virtually all areas of intellectual and cultural life.

While most civilizations had long held "heathens," "infidels," and other outsiders in disdain, it was only in the sixteenth and seventeenth centuries that our current concepts of "race" began to develop. With the advent of racial thinking and philosophies, "races"—crudely labeled "Caucasian, Mongolian, Ethiopian, American, and Malay" by one important racial thinker in 1795—were now

[36]Jones, *Genocide*, 75. See also Brendan C. Lindsay, *Murder State: California's Native American Genocide, 1846–1873* (Lincoln, NB: University of Nebraska Press, 2012). Other cases of near-total genocide include the destruction of the Aboriginal population of Tasmania, an island to the south of southeast Australia during the first third of the 1800s. The indigenous Tasmanian population was reduced from a few thousand to 300 by 1835 and to fewer than two dozen by mid-century. Powell, *Barbaric Civilization*, 210, 216. Cambodia's genocidal Khmer Rouge regime (see Chapter 3) exterminated virtually the entire Vietnamese population of its country. New England's Pequot War of 1634–1638 resulted in the killing, disbursement, or selling into slavery of nearly the entire Pequot people—who numbered less than 10,000 at the beginning of the war—and therefore the Pequots' eradication, an explicitly stated goal of the English colonial settlers who defeated them. Kiernan, *Blood and Soil*, 227–236. These near-total genocides were made possible not only by the exterminatory goals of the perpetrators but by the small, geographically concentrated populations of the victims.

defined.[37] Paradoxically, these new ideas about race, and the accompanying belief in white supremacy, were sometimes driven by forces of progress and modernization. The Scientific Revolution and the Enlightenment engendered a quest to classify everything in nature, which contributed to the compulsion to classify human beings by race. Meanwhile, the anti-slavery abolitionist movement of the early 1800s obliged defenders of slavery to formulate new arguments, which now invariably rested upon skin color or "race." Racism is crucial to our understanding of modern genocide not simply by "dehumanizing" future victims, but by dividing the human race into rigid categories, with supposedly fixed, unchanging characteristics. Thus, unlike in previous centuries, to be a "Jew" or an "African" was supposedly to "always" possess certain traits—traits that invariably derived from common prejudices.

European racism was also fueled by Social Darwinism, which applied Charles Darwin's theories on natural selection to "races." While Darwin analyzed genetic variation and competition in nature, Social Darwinist thinkers saw competition among races as the driving force in history. It was Herbert Spencer, a leader of this new philosophy, who coined the phrase "survival of the fittest." Social Darwinism invested racism with ever greater potential for violence: Competition among races is the driving force in history, it argued, and thus humanity benefited from the inevitable disappearance of supposedly inferior peoples. Some American and European statesmen developed a wistful, elegiac way of referring to the "vanishing races," as if the causes of their disappearances were completely mysterious.[38] But such subterfuge was usually not necessary: It became perfectly acceptable to speak without embarrassment about the eradication of "inferior" peoples. Referring to the "savage races" in 1867, one prominent British writer and theologian, Frederic William Farrar, intoned, "They are without a past and without a future,

---

[37]Johann Friedrich Blumenbach identified four "races" in his 1775 doctoral dissertation and added a fifth, the Caucasian, in 1795. These writings were highly influential. Robert Bernasconi and Tommy Lee Lott, eds., *The Idea of Race* (Indianapolis: Hackett, 2000), 27. In recent years, scientists and scholars have debunked not only such notions of racial hierarchies but also the idea that there is any basis for the persistent belief in race. From a 1998 statement of the American Anthropological Association: "Human populations are not unambiguous, clearly demarcated, biologically distinct groups. Evidence from the analysis of genetics (e.g., DNA) indicates that most physical variation, about 94%, lies *within* so-called racial groups. Conventional geographic 'racial' groupings differ from one another only in about 6% of their genes. This means that there is greater variation within 'racial' groups than between them." Available here: http://www.aaanet.org/stmts/racepp.htm (accessed June 12, 2013).

[38]See Patrick Brantlinger, *Dark Vanishings: Discourse on the Extinction of Primitive Races* (Ithaca, NY: Cornell University Press, 2003). Thomas Jefferson was given to the most astonishingly obtuse ruminations, masking the Indians' fate in passive language: "It is to be lamented then, very much to be lamented, that we have suffered so many of the Indian tribes already to extinguish"; the whites had "suffered," he continued, because they had neglected to collect a scientific record of the languages of the vanishing peoples. Thomas Jefferson, "The Prehistoric Origins of the Races of America: Notes on Virginia," in Jefferson, *Letters of Thomas Jefferson Concerning Philology and the Classics*, ed. Thomas Fitzhugh (Charlottesville, VA: University of Virginia, 1919), 3.

Statue of Leopold II

This monument to Leopold II still stands in Arlon, southern Belgium—indeed, one can still find large statues of the king in Brussels and elsewhere throughout the country. The inscription reads, in translation: "I have undertaken the work of colonialization for the sake of civilization and for the benefit of Belgium." By the end of the nineteenth century, more Europeans (and Americans) were able to see through these rationalizations and a powerful human-rights movement emerged in opposition to the atrocities in the Congo.

doomed . . . to a rapid, an entire, and, perhaps for the highest destinies of mankind, an inevitable extinction." They pass through the world "learning nothing, inventing nothing, improving nothing," and their disappearance will leave "no trace of their existence" beyond their physical remains.[39] By the end of the nineteenth century, no less a figure than the British prime minister, Lord Robert Cecil (aka The Marquess of Salisbury), could express similar genocidal fantasies without fear of embarrassment or censure: "One can roughly divide the nations of the world into the living and the dying."[40] When Adolf Hitler later asserted that "the victory of the best race" is "the precondition of all human progress," he was simply articulating the viewpoint of most European elites of the era.[41]

The prevalence of racism in Western societies helps us understand—if not condone—the European powers' cavalier disregard for the lives of their colonial

---

[39]Frederic William Farrar, "Aptitudes of Races," in *Transactions of the Ethnological Society of London*, Vol. V (London: John Murray, 1867), 120.

[40]"Living and Dying Nations: From Lord Salisbury's Speech to The Primrose League, May 4," *The New York Times*, May 18, 1898. (PDF of article [http://query.nytimes.com/mem/archive-free/pdf?res=F20C1FFF345911738DDDA10994DD405B8885F0D3] accessed June 21, 2013).

[41]Adolf Hitler, *Mein Kampf* (Boston: Houghton Mifflin Company, 1998), 317.

subjects, an attitude that filtered down through their respective military forces.[42] One British army pilot, instructed to bomb any group of ten or more people as the British administration suppressed a revolt in India in 1938, commented, "In my case I can remember actually finding nine people and saying 'That's within ten percent and that's good enough,' so I blew them up."[43] In 1919, as Britain was combating a revolt by the Kurdish people in northern Iraq, future prime minister Winston Churchill opined, "I do not understand the squeamishness about the use of gas. . . . I am strongly in favour of using poisonous gas against uncivilised tribes."[44] European racism was expressed not only in such brutish proclamations, but in the paternalistic and narcissistic attitude set forth in Rudyard Kipling's 1899 poem "The White Man's Burden"—that the colonized peoples were not only "half-devil" but "half-child" in need of the benevolent, selfless assistance of the "civilizers."[45] Centralized states, and ideologies of nationalism, arose more or less simultaneously in much of Europe, and nations were often defined in racial terms; that is, in the view of many Europeans, a nation comprised members of a single "race," with common cultural and linguistic traditions, rather than peoples of varying ethnicities or religions who were united in citizenship and legal equality. Thus, racism often lent individual nationalisms a belligerent, exclusive character.

MODERN IMPERIALISM

It was hardly coincidental that racism flourished during the same era that European nations were engaged in the imperialist land grab now known as the "scramble for Africa." From the 1860s until World War I, the leading European powers competed for land and resources on the African continent. While Europe enjoyed

---

[42]This chapter discusses racism as it relates to European colonialism and genocide, but it should be emphasized that racism is not monopolized by Western civilization. Many other cultures have developed their own racist ideologies and attitudes, often with destructive results. The Japanese example is briefly discussed later in this chapter. For more on racial ideologies and minorities in modern Japan, see Michael Weiner, ed., *Japan's Minorities: The Illusion of Homogeneity* (New York: Routledge, 2009). For an analysis of some important distinctions between European and Japanese racial philosophies and obsessions in that era, see John Dower, *War Without Mercy: Race and Power in the Pacific War* (New York: Pantheon, 1986), 203–290.

[43]Nicholas Baker, *Human Smoke: The Beginnings of World War II, the End of Civilization* (New York: Simon & Schuster, 2008), 85.

[44]Martin Gilbert, *Winston S. Churchill*, Vol. 4 (1977), 490, 504; Baker, *Smoke*, 7.

[45]As US forces were imposing their rule on the Philippines at the turn of the century, Albert Beveridge, in an address to his colleagues in the US Senate, proclaimed that the Filipinos were "children" who "are not capable of self-government. How could they be? They are not of a self-governing race. They are Orientals, Malays, instructed by Spaniards." Senator Beveridge, who was later a Pulitzer Prize–winning historian, continued: "Savage blood, Oriental blood, Malay blood, Spanish example—are these the elements of self-government?" Albert J. Beveridge, speech to the US Senate, January 9, 1900: https://www.mtholyoke.edu/acad/intrel/ajb72.htm (accessed August 13, 2012).

Mutilated Congolese
Portrait of two mutilated children—two of the many millions of victims of atrocities committed under King Leopold II's "rubber terror." Yoka (standing) had his right hand amputated for failing to meet a quota for rubber. This tactic had been used 400 years earlier by Columbus's men in the Caribbean, who demanded high quotas of fold from the enslaved locals. Mola (left) lost both hands to gangrene after mercenaries tied them too tightly. Equateur province, Congo Free State, c. 1905.

a century of relative continental peace from 1815 to 1914,[46] European powers extended their control from 35 to 85 percent of the world's territory. Racism was not the only motivating factor, but it certainly fueled—and helped justify—the seizure of huge tracts of land in Africa, with deadly consequences. As one scholar observed, racism "provide[d] ideological legitimation for a vast project of conquest and genocide."[47]

However, it was not only racial philosophies or mentalities that arose during this period of the "New Imperialism." More tangibly and lethally, European colonizers implemented murderous and even genocidal practices that foreshadowed the carnage of the twentieth century. The gravest crimes of the "New Imperialism" occurred under the Belgian administration of King Leopold II, who took control of the Congo in the 1870s; established an administration called the "Congo Free State" in 1885; and governed the huge territory as his personal property until 1908. In pursuit of ivory and rubber, as well as the status afforded a major colonial power, Leopold's authorities, complemented by a motley assortment of adventurers, inflicted terrible violence upon the Congolese people. (The monarch himself never set foot on the African continent.) Much of the population was enslaved, and Leopold's men imposed production quotas for harvesting rubber; the hapless

---

[46]"Relative" to the subsequent century's two world wars and the preceding centuries' wars between Europe's major powers.
[47]Enzo Traverso, *Origins of Nazi Genocide* (New York: New Press, 2003), 63.

slave laborers who failed to meet these quotas had their hands chopped off.[48] Beatings, lashings, and periodic massacres also characterized Leopold's rule, and starvation and disease were the predictable consequences of the Belgians' destruction of community life and commerce.

As many as 10 million Congolese ultimately perished under Leopold's rule—which exceeded in magnitude, but not in cruelty and exploitation, the tactics of French, British, and other European colonizers elsewhere on the continent. The Congolese catastrophe, which calls out for greater attention, was little known to the public or even to historians—outside central Africa, that is—before the publication of a 1998 book (Adam Hochschild's *King Leopold's Ghost*) and remains, in comparison to the Holocaust and other comparable calamities, relatively unknown.

Yet for a few years at the end of the nineteenth and beginning of the next century, it was quite well known. A vigorous human rights campaign brought attention to the "rubber terror" in the Congo, which for several years was an international scandal. Led by British journalist E. D. Morel and Irish humanitarian Roger Casement, the movement gained the active support of such cultural luminaries as Mark Twain and Joseph Conrad, whose *Heart of Darkness* was inspired by the author's revelations, while working on a ship in the Congo in the 1890s, about the moral corruption and brutality of colonialism.[49] The Congo human rights scandal receded in European consciousness during World War I, in part because of Belgium's suffering after the 1914 German invasion. German atrocities, which were abundant, were exaggerated for Allied propaganda value; ironically, one such exaggeration was the story that the Germans cut off the hands of Belgian children. At that time, "no one in the Allied countries wanted to be reminded that, only a decade or two earlier, it was the King of Belgians whose men in Africa had cut off hands."[50]

Roger Casement's 1904 report, written after extensive travel and investigation, had been instrumental in raising awareness of the Congo's miseries. A few years later, again after his own investigation, Casement exposed another abomination that had much in common with Leopold's reign of terror: "the systematic starvation, whipping, torture, and murder of thirty thousand Indian victims in a decade's time," as Casement's 1911 report revealed, in the Putumayo region of

---

[48]Roger Casement, *Correspondence and Report from His Majesty's Consul at Boma Respecting the Administration of the Independent State of the Congo* (London: Harrison and Sons, 1904), 21–80.
[49]Adam Hochschild, *King Leopold's Ghost: A Story of Greed, Terror, and Heroism in Colonial Africa* (New York: Mariner Books, 1998). Before Morel's success in making the Congo a cause célèbre, other humanitarians had discovered and attempted to expose the abuses. Perhaps most notable were the efforts of an African American journalist, historian, and activist, George Washington Williams. See Hochschild, 101–114.
[50]Ibid., 296.

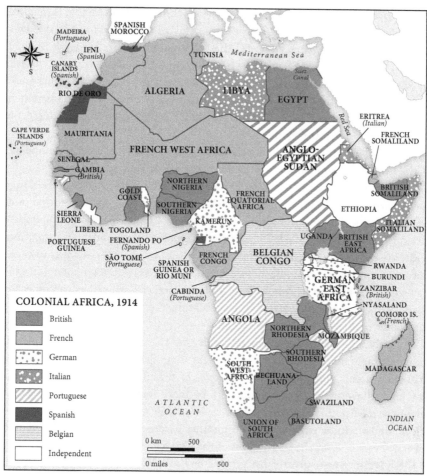

Colonial Africa, 1914

the Amazon.[51] These crimes unfolded during the time of the Congo travesties and were driven by greed for profit for the same natural resource: rubber. Casement's report, which followed reports by Peruvian and English periodicals, again helped spark a human rights scandal, which gained considerable attention for a few years (1907–1914). The report described some atrocities that were strikingly similar to those in Leopold's Congo, such as the brutal enforcement of rubber quotas: "When the time comes to deliver the rubber, these unhappy victims appear with their loads upon their backs, accompanied by their women and children, who

---

[51]Michael Edward Stannard, *Red Rubber, Bleeding Trees: Violence, Slavery, and Empire in Northwest Amazonia, 1850–1933* (Albuquerque: University of New Mexico Press, 1998), xv–xvi.

help them to carry the rubber. When they reach the section the rubber is weighed. They know by experience what the needle of the balance should mark, and when it indicates that they have delivered the full amount required, they leap about and laugh with pleasure. When it does not, they throw themselves face downwards on the ground and, in this attitude, await the lash, the bullet, or the machete."[52] Again, though, to those outside the region these travesties, which had momentarily stirred the consciences of humanitarians, would be ignored and forgotten once the European war began.

These tragedies highlight the connection between genocidal conditions and one of the iconic developments of the modern era: the invention of the automobile, which generated demand for rubber. Slavery, starvation, and murder in the Congo and Amazonia also suggest that modern Western labor systems created and profited from genocidal conditions, which were integral to the expansion of capitalism into colonial or postcolonial lands. Further, the exclusion or marginalization from Western scholarship and knowledge of the Putumayo disaster—which involved the decimation of several indigenous groups—as well as the Congo exemplifies the way that such brutalities, when far from the heartland of Europe, can be easily overlooked, thereby inadvertently perpetuating the hierarchies that produced such catastrophes in the first place.[53]

Similarly obscure in the annals of history are the deaths of many millions of Indians, Brazilians, and Chinese from famine under British rule (or resulting from British economic policy) in the last quarter of the nineteenth century—deaths that could have been greatly minimized by more humane governance, or that might not have occurred at all if not for the economic distortions and exploitation of colonialism. India experienced few famines before British rule, but it endured several severe ones in the last quarter of the nineteenth century. The human tolls of these famines were greatly exacerbated by the callous responses of British administrators, who—guided by the ultra-free-market economic philosophy of the time—were, with rare exceptions, miserly in their efforts to alleviate starvation during the worst disasters. In one case, the British official presumably responsible for relief efforts declared: "The doctrine that in time of famine the poor are entitled to demand relief would probably lead to the doctrine that they are entitled to such relief at all times."[54] Another official, Sir Richard Temple, required starving

[52]W. E. Hardenburg, *The Putumayo, the Devil's Paradise: Travels in the Peruvian Amazon Region and an Account of the Atrocities Committed upon the Indians Therein* (London: T. Fisher Unwin, 1912), 217. Hardenburg's book included extensive excerpts, including this one, from Casement's report. Casement's extraordinary life—the aristocrat-turned-revolutionary was executed by the British authorities for his role in the 1916 "Easter Uprising" in Dublin—is rendered in literary form in Mario Vargas Llosa's novel *The Dream of the Celt* (New York: Farrar, Straus and Giroux, 2012).
[53]Thanks to my colleague Nicola Foote for this formulation. Nicola Foote, email to John Cox, August 4, 2013.
[54]Government of India and the Parliament of Great Britain, *Report of the Indian Famine Commission, 1878, Part I: Famine Relief* (London: G.E. Eyre and W. Spottiswoode, 1880), 59.

Uncle Sam and the "White Man's Burden"

"School Begins," *Puck* magazine, 1899. The caption reads, "Uncle Sam (to his new class in Civilization)—Now, children, you've got to learn these lessons whether you want to or not! But just take a look at the class ahead of you, and remember that, in a little while, you will feel as glad to be here as they are!" The "White Man's Burden" was taken up by the United States after seizing several colonies—depicted as the children in the first row—as the spoils of its victory in the War of 1898. Note the supposedly untamable American Indian and Chinese immigrant in the doorway.

Indians to travel to camps for work on railroad and canal projects, whereupon he offered a meager diet that provided fewer calories per day for heavy labor than given slave laborers at the Nazis' Buchenwald concentration camp.[55] At the time, an Indian economic historian calculated that at least 15 million people died in six of the worst famines in his country between 1877 and 1900.[56] All told, this age of imperialism claimed at least 50 million victims in the late nineteenth and early twentieth centuries.

This era is crucial to understanding the precursors and influences of modern genocide. Nazi Germany did not have to invent the concentration camp, which we tend to associate only with Hitler: As already noted, Spanish colonizers in Cuba, British settlers and authorities in South Africa, and American forces in the Philippines all employed mass incarcerations in concentration camps while combating insurgencies around the turn of the century. It was also at that time that the leading imperial

---

[55] Mike Davis, *Late Victorian Holocausts: El Niño Famines and the Making of the Third World* (New York: Verso, 2001), 38.
[56] Romesh Chunder Dutt, *The Economic History of India Under British Rule*, Vol. 1 (London: Kegan Paul, Trench, Trübner, 1902), viii. Earlier in the century, British policy had also exacerbated the effects of Ireland's potato blight and "Great Famine" (1845–1852), which killed roughly 1 million Irish people (of a pre-famine population of less than 7 million) and compelled an equivalent number to leave their homeland, thus reducing Ireland's population by one-quarter.

powers developed lethal new technologies, often trying them out upon their colonial subjects. Aerial bombing and other technologies led to heavily one-sided, murderous encounters, such as the Battle of Omdurman in Sudan in 1898, in which 48 British troops were killed, while more than 10,000 Sudanese perished.[57] "Like other colonial powers," noted Sven Lindqvist in a scathing indictment of racism and imperialism, "the British had already been bombing restless natives in their territories for several years" by World War I. "It began with the Pathans on India's northwestern border in 1915. . . . The British combed revolutionaries in Egypt and the rebellious Sultan of Darfur in 1916. The 1917, bombers put down an uprising" on India's border with Afghanistan, and in 1920 "Enzeli [a major port city] in Iran was bombed in an attempt to create a British puppet state."[58]

Genocide sometimes accompanied—or resulted from—European colonialism, especially once the colonizers determined that they wanted the land, rather than the forced labor, of local populations. The commanding German officer responsible for the Herero and Nama Genocide of 1904–1908, General von Trotha, wrote to fellow officers: "The exercise of violence with crass terrorism and with cruelty is my policy. I annihilate the rebellious tribes with streams of blood. . . . Only on this seed can something new emerge that will remain."[59] After the genocide, von Trotha wrote a public statement in a local (South-West African) newspaper that proclaimed that, while in earlier stages of colonization the Europeans needed the labor of the natives, "later they must disappear" to make room for European settlers and in accord with the "law of the survival of the fittest."[60] In a war that is less well-known than the Herero genocide, the Germans were simultaneously suppressing the "Maji-Maji Revolt" in East Africa, killing more than 200,000 people and employing tactics that would later be part of Western counterinsurgency strategies during the Cold War: destroying villages and crops and otherwise attempting to eliminate the rebels' base of support.[61]

MASS ATROCITIES IN THE SOVIET UNION AND ASIA

In addition to the Nazi Holocaust and other episodes that are uniformly characterized as genocide, the last century witnessed other instances of mass killing on

[57]Lindqvist, *Exterminate*, 21.
[58]Lindqvist, *A History of Bombing* (London: Granta, 2001), 42–43.
[59] Dominik J. Schaller and Jürgen Zimmerer, "Settlers, Imperialism, Genocide: Introduction," *Journal of Genocide Research* 10, no. 2 (June 2008), 193.
[60]Ibid., 195.
[61]Bridget Conley-Zilkic and Alex de Waal, "Setting the Agenda for Evidence-Based Research on Ending Mass Atrocities," Journal of Genocide Research 16, no. 1 (March 2014), 63; Dominik J. Schaller, "Genocide in German Southwest Africa and German East Africa," in A. Dirk Moses, ed., Empire, Colony, Genocide: Conquest, Occupation, and Subaltern Resistance in World History (New York: Berghahn, 2008), 296–324. The Maji-Maji Revolt and its suppression are awaiting a thorough study; in the meantime, this 1976 article is probably the best summary: Detlev Bald, "Afrikanischer Kampf gegen kononalie Herrschaft: Der Maji-Maji-Aufstand in Ostafrika," *Militärgeschichte Mitteilungen* 19 (1976), 23–50.

Mayan women call for justice

Demonstration in Guatemala City, 2013. The former Guatemalan military ruler Rios Montt was tried for genocide and crimes against humanity and, convicted in May 2013—the first time a former head of state was convicted of such charges in his own country. A few days later, however, the Constitutional Court annulled the verdict because of a technicality, and a retrial was set for January 2015 but it was suspended. The legal proceedings have prompted large demonstrations, often under the slogans "Si hubo genocidio" and "Nunca más": "Yes, there was genocide" and "never again."

scales that were unprecedented, but that may not fall into the category of genocide. Under Joseph Stalin in the 1930s, the Soviet regime committed its gravest
offenses against its own peoples. Beginning in 1929, the USSR, encompassing historically underdeveloped and agrarian lands, embarked upon a wildly accelerated
drive to industrialize and "catch up with the West." This rapid industrialization
was accompanied by forced collectivization of the peasantry, and the government
announced a campaign to destroy the entire social class of "kulaks." There was,
however, no single, stable definition of *kulak*. The term is often translated as
"wealthy" or "prosperous" peasant, but many people designated as kulaks were far
from wealthy; owning a single cow could cause a peasant to be deemed a kulak,
with lethal consequences. As many as 10 million "kulaks" and their family members were deported to the harshest regions of Siberia or interred at dismal labor
camps, such as the infamous Kolyma, which closely resembled the Nazis' most
notorious camps in its daily routine.

The Soviet government presided over a famine that killed several million
Ukrainians in 1932–1933. Of Stalin's many crimes, the Ukrainian famine—the
Holodomor ("killing by hunger"), as Ukrainians still bitterly call it—most closely

matches our understanding of "genocide," although this designation is still hotly debated: Was it an intentional effort to destroy a nationality that was restive and, from Stalin's point of view, too nationalistic? Newly discovered evidence continues to influence the debate on this question, but, at the very least, the *Holodomor* was the result of official miscalculation and criminal incompetence and indifference. The neighboring republic of Kazakhstan also suffered greatly; as many as 1 to 2 million Kazaks, out of a population of only 4 million, died during the famine there in the early 1930s. And the Stalinist leadership concluded the 1930s with the "Great Terror," a far-ranging search for "enemies" that gathered lethal momentum and ultimately claimed the lives of roughly 700,000 people.[62] And, as we will see in subsequent chapters, in no case has genocide or murderous persecution been driven solely by the will of a totalitarian state; in each case, there was some degree of support and participation by common people. In its campaigns against the kulaks and the "enemies of socialism," Stalin's regime succeeded in generating widespread enthusiasm and complicity. Many victims of the Great Terror were turned in by neighbors or coworkers who sought to profit or to protect themselves, or who acted out of genuine, if deluded, conviction. We see similar patterns of behavior during many other periods of repression and hysteria, dating at least as far back as the Spanish Inquisition.

Another 1 million Soviet citizens languished in the USSR's extensive camp network, the Gulag, by the end of the 1930s, and by the time of Stalin's death in 1953 the camps had incarcerated more than 10 million people. In a cruel twist of fate, many thousands of Soviet war veterans who had somehow survived Nazi prisoner-of-war camps (Chapter 2) were, upon their return, imprisoned in the Gulag under charges of collaboration with the Germans. The organizer of an uprising in the Nazis' Sobibor death camp, for example, was jailed for five years by his own government after the war, a victim of the paranoid and anti-Semitic atmosphere of Stalin's final years.[63]

The Ukrainians were not the only national or ethnic group to be singled out under Stalin's reign. During the last two years of World War II, Stalin's government carried out wholesale deportations of several national or ethnic minorities who were falsely accused of sympathizing with the German invaders. Chechnya, a predominantly Muslim region deep in Russia's southwest corner, was nearly emptied of its Chechen and Ingush populations, with 500,000 residents driven into exile, and many tens of thousands of Tatars, Greeks, Turks, Karachais, Balkars, and other peoples deported because of their ethnicities.[64] All told, roughly 1 million people were uprooted from their homelands, usually sent to distant camps or settlements. And earlier in the war the Soviet regime had exiled an additional 1 million Germans

[62] Jones, *Genocide*, 130.
[63] Thomas Blatt, "Excerpts from an Interview with Alexander Aronowicz Pechersky": http://www.sobibor.info/hero.html (accessed July 31, 2013).
[64] Alexander Statiev, "Soviet Ethnic Deportations: Intent Versus Outcome," *Journal of Genocide Research* 11, no. 2–3 (June-September 2009), 246.

and 400,000 Poles.[65] This brief catalog of his crimes inadequately conveys Stalin's malign contributions to the murderous twentieth century. The influence, direct and indirect, of Stalin and his brand of "communism" is seen in tyrannical, inhumane regimes from Maoist China and Khmer Rouge-era Cambodia to Ethiopia's bloody Mengistu dictatorship (1974–1991), which was responsible for hundreds of thousands of deaths through political terror, violent repression, and famine; and Stalinism is also responsible for the corrupt, brutish Eastern European governments that took power after World War II. (See Chapter 3 for more on the emergence and character of Stalinism.)

By the 1970s, the *Shoah*—the Hebrew term that designates the Holocaust—had emerged in Western public consciousness and collective memory as the central moral drama and greatest calamity of World War II. While this is justified, the war unleashed other massive, genocidal crimes. For example, Japanese forces, guided by their leaders' own set of racial obsessions and imperial ambitions, killed approximately 200,000 Chinese during the notorious 1937 "Rape of Nanking," and murdered an additional 4 to 6 million during their occupation of China, which only concluded with the end of the war in 1945. Japan's full-scale invasion of China proper in 1937 can be considered the beginning of World War II (some date the world war to the Japanese invasion of China's northeastern region of Manchuria six years earlier). By 1942 Japan's huge empire extended west to Burma, north beyond Korea into Manchuria, south to Indonesia (the Dutch East Indies), and farther east into other Pacific islands. The Japanese government and military committed vast crimes throughout its realm. In addition to mass killings in countries it ruled or invaded during the war, these included forced labor on vast projects, which took the lives of tens of thousands of (mostly Asian) prisoners; systematic, widespread imposition of sexual slavery; and cruel medical experiments that rivaled those of the Nazis.[66]

The final chapter of World War II's unprecedented carnage was the bombing of Hiroshima and Nagasaki—the first and only use of nuclear bombs to date, claiming at least 200,000 lives, among them tens of thousands of Koreans and members of other nationalities, including a small number of Dutch prisoners of war (POWs). The Americans' decision is still debated, as is the role of the bombings in bringing the war to a close; it is likely that the USSR's entry into the Pacific war,

---

[65]Ibid., 244, 246. Also see Norman Naimark, *Stalin's Genocides*.
[66]"Unit 731," established in Manchuria, was the site of the most notorious experiments. Japanese scientists oversaw a vast program "dedicated to developing biological weapons, including plague, anthrax, and typhus," wrote one historian. "POWS and Chinese victims were frozen, placed inside pressure chambers to see how long it took before their eyeballs popped from their sockets, or were tied to stakes and bombarded with test weapons. Children as young as 3 years of age" were among the victims; others "underwent vivisection without anesthetic." As many as 200,000 Chinese were killed in such experiments. Joanna Burke, *The Second World War: A People's History* (Oxford: Oxford University Press, 2001), 69–70. After the war, US authorities gave amnesty to thousands of Unit 731 perpetrators, on condition that they reveal the knowledge and data they collected from these experiments. Ibid., 70, and Jones, *Genocide*, 74.

by invading Japan's puppet state in Manchuria on August 8, exerted a greater influence in bringing about Japan's surrender. There is little room for debate about the fierce anti-Japanese racism that was a factor in Truman's decision. In a communication to his secretary of war, Henry Stimson, a few weeks earlier, Truman referred to the "Japs" as "savages, ruthless and fanatic"; two days after the bombing of Nagasaki, the president stated, "When you have a beast you have to treat him like a beast."[67] Such language was not an aberration. In his important 1986 book *War Without Mercy: Race and Power in the Pacific War*, historian John Dower used contemporary accounts, letters, and texts from popular culture to uncover and analyze the extent of racial hatred that fueled the US war against Japan and that facilitated such atrocities as "mutilating Japanese war dead for souvenirs, attacking and sinking hospital ships, shooting sailors who had abandoned ship and pilots who had bailed out . . . and torturing and executing prisoners."[68] Shortly before being named commander of the South Pacific Force, Admiral William Halsey exhorted his troops with such slogans as "Kill Japs, kill Japs, kill more Japs."[69] In popular culture, the Japanese were "perceived as a race apart, even a species apart," argued Dower; "and an overpoweringly monolithic one at that," while the conflict in the Pacific was regularly described as "a racial war."[70] The US Army produced now-infamous posters that called for "every murdering Jap" to be "wiped out"—posters that were replete with grotesque racist caricatures. A button bluntly proclaiming "We'll Bomb Each Jap Right Off the Map" could be produced and worn without embarrassment or reproach.[71] "By the final year of the war, one out of four US combatants stated that his primary goal was not to help bring about Japan's surrender, but simply to kill as many Japanese as possible."[72] These murderous sentiments were shared by civilians at home: In a December 1944 public opinion poll in the United States, 13 percent answered, "Kill all Japanese people" to the question "What do you think we should about Japan as a country after the war?"[73]

---

[67] Tsuyoshi Hasegawa, "Were the Atomic Bombings Justified?," in Yuki Tanaka and Marilyn B. Young, eds., *Bombing Civilians: A Twentieth-Century History* (New York: The New Press, 2009), 124, 128.

[68] John W. Dower, *War without Mercy: Race and Power in the Pacific War* (New York: Pantheon, 1986), 61–62.

[69] Quoted in Dower, 36.

[70] Ibid., 8.

[71] "World War II Home Front: Anti-Japanese," an online collection of anti-Japanese propaganda materials produced in the Unites States during the war. http://www.authentichistory.com/1939-1945/2-homefront/3-anti-jap/index.html (accessed January 20, 2013). Shortly after the August 1945 atomic bombings, popular toy company A.C. Gilbert produced a game called "Atomic Bomb," a puzzle "which let players reenact the bombing of Japan." From online exhibit by the Wisconsin Historical Society, "Living Under a Mushroom Cloud: Fear and Hope in the Atomic Age": http://www.wisconsinhistory.org/museum/atomic/fear.asp (accessed January 20, 2013).

[72] Dower, *War without Mercy*, 53.

[73] Gary Paul Bass, *Stay the Hand of Vengeance: The Politics of War Crimes* (Princeton, NJ: Princeton University Press, 2000), 198.

Darfur refugee camp, 2009
Abu Shouk refugee camp, Darfur, 2009. Much of the world turned its attention to Darfur in the early 21st century—at least temporarily. Yet very little was done to alleviate or end the slaughter and suffering. As in other cases, months and years were wasted at the UN in semantic debates. The violence diminished somewhat in the first year or two of the 2010s but since May 2011 it has worsened, and extended to the border region separating Sudan from the new state of South Sudan. (See "Timeline of Genocide and Genocidal Crimes Against Humanity" for more information.)

POST–WORLD WAR II GENOCIDE

Revelations of Nazi atrocities shook humanity's faith in progress and reason and brought about, for the first time, extensive international attention to this age-old blight, and in 1948 the United Nations held its convention on genocide. If it is possible to conclude that anything positive emerged from the ashes of Auschwitz, it is that racism and anti-Semitism were largely discredited (although they did not disappear), and for the first time the world's attention was focused on genocide.

The earnest, well-meaning injunction "never again" (in German: *nie wieder*) has often been invoked after the extent of the Holocaust became known. Yet this lofty term must ring hollow to the families of the many millions of victims of genocidal violence in the postwar world. It is impossible to conclude that the "international community" has learned from the Holocaust when we survey the numerous cases of mass killing in the postwar world, and the near-total absence of effective international action in response.

The Cold War served as a cover or justification for the world's superpowers to install, finance, or at least condone murderous regimes in their respective spheres of influence. In Guatemala, the US administration, alarmed by the moderate land reforms of a left-leaning government, overthrew the democratic state in 1954 and installed a military dictatorship that murdered tens of thousands of real and perceived opponents over the next four decades. This dictatorship's violence reached a grisly crescendo under Generals Lucas Garcia and Rios Montt between 1981 and 1983.[74] A pattern that was all too familiar in Central and South America in the 1970s and 1980s unfolded: Facing a left-wing guerrilla movement, the military's "counterinsurgency" campaigns targeted civilian populations that supposedly provided support for the guerrillas. Guatemala's Mayan Indians—long oppressed in the country's highly stratified and racist society—suffered the brunt of this campaign, and tens of thousands of Indians were killed by government troops or allied "death squads." Also enjoying US patronage during the Cold War, other Latin American dictatorships from El Salvador to Uruguay massacred hundreds of thousands of peasants, trade unionists, political activists, and other civilians in the name of anti-communism and counterinsurgency. Some regimes, such as the Chilean, Argentine, and Bolivian dictatorships, employed Nazi war criminals, who claimed expertise and experience in fighting "communism."

Indonesia's military dictatorship (1966–1998) also received the steadfast support of the West, despite coming to power through a fearsome bloodbath that claimed about 500,000 civilians and political opponents, many of whose names were provided to the army by the US Central Intelligence Agency (CIA). Indonesia invaded tiny East Timor in 1975 and conducted a wave of genocidal actions until the island's independence in 1999. During the most intense period of this protracted genocide—from 1975 to 1980—massacres, aerial bombings, and state-engineered famine killed close to one-quarter of East Timor's 620,000 people.[75] "Pray for us, that God will quickly send away this scourge of war," wrote a Timorese inhabitant in a 1978 letter. "The mountains shake with bombardment, the earth talks with the blood of the people who die miserably."[76] The Indonesian occupation finally ended after a 1999 referendum, in which the large majority of East Timorese voted for independence. But before leaving, Indonesian troops and allied paramilitary forces indulged in a final orgy of burning, looting, and mayhem, driving some 300,000 people into flight and killing another 1,500.[77]

The Soviet Union's postwar sphere of influence was smaller than that of its Cold War adversary, the United States. Until their regimes collapsed like so many houses of cards in 1989–1990, the USSR's Eastern European clients effectively suppressed

---

[74]Israel also provided economic and military assistance to the Guatemalan dictatorship and army during this time. See Jane Hunter, "The Israeli Role in Guatemala," *Race & Class* 29 (1987), 35–54; and Jane Hunter and Jane Power, *No Simple Proxy: Israel in Central America: A Report* (Washington, DC: Washington Middle East Associates, 1987).

[75]Kiernan, *Blood and Soil*, 578.

[76]John G. Taylor, "'Encirclement and annihilation': The Indonesian Occupation of East Timor," in Kiernan and Gellately, *Specter*, 166.

[77]Kiernan, *Blood and Soil*, 581.

their respective peoples through police-state tactics. They were not reticent to use violence when deemed necessary; rather, they were able to maintain power for forty years without recourse to the wanton slaughter employed by many Western allies in the underdeveloped world. But the record of postwar state Communism was hardly bloodless. Chapter 3 examines the genocide committed by Cambodia's Communist Party (Khmer Rouge) government in the late 1970s. The human toll of the Khmer Rouge's atrocities was surpassed, though, by China's Communist government during the reign of Mao Zedong (Tse-Tung) from 1949 to 1976. While none of his policies clearly fit the "genocide" label, Mao's reign—"the worst non-genocidal regime," in one historian's astute judgment—was responsible for the deaths of tens of millions of people through famine and mass murder.[78] The most lethal famine— and indeed, the worst in all of modern history—occurred from 1959 to 1961, result-ing from the so-called Great Leap Forward, a criminally incompetent, chaotic adventure in rapid industrialization and forced collectivization. More than 20 mil-lion people, and possibly twice that number, perished. Such calamities did not disturb the "Great Helmsman," as Mao was known: "Even if half the population of the world was wiped out this would not be a total disaster," he casually uttered.[79] Subsequent campaigns of political hysteria and mass repression—most ruinously, the Cultural Revolution (1966–1976)—claimed many hundreds of thousands of lives in Mao's final decade. His successors have retained a highly repressive state that deals harshly with ethnic and national minorities, such as the Tibetans and, less known to the outside world, the Uyghurs and other Muslim peoples in north-west China.

And while the peoples of the Soviet Union never again experienced the inten-sity of Stalin's murderous repression, Moscow unleashed a fearsome war on Afghanistan in the 1980s. Some observers have designated the Soviet war as geno-cide, based not only on the tremendous human toll (somewhere between 1.5 and 2 million Afghanis were killed, 90 percent of them civilians) but also on evidence of the systematic massacres of noncombatants, the forced transfer of children, and other actions that fit elements of the UN definition of genocide. The legacy of that war is all too evident in today's Afghanistan, still plagued by the lawlessness and brutal power struggles that were fomented and unleashed during the Soviet war,

---

[78] The quotation is from Jean-Louis Margolin, "Mao's China: The Worst Non-Genocidal Regime?," in Dan Stone, ed., *The Historiography of Genocide* (London: Palgrave Macmillan, 2008), 438–467. Much has been written on Maoist China; among recent books, these are recommended: For the "Great Leap Forward," Frank Dikötter, *Mao's Great Famine* (New York: Walker & Company, 2011); on the Cultural Revolution, Roderick MacFarquhar and Michael Schoenhals made an important contribution with their 2006 *Mao's Last Revolution* (Cambridge, MA: Belknap Press of Harvard University Press); for a comprehensive over-view and appraisal of Mao's tenure in power, Timothy Cheek, ed., *A Critical Introduction to Mao* (New York: Cambridge University Press, 2010).

[79] Kiernan, *Blood and Soil*, 530–531. The Soviet Union's experiments in forced, rapid collectiv-ization and industrialization heavily influenced Mao's policy. For other reasons, the two Communist Party superpowers underwent an acrimonious split, which became visible by the end of 1961.

and exacerbated by US and Pakistani funding and training of violent Islamist radicals. As widely remarked upon at the time, the Soviet Union had been lured into its own Vietnam; that is, a misguided adventure, stumbled into by policymakers who were overly infatuated with military power but possessed little sense of history—and an "adventure" doomed to fail and to undermine the power and prestige of the superpower.[80] For little clear strategic purpose[81]—save to uphold US prestige and halt the presumed advance of communism—the United States eventually deployed more than 500,000 troops to the war in Vietnam (usually dated 1964–1975, from the time of the heavy commitment of US troops to the collapse of the Republic of South Vietnam).

The US military employed several tactics that targeted civilians as well as combatants and resulted in massive casualties: the creation of "free-fire zones," in which anything moving could be bombed or strafed; the copious use of chemical warfare; internment in camps; the wholesale destruction of villages; and campaigns, coordinated with the South Vietnamese dictatorship, to wipe out perceived political enemies (such as the "Phoenix Program," which led to the torture and murder of nearly 100,000 Vietnamese). A March 1968 massacre of hundreds of Vietnamese civilians in the village of My Lai became emblematic of US atrocities. This massacre was far from an isolated incident: In 1971, a US colonel admitted that "every unit of brigade size has its My Lai hidden someplace."[82]

Predictably, a war of this nature corrupted many of the American soldiers, some of whom indulged in such grisly practices as the collection of body parts, a form of trophy-taking that has been chronicled in other wars dating to antiquity. The combat in Vietnam provides telling examples of the brutalization and dehumanization of

---

[80]Afghanistan's sad saga of unrelenting violence has now spanned more than thirty years. The US invasion of October 2001 wrought additional strife and instability. American forces quickly toppled the reactionary, oppressive, misogynist Taliban government, but put in its place an unusually corrupt, weak central government. Large regions were quickly seized by the warlords who had ruled most of the country before the Taliban took power in 1996, while other areas fell back into the hands of Taliban factions. As this book goes to press in late 2015, it is difficult to be optimistic about Afghanistan's near future.

[81]In a March 24, 1965 memo, Assistant Secretary of Defense for International Security Affairs John McNaughton summarized US goals thus: "70%—To avoid a humiliating US defeat (to our reputation as a guarantor). 20%—To keep SVN (and then adjacent) territory from Chinese hands. 10%—To permit the people of SVN to enjoy a better, freer way of life. ALSO—To emerge from crisis without unacceptable taint from methods used. NOT—To 'help a friend,' although it would be hard to stay in if asked out." *The Pentagon Papers: The Senator Gravel Edition*, Vol. 3 (Boston: Beacon Press, 1971), 349.

[82]Jerry Kuzmarov, *The Myth of the Addicted Army: Vietnam and the Modern War on Drugs* (Amherst, MA: University of Massachusetts Press, 2009), 33. The colonel, Oran Henderson, made these comments on May 24, 1971, during a court martial that was brought against him for serving as commanding officer of the unit. He was acquitted. Nick Turse, "A My Lai a Month," *The Nation* December 1, 2008: http://www.thenation.com/article/my-lai-month?page=full# (accessed July 22, 2012). Two recent well-researched books have chronicled, in extensive detail, American atrocities in Vietnam: Bernd Greiner, *War Without Fronts: The USA in Vietnam* (New Haven, CT: Yale University Press, 2010) and Nick Turse, *Kill Anything That Moves: The Real American War in Vietnam* (New York: Picador, 2013).

war, especially those with colonial and racial overtones. "The only thing they told us [in basic training] about the Viet Cong was they were gooks," said one US veteran later. "They were to be killed. Nobody sits around and gives you their historical and cultural background. They're the enemy. Kill, kill, kill. That's what we got in practice. Kill, kill, kill."[83] Ultimately, somewhere between 3 and 5 million Vietnamese were killed during the US war, which failed to prevent the victory of the nationalist and Communist forces in 1975.[84]

Addressing an international tribunal on US war crimes in Vietnam, Jean-Paul Sartre pointed to several factors that lent a genocidal character to the American assault. Any war in the modern epoch, the French philosopher suggested—and especially a war with a colonial component—would become a "total war," engulfing civilians as well as soldiers. All members of the "enemy" nation would inevitably be viewed as the enemy. And "against partisans backed by the entire population, colonial armies are helpless," Sartre added, and their only hope for victory will be "to eliminate the civilian population."[85]

Vietnam, Cambodia, and Laos were not the only nations in their region to experience such atrocities. In 1971, in a futile attempt to maintain control of East Pakistan—which would soon become the independent state of Bangladesh—Pakistan's military government conducted a series of well-organized massacres, replete with mass rapes and the wholesale destruction of villages, that assumed genocidal dimensions, ultimately killing at least 1 million people and perhaps two or three times that number.[86]

In Southwest Asia or the Middle East, the dictatorship of Saddam Hussein singled out the Kurdish people of northern Iraq for destruction during the 1986–1989 "Operation Anfal."[87] This campaign reached its murderous apex in 1988,

---

[83]Christian Appy, *Working-Class War: American Combat Soldiers and Vietnam* (Chapel Hill, NC: University of North Carolina Press, 1993), 107.

[84]The most accurate estimates probably come from a study conducted by researchers from Harvard Medical School and the Institute for Health Metrics and Evaluation at the University of Washington. It concluded that 3.8 million Vietnamese people were killed: http://www.bmj.com/content/336/7659/1482 (accessed May 12, 2014). Historian and journalist Nick Turse, author of one of the most exhaustive accounts of the conduct of the American war, wrote that even this "staggering figure may be an underestimate." https://portside.org/2014-05-08/four-decades-after-vietnam (accessed May 12, 2014).

[85]Jean-Paul Sartre, "On Genocide," presented at the Russell International War Crimes Tribunal, June 1967: http://www.sartre.org/Writings/genocide.htm (accessed August 11, 2012). Sartre was probably using the term "genocide" for polemical rather than purely analytical purposes; nonetheless, his argument has force.

[86]For sexual violence by the Pakistani army in Bangladesh in 1971, see Yasmin Saikia, *Women, War, and the Making of Bangladesh: Remembering 1971* (Durham, NC: Duke University Press, 2011); Sultana Kamal, "The 1971 Genocide in Bangladesh and Crimes Committed Against Women," in Indai Lourdes Sajar, ed., *Common Grounds: Violence Against Women in War and Armed Conflict Situations* (Quezon City, Philippines: Asian Center for Women's Human Rights, 1998); Lisa Sharlach, "State Rape: Sexual Violence as Genocide," from Samuel Totten and Paul R. Bartrop, eds., *The Genocide Studies Reader* (New York: Routledge, 2009), 182–184.

[87]Al-Anfal, which means "The Spoils of War," is the eighth sura of the Qur'an.

when Iraqi forces used poisonous gas in a full-scale assault, killing more than 100,000 Kurds, according to the most reliable recent estimates. The Kurdish town of Halabja, where in March 1988 at least five thousand civilians were killed by gas dropped from the air, came to symbolize these atrocities, which were reminiscent of the German bombing of Guernica, in northern Spain, in 1937. The offensive against the Kurds and other minorities within Iraq provoked little protest from the major Western powers, which at the time considered Hussein an ally.

In more recent years, the government of the East African nation of Sudan, in loose coordination with a dreaded militia called the *janjaweed*, has conducted large-scale rape, murder, and forced removals against the Fur and other peoples of the country's Darfur region. The conflict arose from a set of issues that is far more complex than the "Arab vs. African" framework usually invoked in the English-speaking news media. These issues include a fierce competition for land amid an environmental crisis that has made natural resources scarcer than ever. The more immediate cause was a June 2003 uprising, which the government of Omar al-Bashir—which had responded with wildly disproportionate violence to previous threats—sought to extinguish with harsh repression that quickly evolved into a wide-ranging campaign against several ethnic groups. The bloodletting in Darfur is further complicated by warfare in other regions of the country, especially in nearby regions of the south, throughout the first decade of the twenty-first century. By early 2015, some 350,000 Darfuris had died and nearly 3 million had been displaced.[88] In July 2011 a peace agreement was signed by the al-Bashir government and an umbrella group representing the major rebel factions; in that same month, South Sudan became an independent nation. Neither development brought a permanent cessation to hostilities in the region; al-Bashir's government launched attacks on Nuba and Dinka Ngok peoples at the very time it was negotiating the 2011 agreement. Disease has been the principal culprit in the humanitarian calamity—although it must be stressed that these diseases and their effects arise from the conditions that the Sudanese government has knowingly created by driving its victims into flight. According to a 2010 report, "diarrhea spread by filthy water, pneumonia picked up in swirls of desert dust and fire smoke, malaria carried into their tents by mosquitoes and other maladies from years of rough living" are responsible for a majority of the deaths.[89]

While considerable media and popular attention was devoted to Darfur, an even larger tragedy unfolded a few hundred miles to the southeast, where since 1996 more than 6 million people have perished in a series of wars in Congo, the

---

[88]See Olivier Degomme and Debarati Guha-Sapir, "Patterns of Mortality Rates in Darfur Conflict," *The Lancet* (January 23, 2010), 294–300. "We estimated the excess number of deaths to be 298, 271." The report concluded that while "violence was the main cause of death during 2004, diseases have been the cause of most deaths since 2005, with displaced populations being the most susceptible."

[89]Donald G. McNeil, Jr., "New Study Estimates That Disease Caused 80% of Deaths During Years of Darfur Strife," *The New York Times*, January 23, 2010, A4.

large majority of them during the "Second Congo War" of 1998–2003. (More in Chapter 4.) While most of these killings have resulted from a multiparty scramble for natural resources and political power, some victims have been singled out for their inclusion in identifiable ethnic groups. The Rwandan government, led by the political and military force that put an end to its own country's genocide by overturning the Hutu-extremist regime in 1994, is largely responsible for the warfare in neighboring Congo. Perhaps this moral and political confusion is one reason the Congo war has garnered so little attention outside of Africa.

For the first two generations after World War II, Europeans could take solace in the knowledge that such horrors no longer plagued their own continent. But a development that seemed to herald greater peace and unity in Europe—the collapse of Communist party regimes between 1989 and 1991—instead brought about a catastrophic war in Yugoslavia. Following the collapse of the Soviet Union and its allied states, most countries made painful, uneven transitions to free-market economies and multiparty political systems. In some cases, political, economic, and social crises generated powerful nationalist sentiments and movements.

Most disastrous was the example of Yugoslavia, where the disintegration of the state gave way to a bitter struggle for land and power, pitting the dominant Orthodox Christian Serbian population against the Roman Catholic Croatians and the Bosnian Muslims, who ultimately suffered the most. Grievous crimes were committed by all states and militias involved. Yet Serbia's nationalist, racist government, led by Slobodan Milošević and its allied Bosnian Serb militias, and their drive to forge a "Greater Serbia" through conquest and expulsion, bear greatest responsibility fix, with the Croatian forces a not-too-distant second. The wars of 1991 to 1995 killed more than 100,000 people, mostly civilian, while another million or so people were internally displaced. I argue, with most genocide scholars, that despite the complexities Serbian policies and actions earned the "genocide" label is not easy to assign here, but specific incidents, such as a massacre of more than eight thousand Bosnian Muslim men and boys by Serb forces in July 1995, fit the standard definitions. This massacre also exposed the dismaying impotence of the "international community": As in Rwanda the previous year, European peacekeeping troops stood idly by as the atrocities multiplied.

The Yugoslav wars introduced a problematic new term into our political lexicon: "ethnic cleansing." This wording was quickly adopted by diplomats and politicians, commentators, and scholars. The phrase is tainted by its probable origins—that is, as a term coined by perpetrators to advocate or celebrate their misdeeds. It was reportedly used by Serbian nationalists (*Chetniks*), as well as by Hitler and other Nazi leaders, during World War II.[90] And, as genocide historian Martin Shaw pointed out in a 2007 book, the term "ethnic cleansing" accepts and embeds, rather

---

[90]Norman Cigar, *Genocide in Bosnia* (College Station, TX: Texas A & M University Press, 1995), 18; Kiernan, *Blood and Soil*, 440.

than critiques, the perpetrators' notions of racial or ethnic "hygiene."[91] But this term nonetheless succinctly embodies a crime that is often integral to genocide (and which in itself is genocidal).

WHY DO HUMANS COMMIT GENOCIDE?

Finally, this book will consider the most troublesome question that arises from any study of genocide: How can seemingly ordinary human beings be lured or coerced into committing cruel acts? The concluding chapter will consider some historical, sociological, and psychological perspectives on this question.

The term "evil-doer" came into wide use in the United States after the September 11, 2001, terrorist attacks. But the notion that we can simply label some people "evil," and that this is all we need to know about their motives, is superficial, as well as erroneous. "If only there were evil people somewhere, insidiously committing evil deeds," wrote the Russian author Alexander Solzhenitsyn, we could simply "separate them from the rest of us and destroy them. But the line dividing good and evil cuts through the heart of every human being."[92]

In recent years, historian Christopher Browning, psychologist James Waller, and others have shared some illuminating insights into this problem of individual participation. In *Ordinary Men: Reserve Police Battalion 101 and the Final Solution* (1991), Browning examined the actions of German troops who conducted massacres of Jewish civilians in Poland. Few of these murderers were fanatical Nazis or racists. Rather, they succumbed to combinations of "wartime brutalization, racism," the "routinization" of their grisly tasks, "careerism, obedience to orders, deference to authority, ideological indoctrination, and conformity"—factors that were all present, "in varying degrees," but none of which fully explains their motivations.[93] "If the men" of the battalion that Browning studied "could become killers under such circumstances, what group of men cannot?" *Ordinary Men* solemnly concluded.[94] Waller's 2007 *Becoming Evil: How Ordinary People Commit Genocide and Mass Killing* argues persuasively that we must go beyond the historical and cultural factors that genocide scholars have dwelt upon and examine deeper, long-standing psychological forces. Adam Jones, the author and editor of several recent books on genocide, points out that humiliation, greed, narcissism, and fear can each— singly or in combination—serve as powerful inducements for the sort of murderous, cruel behavior that genocide requires.

Perhaps out of a justified aversion to one-dimensional structural explanations, historians can be slow to investigate or detect larger economic contexts. But a

---

[91] Martin Shaw, *What is Genocide?* (Cambridge, UK: Polity, 2007), 49.
[92] Waller, *Becoming Evil*, 171.
[93] Christopher Browning, *Ordinary Men* (New York: Harper, 1993), 159.
[94] Ibid., 189.

survivor of the Rwandan genocide vividly illustrated the psychological and social effects of extreme underdevelopment and poverty in the villages where he had lived in Central Africa:

> *Women get so exhausted from walking miles for the family's water every day, cooking, and otherwise caring for the family, that by the time they're thirty they are old ladies. . . . Almost everyone has worms. . . . Can you imagine that kind of life? It's terrible. How are you going to think right? With pain everywhere. So it's been really hard to blame the people who have been slaughtering each other, though I do blame people all the time. They were not themselves. They were something else.*[95]

As noted, the concluding chapter delves more deeply into these questions of individuals' motivations, as well as factors that lead impersonal institutions, including governments and armies, to commit mass atrocities. Before the twentieth century, genocide usually occurred for utilitarian purposes; that is, the perpetrators determined that it was in their interest to remove a group or groups that stood in the way of expansion, conquest, or some other political goal. But in the last century it was ideological goals, often driven by racism or some variant of extreme nationalism—or by a utopian quest to reorder society in accord with an ideology—that fuelled most genocidal atrocities. Other societal factors often include "popular historical grievances, previous social traumas, ingrained poverty, educational deprivation, sudden political or economic destabilization, colonial occupation, and war," wrote Robert Gellately and Ben Kiernan, which often "foster the growth of sociopathic political movements."[96] Each of the genocides examined in the following four chapters demonstrates another dynamic that has led to dangerous volatility and even genocide: strong national ambitions accompanied by a deep sense of insecurity or vulnerability. For example, Cambodian nationalists of the 1970s—and German nationalists of the 1930s—were gripped by grandiose national ambitions, while simultaneously wracked with excessive anxiety over their country's weakness and vulnerability to internal or external attack.[97]

This brief survey cannot begin to do justice to these complex issues, but I hope it has at least suggested some of the cultural, social, and historic forces that have conspired to disfigure human history through repeated occurrences of genocide, the gravest crime imaginable. But we should enter this field of inquiry with great humility. While we will attempt to understand this pathology of genocide and its

---

[95]Tracy Kidder, *Strength in What Remains: A Journey of Remembrance and Forgiveness* (New York: Random House, 2009), 187.
[96]Kiernan and Gellately, *Specter*, 374–375.
[97]Ben Kiernan, "Myth, Nationalism and Genocide," *Journal of Genocide Research* 3, no. 2 (2001), 190.

origins, we may still find ourselves agreeing with Isaac Deutscher. The Polish-Jewish historian, whose parents died in Auschwitz, once said that the Holocaust might "forever baffle and terrify mankind with a huge and ominous mystery of the degeneration of the human spirit."[98] This mystery surely extends to the other genocides this book confronts.

---

[98]Isaac Deutscher, *The Non-Jewish Jew and Other Essays* (New York: Hill & Wang, 1968), 164.

1
THE ARMENIAN GENOCIDE

The old is dead and the new cannot be born; in this interregnum, many morbid symptoms appear.

—Antonio Gramsci

AS THEIR EMPIRE LAY dying in 1915, Ottoman authorities organized the killing of more than 1 million Armenians. Over the next several years, they and their successors murdered additional hundreds of thousands in sporadic attacks. Like the Ottoman Empire itself, this genocide straddled the premodern and modern worlds. The Armenian catastrophe was the century's "first total domestic genocide," as one expert observed, and it served as a horrifying precedent that shared many features of subsequent state-directed mass killings.[1] Centuries-old antagonisms were taken to new, harsher extremes by new theories of race and nation, while modern technology and organization produced scenes of torture and cruelty that equaled those of supposedly more barbaric times.

This chapter traces relations over the preceding centuries between the Muslim and the Armenian Christian populations; the emergence of Armenian nationalism in the nineteenth century, which was perceived as a dire threat by the Ottoman authorities; the 1894–1896 massacres of tens of thousands of Armenians, which helped dehumanize the Armenians in Turkish eyes and paved the way for subsequent atrocities; and the crumbling of the Ottoman Empire and the rise of the "Young Turks," whose efforts to revive and reconstitute the declining empire led directly to the end of the Armenians' millennium-long existence in Turkish lands. Like the German Nazis a few years later, they were determined to protect their

---

[1] Quotation from Robert Melson, *Revolution and Genocide* (Chicago: University of Chicago Press, 1996), 142.

realm "from division and disintegration for all time."[2] Another decisive factor was the onset of "total war" within the European conflagration of 1914–1918, which exacerbated the Ottoman regime's fears of Armenian disloyalty and removed any political and moral constraints.

THE ARMENIANS

From roughly 1000 BCE, the Armenian people inhabited areas that conform to present-day Syria and parts of Iraq, Turkey, and Iran, as well as the modern states of Armenia and Azerbaijan. Armenians believe that, at the dawn of the fourth century CE, the kingdom of Armenia was the first polity to adopt Christianity as its official religion; this is difficult to prove, but its importance lies in its centrality to Armenian identity and national consciousness. The remoteness and roughness of the Armenians' mountainous area produced a distinctive culture and unique language, which for many centuries developed in relative isolation. From the fifth century onward, however, most of historic Armenia was ruled by various foreign empires, including those of the Persians, Byzantines, Seljuk Turks, and Mongols. Mamluk Muslim armies captured the region in 1375, and it was incorporated into the Ottoman Empire in the sixteenth century. With its conquest of Constantinople (now Istanbul) in 1453, the Ottoman Empire had established itself as one of the world's great powers. Ruled by Muslim sultans, its territories spanned "from the gates of Vienna in the north to Mecca in the south" and enveloped numerous ethnic and religious minorities.[3]

Turks were the dominant ethnicity, and the Ottoman Empire itself was sometimes referred to as "Turkey" (and this chapter uses "Ottoman," "Turk," and "Turkey" interchangeably). But as it expanded, the empire encompassed many other ethnic, religious, and national groups, including such Christian peoples as Armenians, Greeks, Serbs, Croatians, and Bulgarians—as well as Kurds, Arabs, and others who were predominantly Muslim.

Islam traditionally taught that Christians and Jews were "peoples of the book"— that they shared the same deity as Muslims; that God had spoken to them through their prophets Moses and Jesus, and had given them holy scriptures; and that, when subject to Muslim authority, they should be treated with tolerance and offered a social-political contract (*dhimma*) outlining their privileges and duties. They thus became *dhimmis*. As dhimmis, Christians and Jews were allowed to practice their

---

[2]Shelley Baranowski, "Against 'Human Diversity as Such': Lebensraum and Genocide in the Third Reich," in Volker Langbehn and Mohammad Salama, eds., *German Colonialism: Race, the Holocaust, and Post-War Germany* (New York: Columbia University Press, 2011), 59.

[3]Quotation from Rouben Adalian, "The Armenian Genocide: Context and Legacy," in William Hewitt, ed., *Defining the Horrific* (Upper Saddle, NJ: Pearson Hall), 97. There were also substantial numbers of Armenians in areas beyond historic Armenia and the Ottoman Empire—for example, in Italy and other parts of southern Europe and the Balkans as well as in Persia (Iran).

religions, but certain civic and religious restrictions were placed on them, and they were subjected to special taxes. Consistent with this approach, the Ottomans established a "millet" system. Each millet corresponded to a religious community, which also tended to be closely tied to ethnicity; thus, the Greek Orthodox and Jewish communities, as well as Armenian and Syrian Christian (Orthodox), and Muslim communities were organized into millets, which theoretically gave them limited autonomy, at least in the realm of law. The Armenians inhabited six "vilayets" (provinces) of eastern Anatolia. (The peninsula of Anatolia constituted a large portion of the Ottomans' Asian territories and makes up most of present-day Turkey, which is much smaller than the Ottoman Empire of the nineteenth century.) A considerable part of Greater Armenia, largely the area east of Anatolia, was seized by Russia, the Ottomans' most bitter enemy, after the brief Russo-Turkish War of 1828–1829. The Treaty of Adrianople, which concluded the war, also mandated demographic shifts that Russia desired; Russia forced Muslims from the Georgian region into the Ottoman Empire, repopulating this area with Armenians who had formerly been under Ottoman rule. One significant result of these complex arrangements—which serve as a reminder that long before "ethnic cleansing" entered our vocabulary, nationalist empires oversaw large-scale population transfers—was that the Armenians' historic homeland was now divided between two hostile, autocratic empires: one Orthodox Christian, the other Sunni Muslim. As elsewhere in Europe and Asia, religious minorities suffered discrimination under Ottoman rule, but despite many forms of prejudice, punctuated by occasional violence, the Armenians' status was legally assured—as long as they and other dhimmis accepted their lot. While they were not treated with complete equality, the Armenians were at least tolerated, if often disdained as "giaours," or infidels. This, however, would change as the empire sank into terminal crisis during the nineteenth century.

By the 1870s, roughly 2 to 2.5 million Armenians lived among the empire's 35 to 40 million subjects. Urban Armenians were concentrated in the large western cities of Constantinople and Smyrna (present-day Izmir), where many belonged to a fairly affluent and successful middle class. This contributed to a misperception that the Armenians were financially successful and, worse yet in the popular imagination, engaged heavily in commercial dealings with outsiders, thus serving as a "link between external and internal Christian forces antithetical to the established order."[4] In reality, most urban dwellers scraped out meager livings as artisans or workers, while the large majority of Armenians were peasants.

A DECAYING EMPIRE CONFRONTS THE MODERN AGE

The Ottoman Empire was labeled "the sick man of Europe" in the 1850s by the Russian tsar, a fierce rival of the Ottomans whose own empire was hardly an exemplar of good health. But the term quickly caught on: The Empire had proved

---

[4]Donald Bloxham, *The Great Game of Genocide* (New York: Oxford University Press, 2007), 41.

incapable of keeping up with the industrial, political, and social modernization that swept much of Europe after the French Revolution. Despite a lengthy period of reforms (the "Tanzimat" of 1839–1876), the Ottomans could not escape the humiliating "sick man" label. Moreover, the empire had not only stagnated socially but also steadily disintegrated, losing Greece, Serbia, and other lands in the early nineteenth century, and additional territories in the 1850s and 1870s. This decline was rendered more pitiable by the not-so-distant memory of Ottoman power and glory; despite its prolonged downfall, the Ottoman Empire was, by some measures, "the most successful empire of modern times," surviving for six long centuries that saw the rise and fall of numerous world powers.[5]

The hopes of Turkish reformers, which had been raised by the limited progress of the Tanzimat, were dashed when Abdul Hamid II proclaimed himself sultan in 1878 and abrogated the 1876 constitution. As sultan, or head of state, Hamid would preside over an oppressive, autocratic regime until 1908. Hamid was deeply paranoid, moreover. Like the rulers of other crumbling empires, including the final tsar of Russia's Romanov dynasty, he solicited the advice of fortunetellers and other charlatans. Each of his meals necessitated elaborate security measures; he employed not one but two tasters—whose job was to ensure the sultan's food was not poisoned—one of many practices evocative of long-bygone despots. In another example, the sultan's veritable army of censors was obliged to take such measures as striking "H_2O" from science textbooks, for fear it could be interpreted as "Hamid the Second is nothing."[6] Hamid's state increasingly depended upon its extensive police and spy network as its public support dwindled.

Hamid harbored a pathological hatred of the Armenians and instituted policies that set precedents for the events that would unfold during World War I. To the sultan, "the very name of Armenia," as a British journalist stationed in Constantinople reported, was "anathema." In a characteristic episode, customs officials, following the sultan's dictates, seized a bible from a visiting American missionary in 1899 and "cut the maps out of his Bible because the name 'Armenia' appeared on them."[7]

Hamid was excessively alarmed over the appearance of small Armenian political parties in the 1880s and early 1890s, in particular the Armenian Revolutionary Federation (ARF), or Dashnaks, and the Hunchaks, a Marxist-oriented group. These new parties were products of an Armenian cultural and political renaissance toward the end of the century, which fostered greater unity among the disparate Armenian communities. Hamid's intolerance of even the most peaceful protest became evident during this time. Ottoman police attacked a peaceful demonstration in 1890 and killed a dozen Armenians, but this was mild compared to the

---

[5]Mark Mazower, quoted in Cathie Carmichael, *Genocide before the Holocaust* (New Haven, CT: Yale University Press, 2009), 10.

[6]Peter Balakian, *The Burning Tigris: The Armenian Genocide and the American Response* (New York: Harper Perennial, 2004), 49.

[7]Ibid., 36.

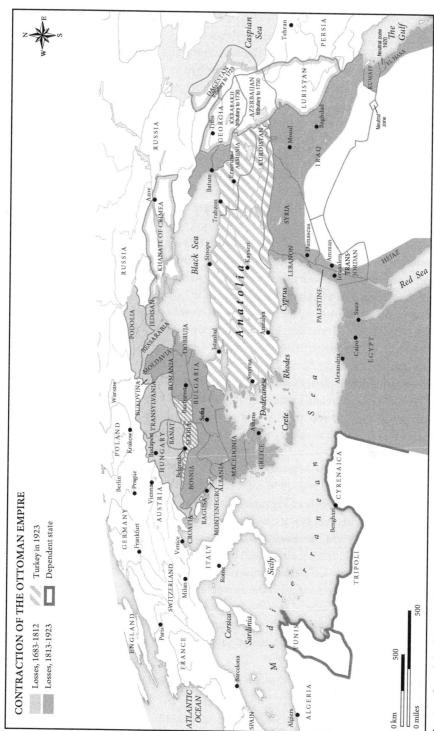

CONTRACTION OF THE OTTOMAN EMPIRE

Losses, 1683-1812
Losses, 1813-1923
Turkey in 1923
Dependent state

Contraction of the Ottoman Empire

suppression of a Hunchak rally in Constantinople five years later that degenerated into a city-wide pogrom, leaving many dozens dead.

This was only the beginning. Hamid earned the sobriquet "the Red Sultan" for presiding over a series of massacres between 1894 and 1896 that claimed more than 200,000 Armenian victims and helped pave the way, organizationally and psychologically, for the genocide to come. The massacres began in Sasun, a remote region with a large Armenian population that had become a hotbed of Hunchak agitation that was aimed principally at the "double taxation" inflicted upon the Armenians. (In addition to taxes to the central authorities, the residents were taxed by local Kurdish chieftains.) Organized resistance to the taxations prompted a harsh response, which one historian has characterized as "the first instance of organized mass murder of Armenians in modern Ottoman history . . . in peace time."[8]

The bloodshed and destruction gained a fearsome momentum. By the end of 1896, some 2,500 villages and towns lay in ruins, and more than 600 churches and monasteries had been destroyed.[9] Many Armenians engaged in self-defensive military operations; in the town of Zeitun, for example, Armenian forces killed several thousand Turkish soldiers. Such resistance only served to provoke intensified repression and murder, including the December 1895 burning to death of 2,500 to 3,000 Armenians, mostly women and children, in a cathedral in Şanliurfa (ancient and medieval Edessa, also known today as Urfa).[10] Meanwhile, other Armenian activists resorted to more desperate measures. In August 1896, three Dashnak activists made a daring, midday attack on a major bank in Constantinople, not to rob it but in hopes that this act would attract attention to their cause. Predictably, though, this action merely provided a pretext for greater violence and, in response, the regime unleashed a pogrom that took the lives of another 5,000 or more Armenians within the capital city.

The massacres of 1894–1896 were crucial precedents to the later genocide for several reasons. Because of organized Armenian political activity and appeals for foreign assistance, these episodes deepened the popular image of the Armenians as a disloyal population. Moreover, the carnage demonstrated that such violence could be carried out without penalty, a lesson not lost on the architects of the 1915–1923 genocide, and they were a key turning point in the radicalization of public attitudes, as well as state policies, toward the Armenians. As social psychologist Irvin Staub observed, "A progression of changes in a culture and individuals is usually required for mass killing or genocide."[11] The pogroms of the mid-1890s also accelerated the marginalization and perceived dehumanization of the Armenian people, revealing

[8]Vahakn Dadrian, *The History of the Armenian Genocide* (New York: Berghahn, 2004), 117.
[9]Balakian, *Burning Tigris*, 110.
[10]Ben Kiernan, *Blood and Soil: A World History of Genocide and Extermination from Sparta to Darfur* (New Haven, CT: Yale University Press, 2007), 399.
[11]Irvin Staub, *The Roots of Evil: The Origins of Genocide and Other Group Violence* (Cambridge, UK: Cambridge University Press, 1989), quoted in Balakian, 114–115.

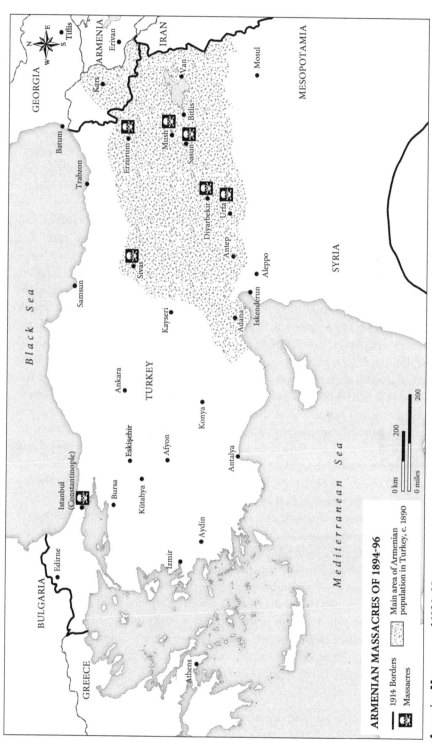

ARMENIAN MASSACRES OF 1894-96

1914 Borders

Massacres

Main area of Armenian
population in Turkey, c. 1890

0 km   200
0 miles   200

Armenian Massacres of 1894–96

a sharp shift in the Ottoman view of the Armenians, as the state "realigned on a more Islamic basis."[12]

EROSION OF THE EMPIRE

These massacres were the result not simply of irrational hatred but of the anxiety within ruling circles, and large segments of Ottoman society, over the empire's seemingly irreversible decline. The empire did not, however, simply crumble of its own accord. This was the age of European expansion and imperialism, and England, Russia, and other powers hastened to profit from Ottoman weakness. In 1876, the prominent Scottish historian and writer Thomas Carlyle, articulating a widely held view, called for "the immediate and summary expulsion of the Turk from Europe." This expulsion that Carlyle and many others craved would not be a peaceful process: As Bulgaria moved toward autonomy from the Ottomans in 1877, Turkish homes and buildings, as well as a mosque, were burned down, while in the city of Filibe that same year witnesses reported that "mosques were turned into latrines." In the early 1900s, Bulgarian gangs slaughtered Greeks and Muslims. But such violence was not confined to Bulgaria, which remained part of the empire until 1908—and it should be emphasized the Turkish forces carried out massacres against Bulgarians during the same period of strife. Russia, with which the Ottomans had fought a series of wars in the eighteenth and early nineteenth centuries, drove into Ottoman territory during the Crimean War of 1853–1856, and its troops often indulged in or instigated large-scale violence and expulsions of Ottoman subjects.[13]

As one historian summarized it, by the late nineteenth century, the Ottomans were "caught between the jaws of Great Power military pressure from abroad and the demand for self-determination of newly conscious national minorities from within."[14] The erosion of the empire's European territories prompted the rulers to look eastward for expansion or at least renewal. And in the view of Ottoman leaders, it was more important than ever that eastern Anatolia, the homeland of hundreds of thousands of Armenians—as well as large numbers of Kurds—remain Turkish.

The Ottomans were losing not only land but also control of their economy to their European rivals. In need of quick funds after its involvement in the Crimean War, the Ottoman government built up a huge debt to European banks, the interest on which consumed half of the empire's annual budget by 1876. In 1881, Abdul Hamid II was compelled to agree to the imposition of the foreign-controlled Public Debt Administration, which gave European powers control over Ottoman fiscal policy and the rights to collect and administer revenues of several provinces—a significant landmark in the empire's decline vis-à-vis its European rivals.

---

[12]Carmichael, *Genocide before the Holocaust*, 17.
[13]Ibid., 14–15.
[14]Melson, *Revolution and Genocide*, 141.

"Who says 'Sick Man' now?"

Abdul Hamid II
English cartoon caricature of Abdul Hamid II (reigned 1876–1909), published after the brief Greco-Turkish War of 1897, which resulted in a rare Ottoman military victory. Western news media delighted in mocking the "sick man of Europe" and its sultan. Much of this mockery and satire was well-founded, but invariably conveyed a sense of Western cultural superiority; European kings and queens, including those with bloody records, such as Leopold II of Belgium, were not subjected to such treatment.

THE "YOUNG TURK" REVOLUTION

This dismal state of affairs, exemplified by the outmoded style and policies of the erratic sultan, inevitably provoked opposition. The "Young Turks"—university and military students and cadets who advocated modernization and reform—coalesced around 1889, the same year that the Committee of Union and Progress (CUP), the major "Young Turk" organization, was formed. The CUP was a politically heterogeneous group that was united in its desire for political and social reform and modernization. As was true of many revolutionary movements, the CUP contained democratic and progressive—as well as autocratic and repressive—elements. The more democratic faction was inclined to address the inequalities among groups within the empire, while the other was fiercely nationalistic and explicitly hostile toward Armenians and other minorities.

The Young Turks gained widespread support among educated elites and, perhaps most important, within the military, and they took power in a largely peaceful revolution in July 1908. Abdul Hamid II stepped aside, retaining only meaningless titles, and was pushed out completely in 1909 after a failed counterrevolution.

The empire's disintegration continued apace under the new regime. The Young Turks had hoped that their initial efforts to build a modern republic would discourage the European drives into Ottoman lands, but "far from being impressed" by the signs of progress in the first months of the Young Turk revolution, the "Great Powers took the opportunity of momentary Ottoman weakness and distraction to grab more territory and to ask for more concessions."[15] Only three months after the July revolution, Bulgaria declared its complete independence; the very next day, Austria annexed Bosnia and Herzegovina, which Austria-Hungary had occupied since 1878. In 1911, Italy occupied Libya, and during the Balkan Wars of 1912–1913, the crumbling empire lost much of its remaining foothold in southeastern Europe.

In the first five years of their rule, the Young Turk government had seen its domain shrink by about one-third and the population decrease by one-fifth. "Of profound significance for the Armenians was the fact that the loss of the European provinces," one historian noted, "in effect, destroyed the multinational and multi-religious character" of the empire.[16] This left the Armenians further exposed and isolated, as they were now the largest remaining Christian minority within the empire. Similar processes unfolded elsewhere in Central, Eastern, and Southern Europe. As Norman Naimark observed, "The collapse of multinational empires and the emergence of nation-states [founded on the principles of self-determination] left ethnic and religious minorities vulnerable to the state-building ideologies of the dominant nationalities."[17]

In April 1909, another development with profound implications for the later genocide occurred: a series of mass killings and destruction that targeted the Armenian population of Adana, a region near the Mediterranean coast on the empire's southern flank. An attempt by Ottoman reactionaries to overthrow the Young Turks sparked generalized fighting, and frenzied mobs attacked Armenians in numerous cities and towns in the region. Turkish soldiers—both counterrevolutionaries and Young Turk troops sent to put down the rebellion—also murdered Armenians with impunity, and by the end of the month some 15,000 to 20,000 Armenians had been killed. Barely a dozen years after the grim events of 1894–1896, the "Adana Massacre," as it became known, heightened the vulnerability, devaluation, and marginalization of the Armenian minority, while drawing additional elements of Turkish society into the mentalities and practices that are indispensable for genocide.

"YOUNG TURK" NATIONALISM AND RACISM

The CUP, especially the dominant ultra-nationalist faction, imbibed the ethnic-based nationalism as well as racist and Social Darwinist theories that prevailed throughout much of Europe during that era. CUP nationalists, led by their ideologist Ziya

---

[15]Ibid., 160.
[16]Frank Chalk and Kurt Jonassohn, *The History and Sociology of Genocide* (New Haven, CT: Yale University Press, 1990), 277.
[17]Norman Naimark, *Fires of Hatred: Ethnic Cleansing in the Twentieth Century* (Cambridge, MA: Harvard University Press, 2002), 18.

Gökalp, believed that the Turks belonged to a "Turanian" section of the "Aryan race." It was significant that they looked not to Ottoman history—tarnished by its ethnic diversity, in their view—but to a romanticized pre-Ottoman and even pre-Islamic Turkish history, and celebrated such figures as Attila, Chinggis Khan, and Tamerlane. Like the Nazis, these racially minded nationalists usurped certain historical figures and events that did not neatly fit into their nation's history but that buttressed their claims to a heroic, glorious past.

Minister of War Enver Pasha was particularly enthralled with Pan-Turanism—the unrealistic, fantastical quest to claim or reclaim large parts of the Caucasus and Central Asia in order to unite all Turkish speakers. One expert on this epoch of history wrote that "in theory Turanism aspired to a size rivaling that of the Ottoman Empire but without that empire's annoying minority problems."[18] It was also significant that a large proportion of CUP leaders came from outlying areas of the empire, which inspired in them a particularly acute sense of alarm over the loss of territories—heightened by the continued erosion of their European lands in the first few years of their rule.[19] Yet it is important to acknowledge some key differences with Nazi racism—especially in light of a tendency among scholars to impose the more familiar model of Nazism and the Holocaust upon the Armenian genocide, which shared similarities and parallels

Enver Pasha

Enver Pasha, minister of war and one of the chief organizers of the genocide. He boasted to U.S. ambassador Morgenthau, "I have no desire to shift the blame onto our underlings and I am entirely willing to accept the responsibility myself for everything that has taken place." Still pursuing his Pan-Turkic nationalist dreams despite the Empire's collapse at the end of World War I, he was killed in battle while leading a revolt in Russia in 1922.

---

[18]In Chalk and Jonassohn, *History and Sociology*, 280.
[19]Donald Bloxham, *The Great Game of Genocide: Imperialism, Nationalism, and the Destruction of the Ottoman Armenians* (New York: Oxford University Press, 2007), 25.

but also had many differences.[20] The genocide of Armenian and other Christian populations was a means to an end—that is, the country's radical demographic reordering and the quest for "permanent security," to borrow the phrase of genocide scholar Dirk Moses.[21] The Jewish Holocaust was to a large degree an end unto itself, driven by an uncompromising racism that was the cornerstone of Nazi thought as well as by a "redemptive anti-Semitism" (see Chapter 2).

WAR AND GENOCIDE

After a brief interlude when the CUP was replaced as the state's rulers, the party's radical, nationalist wing seized power in January 1913, and over the next few months consolidated its control of the most important ministries. Talât Pasha became the minister of the interior, Enver Pasha the war minister, and Jemal Pasha was named minister of the navy. This triumvirate ruled the Ottoman Empire for the next six years.[22] They quickly purged the officer corps, replacing generals and others with their own loyalists and zealots. Talât reactivated the Special Organization, an outfit that would grow to roughly 30,000 members and play an indispensable role in the genocide. The Special Organization had first been formed during the Balkan Wars and was now charged with the surveillance and "neutralization" of domestic enemies.

Talât and his colleagues sought the "Turkification" of all of society. To mobilize and radicalize the people, the party established ultra-nationalist groups such as the paramilitary Association for the Promotion of Turkish Strength, whose principal goal was to train the youth so that Turkey could again be a "warrior nation" and halt the presumed "decay of the Turkish race." The regime began issuing violent threats against the Armenian community, which was rapidly abandoning the hopes it had placed in the Young Turk revolution only five years earlier. A public letter attributed to the Constantinople police chief in November 1913 railed against "you accursed ones," who have "brought many perils on the head of our

---

[20]See Taner Akçam, *The Young Turks' Crime Against Humanity: The Armenian Genocide and Ethnic Cleansing in the Ottoman Empire* (Princeton, NJ: Princeton University Press, 2012), 333–339. As Akçam points out, the word "race" itself was used and understood differently in Ottoman Turkey than in Nazi Germany—or, for that matter, as most of us understand it today. The Turkish word *irk*, Akçam writes, "was often understood in a broader sense than a biological one: depending on the context, it could also signify 'ancestry' or 'ethnicity.' Ibid., 334, citing Nazan Maksudyan, "The *Turkish Review of Anthropology* and the Racist Face of Turkish Nationalism," *Cultural Dynamics* 17 (2005).
[21]See the forthcoming book by A. Dirk Moses, *Genocide and the Terror of History: The Quest for Permanent Security* (New York: Cambridge University Press, 2017). One could call this quest for "permanent security" a "perpetrators' 'never again' syndrome." Mark Levene, *The Crisis of Genocide*, Vol. 2, *Annihilation: The European Rimlands, 1939–1953* (Oxford: Oxford University Press, 2013), 79.
[22]"Pasha" or "Paşa" was an honorary title in the Ottoman Empire, and each of the three acquired this title around the time they took power.

esteemed government" and "paved the way for foreign assault," repeating the delusional, paranoid accusations that would justify the genocide shortly thereafter.[23]

The opposition of most Greeks, Bulgarians, and other minorities to Ottoman rule gave the Pan-Turanists evidence of the failure of multinational Ottomanism. Further driving the radicalism of the CUP leadership was territorial ambition: They coveted eastern lands—which happened to be populated by other groups— to fulfill their nationalist visions. When they declared war on Russia in November 1914, the CUP rulers announced, in terms and categories similar to those the Nazis would use a few years later, their ambitions for "living space" to unite and settle their "race." "The ideal of our nation and people leads us toward the destruction of our Muscovite enemy," read the proclamation, "in order to obtain thereby a natural frontier to our empire, which should include and unite all branches of our race."[24] Another development during this time was the Young Turks' modernization of the Turkish armed forces with the assistance of Germany, whose ruler, Kaiser Wilhelm II, provided several hundred officers, some of whom took leading positions in the Ottoman army and navy. These trends led to a militarization of the government and the emergence of the army as the nation's major political force.

If not for World War I, these developments, ominous as they appear in retrospect, would probably not have culminated in state-directed mass murder. As in other cases examined in this book, warfare was the crucible for genocide. The instability and brutalization wrought by the war gave sustenance to the most belligerent, racist trends of the recent period, while creating an increasingly staunch attraction to using mass murder to address perceived population problems or ethnic conflict. Henry Morgenthau—the US ambassador to the Ottoman Empire, whose reports would provide substantial firsthand documentation of the genocide—wrote: "The conditions of war gave to the Turkish Government its longed-for opportunity to lay hold of the Armenians."[25] Talât himself openly expressed the same view, reportedly telling a German functionary that his regime was "intent on taking advantage of the war in order to thoroughly liquidate its internal foes," the "indigenous Christians, without being thereby disturbed by foreign intervention."[26] How this "liquidation" would occur was not necessarily yet envisaged by the ruling triumvirate and their henchmen; as in the Nazi genocide, it proceeded largely by improvisation and incremental measures that gathered a deadly momentum.

In late September 1914, roughly seven weeks after the outbreak of the European war, the Ottoman government conscripted battle-age Armenian men into the army, with a view toward quickly forcing them into labor units.

---

[23]Balakian, *Burning Tigris*, 172–173.
[24]Arnold Toynbee, *Turkey: A Past and a Future* (New York: George H. Doran, 1917), 31.
[25]Quoted in Dadrian, *History*, 207.
[26]Ibid., 207.

Armenians driven into the Syrian desert
Armenian deportees marching into Syrian desert, 1915; note the near-total absence of possessions or shelter. Armin T. Wegner took this and many other photographs documenting the catastrophe. A low-ranking German officer and medic serving in the region, Wegner (1886–1978) undertook considerable risk to sneak photographs and other evidence of the genocide to Germany and the United States. Wegner's experiences led him to become an outspoken advocate for Armenian rights. Among many other things, he testified for the defense at the 1921 trial of Talât Pasha's assassin (see Source 1.3).

The Ottomans entered the war in November 1914 on the side of the Central Powers of Germany and Austria-Hungary, hoping for territorial gain. Enver himself led an ill-advised invasion of Russia that winter, which ended in disastrous defeat at the Battle of Sarikamish in mid-January. After years of anti-Armenian agitation and propaganda, it was easy for CUP leaders to blame the defeat on the "disloyal Armenians" and to take the opportunity to rid its land of this domestic "enemy" that was ostensibly tied to a foreign enemy.

Almost immediately after the Sarikamish debacle, the state and the army leadership under Enver initiated a series of anti-Armenian measures, many of which had been conceived and planned in advance, that rapidly escalated to genocide. In late February 1915, Armenian troops who had been serving in the Ottoman army were disarmed and assigned to labor battalions. Very soon thereafter, the army—assisted by police units and special killing squads knows as the *chetes*—began conducting mass killings of those Armenian men in the labor brigades. Also in late February, the authorities decreed that all Armenian civilians must relinquish their weapons—an edict that represented a trap, or classic "Catch-22," because anyone turning over a gun would be accused of plotting rebellion, while those who had nothing to hand over were accused of hiding arms. The irony was immense: In some cases, Armenians frantically searched for weapons they could borrow or purchase, in order to have something to give the authorities.

These were the opening attacks of the genocide. By the First of March 1915, large-scale massacres of Armenians, accompanied by widespread rape and looting, had taken place in numerous provinces. The genocide would be driven by a combination of massacres and deportations, the first of which commenced on April 8 from Zeitun (present-day Süleymanli, Azerbaijan).[27] Many tens of thousands of Armenians of the eastern provinces were sent toward the arid desert in the south (present-day Syria); others were marched to concentration camps, which were administered by Şükrü Kaya, a close colleague of Talât. Alongside Talât's Ministry of the Interior, the "Secret Organization" was largely responsible for the deportations and accompanying murders. Dr. Behaeddin Shakir, an anti-Armenian fanatic, who had earlier described the Armenians as "tubercular microbes" infecting society, had been given command of the Special Organization a few weeks before the deportations began. His forces consisted of roughly 30,000 men, including Turkish police, assorted Muslim bands, and criminals released from prison in order to serve.

As the attacks on the Armenians gained intensified, they were institutionalized through such laws as the May 27, 1915 Temporary Law of Deportation, which empowered Enver's war ministry to implement the ethnic cleansing of historically Armenian lands, a key component of the genocide. The deportations, which usually took the form of death marches, now accelerated. In scenes reproduced later during the Holocaust, many of the victims were transported in squalid, heavily overcrowded trains. But most traveled on foot. "Walk, walk, walk," one survivor later said. "The world didn't seem to end."[28] Another said, "My legs became all swollen because I was so tired. Sometimes my mother would carry me; otherwise, my older sister did."[29] Morgenthau reported that the expelled Armenians were quickly reduced to "a stumbling horde of dust-covered skeletons, ravenously looking for scraps of food, eating any offal that came their way, crazed by the hideous sights that filled every hour of their existence, sick with all the diseases that accompany such hardships and privations, but still prodded on and on by the whips and clubs and bayonets of their executioners."[30] Later caravans observed frightful scenes of their predecessors along the roads: "We saw bones everywhere and saw many

---

[27]In late 1914 and again in March 1915 Zeitun had been the site of fighting between Ottoman forces and Hunchak-led militias.

[28]Donald Miller and Lorna Touryan Miller, eds., *Survivors: An Oral History of the Armenian Genocide* (Berkeley: University of California Press, 1999), 82.

[29]Ibid., 82.

[30]Henry Morgenthau, *Murder of a Nation* (New York: Armenian General Benevolent Union of America, 1974), 31.

others who were dying, or on the verge of death," said one survivor, "simply sitting and waiting for their turn." Another said it took effort to "avoid stepping on" bodies of the deceased.[31]

The *chetes*—Special Organization squads consisting largely of released convicts—and other murderers, though, did not always wait for starvation and exhaustion to do their work. One survivor told of how she had walked for several weeks; her grandmother was drowned by Turkish police; two aunts were also killed; her uncle and a neighbor had their throats slit; and she "observed hundreds of young women commit suicide" to escape rape "by drowning themselves in the Euphrates," which like other rivers was "awash with bodies of people who had been killed by the Turks, as well as those who had drowned themselves."[32] In another characteristic episode, the population of the Black Sea port of Trebizond "was taken out to sea and drowned."[33] The murderers often employed fiendishly clever and cruel techniques. US ambassador Henry Morgenthau wrote that an Ottoman official told him that "they had delved into the records of the Spanish Inquisition and other historic institutions of torture and adopted all the suggestions found there."[34]

APRIL 24: THE DECIMATION OF ARMENIAN LEADERSHIP

An important stage in the genocide's expansion was the arrest, transport, and murder of several thousand Armenian elites in late April 1915. Hundreds of leading figures were arrested in Constantinople on the evening of April 24, bussed to nearby military barracks, and then taken to a large prison. One arrestee recalled that it was "like some dream . . . it seemed as if on one night, all the prominent Armenians of the capital—assemblymen, representatives, progressive thinkers, reporters, teachers, doctors, pharmacists, dentists, merchants, and bankers—had made an appointment in those dim cells. . . . More than a few people were still wearing their pajamas, robes, and slippers."[35] Similar, smaller-scale scenes took place in other cities. Many of those captured were murdered with little delay, while others were driven into the countryside to be worked or starved to death. The overnight disappearance of large numbers of prominent citizens had the desired effect of removing potential leaders of any resistance, and it left the Armenian communities leaderless, confused, and traumatized. Because of the significance of these events, the date of April 24 would later be designated by Armenians as "Genocide Remembrance Day."

The Armenians' miseries were compounded by the pillage and violence of Kurdish bands that, encouraged by Turkish authorities, descended upon the caravans,

---

[31]Miller and Miller, *Survivors*, 83–84.
[32]Ibid., 96.
[33]Carmichael, *Genocide before the Holocaust*, 18.
[34]Henry Morgenthau, *Ambassador Morgenthau's Story* (New York: Doubleday, 1919), 307.
[35]Balakian, *Burning Tigris*, 213.

killing many thousands. And in a depressing pattern of behavior that accompanied other genocides, Turkish civilians were also eager to profit from the dispossession and eviction of the victims, who before being driven from their homes were compelled to sell their possessions for paltry sums. As the caravans of Armenians passed through towns on the way to their unknown destinations, they were more likely to inspire plunder than compassion.

In recent years, a concurrent genocide against other Christian minorities—specifically, the Assyrian and Greek populations—has belatedly received attention and been recognized as closely connected to the anti-Armenian persecutions. Greece had won its independence from the Ottomans after a bitter revolution between 1821 and 1832, which deepened the suspicions and hostility directed against those Greeks who remained within the Ottoman Empire (concentrated primarily in Thrace, which bordered Greece; Pontus, along the southern coast of the Black Sea; and Anatolia).[36] Turkey began full-scale attacks and expulsions of the Pontian Greeks in 1916, and resumed a campaign against its Greek populace

Starvation claims two Armenian boys
"A 15-year-old child [and his companion] who died of starvation" according to photographer Armin Wegner; 1915 or 1916, Syrian region. In addition to his advocacy of the Armenian cause, Wegner became an antiwar activist. In the 1930s he courageously spoke out against Nazi antisemitism, for which he was imprisoned in several concentration camps. Wegner was later recognized by Israel's Holocaust remembrance organization, Yad Vashem, as one of the "Righteous Among the Nations"— non-Jews who risked their lives to save Jews during the Nazi era.

---

[36] Jones, *Genocide*, 150.

after World War I. Assyrians, another Christian minority whose civilization can be dated to ancient Mesopotamia, were targeted in multiple waves of repression, deportations, and mass murder between 1914 and 1923. "The Assyrian genocide was "indistinguishable in principle from the Armenian genocide, despite being smaller in scale," wrote Hannibal Travis, one of a small number of scholars whose pioneering research has uncovered this oft-overlooked chapter.[37] The latest, most reliable estimates indicate that as many as 750,000 Greeks and 250,000 Assyrians perished in genocidal violence directed by the Ottoman and postwar Turkish states.[38]

RESISTANCE

Turkish forces and auxiliaries did not conduct these atrocities without resistance. In April 1915, Van, a city that had long been a major center for Armenian life and culture, witnessed some three hundred armed men, backed by roughly one thousand lightly armed men and youths, ferociously defend their small, heavily populated quarter. A survivor of the fighting later described the involvement of various sectors of the population: "Even we children used to go from house to house to gather the brass candle bars" to be melted down for bullets. "Coppersmiths and other craftsmen" produced "two thousand cartridges and bullets a day. An Armenian professor made smokeless gunpowder. Women made uniforms . . . and cooked around the clock," and a boy scout group, which included the future renowned painter Arshile Gorky, "acted as a fire patrol and sanitary unit, and dug thousands of Turkish bullets out of the ground so the artisans could melt them down and recast them. . . . The slogan 'better 10 days' liberty than to die the slaves we've been' circulated through" the quarter.[39]

The battle raged for four weeks, until Russian forces—which included Armenian volunteers—took the city, bringing a temporary halt to the combat, which had killed tens of thousands of Armenians. Substantial resistance and self-defense also took place in Urfa and elsewhere, but it was the Armenians' desperate, ill-fated stand at Van that would earn a central place in Armenian national consciousness to the present day. But in its immediate aftermath, it provided further "evidence" of the Armenians' supposed treachery and rebelliousness, which was perceived as especially dangerous because of their collaboration, in some cases, with Russian forces. It is certainly true that some Armenian soldiers who had served under Ottoman command deserted to the Russian army; but many Muslims also

[37]Quoted in Jones, *Genocide*, 161. See Hannibal Travis, "'Native Christians Massacred': The Ottoman Genocide of the Assyrians during World War I," *Genocide Studies and Prevention* 1, no. 3 (December 2006).
[38]David Gaunt, "The Ottoman Treatment of the Assyrians," in Ronald Grigor Suny, Fatma Müge Göçek, Norman Naimark, eds., *A Question of Genocide* (New York: Oxford University Press, 2011), 244–245.
[39]Balakian, *Burning Tigris*, 205.

Armed resistance in Van
April-May 1915: Armenian resistance in Van, an ancient center of
Armenian social and cultural life in eastern Turkey. The desperate,
temporarily successful month-long battle to defend Van is the most
well-known but far from the only example of Armenian resistance;
and as in the other genocides discussed in this book, unarmed
forms of defiance were also widespread.

deserted, for the reason that soldiers tend to abandon armies that are poorly led
and destined for defeat.

AFTERMATH: STRUGGLES FOR LAND AND JUSTICE

Unlike the other cases in this book, the Armenian genocide did not have a defini-
tive end point. Most of the killing was over by late 1916, but warfare and instability in the area reigned for several more years, prolonging the Armenians' ordeal.
This chaos was exacerbated by a competition among the major powers, in the wake
of the November 1917 Bolshevik Revolution and the collapse of the Ottoman
Empire the following year, for control of western Central Asia. At the war's end
France and Britain scrambled for Ottoman territory, while Britain encouraged and
funded a Greek occupation of part of western Anatolia, generating further warfare
and instability.

An independent Armenian republic was declared in May 1918; it was populated
by survivors and refugees from Ottoman Armenia and perhaps a half million of
their brethren from the part of historic Armenia that Russia had possessed for the
previous century. Armenia was recognized by the terms of the Treaty of Sévres,
the peace treaty signed by the defeated Turks and the victorious Allies in August

1920, but it was subsequently renounced by Mustafa Kemal Pasha, later known as Atatürk (Father of the Turks), who came to power over the next two years and is venerated in Turkey as the father of the modern nation. In a secret communiqué, Mustafa Kemal declared that it was "indispensable that Armenia be annihilated politically and physically."[40] His army invaded the new republic, regaining several former Ottoman provinces; the remainder of the unfortunate young nation was engulfed by the Soviet Union in March 1922.

In the midst of this chaos, the victorious Allies forced the interim Turkish administration—the CUP government had dissolved, and the triumvirate fled the country, at the end of the war—to conduct trials. These trials, which included the indictment of more than one hundred former Turkish officials, were an important milestone in international human rights law, and produced substantial evidence of the genocide that retains its usefulness today. Yet by 1921, as the new Turkish Republic led by Atatürk consolidated itself, there was neither political will nor outside pressure to follow through with adequate punishments. It would fall to Armenian avengers to bring the chief architects of the massacres to a rough form of justice. Soghomon Tehlirian, who had lost most of his family during the genocide, assassinated Talât in Berlin in 1921; probably as part of the same operation, an Armenian killed Jemal the following year. Enver also met his death at the hands of one of his would-be victims: He was killed in an ambush led by an Armenian Red Army commander while fighting against the Soviet Union in the summer of 1922.

ORGANIZED FROM ON HIGH

Few architects of genocide were incautious enough to leave explicit written orders for prosecutors or historians to discover. Even Hitler, as we will see in Chapter 2, was usually careful to avoid written orders. At the time, though, the CUP—through legislation that was not secretive—authorized the major steps of the genocide: roundups, deportation, and confiscation of property. The central government closely supervised the deportations, and provincial governors were hounded by CUP officials to ensure compliance; reluctant officials were replaced by more zealous ones, and sometimes were even murdered, which even the Nazis did not do.

And in recent years, Taner Akçam and other historians have unearthed much additional and overwhelmingly convincing evidence of the systematic nature of the Armenian genocide and its direction by state and army officials at the highest levels. Akçam's 2012 book *The Young Turks' Crime Against Humanity*, which is to date the best-researched account, demonstrated the centrality and zeal of Talât in the organization of the genocides; his July 1915 communication gloated over two

[40] Jones, *Genocide*, 112.

thousand people "slaughtered like sheep."[41] Akçam shows that Enver Pasha ordered the punishment of any state official or employee who allowed aid to reach Armenians.[42] Turkey's official deniers find it increasingly difficult to uphold their fictionalized narrative; the former head of Ottoman archives, a vigorous champion of genocide denial, "could never manage to produce documentation of a single instance of Armenians being re-compensated for losses"—that is, the architects of the deportation fully understood that their victims would not survive.[43]

The architects of the genocide were not always shy in discussing their work. In a meeting with Enver Pasha, US ambassador Morgenthau, going to great lengths to avoid embarrassment for his host, suggested that the massacres were the work of "underlings" beyond the leaders' control. "Enver straightened up at once," Morgenthau later wrote.[44] "I saw that my remarks, far from smoothing the way to a quiet and friendly discussion, had greatly offended him," by implying that "things could happen in Turkey for which he and his associates were not responsible. 'You are greatly mistaken,' he said. . . . 'I am entirely willing to accept responsibility myself for everything that has taken place,'" declared Enver, adding that the Armenians' "hostile attitude toward the Ottoman Empire" justified their treatment.

Enver's uncle, General Halil Kut, who was responsible for the mass murders of Armenians in labor battalions, was similarly indiscreet. In his postwar memoirs, the former general wrote with satisfaction that he had killed 300,000 Armenians: "It can be more or less. I didn't count. . . . I have endeavored to wipe out the Armenian nation to the last individual."[45]

The genocide was well organized and engineered, and driven by modern technology as well as bureaucratic efficiency. The regime made extensive use of new communications and transport systems—the telephone, telegraph, and the railroad in particular. The efficiency and zeal with which the state expropriated the wealth of its victims is one of several striking similarities that this genocide bears with the Holocaust. Only a few weeks after the deportations began, the CUP government created the "Commission on Abandoned Goods" to facilitate the theft of property "abandoned" by the hapless Armenians.[46] And, again, the perpetrators were not always reticent when it came to revealing their misdeeds. Henry Morgenthau recalled a conversation in which Talât asked the astonished ambassador if he could "get the American life-insurance companies"—many Armenians had policies with two New York–based companies—"to send us a complete list of their Armenian

---

[41]Taner Akçam, *The Young Turks' Crime Against Humanity: The Armenian Genocide and Ethnic Cleansing in the Ottoman Empire* (Princeton, NJ: Princeton University Press, 2012), 208–209.
[42]Ibid., 436.
[43]Quoted from Michael Reynolds's contribution to "Review Forum" on *The Young Turks' Crime Against Humanity*, in *Journal of Genocide Research* 15, no. 4 (December 2013), 475.
[44]Chalk and Jonassohn, *History and Sociology*, 271.
[45]Kiernan, *Blood and Soil*, 413.
[46]Adalian, "The Armenian Genocide," 65.

policy holders. They are practically all dead now and have left no heirs to collect the money," which would, "of course . . . [revert] to the State."[47]

HOW MANY VICTIMS?

Even for the most well-documented and thoroughly researched genocide—the Jewish Holocaust—it is impossible to agree upon precise statistics. Largely because there are varying statistics for the pre-1915 Ottoman Armenian population, the estimates for fatalities during this genocide range widely. The most recent and reliable estimates are that between 1 million and 1.5 million Armenians perished between 1915 and 1923, the large majority as a result of state-directed genocide, others as victims of circumstances (usually starvation and illness) arising from war, upheaval, and mass forced migration. This was a larger number than that of all British war deaths—and the Armenians suffered more, proportionately, than any other population during World War I, despite not being among the combatant nations. Somewhere between one-half to two-thirds of the prewar Ottoman Armenian population died.

While precise numbers are elusive, the immediate consequences were not: The Armenian presence in the region, with its 3,000-year history, was nearly totally eradicated and erased from Turkish history, and Armenian civilization would henceforth exist only in scattered remnants throughout its diaspora. "Armenian monuments and churches were dynamited," Norman Naimark chronicled, "graveyards were plowed under and turned into fields of corn and wheat, and the Armenian quarters of cities were torn down and used for firewood and scrap, or occupied and renamed."[48]

Headline announcing acquittal of Talât's assassin
In March 1921 Soghomon Tehlirian, an Armenian whose parents and other relatives were killed during the genocide, assassinated Talât Pasha. Contemplating Tehlirian's desperate act, Raphael Lemkin wrote in his diary, "Why is a man punished when he kills another man? Why is the killing of a million a lesser crime than the killing of a single individual?" Later that year, Tehlirian was acquitted (see Source 1.3). These headlines are from the June 4, 1921 front page of the *New-York Tribune*, which at the time was one of the most widely read newspapers in the United States.

Talaat Slayer Acquitted in Berlin Court

Armenian Boy, Who Laid Murder to Vision of Mother in Dream, Is Freed on Insanity Plea

Shot to Avenge Slaughter of Race

Witnesses for Defense Assert 1,000,000 Have Been Slain in Massacres

---

[47]Chalk and Jonassohn, *History and Sociology*, 283.
[48]Naimark, *Fires of Hatred*, 41.

Today, roughly 3 million Armenians live in their own country, the Republic of Armenia, which after seventy years as part of the Soviet Union became independent in 1991 as the USSR fell apart. About 7 million more Armenians are concentrated in other parts of the world, principally the nearby states of Lebanon, Syria, Russia, and Iran, as well as the United States and France.

GENOCIDE DENIAL

To this day, the Turkish Republic denies that its founders and predecessors organized a systematic genocide of the Armenian population. In the official Turkish version of World War I, Turks as well as Armenians were victims of a brutal conflict; the Armenians, with little valid cause, rose against the Turkish rulers, and also put themselves at the service of foreign powers intent on dismembering the empire; and the Ottoman authorities organized orderly, humane transports of Armenians out of the war zones. If tens of thousands (Turkish officials often cite the figure of 300,000) of Armenians perished, this was largely the result of warfare, usually instigated by armed Armenians, according to the deniers. It is certainly true that suffering abounded on all sides; the other elements of the Turkish narrative, however, are patently false. But the denial of the genocide is essential to the homogenous national identity fashioned by Atatürk's political descendants, who cannot "acknowledge that the new Turkish state had been built not from a war 'against imperial powers' but by expunging 'the Greek and Armenian minorities,'" as the leading experts Peter Balakian and Taner Akçam have pointed out.[49] The Australian genocide scholar Colin Tatz—an uncompromising critic of his own country's genocides of indigenous peoples—has pointed to other motivations that have sustained Turkish denial for so long: The country's leaders do not wish their nation to be tainted by association with that other great European perpetrator of modern genocide, Nazi Germany; a deepening fear that such an admission would open the door to reparations demands from Armenians and others; "fears of fragmentation of social cohesion in a society still in transition." Tatz added that "the state has invested its very soul in denial," thus creating a political incentive that perpetuates this denial.[50]

Unfortunately, Turkey is aided and abetted by US, British, and Israeli diplomacy, which—guided by the fear of alienating a valuable and rare ally in a volatile region—have meekly supported Turkey in its refusal to acknowledge the crime. Further, the Turkish government has funded scholars and research centers in the United States in order to promote its version and lend a scholarly façade to its

---

[49]Balakian, *Burning Tigris*, 371.
[50]Colin Tatz, *With Intent to Destroy: Reflecting on Genocide* (New York: Verso, 2003), 130–131. Tatz was born in South Africa and has lived and worked in Australia most of his life.

ongoing campaign to refute the genocide.[51] Denial of this crucial episode in
Armenian history also represents a denial of part of Turkey's own past—that of a
multinational land, to which Armenians, Greeks, Jews, and others contributed
culturally and otherwise. It should be noted, however, that the Turkish government and its allies are not alone in their hesitancy or outright refusal to confront
a sordid past. There is still a conspicuous reluctance to honestly confront the past
in many other nations whose colonial administrations and armies committed
massive crimes in the nineteenth and twentieth centuries. But because of the implications for the founding ideology of the modern Turkish nation, Turkey's denial
is more rigid and consistent than, for example, Belgium's poor record vis-à-vis
King Leopold's grisly reign in the Congo (see the Introduction).

Fortunately, though, there are many brave Turkish scholars, artists, journalists,
and intellectuals who—at risk to their careers and even freedom—have chal-
lenged their government's falsified official narrative. Shortly before winning the
Nobel Prize for Literature in 2006, the Turkish novelist Orhan Pamuk spoke
strongly about the genocide in several interviews. The government brought charges
of "insulting the Turkish republic" against him, but dropped them amid an international outcry. Turkish historian Taner Akçam has emerged as a prominent
scholarly authority on the genocide, for which he has also faced repression and
harassment. Unbowed, he actually declared himself to be an accomplice to a charge
of "insulting Turkishness" (for referring to the genocide) leveled against journalist
Hrant Dink in 2006. These signs of progress have produced a backlash, sometimes

Funeral march and protest for Hrant Dink
There have been some recent challenges within Turkey to
the government's century-long denial of the genocide. On
January 23, 2007, hundreds of thousands of Turks
participated in a funeral march and protest for Hrant Dink,
the Turkish journalist who wrote honestly about the
genocide and was murdered by a nationalist extremist.
The signs read "We are all Hrant Dink" and "We are all
Armenians."

---

[51]Roger Smith, Eric Markusen, and Robert Jay Lifton, "Professional Ethics and the Denial
of Armenian Genocide," *Holocaust and Genocide Studies* 9, no. 1 (Spring 1995); Balakian,
373–391.

violent; in January 2007 Dink was assassinated by a young ultra-nationalist, who has since been accorded sympathetic treatment by the police and courts.

CONCLUSIONS

Turkish historian Y. H. Bayur observed that "there are very few movements in the world that have given rise to such great hopes" as the Young Turks' constitutional revolution, but "likewise very few movements whose hopes have been so swiftly and finally disappointed." The Young Turks fostered and deepened the prejudices that had afflicted the Armenians for many years, targeting them as a domestic enemy closely linked to the Empire's external enemies. Allegations of Armenian "disloyalty" became a self-fulfilling prophecy; it was hardly surprising, after many years of restrictions and prejudice punctuated by homicidal violence, that many Armenians favored the Russians during World War I, and even joined their forces. Yet Armenian nationalist activism in the years prior to the genocide was actually at a lower level than in the 1890s.

The Armenian genocide resulted from a lethal convergence of factors. The Ottoman rulers were gripped by a combustible mix of vulnerability and desperation alongside unrealistic ambition. This sense of loss and decay was exacerbated by the conspicuous strengthening and expansion of Western European empires in the last three decades of the century; England, France, and even little Belgium became masters of large swaths of land in Africa, while the Ottomans were being pushed out of Europe.

The crumbing of the Ottoman Empire created a dangerous situation for minorities. For the Armenians, it had the effect of "increasingly expos[ing]" them "as a major compact Christian community in the 'Asian' interior," as Donald Bloxham observed.[52] The massacres of the 1890s and of 1909 deepened the Armenians' vulnerability, and in retrospect we can detect a "continuum of genocide," as Bloxham argued, over the course of more than two decades.[53]

As in other cases examined in this book, warfare was a crucial factor that led to genocide, as ruling groups saw the war as an opportunity to realize their fantasies. World War I also created a new, unprecedented context of total war, in which boundaries between combatants and noncombatants evaporated in many theaters of the conflict. Genocidal passions were sometimes displayed upon by civilians as well as military and political leaders. While in Vienna in 1914, for example, at the height of Austria's preparations for war on Serbia, the exiled Russian revolutionary Leon Trotsky reported that the slogans "all Serbs must die" and "Serbia must die" were widely repeated.[54]

---

[52]Bloxham, *Great Game*, 17.
[53]Bloxham, *Great Game*, 156–157.
[54]From Trotsky's autobiography, *My Life* (1930), quoted in Murray Bookchin, *The Third Revolution: Popular Movements in the Revolutionary Era* (London: Cassell, 1998), 127.

The crumbling of the Austro-Hungarian and Russian empires, as well as that of the Ottomans, was a violent process that unfolded over decades and left religious and national minorities vulnerable. Political and military leaders in all these empires, fighting hopeless rearguard actions against historical progress, sought to wipe out internal enemies; the Austrians targeted Serbs, while Russian Jews were subjected to deadly pogroms, and the Ottomans lashed out at their minorities, especially the Armenians. Armenians had the further misfortune of finding their homeland in the middle of a bitter struggle between Russia and the Ottomans. As A. Dirk Moses argued in a 2013 commentary on this genocide, "the aspiration for *permanent security*" distinguishes the crime of genocide from other severe, violent crises. "Permanent security means the destruction or crippling of the perceived threatening 'other.'"[55]

In the post-9/11 world, it has become too easy to blame the culture and traditions of Islam for violent conflict and oppressive tyranny. There is no doubt that, like ruling elites of other faiths, the Hamid sultanate promoted and exploited religious fervor, and that centuries of anti-Christian prejudice helped pave the way for the genocide. Ambassador Morgenthau said at the time that religion strongly motivated the "Turkish and Kurdish rabble" who carried out massacres, but that "the men who really conceived the crime had no such motive. Practically all of them were atheists, with no more respect for [Islam] than for Christianity."[56] Non-Turkish Muslims, such as Kurds and Arabs, also historically suffered in the Ottoman Empire and were also victimized by the Young Turk regime—and by its successor, the Turkish Republic under Mustafa Kemal (Atatürk). Fanaticism in the service of various religions has often contributed to mass killing, or provided a pretext or a belief system to be exploited by unscrupulous leaders. But while religion was a factor in the Armenian genocide, it was somewhat weaker than other factors examined here.

The deportations and massacres of the Armenians were widely reported at the time, although contemporaries lacked the vocabulary to fully describe or characterize the events—the term "genocide," after all, had yet to be coined. Within a few years, though, knowledge of the Turkish atrocities began to fade, as the Western nations, beset by their own unresolved social and political crises, stumbled inexorably toward a new, even greater conflict.

---

[55]A. Dirk Moses, "Genocide vs. Security: A False Opposition," in Review Forum on Taner Akçam's *The Young Turks' Crime Against Humanity, Journal of Genocide Research* 15, no. 4 (December 2013), 493.
[56]Carmichael, *Genocide before the Holocaust*, 85.

PRIMARY SOURCES
AND STUDY QUESTIONS

Source 1.1: Firsthand account by a Turkish army officer on the deportation of Armenians from Trebizond and Erzerum, December 26, 1916

In December 1916 a Turkish army officer, Lt. Sayied Ahmed Moukhtar Baas, wrote this memo about atrocities he had witnessed the previous year while stationed at Erzerum (spelled Erzeroum in this translation), a large city in the east of the Ottoman Empire that served as a deportation site during the genocide, and then Trebizond (also known at the time as Trabzon), a city and province 175 miles to the north that was also the site of mass killings of Armenians. The memo was circulated within the British cabinet.

In July 1915 I was ordered to accompany a convoy of deported Armenians. It was the last batch from Trebizond. There were in the convoy 120 men, 700 children, and about 400 women. From Trebizond I took them to Gumish-Khana.[57] Here the 120 men were taken away, and, as I was informed later, they were all killed. At Gumish-Khana I was ordered to take the women and children to Erzinjian. On the way I saw thousands of bodies of Armenians unburied. Several bands of "Shotas" met us on the way and wanted me to hand over to them women and children.[58] But I persistently refused. I did leave on the way about 300 children with Moslem families who were willing to take care of them and educate them. The "Mutessarrif" of Erzinjian ordered me to proceed with the convoy to Kamach.[59]

At the latter place the authorities refused to take charge of the women and children. I fell ill and wanted to go back, but I was told that as long as the Armenians in my charge were alive I would be sent from one place to the other. However I managed to include my batch with the deported Armenians that had come from Erzeroum. In charge of the latter was a colleague of mine. . . . He told me afterwards that after leaving Kamach they came to a valley where the Euphrates ran. A band of Shotas

---

SOURCE: Courtesy of the Armenian National Institute.

[57]Approximately 45 miles away.

[58]Also spelled "*chetes*," these were special militias employed by the Ottomans to carry out deportations and massacres. Many of their members were violent criminals who were released from prison; additionally, many *chetes* had participated in violent expulsions of Greeks in 1914. They were recruited and organized by the Special Organization, set up by the Young Turks to implement the atrocities, but the CUP leadership could claim—because the *chetes* were not regular troops, and often made little pretense of military discipline—that they were simply bandits, unconnected to the government.

[59]In the Ottoman Empire, a "Mutessarrif" was a regional governor.

sprang out and stopped the convoy. They ordered the escort to keep away and then shot every one of the Armenians and threw them in the river.

At Trebizond the Moslems were warned that if they sheltered Armenians they would be liable to the death penalty.

Government officials at Trebizond picked up some of the prettiest Armenian women of the best families. After committing the worst outrages on them they had them killed. Cases of rape of women and girls even publicly are very numerous. They were systematically murdered after the outrage.

The Armenians deported from Erzeroum started with their cattle and whatever possessions they could carry. When they reached Erzinjian they became suspicious seeing that all the Armenians had already been deported. The Vali[60] of Erzeroum allayed their fears and assured them most solemnly that no harm would befall them. He told them that the first convoy should leave for Kamach, the others re-maining at Erzeroum until they received word from their friends informing of their safe arrival to destination. And so it happened. Word came that the first batch had arrived safely at Kamach, which was true enough. But the men were kept at Kamach and shot, and the women were massacred by the Shotas after leaving that town.

Questions

1. What are the implications of the officer's statement, toward the end of the first paragraph, that he left 300 children with Muslim families?
2. He also reports that Turkish Muslims were threatened with death if they helped the Armenians. What does this tell us about the government's intentions, as well as about public opinion among non-Armenians toward the atrocities?
3. Sexual violence is an all-too-common feature of such atrocities, especially during wartime. What are some of the reasons or goals for allowing (or organiz-ing) mass rape of the victims?

Source 1.2: US ambassador reports on the genocide, 1919

Henry Morgenthau, Sr. (1856–1946) served as ambassador to the Ottoman Empire from 1913 to 1916. Once the expulsions and genocide were underway, he began to collect hun-dreds of eye-witness reports and other documentation on the atrocities. He was in a deli-cate position, conducting diplomatic meetings with the architects of the genocide, whose crimes he was now aware of, and simultaneously attempting to convince the Woodrow Wilson Administration to take some decisive action. He finally resigned in frustration and disgust in 1916, stating, "I found intolerable my further daily association with men,

---

[60]Ottoman administrator or governor of a subprovince (*vilayet*).
SOURCE: Courtesy of the Armenian National Institute.

however gracious and accommodating . . . who were still reeking with the blood of nearly a million human beings."[62]

Morgenthau did not cease his advocacy on behalf of the Armenians, though: He energetically publicized Ottoman atrocities and raised money for the victims for the next several years. During World War II, his son, US Treasury Secretary Henry Morgenthau, Jr., beseeched President Roosevelt to take measures to help Europe's beleaguered Jews, also with only limited success. He also helped to create the War Refugee Board, which is credited with saving as many as 200,000 Jews.

These excerpts, from 1919, are from the senior Morgenthau. While justly praised for his courageous efforts to alert the world to the Armenians' plight, Morgenthau was also a product of his time, illustrated by his use of terms like "Armenian race" and "Mohammedan" (an antiquated term for Muslims, which presumes that they worship Muhammad as a deity).

One day I was discussing these proceedings with a responsible Turkish official, who was describing the tortures inflicted. He made no secret of the fact that the Government had instigated them, and, like all Turks of the official classes, he enthusiastically approved this treatment of the detested race. This official told me that all these details were matters of nightly discussion at the headquarters of the Union and Progress Committee. Each new method of inflicting pain was hailed as a splendid discovery, and the regular attendants were constantly ransacking their brains in the effort to devise some new torment. He told me that they even delved into the records of the Spanish Inquisition and other historic institutions of torture and adopted all the suggestions found there. . . .

. . . The Young Turks displayed greater ingenuity than their predecessor, Abdul Hamid. The injunction of the deposed Sultan was merely "to kill, kill," whereas the Turkish democracy hit upon an entirely new plan. Instead of massacring outright the Armenian race, they now decided to deport it. In the south and southeastern section of the Ottoman Empire lie the Syrian desert and the Mesopotamian valley. Though part of this area was once the scene of a flourishing civilization, for the last five centuries it has suffered the blight that becomes the lot of any country that is subjected to Turkish rule; and it is now a dreary, desolate waste. . . .

The Central Government now announced its intention of gathering the two million or more Armenians living in the several sections of the empire and transporting them to this desolate and inhospitable region. Had they undertaken such a deportation in good faith it would have represented the height of cruelty and injustice. . . . [But] They knew that the great majority would never reach their

---

[61]Michael Oren, *Power, Faith, and Fantasy: American in the Middle East, 1776 to the Present* (New York: Norton, 2007), 337.

destination and that those who did would either die of thirst and starvation, or be murdered by the wild Mohammedan desert tribes. The real purpose of the deportation was robbery and destruction; it really represented a new method of massacre. When the Turkish authorities gave the orders for these deportations, they were merely giving the death warrant to a whole race; they understood this well, and, in their conversations with me, they made no particular attempt to conceal the fact. . . .

I am confident that the whole history of the human race contains no such horrible episode as this. . . . Perhaps the one event in history that most resembles the Armenian deportations was the expulsion of the Jews from Spain by Ferdinand and Isabella. . . . [62] Yet all these previous persecutions seem almost trivial when we compare them with the sufferings of the Armenians, in which at least 600,000 people were destroyed and perhaps as many as 1,000,000. And these earlier massacres when we compare them with the spirit that directed the Armenian atrocities, have one feature that we can almost describe as an excuse: they were the product of religious fanaticism and most of the men and women who instigated them sincerely believed that they were devoutly serving their Maker. Undoubtedly religious fanaticism was an impelling motive with the Turkish and Kurdish rabble who slew Armenians as a service to Allah, but the men who really conceived the crime had no such motive. Practically all of them were atheists, with no more respect for Mohammedanism than for Christianity, and with them the one motive was cold-blooded, calculating state policy.

Questions

1. If the plight of the Armenians was known to the world, why was very little assistance forthcoming?
2. What motives or underlying beliefs, in addition to his humanitarian concern, might have motivated Morgenthau?
3. Does he reveal any prejudices of his own? What is the significance of the final two sentences in this excerpt?

Source 1.3: The trial of Soghomon Tehlirian, assassin of Talât Pasha

On March 15, 1921 in Berlin, Germany Soghomon Tehlirian assassinated Talât Pasha, former Ottoman Interior Minister and one of the genocide's chief organizers. Tehlirian

---

[62]Soon after conquering the last outpost of Muslim-ruled Spanish territory in 1492, the Spanish king and queen ordered the expulsion of Spain's Jewish population. Estimates of the number of Spanish Jews vary widely; they were probably in the hundreds of thousands.
SOURCE: Courtesy of the Armenian Center for National and International Studies.

was an Armenian, born in 1897 in eastern Anatolia, and he had lost much of his family during the height of the genocide, in 1915. He suffered serious wounds during the attack that killed his parents, brother, and sister.

The trial was held over two days in June 1921. More than one-fourth of the testimony consisted of detailed descriptions by expert witnesses about anti-Armenian persecutions and massacres in the 1890s and as during World War I. Much of the trial focused on the issues of premeditation; the defendant's mental state; and "extenuating circumstances." There were lengthy testimonies from medical experts, speculating about the defendant's psychological state (the trauma induced by the murder of his family and his knowledge of the larger massacres).

In its closing statements, Tehlirian's defense presented an extensive condemnation of Talât and his role in the deportations and massacres, suggesting that Tehlirian should be freed in the interests of a broader, moral conception of justice. His lawyers also argued that the murder was not premeditated. The district attorney, on the other hand, defended Talât and his government as allies of Germany during the war, and argued that the Armenian population of Armenia was disloyal to its Ottoman rulers. In short: The trial was heavily marked by overtly political arguments.

The jury deliberated for only one hour before pronouncing Tehlirian innocent. He later moved to Belgium, and after World War II settled in San Francisco where he died in 1960.

PRESIDING JUSTICE: How did your parents, brothers, and sisters die? . . .

TEHLIRIAN: While we were being plundered, they started firing on us from the front of the caravan. At that time, one of the gendarmes pulled my sister out and took her with him. My mother cried out, "May I go blind." I cannot remember that day any longer. I do not want to be reminded of that day. . . . They took everyone away . . . and they struck me. Then I saw how they struck and cracked my brother's skull with an axe.

PRESIDING JUSTICE: Your sister, the one whom they pulled and took with them, did she return?

TEHLIRIAN: Yes, they took my sister and raped her.

PRESIDING JUSTICE: Did she return?

TEHLIRIAN: No.

PRESIDING JUSTICE: What did you do?

TEHLIRIAN: I was struck on the head and fell to the ground. I have no recollection of what happened after that.

PRESIDING JUSTICE: Having fallen, did you remain at the site of the massacres?

TEHLIRIAN: I do not know how long I stayed there. Maybe it was two days. When I opened my eyes, I saw myself surrounded by corpses. . . .

PRESIDING JUSTICE: Among the dead, did you find the bodies of your parents, brothers, and sisters?

TEHLIRIAN: I saw my mother's body; she had fallen face down. My brother's body had fallen on top of me.

Later:

PRESIDING JUSTICE: When did the idea first occur to you to kill Talât?[63]

TEHLIRIAN: Approximately two weeks before the incident. I was feeling very bad. I kept seeing over and over again the scenes of the massacres. I saw my mother's corpse. The corpse just stood up before me and told me, "You know Talât is here and yet you do not seem to be concerned. You are no longer my son."

PRESIDING JUSTICE (repeats those words to the jury): So what did you do?

TEHLIRIAN: I woke up all of a sudden and decided to kill that man.

Tehlirian described the assassination, which he carried out on a street in Charlottenburg, a relatively affluent neighborhood of Berlin.

The court also heard extensive testimonies from other Armenian victims of the massacres of the 1890s as well as of the genocide. Several expert witnesses also testified, describing Ottoman policy and atrocities against the Armenians over the previous decades and the centralized and systematic character of the expulsions and massacres during World War I.

Dr. Johannes Lepsius informed the court that a postwar trial in Constantinople, which was organized under pressure by the postwar British occupation, had found Talât [Istanbul] and others guilty of grave crimes and sentenced him and three others to death. The defense later implied that this helped justify the assassination.

On the trial's second day:

DISTRICT ATTORNEY: He [Talât] was the faithful ally of the German people. . . . The government in Constantinople had received word that the Armenians were thinking of betraying the government and plotting with the Allied Powers. . . . Thus, for defensive and military reasons, the government in Constantinople considered it necessary to deport the Armenians. As to the character of these deportations, we should take into consideration . . . that Asia Minor is not exactly a place in which conditions characteristic of civilized peoples prevail.

DEFENSE ATTORNEY JOHANNES WERTHAUER: The whole world is watching us, and the decision that you will render will be such that perhaps thousands of years from now it will still be regarded as a wise and just decision.

Two articles later occurs another article that explains imperative self-defense. Imperative self-defense we understand to mean defending oneself against an attack. . . . [64]

---

[63]Tehlirian had earlier testified that "when I was in Constantinople [shortly after the war], I became convinced that he was the person responsible from reading the newspapers."

[64]The lawyer added that "the experiences of terror and panic suffered by the defendant" could also have pushed him "into the realm delimited by the concept of self-defense."

. . . Is it not true that one of those individuals just recently fled from Germany too? According to the papers, Enver has again gone to Russia to forge new projects with the Bolsheviks, one of whose aims is to wage war against the Armenians and annihilate them.[65] If Talât, as he of course wished, had followed Enver, most probably new atrocities would be committed against the Armenians within a few weeks.

If an individual, as a liberator of his people, kills a man who engages in dangerous and criminal activity against that people, certainly this is how he would reflect on it: "This man is an enemy to the Armenian people. If he leaves Germany and, like Enver, joins the Bolsheviks, our women and children shall be massacred again." In this sense, we find that the concept of imperative self-defense is relevant to the defendant's act. . . .

You cannot hold Tehlirian responsible for his actions. He did what he had to do. . . . Whether the compulsion that drove Tehlirian should be called a diabolic or a moral force, whether it emerged out of a healthy or diseased mind, is a matter which you will have to determine.

When you take all factors into consideration . . . ask yourself the following questions: What will be the result of my decision? What will be its consequences, not from a political or other such point of view, but with respect to supreme justice or to charity, which is what we live for and which makes life worth living?

The trial then moved to the "Instructions to Jury" and, an hour later, the reading of the verdict.

PRESIDING JUSTICE: Therefore, the following sentence is issued: "The defendant is acquitted at the expense of the state treasury." (Renewed commotion and applause)

The transcript concludes that Tehlirian was congratulated by "the public in attendance" as well as by his legal team.

Questions

1. Does the judge reveal his own sympathies—and if so, how?
2. What are your own views about one of the defense's final arguments—that the assassination was morally justifiable? Consider the argument "preventive self-defense." Can you understand how Tehlirian (who had no previous record of violence or aggression) was driven to this act?
3. Would it strike you as unusual, in a murder trial, for the court to entertain such politicized or philosophical arguments, when the facts are not in dispute?

---

[65]After going into exile in late 1918, the former war minister engaged in assorted intrigues with the German and Russian governments, the aims of which are murky, in part because his actions were often rash and unpredictable. In 1921, for example, he told Lenin he would fight on behalf of his government, but later switched sides. Enver was ultimately killed, ironically, by an Armenian serving in the Red Army.

Source 1.4: Proclamation ordering deportations of the Armenians, June 1915

In late May 1915 the Ottoman Parliament passed a law—without a single dissenting vote—that decreed the expulsion and legalized theft of the Empire's Armenian people. The proclamation contains some features common to the other case studies in this book, for example, the accusation that the targeted population, in tandem with a foreign power, are attempting "to destroy the peace and security" of the realm. The US Consul General serving in Trebizond (Oscar S. Heizer), who was sympathetic to the Armenians, and along with Morgenthau did much to publicize the atrocities, obtained the original and it was translated at the US State Department.

Our Armenian fellow countrymen . . . having taken up with a lot of false ideas of a nature to disturb the public order, as the result of foreign instigations for many years past, and because of the fact that they have brought about bloody happenings and have attempted to destroy the peace and security of the Ottoman state, of their fellow countrymen, as well as their own safety and interests, and, moreover, as the Armenian societies now have dared to join themselves . . . to the enemies now at war with our state, our government is compelled to adopt extraordinary measures and sacrifices, both for the preservation of the order and security of the country, and for the continuation of their existence and for the welfare of the Armenian societies. Therefore, as a measure to be applied until the conclusion of the war, the Armenians have to be sent away to places which have been prepared in the interior vilayets,[66] and a literal obedience to the following orders, in a categorical manner, is accordingly enjoined upon all Ottomans:

1. With the exception of the sick, all Armenians are obliged to leave, within five days from the date of this proclamation, and by villages or quarters, under the escort of the gendarmerie.
2. Although they are free to carry with them on their journey the articles of their movable property which they desire, they are forbidden to sell their landed and their extra effects, or to leave them here and there with other people. Because their exile is only temporary, their landed property, and the effects which they will be unable to take with them will be taken care of under the supervision of the government, and stored in closed and protected buildings. Anyone who sells or attempts to take care of his movable effects or landed property in a manner contrary to this order shall be sent before the Court Martial. They are only free to sell to the government, of their own accord, those articles which may answer the needs of the army. . . .

SOURCE: From Leslie A. Davis, *Slaughterhouse Province: An American Diplomat's Report* (Athens, Greece: Aristide D Caratzas Pub, 1989).
[66]"Vilayets" were administrative units or provinces in the Ottoman Empire.

3. Since the Armenians are obliged to submit to this decision of the government, if some of them attempt to use arms against the soldiers or gendarmes, arms shall be employed only against those who use force, and they shall be captured dead or alive. In like manner, those who, in opposition to the government's decision, refrain from leaving, or hide themselves here and there, if they are sheltered or are given food and assistance, the persons who thus shelter them or aid them shall be sent before the Court Martial for execution.

4. As the Armenians are not allowed to carry any firearms or cutting weapons, they shall deliver to the authorities every sort of arms, revolvers, daggers, bombs, etc., which they have concealed in their places of residence or elsewhere. [Those who disobey this order] will be under heavy responsibility and receive severe punishment.

5. The escorts of soldiers and gendarmes are required and are authorized to use their weapons against and to kill persons who shall try to attack or to damage Armenians in villages, in city quarters, or on the roads for the purpose of robbery or other injury.

6. Those who owe money to the Ottoman Bank[67] may deposit in its warehouses goods up to the amount of their indebtedness.

Questions

1. How did the author(s) justify these orders? What would be the likely result of Order 2?
2. Why do you think the Armenians were ordered to entrust their property to the government, while being prevented from selling their goods to anyone else?
3. Do you see evidence that the author(s) of these orders knew they might come to the attention of the outside world?

---

[67]The central bank, similar to the Federal Reserve in today's US system.

2

THE HOLOCAUST

Auschwitz is outside of us, but it is all around us, in the air. The plague has died away, but the infection still lingers. . . . Rejection of human solidarity, obtuse and cynical indifference to the suffering of others, abdication of the intellect and of moral sense to the principle of authority, and above all, at the root of everything, a sweeping tide of cowardice which masks itself as . . . love of country and faith in an idea.

—Primo Levi

AS WE SAW IN Chapter 1, the Armenian genocide was widely reported and was known to the world. Twenty years later, though, this knowledge had evaporated. Hitler is reputed to have stated, one week before the German invasion of Poland that would set the Holocaust in motion, "Who still speaks today of the annihilation of the Armenians?"[1] Within two years of this brutish and cynical pronouncement, Hitler's regime initiated a genocide that, in its organization and in its origins in extreme racism and nationalism, bears many similarities to the Turkish massacres.

Like other genocides, the Holocaust had unique features; and, like others, it left in its wake profound and disturbing philosophical questions. How could a seemingly civilized, modern nation—the "land of poets and thinkers" (*Dichter und Denker*) as it was known—embark upon this barbaric crime, marshaling its immense resources for such a diabolical purpose? To contemplate the madness of Hitler and his chief accomplices is disturbing enough; even more troubling is the involvement of hundreds of thousands of people who were not fanatical Nazis. How and why did they accommodate themselves to this regime and its crimes; how did "ordinary" men and women commit such gratuitously cruel acts; and how was the rest of the world able to turn a blind eye?

---

[1]Norman Naimark, *Fires of Hatred: Ethnic Cleansing in Twentieth-Century Europe* (Cambridge, MA: Harvard University Press, 2002), 57.

In a strange way, it would be comforting to believe that the Holocaust was simply the work of one madman, or perhaps a consequence of a flaw in the German national character. Yet a closer look at the Holocaust and its place in history leads to disturbing conclusions about the malignant potential of modern industrialized society, and indeed of Western civilization—as well as about such features of this civilization as bureaucratization, careerism, excessive deference to authority, and other values that were not the monopoly of Nazi or pre-Nazi Germany. The Holocaust was a product not simply of German history, but of Western history. The Nazis invented little, if anything, either in the realm of ideology or in colonial practice— although they took certain trends in Western history to their most deadly extremes.

ANTI-JEWISH PREJUDICE IN HISTORY

Prejudice and discrimination have plagued the Jewish people throughout much of its history, which can be traced. Their origins can be traced to roughly 3,000 years ago. Anti-Jewish sentiment often arose from the notion that Jews did not assimilate into the dominant culture, and clung to their own religious practices rather than accepting the practices and beliefs of their immediate neighbors. Persecution flared into violent suppression during the first century CE, and the Roman authorities crushed a Jewish rebellion (66–70 CE) and destroyed the Second Temple. In the first century CE, a new faith eventually known as Christianity split off from Judaism and began to develop its own scriptures and theology. Based upon some accounts of Jesus's trial and execution in the New Testament—accounts that biblical scholars and historians have shown to be wildly inaccurate in their depiction of a weak and compassionate Pontius Pilate being ordered about by Jewish priests— Christian theology blamed the Jews collectively for the death of Jesus. Matthew 27:25 was often cited; after Pilate "washes his hands," the Jewish crowd declares, "His blood shall be on us and on our children."[2] Christian teaching further stigmatized the Jews for failing to accept the divinity of Christ. The fact that Jesus was born and died a Jew would be forgotten in coming centuries.

Throughout the first four or five centuries of the European Middle Ages (roughly 600–1500), a majority of Jews lived under Islamic rule—in Muslim polities that were located in North Africa, Mesopotamia (present-day Iraq), Syria, Iran, Anatolia (present-day Asian Turkey), and that region of Spain then known as Al-Andalus. Generally, Jews found tolerance and opportunity under Muslim domination. While never creating a perfectly harmonious relationship, Muslim rulers were guided by the Islamic belief that Jews shared the same God and should be treated with respect. Jews, along with other non-Muslim subjects,

---

[2]Despite the rejection of the "Christ killer" myth by all mainstream Christian denominations over the last fifty years, Chapter 19 of John (in which Pilate does not want to execute Jesus but finally succumbs to the demands of the Jewish priests and mob) is still commonly read in Catholic churches as part of the Good Friday liturgy.

were nonetheless compelled to pay special taxes, endured restrictions on their public religious and social activities, and were not immune from harsher repression or violence during times of trouble.

In Christian Europe throughout the Middle Ages, religious and cultural anti-Semitism persisted and was the basis for additional forms of discrimination. Jews were usually barred from owning land and from military service. In a classic example of a self-fulfilling prophecy, these restrictions served to create or validate certain stereotypes (e.g., that Jews were cowardly and devious and incapable of honest work or agricultural labor, preferring parasitical financial dealings). By the late twelfth century, the creation and spread of fantastic allegations, most notably the infamous "blood libel" myth—the allegation that Jews abducted and murdered Christian children in order to use their blood in religious rituals—intensified the anti-Jewish sentiments that were embedded in Christian theology and popular culture, and sometimes provoked murderous pogroms. By this time, we see a pattern in place that has continued to the present day: Social crisis and instability, especially when combined with religious zealotry, proved to be especially dangerous for Jews. The First Crusade (1096–1099) provides an example of the perils to Jews of Christian zeal, but it also serves as an example of the complexity of Christian-Jewish relations. In 1096, Crusader forces attacked the Jewish communities of Mainz, Worms, and Cologne in an effort to forcibly baptize the "unbelievers" residing in these cities. Although some Christians attempted to protect them, as many as 3,000 Jews died as a consequence of these attacks—attacks that were made possible because of the weakness of local authorities and the overall hostility of Christian burghers in the three cities who saw the Jews as a threat to their economic well-being and made common cause with the Crusaders.[3] Elsewhere, this was largely not the case, as the local authorities and inhabitants of most other cities and towns in Europe managed to deflect the Crusaders' zeal to force baptism upon Jews as they marched eastward toward Jerusalem. What might surprise many modern readers is that most of the deaths in these three Rhineland cities were by suicide or at the hands of relatives, who chose martyrdom for themselves and their loved ones rather than enforced conversion to Christianity.

Although violence against Jews was sporadic and localized during the Age of the Crusades, and almost always due to local social and economic circumstances, by the Late Middle Ages (1300–1500), "Passion Plays" enacting the execution of Jesus often culminated in anti-Jewish violence. The "Black Death" of the mid-fourteenth century is another example of a social crisis that produced pogroms against Jews, who were accused of poisoning the wells and streams to bring about the calamity. In numerous instances in French, German, and Italian villages, Jews were burned

---

[3]Robert Chazan, *In the Year 1096: The First Crusade and the Jews* (Philadelphia and Jerusalem: The Jewish Publication Society, 1996), 129. See also Chazan's *European Jewry and The First Crusade* (Berkeley: University of California Press, 1987).

to death, sometimes in their synagogues and sometimes after being rounded up and forced to confess to the outlandish allegations.[4] Notably, the anti-Jewish violence was often instigated by political and economic elites, belying the image of spontaneous blind fury arising from mobs of ignorant lower-class people.[5] This practice of blaming or scapegoating Jews for social or economic problems is a long-standing, recurring tradition that would again be evident in pre-Nazi Germany.

The histories of relations between adherents of various "conflicting" faiths, though, are always more complex and varied than popularly believed: It is much easier to focus on the violent episodes than to detect the deeper patterns. The long history of Jewish-Muslim coexistence and even synthesis has been forgotten in recent years; similarly, it is important to stress that, while the history of antagonism summarized earlier is important for our understanding of the Holocaust's background and influences, it is an incomplete account of many centuries of Jewish life within Europe. European rulers and authorities often protected their Jewish subjects, who provided necessary professional and financial services, and the exclusion of Jews from feudal obligations had the beneficial impact of sparing them from the continent's nearly ceaseless warfare. Sometimes in their own communities segregated from the dominant societies, but often in coexistence with Christians, European Jews had a long, rich, highly diverse and vibrant history. Our knowledge of the terrible events of 1933–1945 can prevent us from recognizing that simple fact, and to view those thousands of years of history merely as a prelude to an inevitable catastrophe.

Although various secularizing trends began to weaken the ideological hold of anti-Judaism in early modern Europe, it was rejuvenated and given a more lethal potential by the racial ideologies that dominated European thought during the 1800s. While Jews had previously been viewed as a religious or ethnic group, they now came to be seen by many Europeans as a "race." Therefore, the negative qualities that had been falsely associated with Jewry were now depicted as genetic, and therefore immutable and unchanging. This "racializing" of anti-Semitism would later have lethal consequences: during times of persecution and pogroms, a Jew could no longer convert to escape his or her fate—an emotionally difficult option, but an option nonetheless for previous generations. By the turn of the twentieth century modern and premodern forms of Judeophobia converged, and were given new force by racism and other anxieties stirred by the rapid and, to some, unnerving political and cultural trends of that era. By the end of the nineteenth century, modern anti-Semitism, while imbibing and perpetuating many stereotypes and motifs from earlier centuries, had become a political force in much of Europe, and

---

[4]Samuel K. Cohn, Jr., "The Black Death and the Burning of Jews," *Past and Present* 196, no. 1 (August 2007), 3–4.

[5]Cohn, "The Black Death," 3–36. An important exception was Pope Clement VI, who in 1348 issued two bulls (official papal edicts) decrying the violence and pointing out that there was no evidence that the Jews were responsible for the Black Death.

"Protocols of the Elders of Zion"
This absurd forgery, concocted by the Russian secret police, purports to expose the "international Jewish conspiracy" to rule the world through myriad ways. It combines age-old anti-Jewish motifs with modern ones, helping explain its appeal to susceptible people. The tract was translated into German shortly after World War I by Alfred Rosenberg, self-styled "philosopher" of race and antisemitism who exerted a strong influence on Hitler in the early years of the Nazi party. The lurid cover on this French edition captures the forgery's themes.

in its racial rather than religious character it differed in character from anti-Jewish prejudice of the late Middle Ages and Early Modern period.

In France, the infamous, prolonged Dreyfus Affair of 1894–1906 symbolized the strength and potency of anti-Semitism as a political weapon. A Jewish army officer, Captain Alfred Dreyfus, was falsely accused of giving secrets to France's enemy, Germany, and sentenced to life imprisonment at the notoriously severe Devil's Island penal colony. Military authorities suppressed evidence pointing to the real culprit; fabricated evidence against Dreyfus; and subjected the captain to gratuitous humiliation, in addition to the unjust conviction. Édouard Drumont, founder of the Anti-Semitic League of France, led a scurrilous, nakedly Judeophobic campaign in the press to impugn Dreyfus. The case exploded into a huge, politically charged controversy, but it was only after nearly a dozen years that the innocent man was exonerated and freed. "The Dreyfus affair was the first indication that a new epoch of progress and cosmopolitan optimism," wrote Adam Gopnik, "would be met by a countervailing wave of hatred that deformed the next half century of European history."[6]

Also at the turn of the century, the Russian secret police concocted a document called "The Protocols of the Elders of Zion"—supposedly the record of a gathering of Jewish leaders bent on world domination, but in reality a clumsy forgery that echoed anti-Jewish stereotypes from the distant past. This document found eager, gullible audiences in Russia and elsewhere. It was translated and distributed

---

[6]Adam Gopnik, "Trial of the Century," *The New Yorker*, September 28, 2009.

in Germany after World War I by, among others, Alfred Rosenberg, a future Nazi leader who was part of a group of German-speaking émigrés from the former Russian empire. Adolf Hitler later asserted that the "Protocols" uncovered the "nature" as well as the "ultimate aims" of the Jewish people.

Anti-Semitism in German-speaking Central Europe, where Jews had lived from at least the fourth century, was not substantially stronger than elsewhere: To the contrary, Germany was ahead of other European states in its legal emancipation of its Jewish population. Shortly after its 1871 unification, Germany passed a law abolishing all restrictions of civil and political rights based on religious differences. Surprising in hindsight, the fact is that by the nineteenth century many European Jews looked to Germany as a "safe harbor," as one Prussian-Jewish politician said, and emigrated there.[7] By the end of the century nearly 600,000 Jews lived in Germany (1 percent of the population), and most of them were well assimilated and considered themselves to be fully German. They "knew their Goethe and Schiller better than [they knew] any Jewish Bible commentator," to quote one observer.[8]

PRECONDITIONS FOR THE HOLOCAUST: WORLD WAR I AND WEIMAR GERMANY

World War I and its conclusion helped lay the groundwork for Nazism's rise to power and its success in scapegoating Jews. The war and its unsatisfactory conclusion strengthened numerous ominous trends: aggressive nationalism, tinged with bitterness and a quest for vengeance or recapture of lost glory; glorification of war and of martial values; racism and anti-Semitism; extreme anti-Communism, intensified by fear of the Bolshevik Revolution and its influence; and a longing for authority rather than freedom. Further, the battlefield's cheapening of life and the overall harshness of the war produced a brutalization of postwar politics, as disoriented, embittered soldiers returned to the home front and the conviction spread that political differences should be resolved by force.

All these factors resulted in a sharp polarization of politics through much of the continent. Moderate, democratic political parties lost ground, as increasing numbers of people sought radical solutions. In Germany, revolutionary uprisings in the northern port city of Kiel, followed quickly by rebellions in Berlin, Munich, and other major cities, brought down the German "Second Empire" and sent the emperor, Kaiser Wilhelm II, into exile in November 1918. A new, democratic government led by the moderate Social-Democratic Party (SPD) took power, but not until left-wing revolutions were bloodily suppressed in early 1919.

---

[7]Konrad Fischer, *The History of an Obsession: German Judeophobia and the Holocaust* (New York: Continuum Publishing Company, 1998), 52.
[8]Michael Brenner, *The Renaissance of Jewish Culture in Weimar Germany* (New Haven, CT: Yale University Press, 1998), 19.

Before the armistice had even been signed, a myth began to circulate that purportedly explained the cause of Germany's capitulation: The brave, selfless, and undefeated soldiers at the front had been betrayed—"stabbed in the back"—by pacifists and socialists as well as domestic politicians who, far from the front, conceded the war. It is ironic that Generals Erich Ludendorff and Paul von Hindenburg, who were largely to blame for Germany's fortunes in the war, were instrumental in promoting this legend. The stab-in-the-back myth converged and drew sustenance from anti-Semitism—for, in the imaginations of Germany's growing number of right-wing nationalists, "the Jew" lurked behind the unpatriotic forces of liberalism and socialism. Anti-Semitic agitators could cite the Jewish background (usually distant) of Karl Marx and of contemporary revolutionaries, such as Rosa Luxemburg, to substantiate their delusional link between Judaism and "Bolshevism."

And, lastly, the war transformed a wayward young Austrian into a single-minded fanatic and gave him a purpose in life: to resurrect and return to greatness his beloved Germany.

ADOLF HITLER AND THE RISE OF THE NAZI PARTY

Historians have searched in vain for the source of Hitler's virulent, obsessive anti-Semitism. This question would not arouse any curiosity if historical events had not lifted him from obscurity. There is no simple explanation for Hitler's violent and deranged worldview. In many ways, he was a product of his time and of his Austrian environment.

Adolf Hitler was born in a town in northern Austria-Hungary, not far from Germany, in April 1889. His early years, which were spent primarily in Linz, were unremarkable: He drifted along aimlessly, seemingly fated to lead the life of a failed pseudo-intellectual. His passion for Richard Wagner's operas—which helped instill in Hitler the belief in a romanticized, mythical, superior "Aryan race"—was unmatched by strong enthusiasm or dedication for any particular career. He dabbled unsuccessfully in painting, but lacked the discipline to hone his modest skills and was rejected by a prestigious art institute in Vienna, where he had moved in 1905 at the age of sixteen. Hitler's time in Vienna corresponded to the final five years of the rule of Mayor Karl Lueger, who was one of many politicians in Austria and Germany who made anti-Semitism the core of their platform and their appeal around the turn of the century. Lueger thereby contributed mightily to his city's overtly anti-Jewish political culture; another prominent anti-Semitic politician, the unruly pan-German racist Georg Schönerer, was also popular and influential in Vienna. While Hitler surely imbibed Vienna's toxic politics, he displayed few signs of strong political convictions or of rabid anti-Semitism at this time in his life. In 1913 he moved to Munich, still disinclined to work but supported by an inheritance from his father, who died ten years earlier.

World War I and its culmination in Germany's defeat transformed Hitler by accentuating his fanaticism, sharpening his animosity toward the Jews, and giving him a sense of destiny. Hitler enlisted in the German army and served in the trenches at the Western Front, where he speechified endlessly about the necessity for greater dedication to the war. Recovering in a hospital from a mustard gas attack, Hitler, who had not risen above the rank of *Gefreiter* (lance corporal), was stunned and enraged by Germany's defeat. The subsequent Versailles Treaty was the cause of "boundless extortion and abject humiliation," he wrote a few years later in his rambling, poisonous 600-page manifesto and quasi-autobiography, *Mein Kampf (My Struggle)*.

It is evident from his writings that by September 1919 at the latest, Hitler had become convinced that "the Jew" was the chief evil in Western society, and that this belief was the cornerstone of an increasingly coherent, if irrational, worldview. In sharp contrast to Marxism, which he excoriated and linked inextricably to Judaism, he saw race and racial conflict as history's principal motor force. His oratory and writings from the early 1920s were filled with the language of biological and racial determinism, and with an anti-Semitism that was expressed in uncompromising, lurid tones. "With diabolic joy in his face, the black-haired Jewish youth lurks in ambush for the unsuspecting girl whom he defiles with his blood," he wrote in *Mein Kampf*. "All great cultures of the past perished only because the originally creative race died off through blood-poisoning," and so on and so forth ad nauseam.[9] Hitler saw the Jews not only as repulsive, sickly, and parasitical, but as an invading force; they were not merely a nuisance, but an existential threat, in large because of their presumed connection to Marxist subversion. Marxism and "Bolshevism" were merely Jewish inventions in his view—a weapon to "enslave and rule the peoples with a brutal fist."[10] If Germany did not defeat the Jewish menace, Germany and Western Civilization itself would instead be defeated. In late 1919, Hitler discovered a group in Munich that would serve as his instrument for the hoped-for regeneration of his adopted homeland: the German Workers' Party, which had originated in small World War I–era circles of racists and self-styled intellectuals. Quickly asserting himself as leader, Hitler renamed the party the "National Socialist German Workers' Party." (NSDAP; "Nazi," an abbreviation of the German for "National Socialist," quickly became the party's informal designation.)

In February 1920, at its first mass public meeting, the NSDAP announced a "25-point program," a mix of ultra-nationalism, anti-Semitism, and half-hearted populism. But these qualities did not sharply distinguish the Nazis, who for most of the decade remained simply one of many small parties on the far right wing of German politics. A premature power grab in Munich in 1923—the "Beer Hall Putsch" of November 8–9, the date of Germany's defeat five years earlier and a sacred date on the Nazi calendar—resulted in the deaths of a dozen Nazi activists

---

[9] Adolf Hitler, *Mein Kampf* (New York: Reynal & Hitchcock, 1941), 448, 396. Some form of the word "poison" appears more than 70 times in this book, which was 642 pages in its original German version, and just over 1,000 pages in its early English-language translations.
[10] Ibid., 449.

and the arrest of Hitler. Symptomatic of the hostility of many German institutions to democracy, the Weimar-era criminal justice system was notoriously sympathetic to rightists. Hitler was allowed to turn his trial into a stage, expounding his views to great publicity, which brought him to the notice of many Germans far from the Nazis' stronghold of Munich.

Hitler served only 9 months in prison, where he was well-treated by his jailers and hosted a steady stream of visitors. He used his leisurely incarceration to compose *Mein Kampf.* While the book is unreliable in its account of his earlier years, it is a clear expression of his beliefs and worldview. Hitler was not an original thinker or theorist; he borrowed heavily from racist and German nationalist mythology, and his only semioriginal idea—the presumed link between Judaism and "Bolshevism"—was imparted to him by right-wing émigrés from Russia who played an important role in the pre–"Beer Hall Putsch" Nazi party. Some of Hitler's closest colleagues and followers were "true believers," while others, especially after 1933, were opportunists who were not necessarily obsessed with race. But of Hitler's adherence to such delusional, hateful beliefs there is no question. He continued to rail against the Jews into the final hours of his life, when he even claimed that British and American military forces were "the troops of Jewry."[11]

Throughout the 1920s, the Nazis were one of many small groups in a chaotic political landscape. But by the end of the decade their cunning use of propaganda—refined by Joseph Goebbels, who joined the party in 1924—and mobilization of street-fighting units, the SA (*Sturmabteilung* or "storm troopers"), distinguished them from the other rightist groups and contributed to their ascent. Capitalizing on the deep polarization of German politics and opinion, the NSDAP finally emerged as a formidable force at the end of the decade. Most of its supporters believed the party's promises to restore Germany's greatness, end the humiliation of its defeat in World War I and of the Treaty of Versailles, reverse the economic instability of the 1920s, and unify the *Volk.*

The Nazis' ascent at the turn of the decade—not coincidentally, as the worldwide economic depression began to set in—can be seen in their success at the ballot box, where their share of the national vote rose from a negligible 2.6 percent in May 1928 to 18.3 percent in September 1930. The Nazi party won more votes than any other party, 37 percent, in the July 1932 elections, which like the multitude of hastily called elections of the early 1930s failed to resolve the deepening political crisis. In this election as well as the subsequent November 6 vote, half the electorate voted for either the Nazis or the Communists, while the centrist parties were pushed to the margins. Petrified by left-wing revolution and lacking options or imagination, traditional conservative elites like Franz von Papen, one of three short-term chancellors as the government sank into near chaos in the early 1930s,

[11]Saul Friedländer, *The Years of Extermination: Nazi Germany and the Jews, 1939–1945* (New York: Harper, 2008), 659.

Hitler at a Munich pro-war rally
Adolf Hitler drifted through the first 25 years of life with little direction. World War I, however—
and its culmination in the German defeat—gave him his purpose in life: to avenge the humiliation
and restore German greatness and dominance. This photograph captures Hitler's elation at the
proclamation of war, at a large rally in Munich on August 2, 1914. It was taken by Heinrich Hoffman,
who later became Hitler's personal photographer, who helped to shape his image in the 1920s.

persuaded the eighty-five-year-old President Hindenburg to offer Hitler the
chancellorship—which Hindenburg did on January 30, 1933.

The conservatives mistakenly thought they could control the "drummer boy," as
they sometimes contemptuously called him. They were not the only ones who failed
to anticipate the ruthlessness and determination with which Hitler would consolidate power. The powerful working-class parties—the Social Democrats (SPD) and
the Communist Party (KPD)—also failed to perceive the danger, and spent more
time denouncing one another than attempting to unite to combat the Nazi threat.

ELIMINATION OF OPPONENTS AND INTENSIFICATION
OF REPRESSION: 1933–1938

The Nazis' first targets were not German Jews per se, but political opponents, particularly members of the large Social-Democratic and Communist movements.
Four weeks after Hitler's appointment, in the early hours of February 27, 1933, the
Reichstag (parliament) building was burned down. Historians believed for years
that the arson was the work of a lone, wayward Dutch radical, but new evidence

suggests that the Nazis may have set the fire. In either case, the fire was convenient for the Nazi leadership, which immediately seized upon it as a pretext to solidify power, decrying the arson as the work of "communists" bent on taking power and unleashing a reign of terror on real and imagined enemies. On March 23, the Reichstag passed the Enabling Law, allowing Hitler to essentially rule by decree. By the end of Hitler's first year, tens of thousands of KPD members were under arrest, many of them subjected to the ghastly symbol of Nazism that would later define its rule throughout Europe: the concentration camp.

This rapid and successful suppression of political opposition greatly impeded, but did not completely destroy, organized resistance to Hitler. Thousands of German Communists and Social Democrats undertook resistance activities, producing and furtively distributing anti-Nazi literature; relaying news to the outside world, and gathering and transmitting news from abroad; taking up collections to help the families of political prisoners; and, within the camps, attempting to maintain morale and foster solidarity among fellow prisoners.

The regime, however, consolidated itself by the fall of 1934, after a vicious purge (the "Night of the Long Knives") of its own SA leadership and others, and the death of President Hindenburg in August 1934, after which Hitler combined the offices of chancellor and president under the title of "Führer" (Leader). Despite the persistence of a scattered underground resistance, the large majority of the German public supported or at least condoned the new regime. Many Germans were swept up in the enthusiasm that was skillfully fomented by Nazi spectacles and mass organizations of various segments of society. The Nazis' ability to reduce unemployment, in part by remilitarizing in violation of Versailles, also won wide support.

In recent years, historians of the Third Reich have abandoned a simple dichotomy between "support" and "resistance," and they now use more nuanced terms—compliance, acceptance, acquiescence, as well as defiance, refusal, and nonconformity—to characterize the great variety of responses and, in some cases, survival mechanisms adopted by the German populace. It is also important to recognize that, while the Nazi police apparatus was efficient and ruthless, it was not omnipresent. The Gestapo (from the German *Geheime Staatspolizei*—Secret State Police) functioned in large part because of the active complicity of many tens of thousands of citizens who willingly betrayed their neighbors. Such impulses can be found in other societies led by powerful dictatorships, such as that of Soviet Russia.

STAGES IN ANTI-JEWISH PERSECUTION

The German-Jewish population totaled about 525,000 in 1933, less than 1 percent of the country's total populace. Berlin had the largest Jewish community, numbering close to 200,000. While only about 2 percent of Germany's bankers and stockbrokers were Jewish, Jews were well represented in small businesses, lending anecdotal evidence to support anti-Semitic myths about Jewish dominance of commerce and finance. German Jews were prominent in the legal and medical professions and were also well represented in the arts. Approximately 80,000 German Jews had served in the world war, and 12,000 had died in service[12]—evidence of Jewish patriotism that made little impact on public opinion, which grew steadily more racist during the 1930s.

Although the Nazis initiated their rule with the ruthless suppression of left-wing organizations, they wasted little time clamping down on the Jewish population, who in the Nazi worldview were responsible for virtually all the ills of society. "The adjective *jüdisch* [Jewish] . . . was attached to every phenomenon of the modern world objectionable to the Nazis," wrote historian Alon Confino, "and then some. Jews were responsible for bolshevism, communism, Marxism" as well as "capitalism, conservatism, pacifism . . . materialism, atheism." The Jews were also responsible for those features of the Weimar Republic that were so abhorrent to the Nazis: its "cabaret and club scene, as well as sexual freedom, psychoanalysis, feminism, homosexuality . . . modernist, atonal, and jazz music" and avant-garde art and film.[13]

During the first six years of the Third Reich, the Nazis steadily increased the legal persecution and social ostracizing of the German Jews. The Nazis' first overt attack upon the Jewish population was the declaration of an April 1, 1933 boycott of Jewish-owned businesses. Nazi storm troopers stood menacingly outside many businesses, which were defaced with slogans such as "The Jews Are Our Misfortune"; but the one-day boycott was not, from Hitler's point of view, a great success, as many Germans ignored it. Within a week, though, the new regime began its legal assault on the Jews, issuing the "Law for the Restoration of the Professional Civil Service" on April 7, which forced Jewish and other "politically unreliable" employees out of government jobs—including positions in law and education. The 1935 "Nuremberg Laws" went further in institutionalizing Nazi racial ideology as the basis for citizenship and political rights. Section 1 banned marriage between Jews and "Aryan" Germans, an important step in isolating the Jews and bringing about their "social death," as some historians have described it, which would make it easier for German gentiles to harden their hearts or ignore the worsening plight of their Jewish neighbors.

The *Kristallnacht* (Crystal Night, or Night of Broken Glass) pogrom of November 9–10, 1938 heralded a violent new stage in anti-Jewish persecutions. Using as a pretext the murder of a Nazi diplomat by a Polish-Jewish teenager in Paris, Goebbels and other Nazi leaders unleashed a wave of violence throughout the Greater Reich (Germany and Austria). The date was no coincidence; the anniversary of the 1923 Munich putsch had long attained a sacred status among Nazis. By the morning of November 10, at least one hundred Jews had been murdered, hundreds of synagogues as well as Jewish-owned businesses had been vandalized or destroyed, and some 26,000 Jewish men were arrested and dragged off to concentration camps. Significantly, these were the first German Jews to be arrested simply

---

[12]David Crowe, *The Holocaust: Roots, History, and Aftermath* (New York: Westview, 2008), 107.
[13]Alon Confino, *A World without Jews: The Nazi Imagination from Persecution to Genocide* (New Haven, CT: Yale University Press, 2014), 33.

Das Ergebnis!

Der Rassestolz schwindet.

Nazi racism

Propaganda photo depicting friendship between an Aryan woman and a black woman as a "loss of racial pride." Nazi racism also targeted the country's very small Afro-German population. As this poster indicates, simple friendships—much less marriage or sexual relations—between "Aryans" and "lesser races" was strongly discouraged and penalized.

for being Jewish. The Nazi regime placed the responsibility for the destruction upon the Jews themselves. It assessed the Jewish community about $100 million for the damage, and another $400 million for the murder of the Nazi diplomat.

Kristallnacht dispelled the hopes of many German Jews that they could endure and outwait the Nazis, and that the relatively tolerant pre-1933 Germany would eventually reappear. Young children later recalled the shock and trauma of having their homes ransacked and their fathers dragged off, sometimes to return several weeks later with dreadful injuries from tortures and beatings in such camps as Buchenwald and Dachau. "My father came from Dachau" at the end of the year, recalled one young boy; "he had several ribs broken on one side."[14]

The Nazi regime pressed its offensive. Before the end of 1938, all Jewish business activity was banned, and Jews were instructed to sell their enterprises as well as any land; to sell their stocks and also certain valuables, such as jewels and artworks; they were banned from most entertainment or cultural venues; and Jewish children were expelled from German schools.[15] By this time, anti-Semitic persecution enjoyed

---

[14]Deborah Dwork and Robert Jan van Pelt, *Holocaust: A History* (New York: Norton, 2002), 101.

[15]Two months after *Kristallnacht* these persecutions would even expand "to the animal kingdom as Jewish veterinarians were allowed to treat only pets owned by Jews; pets owned by [non-Jewish] Germans were now considered Aryan." Confino, 108.

greater public support. The widespread indifference and even opposition to the anti-Jewish boycott of April 1933 had evolved, after several years of propaganda and social separation, into grudging or outright approval of anti-Semitic persecution.

Kristallnacht encouraged Jewish emigration, one of the Nazis' aims. Many more would have fled if the United States, England, and other Western democracies had opened their doors more widely, or even fulfilled the immigration quotas they had set. Nevertheless, by the start of World War II in September 1939, more than one-half of Germany's Jewish population had fled, with the exiles often leaving behind most of their possessions.

WORLD WAR II

The Nazi regime had tormented its Jewish citizens for six years, but it was the war (1939–1945) that led directly to the wholesale mass murder of European Jewry. As the German Reich expanded into Poland and eventually the Soviet Union—countries with much larger Jewish populations than Germany itself—Nazi policy radicalized, and collaborationist or ultra-right governments and movements in Europe also targeted Jews for extermination, sometimes with little encouragement from Berlin. Finally, the war virtually trapped Europe's Jews: While they had some limited options for emigration before the war, escape routes now closed, with minor exceptions.[16]

On September 1, 1939, a week after signing a "Non-Aggression Pact" with the Soviet Union, Germany invaded Poland, initiating World War II. Ten days before, Hitler had instructed his military commanders to "close your hearts to pity."[17] In his mind, the war against Poland was both a war for territory or *Lebensraum* ("living space," a long-cherished goal of certain German elites predating Hitler)—presumably needed for a greater Germany that would encompass ethnic Germans throughout the region—and a racial war against the "dreadful [racial] material," as he viewed the Poles.[18] His chief of staff explained that it was "the intention of the Führer to destroy and exterminate the Polish people."[19]

---

[16]Until May 1940 small numbers of Jews were able to find refuge in Italy; it was also possible if difficult to get into the USSR until the Nazi invasion of June 1941; and some Jews also escaped to Spain and Portugal until those routes closed in October 1941.

[17]Louis Leo Snyder, *Hitler's Third Reich: A Documentary History* (Chicago: Burnham, 1982), 329.

[18]Crowe, *Holocaust,* 159. Friedrich Ratzel, a leader of Germany's procolonial Pan-German League, coined *Lebensraum* in 1897 and developed it further in the last years of his life (he died in 1904). In Ratzel's conception, as in Hitler's, a *Volk* requires *Lebensraum* in order to sustain itself; the German *Volk* must expand its territory by any means, including conquest, in order to obtain resources for an expanding population; and the people and its land must have a strong agricultural basis. Benjamin Madley, "From Africa to Auschwitz: How German South-West Africa Incubated Ideas and Methods Adopted and Developed by the Nazis in Eastern Europe," *European History Quarterly* 35, no. 3 (2005), 432.

[19]Timothy Snyder, *Bloodlands: Europe Between Hitler and Stalin* (New York: Basic Books, 2010), 121.

In the first days of the invasion, special German units, the *Einsatzgruppen*, were unleashed upon Poland's defenseless civilians, both Jews and non-Jews. Augmented by other units, five *Einsatzgruppen* composed of roughly 4,200 men murdered 50,000 Poles, mostly non-Jews, by the end of 1939.[20] These special units would later play a prominent and indispensable role in the murder of Soviet Jews, after the subsequent invasion of that country. On September 7, Reinhard Heydrich, chief of the German Reich Security Main Office and one of the Holocaust's chief organizers, ordered his police and SS forces to wipe out the Polish elite and expel Jews; the "nobility, clergy, and Jews must be killed," he instructed.[21] The Soviet Union, Germany's non-aggression-pact ally, invaded Poland from the east on September 17, and occupied slightly more than half the country with a brutality that rivaled the Nazis'. Of the one and a quarter million Jews in the Soviet zone, about 250,000 were deported to Siberia or Kazakhstan, while the remaining population saw its synagogues, schools, and aid organizations shut down on Stalin's orders.[22]

The Germans annexed much of western Poland into the "Greater German Reich" and established a huge territory labeled the *Generalgouvernement*, or General Government. The General Government was a dumping ground for displaced persons, as well as a colony: In search of profit, career advancement, or adventure, German civilians flooded in, as colonists had poured into African colonies in previous generations. The territory was ruled by Hans Frank, who after the war was hanged for his crimes. In April and May 1940, German troops conquered much of northern Europe and defeated France after a brief struggle. France, like other imperialist powers, had many colonial troops under its command, and African-French troops suffered dreadfully after the defeat. The Nazis killed at least three thousand captured African soldiers, often with gratuitous and grisly cruelty.[23] Displaying their delusional creativity, the Nazis were able to depict certain Africans as real or potential colonizers. At the end of May 1940, shortly after the defeat of France, the Nazi daily *Völkischer Beobachter* ran a photo from 1918 of French colonial troops with the caption: "The black representatives of French civilization march into the Rhineland. Several hours later they throw themselves like wild beasts on

[20]Crowe, *Holocaust*, 160.
[21]Donald Bloxham, *The Final Solution: A Genocide* (New York: Oxford University Press, 2009), 105.
[22]Crowe, *Holocaust*, 193–194.
[23]Raffael Scheck, *Hitler's African Victims: The German Army Massacres of Black French Soldiers in 1940* (New York: Cambridge University Press, 2008), 9. In one of the very few books devoted to this topic, Scheck argues that Hitler conducted a "race war against black Africans in the Western campaign of 1940." This "race war" was not a mere "hiatus between the race wars in the east," Scheck argues, but through the involvement of the regular army and the impetus provided by racist propaganda was connected to "Wehrmacht atrocities in Poland and the full-fledged race war [the Wehrmacht] later conducted in the Balkans and the Soviet Union."

German women and girls. They rape, plunder, murder, and commit arson wherever they can."[24]

At this stage, the Nazi leaders considered various options for how to deal with the millions of Jews who had fallen into their hands. Tens of thousands of Polish Jews were killed or died of conditions imposed upon them by the occupiers, but the Nazis had not yet decided upon systematic mass murder as their answer to the "Jewish Question." They considered some plans that may seem fantastical—such as deporting mass numbers of Jews to the island of Madagascar, off Africa's southeast coast, a scheme that had long fascinated European anti-Semites. As a stopgap, or transitional, measure while debates continued at different levels of the German administration, the Germans instituted a policy of ghettoization. Beginning in late 1939, German forces squeezed Jews into sealed-off quarters of numerous cities. They later extended this policy into other corners of occupied Europe, but the largest ghettos remained in Poland, until their occupants were deported en masse to death camps later in the war. Although many ghettos were being liquidated and their inhabitants sent to death camps by 1942, some ghettos—for example, in Poland's Lublin district—were still being established in that same year.[25]

Miserable, degrading conditions prevailed. The Warsaw Ghetto housed 445,000 Jews in an area constituting 2.4 percent of the city's living space.[26] In Lodz, the second-largest ghetto, an average of more than seven people resided in the average apartment, only one in forty of which had running water. Typhus and tuberculosis augmented starvation as the major killers; and "potato peels became a prized item."[27] Warsaw's thriving ghetto underground press produced harrowing, heart-breaking literature. A young socialist activist and writer named Leyb Goldin wrote a short story that chronicled the emotional, spiritual, and physical devastation he witnessed as well as experienced. "The world's turning upside down," he wrote in the story's despairing finale. "A planet melts in tears. And I—I am hungry. I am hungry."[28] Goldin succumbed to starvation in 1942.

---

[24]Ibid., 151, 11, 106.

[25]The US Holocaust Memorial Museum has undertaken a mammoth project, the seven-volume *Encyclopedia of Camps and Ghettos, 1933–1945*, which has greatly enriched our knowledge of the range and diversity of Nazi camps and ghettos, from small and temporary sites to huge complexes (such as Auschwitz-Birkenau) possessing dozens of subcamps. From the museum's site: "Most people are unaware of the full extent of the Nazi camp and ghetto system. Behind the well-known names, such as Auschwitz, Dachau, Treblinka, and Warsaw, there was a vast universe of facilities, more than 42,000, that formed the heart of the Nazi regime." http://www.ushmm.org/research/publications/encyclopedia-camps-ghettos (accessed July 29, 2015). The first two volumes have been published and total nearly 4,000 pages; another six volumes are planned.

[26]Crowe, *Holocaust*, 176.

[27]Bloxham, *Final Solution*, 112–113.

[28]David Roskies, ed., *The Literature of Destruction* (Philadelphia: Jewish Publication Society, 1989), 434.

OPERATION BARBAROSSA AND THE "FINAL SOLUTION"

In retrospect, there was never any doubt that Nazi Germany, driven by its quest for *Lebensraum* and the imperative of destroying "Judeo-Bolshevism," would attack the USSR when it perceived the time was right. By the summer of 1940, Hitler routinely bellowed to his colleagues that the Soviet Union must be "utterly destroyed" and its occupants, like the Poles, reduced to "a people of leaderless slave laborers."[29] On March 30, 1941, Hitler instructed his generals that the war would be one of "extermination" (a *Vernichtungskrieg*). One June 6, the infamous "Commissar Order" had been issued, calling for the execution "as partisans" of Soviet political officers, Communist Party members, and supposed saboteurs. "In the battle against Bolshevism, the adherence of the enemy to the principles of humanity [*Grundsätzen der Menschlichkeit*] or international law is not to be counted on."[30]

In May 1941, German leaders devised the "Hunger Plan," an avowedly genocidal strategy that called for the "extinction of industry as well as a great part of the population" in "deficit regions"—those areas, some encompassing entire Soviet republics, dependent upon food imported from regions with agricultural surpluses.[31] In those regions and elsewhere in the Soviet Union, the Hunger Plan envisioned the destruction of the cities and the starvation of roughly 30 million people during the first winter of the invasion.[32] The plan's chief author, SS *Obergruppenführer* and long-time party radical Herbert Backe, presented the envisioned consequences with utter clarity at a May 2, 1941, conference of state secretaries of ministries that would be involved in the occupation. Point Two casually announced, "Tens of millions of people will undoubtedly starve to death." "With no evidence of protest or disagreement," reports Stephen G. Fritz is his recent *Ostkrieg*, "key representatives of the German state agreed."[33] "The chilling wartime scheme for the 'reduction' of the Slav population in Nazi-occupied Eastern Europe 'by one-third,'" observes Aristotle Kallis, "serves as an eloquent reminder of the eliminationist focus of the regime's plans" for the Slavic peoples it ruled or hoped to conquer.[34]

---

[29]Robert Gellately, "The Third Reich, the Holocaust, and Visions of Serial Genocide," in Robert Gellately and Ben Kiernan, eds., *The Specter of Genocide: Mass Murder in Historical Perspective* (New York: Cambridge University Press, 2003), 259.

[30]"Der Kommissarbefehl," 6 June 1941 (http://www.ns-archiv.de/krieg/1941/kommissarbefehl .php; accessed April 2, 2014).

[31]Snyder, *Bloodlands*, 163. See also Adam Tooze, *The Wages of Destruction: The Making and Breaking of the Nazi Economy* (New York: Penguin, 2006), 476–485, 538–549.

[32]Document 2718-PS, "File Memorandum on a Conference of Under-Secretaries May 2, 1941," entered into the proceedings of the Trial of the Major War Criminals before the International Military Tribunal, Vol. XXXI, page 84. The forty-two volumes of the official trial records are available through the US Library of Congress's site: http://www.loc.gov/rr/ frd/Military_Law/NT_major-war-criminals.html.

[33]Stephen G. Fritz, *Ostkrieg: Hitler's War of Extermination in the East* (Lexington, KY: University Press of Kentucky, 2011), 61–62.

[34]Aristotle A. Kallis, "Race, 'Value' and the Hierarchy of Human Life: Ideological and Structural Determinants of National Socialist Policy-Making," *Journal of Genocide Research* 7, no. 1 (2005), 16.

Early on June 22, 1941, 3 million German soldiers, backed by thousands of tanks and airplanes, stormed across the USSR's western border in Operation Barbarossa.[35] The German invasion heralded a new stage in the mass murder of Jews, Slavs, and others, and led directly to the systematic, centralized genocide that would later be designated the Holocaust. In the first few weeks after the invasion, German policy evolved from mass murder of Communist and Jewish men to a much broader targeting of all Jews—including women, children, and the elderly. These genocidal actions predated and led to the decision for a continent-wide "Final Solution to the Jewish Problem" later in the year.[36]

In the summer and fall of 1941, after its initial military successes, the Nazi empire found itself ruling over several million more Jews, in addition to those in the General Government.[37] At this point, the Nazi leadership moved quickly toward the decision for a genocidal "final solution" (their term) to the so-called Jewish question. Decisions were now being shaped by a climate of euphoria over the initial successes in the Soviet campaign, tinged with anxiety over what to do with the millions of Jews in German-occupied lands, whose numbers dwarfed those of the Jewish population within Germany. This anxiety would deepen later in the fall as the German advance into Russia slowed and was halted outside Moscow in early November.

After two years, localized mass murder, driven by racial and demographic schemes and the brutality intrinsic to them, evolved into systematic genocide. Once the decision for an exterminatory "final solution" was made and conveyed, by late October 1941, administrators like Hans Frank adapted to it with alacrity.[38] "Gentleman, I must ask you to rid yourselves of all feeling of pity," Frank announced to subordinates in Krakow in December. "We must annihilate the Jews wherever we find them."[39]

In the fall of 1941, the Nazis began constructing death camps, or extermination centers, as they were later known: all located in German-occupied Poland, they were designed specifically for the mass murder of Jews. Chelmno and Belzec, which began operating in December 1941 and March 1942, respectively, were the first. Chelmno was also the first to use gas. Approximately 150,000 people were killed in this fashion—Russians, Poles, and Roma (gypsies) as well as Jews, who

---

[35]The German forces were augmented by roughly 600,000 troops from Finland, Romania, Italy, Croatia, Slovakia, and Hungary.

[36]The most complete and insightful account of Nazi decision-making is Christopher Browning's *The Origins of the Final Solution: The Evolution of Nazi Jewish Policy, September 1939–March 1942* (Lincoln, NE: University of Nebraska Press, 2004).

[37]Roughly 1 million Soviet Jews fled eastward, out of the regions occupied by the Germans, sparing themselves the fate of those in the German zone.

[38]For the timing of the decision and an analysis of the Nazi decision-making process vis-à-vis the Holocaust, see Christopher Browning, *The Origins of the Final Solution: The Evolution of Nazi Jewish Policy, September 1939–March 1942* (Lincoln, NE: University of Nebraska Press, 2004).

[39]Mark Mazower, *Hitler's Empire: How the Nazis Ruled Europe* (New York: Penguin, 2008), 376–377.

The Holocaust: Death Camps, Concentration Camps, and Ghettos
Because of space limitations this map only includes certain major camps and ghettos, and includes some camps administered by Nazi allies, such as the notorious Croatian camp at Jasenovac. The US Holocaust Memorial Museum recently completed a major project to list and describe all the camps and ghettoes, and counted more than 20,000 camps—of widely varying size, duration, and uses—and the Nazis established more than 1,000 ghettos, also of varying types, in its zones in Poland and the USSR alone, in addition to others elsewhere. Nazi allies sometimes created their own Jewish ghettos, for example in Budapest.

were the principal target and the large majority at Chelmno and the other five death camps.

Two years earlier, a program for the murder of Germans deemed to have physical or mental disabilities ("the Unfit")—Operation T-4, which killed tens of thousands

of non-Jewish victims between October 1939 and August 1941—provided a training group for methods of mass killing, as well as for gaining the complicity of many
non-Nazi doctors and other professionals who would later lend their services to
the systematic killing of Jews. After using poison and injections in the first weeks
of the program, the T-4 murderers experimented with carbon monoxide, sometimes pumped into the back of a van, a tactic that would later be employed at
Chelmno. A public outcry within Germany, led by German clergy, induced the
Nazis to announce a halt to T-4 in August 1941—although the killing program had
by then been extended into Poland and the USSR, and was quietly resumed in less
conspicuous, decentralized fashion within Germany itself in 1942. The "euthanasia"
operation, as it was euphemistically termed, claimed the lives of at least 250,000
people, half of them Germans.

Operation T-4 was the outcome of the popular eugenics movement and a deadly
manifestation of an ideology of inequality that was widely accepted in pre-Nazi
Europe and the United States. This ideology devalued not only Jews and other minority peoples or "races." In the spirit of Social Darwinism, which applied Darwin's
theory of a struggle for survival to human interactions, proponents of eugenics
sought to perfect their own "race." These movements attempted to trace the "trans-
mission of social traits, especially undesirable ones, and undertook to classify

Racist eugenics
1934 propaganda slide featuring a mentally ill British black man in an unidentified asylum. The caption
reads: "Mentally ill Negro (British)/16 years of care costs 35,000 Reichsmarks." The quest to perfect
the "Aryan race" by sterilizing or eliminating lesser "races" would lead to the T-4 Operation, which
killed many tens of thousands of Germans who were deemed "unworthy of life" and a drain upon the
economy, as well as a source of racial decline.

individuals, groups, and nations on a scale of human worth," as historian Henry Friedlander wrote in an important book on eugenics and T-4, and then "proposed biological solutions to social problems and lobbied for their implementation."[40] This movement focused its attention on the supposedly feeble-minded ("idiots" or "imbeciles" in the parlance of the time), asserting that low intelligence led to immorality as well as crime.

This was not a fringe movement: It had considerable support among the American populace and educated elites, and legislatures in more than half the states of the country were swayed to enact sterilization laws, beginning with Indiana in 1907. In 1927, the US Supreme Court upheld a Virginia law ordering the compulsory sterilization by state institutions of handicapped patients diagnosed with "hereditary form[s] of insanity or imbecility." Writing for the unanimous majority, Justice Oliver Wendell Holmes declared that American society should "prevent those who are manifestly unfit from continuing their kind . . . three generations of imbeciles are enough."[41] Inspired in part by these American precedents, Hitler's government enacted the "Law for the Prevention of Hereditarily Diseased Offspring" in July 1933. This was the legal basis for the compulsory sterilization over the next twelve years of roughly 400,000 Germans who were deemed (by special medical boards) to possess certain "genetic disorders," a list that included "feeblemindedness" or "mental deficiency," "manic depression," "genetic blindness," and "chronic alcoholism."[42]

AUSCHWITZ, "OPERATION REINHARD," AND THE PEAK OF NAZI GENOCIDE

Reinhard Heydrich and others convened a meeting of senior officials representing various ministries of the government and military on January 20, 1942 in Wannsee, an affluent Berlin suburb. Adolf Eichmann, another key figure in the organization of the genocide, circulated a list of the countries holding the 11 million Jews who were to be killed—a list that included populations that in some cases were very small, such as the 4,000 Jews of Ireland. Albania's population of 200 Jews also did not escape Eichmann's notice.

By the time of the "Wannsee Conference," as it later became known, the genocide was already well underway. The Germans had opened a camp at Auschwitz, outside the town of Oświęcim, Poland, in 1940, and in October 1941 the Germans began a large-scale expansion, adding a second camp, Birkenau, which included more sophisticated gas chambers and crematoria. In the early spring of 1942,

---

[40]Henry Friedlander, *The Origins of Nazi Genocide: From Euthanasia to the Final Solution* (Chapel Hill, NC: University of North Carolina Press, 1997), 4–5.
[41]Justice Holmes, "Opinion" in Buck v. Bell, 274 US 200 (1927), October Term, 207.
[42]"Das Gesetz zur Verhütung erbkranken Nachwuchses," http://germanhistorydocs.ghi-dc .org/sub_document.cfm?document_id=1521&language=german (accessed March 27, 2013). For an English translation of the law: http://germanhistorydocs.ghi-dc.org/sub_document .cfm?document_id=152 (accessed March 27, 2013).

gassing of Jews there was conducted in the two rudimentary huts converted into Bunkers 1 and 2. In the summer of 1942, Himmler approved the construction of four large-scale gas chambers and crematoria, which began to operate in the spring of 1943. As Holocaust expert Christopher Browning noted: "In short, the four large crematoria at Birkenau were the last stage in death camp evolution, and Birkenau does not take its place as the primary killing center (surpassing Treblinka's body count) of Jews until the Hungarian deportations in May-June 1944."[43] The Auschwitz-Birkenau complex eventually included dozens of subcamps and labor camps, and took on the character of a monstrous city unto itself, where more than 1 million Jews—as well as scores of thousands of Poles, Russians, Romanies (gypsies), and others—were murdered. Treblinka consumed the second-largest number of lives, approximately 800,000.

As they began to expand and transform Auschwitz in the autumn of 1941, the Nazis initiated "Operation Reinhard," as it was later dubbed (in honor of Reinhard Heydrich, who was assassinated by Czech resistance operatives in mid-1942). The program's task was to murder the Jews who were trapped in the General Government. Operation Reinhard entailed the construction of four additional death camps—Belzec, Majdanek, Sobibor, and Treblinka. Two million Jews perished in "Operation Reinhard," most of them during the most intensive period of the Holocaust: Between early 1942 and early 1943, roughly half the Nazis' Jewish victims were murdered.

THE NAZIS' COLLABORATORS AND IDEOLOGICAL SOUL MATES

Germany was not obliged to heavily occupy or tightly control every corner of its empire. In some places, such as Slovakia and Croatia, the Nazis installed regimes that would do their bidding; in others—such as the Marshall Pétain's Vichy France government, which controlled most of southern part of the country— collaborationist governments took power. The Croatian dictatorship of the fascist Ustaša party killed 300,000 to 400,000 Serbs, and most of Croatia's 45,000 Jews.[44] These atrocities provoked no protest from the Vatican, which was aware of the atrocities in the heavily Catholic country; some Franciscan friars were directly involved in murders at the Ustaša's infamous Jasenovac death camp. Romania, led by the dictator Ion Antonescu and allied with Germany, rounded up, ghettoized, and murdered 300,000 Jews in Transnistria, a region Romania had seized from a neighboring Soviet republic. And in many other ways, the Holocaust was not a purely German crime; for example, special forces from Ukraine, Latvia, and Lithuania, as well as regular army troops from Hungary and Romania took part in the invasion

---

[43]Christopher Browning, email to author, March 10, 2014.
[44]Friedländer, *Origins*, 229.

Antisemitism in Vichy France

Antisemitism was hardly the monopoly of Germany. This exhibition, "The Jew and France," was staged in Paris in 1941 during the reign of Marshall Pétain's collaborationist regime. Like Nazi-allied or –puppet regimes in Croatia, Slovakia, Romania, Hungary, and elsewhere, the Vichy government fully embraced antisemitism and other values in common with Nazism. The Holocaust was not a purely German crime.

of the USSR and the attendant atrocities, in which millions of non-Jewish as well as Jewish civilians were murdered.[45]

The Nazis and their accomplices and political allies killed somewhere near the well-known figure of 6 million Jewish victims through several means. Five hundred thousand Polish Jews died largely from brutal conditions in ghettos and labor camps during the first two years of German occupation.[46] Mass shootings by the *Einsatzgruppen*, soldiers of the Wehrmacht and Waffen-SS, Order Police and other military police squads, and collaborator units of assorted nationalities killed roughly 1.3 million Jews, close to half that number before the opening of the first death camp, Chelmno, where 200,000 Jews were murdered.[47] In other death camps, the numbers of Jews killed were approximately 800,000 in Treblinka; 500,000 in Belzec; 260,000 in Sobibor; and 130,000 in Majdanek.[48] Death marches and train transportation conditions added at least a quarter million to the toll.

Auschwitz-Birkenau, in the far south of present-day Poland, was the final destination of roughly 1.1 million Jews. The Holocaust is closely associated, in the Western imagination and in cultural representations, with Auschwitz and its highly systematic, brutally efficient, industrialized methods of mass extermination. But the iconic images—transmitted through film, literature, and other cultural representations since the 1970s—of the arrival of the trains, the selection process, and the gas chambers and crematoria create misperceptions that affect scholarship as well as popular knowledge.

The overemphasis on the "industrial" nature of the killing also contributes to erroneous assertions of the utter uniqueness of the Holocaust. The 1994 Rwandan genocide was carried out by grisly and seemingly premodern means—primarily with machetes—but, as we will see in Chapter 4, it unfolded with an efficiency and organization that rivaled that of the Nazis. And within the Nazi camps, disorder often reigned, and hundreds of thousands died of disease as well as arbitrary shootings or beatings by sadistic guards and commandants. "The camp yard was littered with corpses," recalled one survivor of Treblinka.[49]

Finally, the geography of the Holocaust is important: The huge majority of Jewish victims were not German or Western European Jews, and the principal killing fields and camps were to the east and south of Germany. About 3 million Polish Jews—one-half of the total number of Jewish victims—were killed, about an equal number by shootings and by gassing in camps.[50]

---

[45]Crowe, *Holocaust*, 211.

[46]Doris Bergen, *War & Genocide: A Concise History of the Holocaust* (New York: Rowman & Littlefield, 2009), 111.

[47]Bloxham, *Final Solution*, 157; Adam Jones, *Genocide: A Comprehensive Introduction* (New York: Routledge, 2010), 153.

[48]Jones, *Genocide*, 153.

[49]Snyder, *Bloodlands*, 267.

[50]Ibid., 275. Also see the important book by Patrick Desbois that has exerted a huge influence on Holocaust Studies; its title is often invoked as a reminder of the mass shootings

NON-JEWISH VICTIMS

The Nazis' racial fanaticism and grandiose schemes to reorder Europe claimed other victims in addition to the Jews. First among them were ethnic Slavs—Russians and other Soviet peoples, as well as Poles—who had the misfortune not only to be viewed as *Untermenschen* (subhumans), to use the Nazis' ugly terminology, but also to inhabit territory that was coveted by the German leadership. One to 2 million non-Jewish Poles—in addition to Poland's 3 million Jewish victims—were killed by German forces. Russians and other Soviet nationalities fared even worse. The Soviet Union lost more than 25 million citizens in the war. About one-third of this total died in combat, either in the Red Army or in partisan groups, but the majority were civilians. Many millions of non-Jewish Ukrainians, Belarusians, and other Soviet civilians were shot by German forces or starved or froze to death; as many as 1 million Russians perished during the thirty-month-long siege of Leningrad alone.

Had Nazi Germany somehow been defeated in early 1942, the murder of 3.3 million Soviet POWs would have been known to posterity as Hitler's gravest crime. Roughly 1 million of the hapless POWs were shot or gassed, while the others were left to their grim fate in giant, open-air camps, where they succumbed to starvation, disease, beatings, arbitrary executions, or simply froze to death.[51] During the first four months of Barbarossa, most of the captured soldiers were transported in open freight cars. Even after closed cars were deployed in late November, a German document the following month reported that "between 25 to 70 percent of prisoners" died en route, "not least because no one troubled to give them any food," Richard Evans pointedly notes.[52] Those who survived the transport were herded into "camps," for lack of a better word. Even such a monstrous creation as Auschwitz-Birkenau, though, provided greater opportunities for survival. Antony Beevor describes the "camps" as "barbed-wire encirclements under open skies."[53]

While "camp" is misleading, "prisoners of war" is also imprecise. Captured Soviets immediately lost any status or protections afforded POWs under international law by even the most inhumane regimes; in the worst camps, they were viewed and treated in a manner closer to that of the despised, dehumanized Jews, and subjected to appalling torments. "The German guards used the inmates as target practice and set their dogs on them, placing bets on which dog would inflict the worst injuries."[54] A Hungarian officer who visited one camp—or enclosure—reported seeing "tens of thousands of Russian prisoners. Many were on the point

---

that claimed so many millions of victims: Dubois, *The Holocaust by Bullets: A Priest's Journey to Uncover the Truth Behind the Murder of 1.5 Million Jews* (New York: Palgrave Macmillan, 2009).
[51]Michael Mann, *The Dark Side of Democracy: Explaining Ethnic Cleansing* (New York: Cambridge University Press, 2005), 186.
[52]Richard Evans, *The Third Reich at War* (New York: Penguin, 2010), 183.
[53]Beevor, *Second World War*, 209.
[54]Evans, *Third Reich at War*, 183–184.

Soviet POW
What comes to mind when you look at this image? In the 1950s and 1960s, most people in the U.S. and Europe would have thought in generic terms that this was "a victim of Nazi crimes." In fact, this is one of many unfortunate Soviet POWs, who endured their own genocide (more than three million killed) but whose tragedy remains relatively unknown and under-researched.

of expiring. Few could stand on their feet. Their faces were dried up and their eyes sunk deep into their sockets. Hundreds were dying every day."[55] German guards amused themselves by "throwing a dead dog into the prisoners' compound." Russians scrabbled to "fall on the animal and tear it to pieces with their bare hands."[56] Many hundreds of thousands were sent to camps, including Auschwitz-Birkenau, where they—along with Polish POWs—were subjected in September 1941 to the first experiments upon humans in the use of Zyklon B.

In contrast to a mortality rate of 4 percent for British and American POWs held by the Germans, nearly 60 percent of Soviet POWs died in Nazi captivity.[57] Approximately 2 million had perished before the Wannsee Conference was held to determine the "final solution" of the "Jewish question" convened in January 1942,[58] and most of the remaining victims perished before summer of that year. Another 2 million POWs survived the war. Most of them were then arrested upon return to their homeland on suspicion of collaboration with their captors and were sentenced to long terms in the Gulag, where many tens of thousands perished before Stalin's death. Cold War politics conspired to keep this sad tale hidden. It was not in the Soviet Union's interest to draw attention to such a deplorable

[55]Quoted in Alexander Werth, *Russia At War, 1941–1945* (London: Barrie & Rockliff, 1964), 635–636.
[56]Catherine Merridale, *Ivan's War: Life and Death in the Red Army, 1939–1945* (New York: Picador, 2007), 290.
[57]Mann, *Dark Side of Democracy*, 186.
[58]The minutes of the meeting are available on the website of the German Historical Institute. "Das Protokoll der Wannseekonferenz," http://www.germanhistorydocs.ghi-dc.org/sub_document.cfm?document_id=1532 (accessed June 1, 2014); also available in English translation.

example of its own lack of preparedness and weakness in 1941, nor was it a Western priority to remember or honor the terrible suffering and sacrifice of the Soviet peoples. It is worth noting that for each American victim of Pearl Harbor, roughly fourteen hundred Soviet POWs were starved or murdered. Additionally, many tens of thousands of forced laborers died in German workplaces, the majority of them from Slavic lands. More than 300,000 Polish and Russian forced or slave laborers died within Germany, where one-fifth of the total workforce was composed of foreign forced laborers by the fall of 1944.[59]

Roma and Sinti people, popularly known as "Gypsies," also suffered grievously at the hands of the Nazis. Ultimately, somewhere between 200,000 and 1 million were killed in the *Porrajmos* (Devouring), as it is known today by Roma.[60] The Nazis also systematically persecuted homosexuals, in particular gay German men, whom they regarded as "degenerates" who had removed themselves from procreation, and therefore from the reproduction of the "master race." Homosexuals also served as reminders of the permissive society of the Weimar years, which the Nazis viewed with horror, much as far-rightists in other times and places have yearned for a bygone if mythical era dominated by repressive, illiberal values. Heinrich Himmler played a leading role in advocating and formulating policies to persecute gay men. It is worth noting that Himmler was not at all interested in killing non-German gays, whose existence would only curtail the reproduction rates of non-Germans, and therefore these policies were not extended into German-occupied lands. Another key difference with Nazi policy toward Jews, Slavs, and Roma and Sinti, whose "crime" in the Nazi perspective was biologically determined: Himmler believed that gays had learned, and could therefore unlearn, their homosexuality—through the threat, for instance, of the concentration camp. Homosexual men whose sexuality was deemed irremediable often faced castration or death.

As in its attacks on Roma and other groups, the Nazis exploited deep societal prejudices that long predated their reign. The dictatorship ultimately convicted some 50,000 men accused of homosexuality, of whom at least 5,000 died in concentration camps, where they were often ostracized and brutalized by their fellow inmates. If these numbers are small in comparison to those of other victims, one statistic is telling: perhaps 60 percent of gay men who were sent to camps were eventually killed, a higher mortality rate than experienced by political prisoners or other groups singled out for nonracial reasons.[61] And the end of the war brought no immediate recognition: "After liberation of the camps in 1945," writes Doris Bergen,

[59]Tooze, *Wages*, 523, 517.
[60]Estimates for Roma victims vary; pre–World War II census figures are less reliable (or even existent) than for most other European populations. Further, "Roma did not and do not today generally operate as a single, monolithic entity," genocide specialist Mark Levene averred recently, "so much as a mosaic or network of diverse, dispersed, if ethnically and culturally related, peoples." Levene, *The Crisis of Genocide*, Vol. 2: *Annihilation: The European Rimlands, 1939–1953* (Oxford: Oxford University Press, 2014), 136.
[61]The mortality rate in the camps for political prisoners as well as for Jehovah's Witnesses was approximately 40 percent.

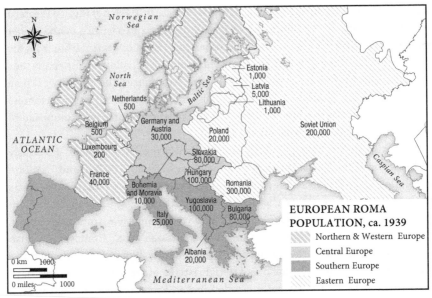

European Roma Population. ca. 1939

"occupation authorities arrested again some gay men, reconvicted them, and sent them back to prison," and homosexual activity was not decriminalized by West Germany for another quarter century.[62] Thus, we can estimate that German Nazism was responsible for the deaths of at least 13 million people, and probably closer to 15 or 16 million.[63] And one can say that Nazism was responsible for the roughly 50 million deaths in the European theater of World War II, where the war was instigated by German policy and actions (in contrast to World War I, which resulted from the policies and actions of multiple parties).[64]

It is entirely appropriate that the Jews retain their prominence in our understanding of Nazi genocide—not because of a misguided competition for suffering, but because of their place in Nazi philosophy and policy. In the Nazi view, it was only the Jews who represented a dire, existential threat that required the most radical measures to destroy. The Nazis viewed some of the other groups as nuisances, social undesirables, or "subhumans" fit only for slavery or removal. But the suffering of Poles, Russians, gypsies, disabled persons, and others was no less

---

[62]Bergen, *War & Genocide*, 203.

[63]In the United States, the figure of 11 million has entered popular consciousness since the late 1970s. This figure arose from the laudable desire to include non-Jews in commemorations of Nazi victims. But it is not based on a clear or sound methodology and is far too low. See Peter Novick, *The Holocaust in American Life* (New York: Houghton Mifflin, 1999), Chapter 10.

[64]The Japanese Empire and its military were responsible for the deaths of at least 10 million people in China, where, after several years of smaller-scale interventions, Japan invaded in force and waged war from 1937 to 1945.

wrenching or deplorable. Compounding their pain, the persistence of anti-gypsy and anti-gay prejudice, among other factors, has to this day prevented those victims from receiving adequate recognition or compensation.

JEWISH RESISTANCE

Jews did not always "go like sheep to the slaughter," to invoke a phrase that was often heard in the first years after the war. Like Hitler's other targets, Jews devised varied strategies for resistance and survival. In the most spectacular and visible examples, Jewish people—usually young, and including both men and women—fought the Nazis with arms in hand. Much more often, they found less visible or spectacular ways to resist, organizing hundreds of clandestine religious schools (*yeshivot*) in Poland; arranging secret libraries and archives throughout the ghetto system; raising money to support prisoners' families; and producing and distributing prohibited literature. All these activities deprived their tormentors of one of their goals: to dehumanize the Jews and destroy their culture and heritage. While historians have gained a deeper and more sophisticated understanding of Jewish resistance in recent years, though, it is important to not exaggerate the phenomenon, which could convey an implicit, unjust condemnation of those who did *not* resist.

The Warsaw Ghetto Uprising of April–May 1943 was the most direct and "successful" effort of this sort. An underground resistance movement had taken form in 1942. When the Germans began a major deportation action on January 18, 1943, the larger of the two resistance groups—the Jewish Combat Organization (ZOB in its Polish initials), led by Mordecai Anielewicz—sprang into action, firing on the Germans. By the time the Nazis decided to liquidate the ghetto and deport its remaining residents to Treblinka—April 19, 1943, the eve of Passover and the day before Hitler's birthday—the ZOB and the other armed resistance group, the Jewish Military Union (ZZW), had about 750 fighters and had acquired revolvers and a few rounds of ammunition for each fighter, as well as about 10 rifles and two machine guns. The ghetto fighters resorted to such inventive tactics as smuggling arms in carts transporting corpses to the cemeteries. The Germans' April 19 deportation *Aktion* was met with a well-prepared military response. Open warfare persisted until April 28, and only on May 16 could the German commanding general, Jürgen Stroop, proclaim success.[65] It is not possible to gain an accurate estimate of German casualties; probably two or three dozen, at a minimum, were killed. Most ZOB and ZZW fighters died, and the overwhelming majority of the ghetto's remaining population was either killed or deported to Treblinka or other camps.

---

[65]At the war's conclusion, General Stroop was arrested by American forces. He was eventually handed over to Poland, where the unrepentant Stroop was tried for war crimes in 1951, convicted, and executed the following year.

Thousands of partisans fought in exclusively Jewish groups such as the celebrated "Bielski Brothers." Led by Asael, Tuvia, and Zus Bielski, the Bielski Brothers group "harried Nazis and saved Jews," as the headline for Zus's 1995 obituary in *The New York Times* stated.[66] Led principally by the charismatic Tuvia, these Belorussian Jewish peasants organized a partisan army that was integrated into a large compound in the Naliboki Forest. The Bielskis sent emissaries and scouts to find Jews and bring them to their compound, and they ultimately saved more than 1,000 people, while judiciously conducting sabotage actions and direct military assaults on the occupiers. Jews also served in disproportionately large numbers in the partisan armies of occupied Europe, where they were a minority and were often not free of anti-Semitism, though fighting a common enemy. Assi Bielski, daughter of one of the leaders of the Bielski Brothers partisan and rescue operation, told me a horrifying story: a Jewish couple fled the Bielski camp and went to a nearby Soviet camp, where they thought their chances of survival were greater; the man was then held captive while the woman was raped by multiple Soviet partisans.[67]

Despite anti-Jewish hostility among many other anti-Nazi fighters, an estimated 20,000 to 30,000 Jews fought in Soviet-led partisan groups,[68] and perhaps one-sixth of the fighters of the French *Maquis* guerrilla fighters were Jewish, although Jews constituted less than 1 percent of the country's population.[69] Even in the most debilitating circumstances imaginable—in the death camps—there were several notable examples of organized resistance. In 1943, Jewish prisoners organized armed revolts in Sobibor and Treblinka; the following year, the underground organization in Auschwitz blew up a crematorium. All told, Jewish prisoners staged armed revolts in five concentration camps and eighteen forced-labor camps, according to Holocaust survivor and scholar Nechama Tec.[70] In most camps, prisoners undertook other, less visible forms of resistance, holding secret political or religious meetings, swapping information, assisting one another, and organizing escapes.

In other ways as well, Hitler's Jewish victims found ways and means to maintain their dignity and humanity in the face of the Nazi assault. "Resistance" entailed

---

[66]Robert Thomas, "Alexander Z. Bielski, a Guerrilla Fighter Who Harried Nazis and Saved Jews, Is Dead," *The New York Times*, August 23, 1995.

[67]Interview by author of Assi Bielski, Charlotte, NC, March 22, 2012. They escaped and returned to the Bielski camp. Tuvia took pity upon hearing their story and did not punish them for desertion; the woman was traumatized and emotionally shattered by this experience for the remainder of her life, and only told this story to Assi and one or two others on her deathbed, sixty years later. Nechama Tec and Peter Duffy have each written books on the Bielski Brothers; the 2008 film *Defiance*, starring Daniel Craig as Tuvia, is surprisingly good. Some Bielski family members served as consultants and have said that "the main fault was that Tuvia was more handsome than Craig." From author's conversations with Assi Bielski and Mickey Bielski.

[68]Rueben Ainsztein, *Jewish Resistance in Nazi-Occupied Eastern Europe* (New York: Barnes & Noble, 1974), 394–395.

[69]Nechama Tec, *Jewish Resistance: Facts, Omissions, and Distortions* (Washington, DC: Miles Lerman Center for the Study of Jewish Resistance of the US Holocaust Memorial Museum, 2001), 2.

[70]Ibid., 1.

Yugoslav partisan

Certificate confirming that Donna Papo, a young Yugoslav, was a member of the partisan army that fought and ultimately defeated the German occupation. Papo had been a member of a left-wing Jewish youth group, and with many of her Jewish friends she joined the partisans. At one point she hid with a Muslim family in Sarajevo for several months, and then returned to the partisan war in the forests; after the war, she served as an officer in the Yugoslav army. An extraordinary story, but its elements are not unique.

much more than armed struggle, and any discussion of Jewish responses should also consider such concepts (which were often not clearly distinct from one another) as defiance, nonconformity, resilience, and various survival mechanisms, including simply a refusal to submit—that is, to attempt to continue civilized life under uncivilized conditions.

BYSTANDERS AND RESCUERS

Primo Levi, an Italian chemist who survived Auschwitz and later wrote with singular insight about the Holocaust's philosophical dimensions, concluded that "the true crime, the collective, general crime of almost all Germans of the time, was that of lacking the courage to speak."[71] Stories about the mass murders began to circulate within Germany by 1941 or 1942, often related by soldiers who were on leave from the front; but most Germans knew just enough to decide that "They wanted *not* to know," Levi wrote.[72] In this respect, the average German citizens

---

[71]Primo Levi, *The Drowned and the Saved* (New York: Vintage, 1989), 182.
[72]Ibid., 181.

conducted themselves much as citizens of other nations while their governments are committing major crimes against humanity.

But the Holocaust was not a purely German crime, as demonstrated earlier in this chapter. It was produced by prejudices and philosophies that flourished throughout the West; it found powerful precedents in the practices of Western imperialist powers; and it was aided and abetted by citizens of all countries occupied by Germany or governed by its allies. And the Holocaust was assisted not only by corrupt, anti-Semitic, or frightened individuals: None of the most powerful Western nation-states and institutions emerged morally unscathed. To the contrary, leaders of the United States and Britain; religious leaders such as Pope Pius XII; and corporate interests of various nations all, to varying degrees, remained silent, if they did not actively applaud or at least profit from the misery of European Jewry.

Yet it is also true that each nation drawn into the war and the Holocaust produced courageous, selfless people who tried to save Jews or otherwise resisted the Nazis. Danish citizens, in a remarkable display of humanitarianism and unity, smuggled nearly the entire Danish-Jewish population (about 8,000 people) to safety in Sweden in October 1943. The Polish organization Żegota (the Polish Council to Aid Jews) saved several thousand Jews, sometimes conducting bold missions, for example, to smuggle Jewish children out of the Warsaw Ghetto. Swedish businessman and diplomat Raoul Wallenberg is justly celebrated for his tireless, highly creative campaign to save Hungarian Jews; by setting up "safe houses," bribing German and Hungarian officials, and various other tactics, he is credited with saving as many as 100,000 Jews from deportation to Auschwitz. Yet no one could rescue Wallenberg: For mysterious reasons, he was arrested by the Red Army after it occupied Hungary at the end of the war, and perished in a Soviet-run prison.

Following the expulsion of Jews from Spain in 1492, there had been a sizeable Jewish presence in the mostly Muslim lands of North Africa for four and a half centuries. During World War II, the French collaborationist regime ruled Morocco and Algeria, and zealously persecuted those regions' Jews. The Germans occupied Tunisia, introducing many of the features of their rule in Europe, such as property confiscations, extortion, deportations, and forced labor. As elsewhere, Hitler's victims did not passively accept their fate. Jews constituted a large majority of Algiers's underground resistance, which, despite the failure of the United States to deliver promised aid, conducted an uprising on November 7–8, 1942, that contributed to the Allies' successful invasion of the city the next day.[73] José Aboulker, the Jewish leader of the city's underground resistance, later recalled the solidarity expressed by Algerian Muslims: "When Jewish goods were put up for public auction, an instruction went around the mosques: 'Our brothers are suffering misfortune. Do not take their goods.'"[74] There are many other examples of Muslims courageously defying Nazism and its agents and rescuing Jews. The leaders of the

[73]Robert Satloff, *Among the Righteous: Lost Stories from the Holocaust's Long Reach into Arab Lands* (New York: PublicAffairs, 2006), 37–40.
[74]Ibid., 108.

Great Mosque of Paris, for example, saved Jews by giving them papers indicating they were Muslim.

Other examples are more surprising: Italian military authorities sheltered several thousand Jews who had escaped German-controlled territories; Spanish diplomats, also serving a government ruled by far-right and fascist politicians, saved Jews in Greece and Hungary by issuing false passes, setting up safe houses, and other means.[75]

THE END OF THE THIRD REICH

The Nazi regime disintegrated in a final orgy of killing and destruction. As the Red Army closed in on Berlin, the Nazis organized exhausting death marches for the luckless inmates of Auschwitz and other camps. Hoping to hide the evidence of their massive crimes, and in some cases exploit prisoners for slave labor in newly built camps, German officials drove many hundreds of thousands of prisoners toward the west, often into camps within Germany such as Buchenwald. An additional 250,000–375,000 people died of starvation, exhaustion, or arbitrary shootings in this final stage of the Holocaust, which began in mid-1944 and accelerated in January 1945 as the Red Army advanced from the east.

The German people also suffered the consequences of a disastrous war waged by a regime that, ultimately, was indifferent to the miseries wreaked upon its own land. "If the German people are not prepared to stand up for their own preservation, fine. Let them perish" blithely remarked the Führer, who on March 19, 1945, pronounced the Nero Order, as it was later labeled, calling for the destruction of his own country's infrastructure lest it fall into Allied hands.[76] (The order was not implemented.) Confused, emotionally drained, and fearful of Soviet reprisals—which would indeed be fearsome—nearly 4,000 people committed suicide in Berlin alone in April 1945.[77] Meanwhile, more than 200,000 Germans and Russians died in the futile, desperate "Battle of Berlin," as the once-mighty Reich was reduced to pressing old men and young boys into service to defend its capital.[78] Hundreds of thousands of German civilians were killed by bombings of large cities such as Dresden and Hamburg, and in a terrible coda to the war, more than ten million ethnic Germans were driven out of countries that had suffered under German occupation; at least 500,000 of these civilians were killed. Only in recent years has it become easier in Germany and elsewhere to acknowledge the extent and gravity of these injustices without appearing insensitive to those who suffered under Nazi occupation.[79]

---

[75]Crowe, *Holocaust*, 344–345.
[76]Snyder, *Bloodlands*, 319.
[77]Richard Evans, *The Third Reich at War* (New York: Penguin, 2009), 732.
[78]See Ian Kershaw, *The End: The Defiance and Destruction of Hitler's Germany, 1944–1945* (New York: Penguin, 2012).
[79]See R.M. Douglas, *Orderly and Humane: The Expulsion of Germans after the Second World War* (New Haven, CT: Yale University Press, 2013).

Hitler's regime collapsed ignominiously in March and April 1945—its final days marked by recriminations and backstabbing within the leadership and vast misery among the German populace. Göring, Himmler, Goebbels, and other Nazi chiefs such as Martin Bormann—men who had once ruled much of Europe—descended into petty infighting, scrabbling for power where little still existed. Hans Frank and his staff, who led an opulent and decadent existence in a Polish castle, abandoned their dwellings in such haste that, intoxicated as they fled, they drove into a gate, leaving behind obscene quantities of liquor, spoiled meat and sausages, as well as silver, paintings, and other spoils of their rule.[80] Alfred Rosenberg, a veteran of the early days of the Nazi movement, turned up in Berlin completely drunk two days after Hitler's death, was turned away by the temporary head of state, tripped over himself, and ended up in a hospital. (He was executed in October 1946 after conviction at Nuremberg for major war crimes.)

As for the Führer—once master of two-thirds of Europe, if one includes collaborationist and puppet states—he spent his last ten days at the center of a surreal drama in a sprawling bunker under the streets of Berlin. The day after marrying his mistress, Eva Braun, in a bizarre and depressing ceremony, he and his new wife committed suicide. Hitler's long-time, loyal accomplice and henchman Goebbels and his wife followed suit the next day, but only after poisoning their six children.

Several of the central leaders of the Nazi state would die either by their own hand or by legal execution after the first Nuremberg war-crimes trial (1945–1946), presided over by a tribunal organized by the Allied victors. The "Trial of the Major War Criminals" concluded with the executions of ten state or military officials, in addition to Göring, who was sentenced to death but committed suicide in prison, and Martin Bormann, a close aide to Hitler who was sentenced to death in absentia. (Three defendants were acquitted.) The Nuremberg tribunal conducted subsequent trials, as did other European or German courts; in 1947, for example, Poland tried forty-one Auschwitz officials and functionaries, twenty-three of whom were executed. A "Second Auschwitz Trial," as it is known in Germany, began in Frankfurt in 1963, and featured twenty-two defendants, six of whom received life sentences. These numbers are very small, when one considers that some 7,000 or more SS members worked at the camp. Ultimately, the large majority of the chief culprits and architects of the Holocaust, and their thousands of accomplices—including camp commanders, Wehrmacht generals, corporate and other civilian officials who were directly responsible for mass murder—escaped justice, often returning to prestigious and lucrative positions in postwar West Germany (and a few in Communist-ruled East Germany, despite its official ideology of "antifascism"). Many others, such as the infamous Klaus Barbie, Gestapo torturer stationed in France whose cruelty earned himself the appellation "Butcher of Lyon," escaped

---

[80]Mazower, *Hitler's Empire*, 529.

Europe in ruins
Dead German soldier in front of Berlin's Brandenburg Gate, May 1945. For the second time in the first half of the century, Europe had destroyed itself. The First World War was an unprecedented calamity, but the Second World War's devastation was much worse, and much broader: it was truly a "world" war. After inflicting the horrors of colonialism, modern imperialism, and slavery upon much of the world, Western Civilization, so to speak, had turned upon itself.

justice with the assistance of the Vatican and other powerful institutions (including the US secret service, which valued these Nazis' skills in combatting "Communism" once the Cold War set in).[81]

CONCLUSIONS

The Allied victory prevented Hitler from achieving his goal of a "*Judenfrei*" (Jew-free) Europe, but the Nazis had killed two-thirds of the continent's Jewish people, largely eradicating centuries of tradition and culture that had contributed mightily to European culture, science, and literature—above all, perhaps, in Germany. A friend

---

[81]See Gerald Steinacher, *Nazis on the Run: How Hitler's Henchmen Fled Justice* (Oxford: Oxford University Press, 2011).

of mine, Rabbi Bruce Diamond, has said, "For all we know, the cure for AIDS may have gone up through the chimneys of Auschwitz."

For those fortunate few who survived the camps, the term "liberation" was not really apt; most camps were abandoned before the Allied forces arrived, and many of the emaciated, starved, frozen survivors died within a few days or weeks. "Behind the barbed wire and the electric fence, the skeletons sat in the sun and searched themselves for lice," reported the American journalist Martha Gellhorn from Dachau. "They have no age and no faces; they all look alike and like nothing you will ever see if you are lucky."[82]

In the war's aftermath, the traumatized survivors searched—usually in vain— for surviving family members. A quarter of a million survivors were housed in Allied- or UN-administered "Displaced Persons" (DP) camps in Germany, Austria, and Italy, where many languished for as long as six or seven years. Other survivors emigrated to the United States or Palestine, where the state of Israel was established in 1948. Several thousand actually returned to Germany, and in recent years, after the Berlin Wall was brought down and the country was reunited, the German-Jewish population has increased nearly five-fold, to roughly 125,000. Today's Jewish community, though, which is composed largely of Russians who have immigrated to Germany since 1991, is cut off from the vibrant pre-1933 traditions of German Jewry, which can never be rebuilt or resurrected. Only a few thousand Jews—many of whom decline to identify themselves as such, because of persisting anti-Semitism—reside today in Poland, home to the world's largest Jewish population before World War II.[83]

As revelations of Nazi atrocities surfaced, the well-meaning injunction "never again" was often repeated, stressing a newfound international commitment to detect and put an end to such wholesale, mass atrocities. George Fredrickson, a historian of race and racism, noted with bitter irony, "Hitler . . . gave racism a bad name. The moral revulsion of people throughout the world against what the Nazis did, reinforced by scientific studies undermining racist genetics (or eugenics), served to discredit the scientific racism that had been respectable and influential in the United States and Europe before the Second World War."[84] But if the Holocaust was the defining genocide of the twentieth century, it was far from the final one. In the late 1970s, as the Holocaust was becoming widely known, discussed, and analyzed, a regime in Southeast Asia claiming the mantle of Communism—ostensibly the political opposite of Nazism—killed nearly a quarter of its own population.

---

[82]From Martha Gellhorn, *The Face of War* (New York: Simon & Schuster, 1959), quoted in Jens Meierhenrich, *Genocide: A Reader* (New York: Oxford University Press, 2014), 254.
[83]Interview by author of Tadeusz Jakubowicz, president of the Jewish Community Center of Krakow, March 1, 2014, at the organization's headquarters.
[84]George Frederickson, "The Historical Origins and Development of Race." Fredrickson wrote this brief article for a website that accompanied the 2003 PBS series, "Race: The History of an Illusion." http://www.pbs.org/race/000_About/002_04-background-02-01.htm (accessed June 23, 2014).

PRIMARY SOURCES
AND STUDY QUESTIONS

Source 2.1: Excerpts from the 1920 program of the National Socialist German Workers Party (NSDAP)

At a rally attended by 2,000 people in Munich on February 24, 1920, Adolf Hitler presented "The Program of the NSDAP," also known as the "25-Point Program." The program was written by Hitler and two or three others, including Dietrich Eckart and Gottfried Feder, who had formed the German Workers Party (DAP) before Hitler joined.

1. We demand the uniting of all Germans within one Greater Germany, on the basis of the right to self-determination of nations.
2. We demand equal rights for the German people (*Volk*) with respect to other nations, and the annulment of the peace treaty of Versailles and St. Germain.
3. We demand land and soil (Colonies) to feed our People and settle our excess population.
4. Only Nationals (*Volksgenossen*) can be Citizens of the State. Only persons of German blood can be Nationals, regardless of religious affiliation. No Jew can therefore be a German National.
5. Any person who is not a Citizen will be able to live in Germany only as a guest and must be subject to legislation for Aliens.
6. Only a Citizen is entitled to decide the leadership and laws of the State. We therefore demand that only Citizens may hold public office, regardless of whether it is a national, state or local office.
7. We demand that the State make it its duty to provide opportunities of employment first of all for its own Citizens. If it is not possible to maintain the entire population of the State, then foreign nationals (non-Citizens) are to be expelled from the Reich.
8. Any further immigration of non-Germans is to be prevented. We demand that all non-Germans who entered Germany after August 2, 1914, be forced to leave the Reich without delay.
9. All German Citizens must have equal rights and duties.

SOURCE: Translated by the author from the German-language original, available at Wikisource: http://en.wikisource.org/wiki/Program_of_the_NSDAP (accessed June 23, 2015). English translations available at the Jewish Virtual Library, Wikisource, and elsewhere.

. . . We therefore demand:

11. The abolition of all income obtained without labor or effort.
13. We demand the nationalization of all enterprises (already) converted into corporations (trusts).
14. We demand profit-sharing in large enterprises.
16. We demand the creation and maintenance of a sound middle class; the immediate communalization of the large department stores, which are to be leased at low rates to small tradesmen. . . .
18. We demand ruthless battle against those who harm the common good by their activities. Persons committing base crimes against the People, usurers, profiteers, etc., are to be punished by death without regard to religion or race.
23. We demand laws to fight against *deliberate* political lies and their dissemination by the press. In order to make it possible to create a German press, we demand:
    . . . All editors and editorial employees of newspapers appearing in the German language must be German by race . . .
    Newspapers which violate the public interest are to be banned. We demand laws against trends in art and literature which have a destructive effect on our national life, and the suppression of performances that offend against the above requirements.
24. We demand freedom for all religious denominations, provided that they do not endanger the existence of the State or offend the concepts of decency and morality of the Germanic race.
    The Party leadership promises to take an uncompromising stand, at the cost of their own lives if need be, on the enforcement of the above points.

Questions

1. How many of these points are aimed at Germany's Jewish population? How is the program's anti-Semitism phrased?
2. How do the Nazis define "citizenship"? What are the implications of this definition?
3. After taking power, the Nazis rapidly destroyed Germany's once-powerful trade unions and carried out many other policies that were hostile to working-class people. Yet this program contains language that seems to sympathize with the plight of poor or middle-income people. Which points express this populism? What do the Nazis claim they will do to help working- and middle-class people?
4. What segments of the population is this program calculated to attract?

Source 2.2: Proclamation by Jewish "United Partisans Organization" of Vilna, Lithuania, September 1, 1943

Vilna, Lithuania, became the site of a large Jewish ghetto after the Germans occupied the city in June 1941. Zionists, Communists, and others organized a resistance group, the "United Partisans Organization" (FPO in its Lithuanian initials). In September 1943 the Nazis began a mass deportation "Action," and the FPO responded by calling on the Jews of Vilna to refuse to report for deportation and to join the partisans in an armed struggle in the nearby forests. Some of the language in this statement was used in earlier appeals from the FPO.

Jews, Prepare for Armed Resistance!

The German and Lithuanian hangmen have reached the gates of the ghetto. They will murder us all. They will take us, group by group, through the gates.

That is how they took them in their hundreds on the Day of Atonement.

That is how they took them at the time of the White, the Yellow and the Pink papers.[85]

That is how they took our brothers, sisters, fathers, mothers, our children.

That is how they took tens of thousands away to their death.

But we will not go!

We will not let them take us like animals to slaughter.

Jews, prepare for armed resistance!

Do not believe the false assurances of the murderers, do not believe the words of the traitors. Whoever is taken through the gate of the ghetto has only one road ahead—Ponary. *And Ponary is death.*[86]

Jews, we have nothing to lose.

Death is certain. Who can still believe that he will survive when the murderers kill systematically? The hand of the hangman will reach out to each of us. Neither hiding nor cowardice will save lives.

Only armed resistance can save our lives and honor.

Brothers, it is better to fall in battle in the ghetto than to be led like sheep to Ponary.

SOURCE: Courtesy of Yad Vashem's Moreshat Archives. English translation available at the Jewish Virtual Library.

[85]German authorities had issued documents in those colors.

[86]A forest about 8 miles from Vilna, where the Nazis had massacred tens of thousands of Lithuanian Jews in the previous two years.

Know that in the ghetto there is an organized Jewish force which will rise up with arms in its hands.

Rise up for the armed resistance!

Don't hide in the *malines*.[87] You will fall there like mice in the hands of the murderers.

Jewish masses

Out into the streets!

Those who have no arms get hold of an axe.
Those who haven't an axe take hold of an iron bar or a cudgel!

—*For our murdered children,*
—*For our parents,*
—*For Ponary.*

Strike the murderers!

In every street, in every yard, in every room, within the ghetto and outside the ghetto.
Strike the dogs!
Jews, we have nothing to lose. *We can save our lives only if we kill the murderers.*
Long live liberty! Long live armed resistance!
Death to the murderers!

Command Staff
United Partisans Organization—F.P.O. (*Fareinikte Partizaner Organizatsie*)
Vilna Ghetto
September 1, 1943

Questions

1. Large non-Jewish resistance forces in France, Yugoslavia, and elsewhere fought the Germany army with the aim of defeating it and liberating their countries. What are the stated or implied goals of the FPO? In what ways are their demands less ambitious than those of the French or Yugoslav partisans, and why?
2. Who do you think would have been receptive to this appeal?
3. The authors of this statement were well aware that their population was powerless and "weak" and that the Nazis depicted them in degrading terms. In the background is the long-standing persecution of Jewish people in Lithuania, Poland, and other neighboring lands, which was based on anti-Semitic stereotypes and caricatures similar to those employed by the Nazis. How did the FPO seek to undermine or overturn those stereotypes?

---

[87]A "maline" was a bunker used for hiding.

Source 2.3: Heinrich Himmler, speech to SS leaders, Posen, Poland, October 4, 1943

Himmler held several titles, most important "Reichsführer-SS," commander of the SS. After Hitler himself, Himmler is considered the second-most-powerful figure in Nazi Germany, and he was principally responsible for implanting the "Final Solution." This is an excerpt from a much longer speech he delivered in Posen (today called Poznan, in the western part of modern-day Poland), which was incorporated into the Third Reich during its occupation by the Germans (September 1939–February 1945).

I want to also mention a very difficult subject . . . before you, with complete candor. It should be discussed amongst us, yet nevertheless, we will never speak about it in public. Just as we did not hesitate on June 30 to carry out our duty as ordered, and stand comrades who had failed against the wall and shoot them—about which we have never spoken, and never will speak.[88]

I am talking about the evacuation of the Jews, the extermination of the Jewish people. It is one of those things that is easily said. "The Jewish people is being exterminated," every Party member will tell you, "perfectly clear, it's part of our plans, we're eliminating the Jews, exterminating them, a small matter." And then along they all come, all the 80 million upright Germans, and each one has his decent Jew. They say: all the others are swine, but here is a first-class Jew.[89]

And, none of them has seen it, has endured it. Most of you will know what it means when 100 bodies lie together, when 500 are there or when there are 1000.

And . . . to have seen this through and—with the exception of human weakness—to have remained decent, has made us hard and is a page of glory never mentioned and never to be mentioned. Because we know how difficult things would be, if today in every city during the bomb attacks, the burdens of war and the privations, we still had Jews as secret saboteurs, agitators and instigators. We would probably be at the same stage as 16/17,[90] if the Jews still resided in the body of the German people.

We have taken away the riches that they had, and . . . I have given a strict order, [and] we have delivered these riches to the Reich, to the State. We have taken nothing from them for ourselves. . . . A number of SS men have offended against this order. They are very few, and they will be dead men *without mercy!*[91]

We have the moral right, we had the duty to our people to do it, to kill this people who would kill us.[92] We however do not have the right to enrich ourselves with

SOURCE: Courtesy of (NIZKOR). Transcript and audio recording available at : http://www .nizkor.org/hweb/people/h/himmler-heinrich/posen/oct-04-43/ausrottung-transl-nizkor.html

[88]Himmler refers here to the "Night of the Long Knives" of 1934.
[89]On the audiotape of this speech, some laughter can be heard after that sentence.
[90]Himmler refers to 1916-1917, implying that during that stage of World War I "the Jews" were sabotaging Germany's war effort.
[91]Himmler shouted this remark with great emphasis.
[92]The German word "umbringen" has been translated here as "to kill."

even one fur, with one Mark, with one cigarette, with one watch, with anything. That we do not have. Because we don't want, at the end of all this, to get sick and die from the same bacillus that we have exterminated. I will never see it happen that even one . . . bit of putrefaction comes in contact with us, or takes root in us. On the contrary, where it might try to take root, we will burn it out together. But altogether we can say: We have carried out this most difficult task for the love of our people. And we have suffered no defect within us, in our soul, or in our character.

Questions

1. Why do you think Himmler stressed the order against plundering?
2. Himmler stated that the mass murder of Jews, which he says will be a glorious chapter in history, must nonetheless remain a secret. What are some possible reasons that he believed this "page of glory" must never be discussed?
3. Although he was addressing a group of battle-hardened soldiers, Himmler seems to have believed it necessary to give them a justification for their orders. How does he attempt to rationalize the mass murder of Jewish civilians?

Source 2.4: Interview with Julia Lentini (née Bäcker), Romani survivor

Julia Bäcker was born into a large Sinti and Roma family in 1926 and grew up in two small towns in western Germany. Like many gypsies in her town, she spoke Romani at home and German at school and with friends. Her father was a craftsman and horse trader. In March 1943, the entire family—she had fourteen siblings—was deported to Auschwitz. Three months earlier, Heinrich Himmler had ordered the deportations of Roma and Sinti out of the greater German Reich; roughly 25,000 of them were sent to Auschwitz, where they inhabited a special "Gypsy family camp." Like many others in the "gypsy camp," both of Julia's parents as well as a sister died of disease and starvation within a few months in the camp, and in early 1944—not long before the SS leadership decided to murder all the remaining gypsies—Julia and her surviving siblings were transported to the Schlieben concentration camp in Germany. After the war, she married an American soldier, taking the name Lentini. These comments are from an interview she gave to the USC Shoah Foundation in 1995.

In these excerpts, Lentini described her family's deportation to Auschwitz and conditions there; her subsequent transport to Schlieben; and the end of the war and its immediate aftermath. She frequently used German expressions and terms in the interview, and she retained a German accent.

The Bürgermeister[93] knocked on our door. "I've heard there are some authorities out here; they've surrounded your house, they want to bring your family in, they

---

SOURCE: Courtesy of the University of Southern California Shoah Foundation Institute for Visual History and Education.
[93]Mayor.

want to take them to Frankfurt. You'll probably be gone for about three or four days." "What about the animals?" we asked. "It's all taken care of. Just pack a little something for three days," he said to my mother.

The neighbors, they didn't know what was going on. We didn't make a big commotion. Because my dad said, "Well, we have to do what's been ordered." My mother said, "Stay together; carry the small ones. Let's all of us stick together so we don't get lost or separated."

We got there at night, and I tell you, all those bright lights and dust. . . . They put us in those big barracks, with 800 or 1,000 people. The children were sleepy and crying; what they were doing, they were putting the numbers on us, before they put us in blocks. Then, the worst thing was the delousing.[94] I told you how innocent we were raised. Here's my mother, with her children. . . . All she had to say was, "Stay together, kids; hold hands, carry the small ones; let's stick together so we don't get lost." That was the beginning of the end for her.

We had to go in quarantine; we couldn't go with our parents. "You're in no. 1 block, your parents are in no. 5," they told us. I didn't get to see them [my parents] for six weeks. We had to cook for those Nazis. I worked in the *Magazin*.[95] Already six weeks later, I see my dad. My dad was a big man. My mom said, "Ach, don't worry. He could lose some pounds anyway." She didn't want to get the kids upset; she said, "It's going to be okay."

In the barracks there were 500 people. It was very tight; there were open pits for toilets. There were even some people lying dead. You don't even notice those odors after a while. You adapt; otherwise, you're finished right then and there.

We were about one day, one night on the train [from Auschwitz to Schlieben in January 1945].[96] "What's going to happen to us? Where are they going to put us?" As the rumors went: the worst camp is where we were; wherever we were going to go was supposed to be a little better.

I was picked again for the kitchen, I couldn't believe it. [She smiles while recalling this.]

Interviewer: "Were you happy?" Well, I didn't have to go a munitions factory, I figured it would be better for me. There was an old man, an old German SS man. He didn't look so mean. I said, "How are things going out there?" He said, "My wife is dead, we were bombed." So, he was a little talkative, the man. Second day, I had a little confidence, I said [to myself], "gosh, maybe I should take one of those cans." It was like dog food in the camps [that they fed us], you know.

At work one day, I took a can and stuck it under my arm. "Halt!" A woman [guard] approached me. "Well . . . where did this come from?" She took my name and number, and wrote down what I said. The next night at this Appell, when the

---

[94]During "delousing" they were forced to strip naked.
[95]Storage room.
[96]A camp in Germany, approximately 300 miles northwest of Auschwitz. She was separated from her siblings at this point.

whole camp has to come out, they called my number out.[97] "Oh, god, what are they going to do to me now," I thought. In front of all these people, the whole camp.

I had to walk there, to the bench. The two Nazis told me to get close to the bench [and] to bend over from my waist down and put my feet under a board, they tied my hands. [In the interview, she demonstrates, leaning over with her hands stretched in front of her.] Then he [a Nazi guard] called out, "*Hundertfunfzig.*"[98] "Don't anybody ever get the idea that you can do this." I had to count [the lashes as they were administered]; I lost count after 75; the blood was splashing through my dress then.

[She was then sent to the infirmary. By this time, Allied troops were approaching.] Bombs and explosions blew all the windows out of the sick-block. I picked her [another female prisoner, who couldn't walk] up on my back. She fell off of me, she laid there . . . But that girl, she survived all that. It was almost toward the end [of the war]. About a week later, the old [German SS] man was still there. "The Russians, they won't be long" he said. He hid himself in the storage; the other prisoners hid him [after the other Germans abandoned the camp], that's how much they liked him. He was a very good man.

If anyone survives here: Go back to our house. If the house isn't there, go to the spot, that's where we'll all meet. And that's exactly what we did. It took some of us three weeks, others three months. We were separated, in different camps. The house was still there; some big-shot Nazi took it over, they took all the stuff, nothing was left in there. But what's material things? We had our lives.

Interviewer: "What was the reaction of the Germans; were they glad to see you?" Oh, yeah, and of course they didn't know; maybe the big shots knew, but the little neighbors didn't. The ones we had had gone to school with, had *Kaffeetrinken* with.[99] The Bürgermeister and the rest all knew, I'm sure.

I thought I wasn't capable of loving anymore, anybody. And I really didn't think there was a god. I didn't pray. . . . The god I was taught [about] wouldn't let that happen. And I had to learn to trust people again, and accept that this was a certain time in my life.

Questions

1. She was in her late teens during the events she describes. How might her age at the time—and the fact that this interview took place fifty years later—shape her testimony?
2. Does she condemn all Germans or camp guards she had contact with? Why or why not?
3. How and why did she greet some of her experiences with humor?
4. What were some survival mechanisms employed by Julia and others? How could a work assignment help or hurt an inmate's chances of survival?

---

[97]The "Appell" was the roll call, usually taken in the mornings but sometimes in the evenings.
[98]150 [lashes].
[99]Literally, "to drink coffee"; German social tradition, also called *Kaffee und Kuchen*, when Germans take an afternoon break and have coffee and a piece of cake or pastry.

3
THE CAMBODIAN GENOCIDE

"The Angkar is our savior! The Angkar is our liberator! We are strong because of the Angkar!" Having heard it many times, I knew when to break into the obligatory claps and screams. "Our Khmer soldiers today killed five hundred Youns trying [to] invade our country! The Youns have more soldiers, but they are stupid and are cowards! One Khmer soldier can kill ten Youns!" "Angkar! Angkar! Angkar!" we scream our replies.

—Loung Ung[1]

LOUNG UNG WAS A young girl living in the Cambodian capital, Phnom Penh, when the Khmer Rouge took power in April 1975. Herded with her family and hundreds of thousands of others onto a perilous trek into the countryside, she was one of the "lucky" ones: Ung survived and now lives in the United States, but her family was decimated. Her recollection of a rally in her village condenses several important elements of the Cambodian genocide of 1975–1979: the religious-like veneration of the party, as well as its shadowy nature (it did not even reveal its formal name until after coming to power); the regime's bitter, violent hatred toward neighboring Vietnam and Cambodia's ethnic Vietnamese population; the shrill militarism and nationalism of the Khmer Rouge; and the party's attempt to indoctrinate, if not eliminate, huge sections of the population.

Right-wing ideologies fueled the genocides examined in this book's first two chapters. In Cambodia, though, it was a party and state that proclaimed itself "communist" that committed genocide. The Khmer Rouge, also known as the Communist Party of Kampuchea (Cambodia), and its leader, Pol Pot, orchestrated

---

[1]Loung Ung, *First They Killed My Father: A Daughter of Cambodia Remembers* (New York: Harper, 2000), 130. "Angkar" refers to the leadership of the Khmer Rouge. "Yuon" is a Cambodian term for Vietnamese people, who were singled out for destruction by the Khmer Rouge.

the genocide—actually, a series of genocides against various groups—that claimed the lives of approximately 2 million people. As a percentage of a country's populace, this was one of the most devastating genocides in world history.[2] Victims were driven to sites throughout the countryside where they died en masse of overwork, starvation, executions, and massacres in Cambodia's notorious "killing fields."[3]

ANGKOR AND PRECOLONIAL CAMBODIA

Since the dawn of recorded Cambodian history some twenty centuries ago, Cambodians have inhabited, without great geographic alteration, a large area of mainland Southeast Asia, a region they have long shared with the more numerous Vietnamese, Malay, and Thai peoples, as well as Laotians and others. By the early years of the Common Era, a distinct Cambodian, or Khmer, civilization and language existed.[4] Cambodia underwent a relative golden age from the ninth to the early fifteenth centuries, the period of the Khmer Empire. During this 600-year span, Khmer civilization reached its cultural and military pinnacle in Angkor, a kingdom in the inland northwest of historic Cambodia that was at times the mightiest of the competing kingdoms in Southeast Asia. After 1431, the Khmer Empire declined in power. Much of Cambodia came under Thai and Vietnamese rulers for most of the following four centuries. Latter-day nationalists, including the Khmer Rouge, invoked the glories of this bygone era, and Angkor would serve as a mythologized reminder of Cambodian greatness, overcome by foreign enemies and supposedly forgotten by its own people.

From the late 1600s into the middle of the 1800s—a period sometimes called Cambodia's "dark ages"—most of Cambodia was at the mercy of the more powerful Buddhist Thai (or Siamese) and Confucian-Buddhist Vietnamese kingdoms, both of which seized territory from their weaker neighbor and installed pliable rulers on its throne. Cambodians occasionally carried out anti-Vietnamese massacres, setting precedents for the 1970s genocide, when the ethnic Vietnamese population

---

[2]According to the latest and most reliable figures, 23 to 30 percent of Cambodia's population (which was 7.3 million in 1975) died under the Khmer Rouge. The victims of the Armenian and Rwandan genocides constituted roughly 8–10 percent of their respective nations' populace—although, in the Rwandan case, this represented more than two-thirds of the Tutsi population. War, genocide, and atrocities by Hitler's and Stalin's armies claimed about 16–17 percent of Poland's population and an even higher percentage of Belarus's. The Nazis' six million Jewish victims inhabited many different countries; about half of them were Polish; and the Holocaust killed more than 60 percent of Europe's Jewish population.
[3]The term "killing fields" was popularized in the United States and elsewhere by the 1984 film of that name, which was based on a book, also titled *The Killing Fields*, about the Cambodian journalist and genocide survivor Dith Pran. "Killing Fields" is an accurate and vivid expression, and since its popularization it has been applied by writers and historians to other instances of mass violence ranging from open-air massacres during the Holocaust to atrocities in recent years in Congo.
[4]Khmer is the language and ethnicity of the majority of the people of Cambodia.

Angkor Wat
The marvelous Angkor Wat compound in the northern Cambodian province of Siem Reap. Built in the early twelfth century at the height of the powerful Khmer Empire, Angkor Wat showcases the cultural achievements of that age. The Khmer Rouge promised to restore the glories and might of that bygone period, and while in power the KR included an image of Angkor Wat in the national flag. A yearning to resurrect a "golden age"—invariably, a mythical one—animates many reactionary movements, including the ones examined in the last two chapters of this book.

remaining in the country was killed in its entirety. In 1751, for example, the Khmer king ordered an extensive, murderous pogrom.[5]

It is important to note, however, that the relations between Cambodians and Vietnamese were far more complex than can be summarized in these few sentences, which focus on trends that are relevant to our understanding of the genocide in the 1970s.

CAMBODIA AND INDOCHINA UNDER FRENCH COLONIALISM

Cambodia remained under the control, direct or indirect, of Vietnam and Thailand well into the mid-nineteenth century. King Duang (also known as Ang Duong), a relatively strong and independent ruler, and his successor King Norodom welcomed French patronage and economic ties in order to counter Vietnamese and Thai influence. This opened the door, however, for France to impose a protectorate in 1863.

For the next two decades or so Cambodia remained a monarchy, but in reality its government was run by young French naval officers. This arrangement was no

---

[5]Ben Kiernan, *Blood and Soil: A World History of Genocide and Extermination from Sparta to Darfur* (New Haven, CT: Yale University Press, 2007), 158–160. During some periods of these "dark ages," local Khmer rulers were able to exert control over portions of their country, usually because of warfare that preoccupied Siam (Thailand) and Vietnam. The mid-1700s was one such period.

more burdensome or onerous for the average Cambodian than previous periods of subordination to outside powers. But in the 1880s, as part of a broader policy to assert itself in the region, France decided to forgo certain diplomatic niceties and charades, tighten its control, and exploit Cambodia's resources more thoroughly.[6] This prompted a lengthy rebellion in 1885–1888, which succeeded only in inducing the French to cultivate a broader layer of local advisers who would be loyal to the colonial power rather than to the weak king. After France established a protectorate in Cambodia, it employed many Vietnamese as subordinate officials in the French colonial administration, thereby perpetuating an image of the Vietnamese population as outsiders who possessed inordinate and illegitimate control.

In the 1890s, France created a federation of colonies called French Indochina, which included Cambodia as well as Vietnam and Laos. Although the Khmer peasantry was heavily burdened by taxes, the French administration made little pretense of funding education, health care, or infrastructure development in Cambodia. In 1915 and early 1916, tens of thousands of peasants descended on the capital, Phnom Penh, to present their grievances to the king, Sisowath I. The "1916 Affair," as it became known, resulted in little immediate alleviation of the peasantry's suffering, but it proved that provincial leaders could rapidly mobilize the peasantry in order to press political demands.[7]

In the final months of World War II, Japan attempted with short-lived success to take control of French Indochina, but after Japan's defeat in August 1945 France reasserted its control. A powerful nationalist movement in Vietnam, spearheaded by a coalition of forces known as the Viet Minh—led by Ho Chi Minh, the central figure in the Communist Party—eventually defeated the French, after a decisive battle in 1954. The country was then partitioned between the Communist-led North Vietnam and a South Vietnamese dictatorship that was heavily supported by the US government. Elections to reunify the country were planned for 1956, but rejected by the South Vietnamese government and never held. South Vietnamese resistance forces (the National Liberation Front, aka the "Viet Cong"), organized out of the now-dissolved Viet Minh and supported by North Vietnam, waged a struggle against the government that eventually pulled the United States into a lengthy, devastating war in Vietnam (1964–1975) that killed millions of Vietnamese, destabilized the entire region, and heavily influenced Cambodia's fate.

Other important social and political changes were underway in Cambodia in the 1950s and 1960s. An increasing proportion of the peasantry was reduced to the level of landless tenants and sharecroppers.[8] This was a new group of rootless, destitute rural people who lived in desperate straits and would have little to lose, and potentially much to gain, from radical change.

---

[6]David Chandler, *A History of Cambodia* (Boulder, CO: Westview Press, 1993), 172–176.
[7]Chandler, *A History*, 188–189.
[8]Ben Kiernan, "The Cambodian Genocide, 1975–1979," in Samuel Totten and William S. Parsons, eds., *Century of Genocide: Critical Essays and Eyewitness Accounts* (New York: Routledge, 2004), 349.

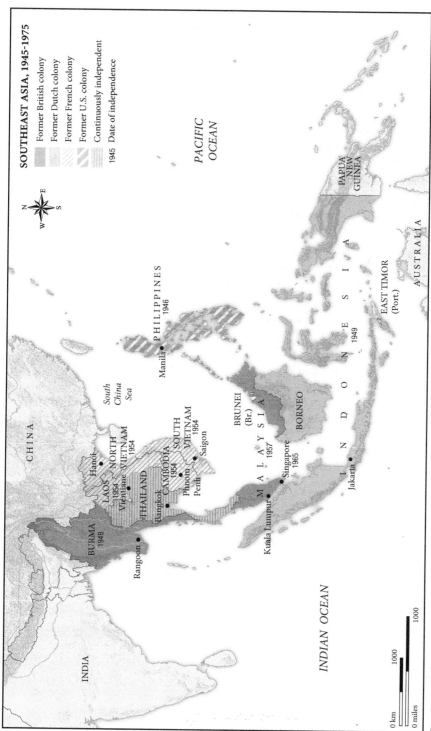

Southeast Asia, 1945–1975

SOUTHEAST ASIA, 1945-1975

Former British colony
Former Dutch colony
Former French colony
Former U.S. colony
Continuously independent
1945 Date of independence

PACIFIC OCEAN

INDIAN OCEAN

CHINA

INDIA

BURMA
1948

Rangoon

THAILAND

Bangkok

LAOS
1954

Vientiane

Hanoi

NORTH VIETNAM
1954

CAMBODIA
1954

Phnom Penh

SOUTH VIETNAM
1954

Saigon

South China Sea

PHILIPPINES
1946

Manila

MALAYSIA
1957

Kuala Lumpur

Singapore
1965

BRUNEI
(Br.)

BORNEO

INDONESIA

Jakarta

1949

EAST TIMOR
(Port.)

PAPUA NEW GUINEA

AUSTRALIA

0 km   1000
0 miles   1000

EMERGENCE OF THE COMMUNIST PARTY OF CAMBODIA

In 1951, the Vietnamese Workers Party (i.e., Communist Party) and its anti-French Khmer allies set up the "People's Revolutionary Party of Kampuchea" (PRPK). In its first years the party was led by Khmer Buddhist monks as well as Vietnamese Communists: two groups in which membership would later be very dangerous. The control initially exercised by the Vietnamese Communists eventually fueled resentment among some Cambodian party members, especially a younger, elite, French-educated group who took control of the party after 1954. A 1960 party congress marked the first major step toward the latter group's independence from the Vietnamese Communists, and in 1966, under its leadership, the Cambodian party changed its name to the Communist Party of Kampuchea (CPK). It was later given the appellation "Khmer Rouge" (Red Khmers) by others.[9]

The organization's precise name is made even more confusing by its leaders' belief that the name and character of the group should remain hidden from the public, and their adoption of other names and guises at certain junctures. Most Cambodians, for example, only heard of the mysterious "Angkar" (organization) during the first two years of Khmer Rouge rule (1975–1977). It was only after nearly two and a half years in power that the party proclaimed its name (the CPK) and the name (actually a pseudonym) of its secretary, or top leader, Pol Pot—and even after being ousted in 1979 he did not acknowledge his true identity. For the sake of clarity, this chapter will refer to the party by the name most widely associated with it from the time it gained international notoriety: the Khmer Rouge or its abbreviation (KR).

"BROTHER NUMBER 1": POL POT

Saloth Sar—the future Pol Pot—was born in 1925 to a fairly prosperous farming family of Khmer descent that had connections to Cambodia's royal family. He led a relatively comfortable and affluent childhood and attended an elite Catholic school in Phnom Penh. One of Saloth Sar's cousins had grown up as a palace dancer and had a son with Prince Monivong shortly before he became king in 1927; afterward, she played a prominent role in his palace. One of his sisters also became a consort of the king, and beginning in 1928 his oldest brother worked as a palace clerk. In 1935, Saloth Sar joined his siblings in Phnom Penh, where he attended an exclusive Catholic school. His family's connections to the Cambodian elite then helped him to enter a succession of leading schools in his teenage years. In brief, he grew up in a privileged setting, distant from the experience of the average Cambodian and with little knowledge of

---

[9]In the Khmer language, the nation is "Kampuchea." "Cambodia" derives from the French word for the country. For the sake of clarity and consistency, this book uses "Cambodia."

peasant or village life. Acquaintances and schoolmates from his youth recalled him as an average student but also a pleasant, unassuming, calm young man, with little indication of the fanaticism and cruelty that would characterize his rule and his personality in the 1970s.

Saloth Sar was one of roughly one hundred Cambodians who studied in France in the late 1940s and 1950s. About two dozen of them, including several future leaders of the KR, joined the French Communist Party. This was a formative time in Sar's life and marks the beginning of his political activity and thought. With several other Cambodian students, he spent the summer of 1950 in Yugoslavia, which at the time seemed to be steering a path toward a socialism that was independent of the USSR, whose leaders scorned the disobedience and nationalism of the Yugoslav Communists. Sar joined the French Communist Party in Paris before returning in 1953 to his homeland, where he became active in the PRPK, later known as the CPK (see earlier). In 1952, he gave himself the first of several pseudonyms he would employ, and one that evinced his emerging fixation with race: "the Original Khmer" (*Khmaer Daem*).[10]

Like other large Communist parties, the French Communist Party (CP) was largely under the control of Moscow. Indeed, in the early 1950s the French CP was unusually loyal to Moscow and deeply Stalinist in its internal culture. The "Marxism" imbibed by Sar and his Cambodian comrades was therefore the Stalinist variant, with little surviving of pre-Stalinist Marxism. Stalinist French Communism was not the only political influence upon Saloth Sar while he was in France: Along with several other future Khmer Rouge leaders, he was also drawn to European ideas about race. French colonialists and racial thinkers disdained modern Cambodian society, yet invoked an idealized image of a distant past, which they associated with an idealized "Khmer soul." One of Sar's early Cambodian mentors, too, taught that Khmer "ancient culture" had been contaminated by such outside influences as Buddhism and Hinduism, which had been imported from India.[11] Despite its origins in colonialism, and imperialism, Saloth Sar and his colleagues readily accepted such racial thinking and categories. Fused with other elements of racial and nationalist mythology, this created the extremely xenophobic, violent nationalism that defined the Khmer Rouge in the 1970s.

In 1956, after returning to Cambodia, Sar married Khieu Ponnary, sister-in-law of Ieng Sary, another of the future Khmer Rouge leaders who joined the movement while in Paris a few years earlier; Sar had become close to both of them during their time in France, where Sary played a leading role among the leftist Cambodian students. Saloth Sar took over the party by the spring of 1963. Sar's ascent to the leadership was eased by the death of long-time leader Tou Samouth in July of the

---

[10]Ben Kiernan, *How Pol Pot Came to Power: Colonialism, Nationalism and Communism in Cambodia, 1930–1975* (New Haven, CT: Yale University Press, 2004), xxi.
[11]Kiernan, *Blood and Soil*, 543.

Pol Pot

Pol Pot being interviewed by ABC News shortly after being deposed, somewhere in a Cambodian jungle in January 1980. Like most genocidal murderers, his personality and motives cannot be fully explained. This image seems to convey the pleasant, calm demeanor that former friends as well as students from his days as a schoolteacher recalled; yet he was capable of the most bloodthirsty, cruel proclamations and decisions. This photograph also reminds us of America's indulgent attitude toward the despot. Most other criminals of his stature, if discovered in hiding only three weeks after their ouster, would be seized rather than peacefully interviewed.

previous year. Mystery continues to surround Samouth's disappearance and murder. For years, it was blamed on agents of the Cambodian government, quite possibly future head of state Lon Nol, who would be ousted by the Khmer Rouge in 1975; some experts including Ben Kiernan argue that Sar and the group around him were involved.[12]

One of Saloth Sar's chief goals was to move his party away from its Vietnamese origins and influence. Sar was not alone in resenting the subordinate position assigned to them by the much more powerful Vietnamese Communists, who instructed their Cambodian comrades to wage a political rather than an armed struggle, while waiting for the victory in Vietnam before attempting to take power.[13] These priorities were made abundantly clear to Sar when he visited North Vietnam for talks with senior party leaders in 1965. Soon afterward, he received a friendlier reception in China. His visit coincided with the onset of the Cultural

[12]Ben Kiernan, *The Pol Pot Regime: Race, Power, and Genocide in Cambodia Under the Khmer Rouge, 1975–79* (New Haven, CT: Yale University Press, 2008), 13–14.
[13]Chandler, *A History*, 242.

Revolution, an explosion of political violence and hysterical persecutions that Sar found inspiring. Sar and other top Communists such as Ieng Sary spent most of the remainder of the 1960s in hiding, in isolated parts of eastern and northeastern Cambodia. This isolation and insularity—they spent much of their time speaking not to the masses, but to each other—fostered the party leaders' secretive style, distrust of outsiders, and detachment from the concerns and daily struggles of their own country-people.

CAMBODIAN POLITICS IN THE 1950s AND 1960s

Cambodia gained its independence in 1953–1954 under the leadership of Norodom Sihanouk (reigned as king 1941–1955 and 1993–2004; died in 2012). During his long political career, Norodom Sihanouk held a variety of titles, including "king" and "prime minister." Born to the royal family in 1922, the erratic, vain prince—through most of his life, he was commonly referred to as "Prince Sihanouk"—exerted a tremendous influence over Cambodian politics for over a half century. Unhindered by excessive principle or a consistent political philosophy, he was the ultimate political survivor, adapting himself both to the Khmer Rouge and, eventually—after years in opposition to it—the pro-Vietnamese government that overthrew and succeeded it. Through most of the late 1950s and 1960s, Sihanouk proclaimed himself a nationalist who, like other such figures in the Third World at the time, refused to take orders from the world's two superpowers. This was during the height of the "Non-Aligned Movement," associated with leaders like Nasser in Egypt and Sukarno in Indonesia whose popularity was based largely on their independence and defense of their nations' sovereignty.

Other political movements developed in Cambodia during this period. The most important included the Democrats, a liberal, reformist movement that gained widespread support in the 1950s. Farther to the left was the Pracheachon, essentially a front for the Communist Party. The appeal of the Left prompted Sihanouk to form Sangkum, a party that included right-wing but also some leftist elements. Sihanouk's policies toward the Left vacillated unpredictably but cannily; at times he repressed them through heavy-handed measures, at other times he co-opted some of their leaders and paid lip service to left-wing causes and concerns.

Sihanouk was skillful in dividing or suppressing his political opponents, but he was less adroit at finding competent advisers or administrators to attend to the daily affairs of state. By the late 1960s his government was tottering, as Sihanouk had taken to pastimes such as film-making, producing films of dubious merit with titles like *The Little Prince of the People* and *La Joie de Vivre*. He was taken by surprise when his army commander, Lon Nol, carried out a peaceful coup d'état while the prince was vacationing in France in March 1970.

Norodom Sihanouk
Norodom Sihanouk (left) visiting Romania
and its Communist Party dictator, Nicolae
Ceauşescu (far right, with wife Elena
at his side), in 1972. At various times
Sihanouk played all sides in the Cold War,
aligning himself with anti-Communists
when it served him, and at other times
(or simultaneously) touting his "leftist"
credentials by consorting with
Communists and Stalinists such as the
Romanian dictator—who was similarly
unburdened by scruples.

WAR IN VIETNAM AND CIVIL WAR IN CAMBODIA

Events in neighboring Vietnam exerted a profound influence on Cambodia and on
the rise of the Khmer Rouge. In its final years, the US war in Vietnam destabilized
Cambodia and contributed indirectly but powerfully to the rise of the Khmer
Rouge. After France's defeat by Vietnamese nationalist forces in 1954, the US government, fearing the advance of nationalism and anti-imperialism in Asia, became
increasingly involved in the region. The Eisenhower, Kennedy, and Johnson administrations supported the South Vietnamese military dictatorship of Ngo Dinh
Diem, and sent tens of thousands of military advisers to assist its struggle against
nationalist and Communist forces. From 1964 onward, the US government committed large numbers of soldiers; by the end of the decade the Johnson and Nixon
administration had deployed roughly half a million troops there.

The war was never strictly limited to the territory of Vietnam. The US Air Force
used its bases in Thailand and the Philippines, and the Vietnamese Communist-led
forces—the National Liberation Front (the Viet Cong) and the North Vietnamese
Army—had bases and supply routes in Cambodia. In order to disrupt supply routes
and rout Vietnamese forces, the US military began conducting bombing raids on
Cambodia in late 1965. The sorties were greatly expanded in late 1969, and by
1973 the United States had conducted at least 230,000 bombing sorties over the
country—which until 1970 was neutral in the war—dropping roughly 500,000
tons of bombs. This figure equals or surpasses the tonnage dropped by the United
States in the Pacific Theater of World War II, including the attacks on Hiroshima
and Nagasaki.[14]

---

[14]Ben Kiernan and Taylor Owen, "Roots of US Troubles in Afghanistan: Civilian Bombing
Casualties and the Cambodian Precedent," *The Asia-Pacific Journal*, 26-4-10, June 28, 2010
http://www.japanfocus.org/-Ben-Kiernan/3380 (accessed June 23, 2012).

Meanwhile, Lon Nol was faced with strong domestic opposition and a guerilla war that began soon after the general took power and quickly expanded into a civil war. The government was weak from the start and was kept alive by vast military and economic aid from the United States. The Indochinese war's intrusion into Cambodia undermined the Lon Nol regime by revealing its ineptitude and corruption, as World War I had revealed similar features of Russia's monarchy. Additionally, the devastation and arbitrariness of the American bombing drove many thousands of Cambodians to support an insurgency that had little previous support. By 1973, the US administration was aware that the Khmer Rouge was using the massive bombings as a powerful recruitment tool; a high-ranking CIA official said that year that the "damage caused by B-52 strikes was the main theme of their propaganda."[15] A former KR officer later recalled that after bombings, his comrades "would take the people to see the craters, to see how big and deep the craters were. . . . That was what made it so easy for the Khmer Rouge to win the people over. . . . It was because of their dissatisfaction with the bombing that they kept on cooperating with the Khmer Rouge. . . . Sometimes the bombs fell and hit little children, and their fathers would be all for the Khmer Rouge."[16]

During the civil war of 1970–1975, the Khmer Rouge also benefitted from Vietnamese arms and training and from an alliance of convenience with the deposed Prince Norodom Sihanouk. With Chinese encouragement, the former prince came into closer alliance with the Khmer Rouge under the auspices of the "National United Front of Kampuchea." Despite the numerous failures and embarrassments of his last years in power, he remained popular among many rural people, and his name helped to raise support for the guerilla struggle. Meanwhile, the Khmer Rouge—on the front lines of the war, while the prince whiled away his time in comfortable exile in China and North Korea—steadily eclipsed him as the real power behind the war against Lon Nol.

Within the first two years of the civil war the government was losing its grip, and the conflict had taken a brutal character, with both sides committing vast atrocities. For General Nol's state, this brutality was matched by corruption; many of Nol's commanders and provincial governors sold arms and other contraband to KR forces. US bombing intensified after the American pull-out from Vietnam in early 1973, killing or maiming additional thousands of civilians and deepening the unpopularity of the Lon Nol government. Cambodia was now "the only war in town," as one US official candidly stated.[17] Meanwhile, the KR maintained the charade of a national liberation front, with Sihanouk as a figurehead.[18]

---

[15]Ibid.

[16]Kiernan, *Pol Pot Regime*, 23.

[17]Chandler, *Brother Number One*, 100.

[18]Even after taking power, the KR found it useful to give Sihanouk a symbolic but meaningless title; he resigned in April 1976 but was kept under house arrest at his palace in the capital until the end of the regime nearly three years later.

While the Cambodian government proved itself incapable of fighting the Khmer Rouge, it *was* capable of afflicting its own Vietnamese population. Through massacres, refugee flight, and expulsions, the number of ethnic Vietnamese was reduced from approximately 450,000 to about 140,000 in the first year of Lon Nol's regime.[19] Like the KR, the Lon Nol regime was infatuated with racial thinking. The general acclaimed the greatness of the "Khmer-Mon race," a subject to which he devoted several periodicals and official committees.[20]

The KR launched its final offensive on the first day of 1975, and on April 17 KR forces swept into Phnom Penh—which was overwhelmed with war refugees, its population tripling to more than 2 million. After five years of civil war accompanied by American bombing, KR troops were initially greeted with joy by much of the populace. Who were the mysterious, black-clad, grim young men who entered Phnom Penh on the day of liberation? What was the nature of the political force that toppled Lon Nol, and that kept not only the identity of its leaders, but even its very name, shrouded in mystery?

MARXISM, STALINISM, AND MAOISM

Though it called itself a communist party, the KR represented a brand of socialism that was indebted to Stalin and Mao and that would have been unrecognizable to Karl Marx or to most traditional socialists or communists. During the nineteenth century, substantial labor movements and socialist parties developed in Germany, England, France, the United States, and elsewhere in the industrialized world. Modern socialism arose out of Europe's Industrial Revolution, as a response to the inequities and social ills produced by early industrial capitalism, such as dangerous and oppressive workplaces, child labor, and squalid working and living conditions in the rapidly growing cities. Socialism was both an ideology and a political movement, and it was given a theoretical framework by Karl Marx, his friend and colleague Frederick Engels, and their intellectual heirs. While there were multiple, competing versions or interpretations, in its essence socialism represented the quest for economic and social equality and the empowerment of the working classes. Socialists were often at the forefront of democratic reform movements, such as the women's suffrage and peace movements of pre–World War I Europe. Socialism and Marxism also articulated, in a modern form, age-old human aspirations for egalitarianism and social justice.

The first state to ostensibly put socialism into practice was the Soviet Union, where V.I. Lenin's Bolshevik party took power in 1917. A bitter civil war (1918–1921)

---

[19] Kiernan, *Blood and Soil*, 548.
[20] Marie Alexandrine Martin, *Cambodia: A Shattered Society* (Berkeley, CA: University of California Press, 1994), 130. Mon-Khmer is a language group or family; the general switched the terms around in order to emphasize "Khmer." A "Khmer-Mon" or "Mon-Khmer" race or ethnicity seems to have been entirely an invention of Lon Nol's. Colin Mackerras, *Ethnicity in Asia* (New York: Routledge, 2003), 197.

induced the Bolsheviks to impose harsh methods that led to the institutional-ization of repressive apparatuses such as the Cheka (the secret police, later known by other acronyms such as the GPU and eventually the KGB). As the revolution's initial democratic promise evaporated, Bolshevik leaders grew enamored of repres-sion for its own sake and came to believe that virtually anything was permissible if it protected the revolution and defeated the "counterrevolutionaries"—a category that grew ever wider and more imprecise. Dedicated socialists and anarchists were labeled "oppositionists" or "class enemies" if they opposed the Bolsheviks' repres-sive methods.[21] Lenin died in 1924, and Joseph Stalin assumed power over the next few years, persecuting and eventually murdering many of the revolutionaries of the 1917 generation and consolidating a one-party, police-state dictatorship. By the 1930s, the titles of Marxism, socialism, and communism were indelibly cor-rupted by association with Stalinism, which replaced the values of earlier variants of socialism with hollow, hypocritical slogans. Anti-Stalinist or independent so-cialist and communist groups existed in much of the world, but these groups were small and lacked the stature and support of the USSR, which could claim to be the world's first and, until after World War II, only "socialist" society.

Pol Pot would later admit that, while he read "the big, thick works of Marx . . . I didn't really understand them at all." He may have preferred some of Stalin's writings, such as the Soviet leader's ponderous *Dialectical and Historical Materialism*, parts which of he occasionally plagiarized.[22] According to a journalist who spent many years in Cambodia and conducted numerous interviews with KR leaders, Pot's "public declarations in his four years in power were couched in the wooden language of ill-digested Marxism-Leninism," perhaps the product of an intellect "dulled by decades of hearing and speaking only theoretical rev-olutionary claptrap."[23] It is also noteworthy that, in contrast with the other "Marxist" parties that took power during the last century, KR leaders produced few writings or texts that might have given evidence of their philosophy and its evolution.

In several other fundamental ways, Pol Pot's thinking and CPK ideology devi-ated sharply from any previous variant of Marxism. For Pol Pot and the Khmer Rouge, race and nation were far more important than class, which they treated with surprising imprecision. Like Stalin's and Mao's parties, the CPK applied class

---

[21]Victor Serge's writings offer many poignant examples of selfless, honest revolutionaries who suffered under Stalin's reign. See Serge, *Russia Twenty Years After* (republished in 1997) and Serge, *Memoirs of a Revolutionary* (after being out of print for many years, this master-work was republished by New York Review Book Classics in 2012 with an introduction by Adam Hochschild).
[22]See Kiernan, "Kampuchea and Stalinism," in Colin Mackerras and Nick Knight, eds., *Marxism in Asia* (New York: Palgrave Macmillan, 1985), 232–249. Pot was therefore pla-giarizing from an already-plagiarized, unoriginal text: For this 1938 pamphlet, Stalin borrowed heavily from Lenin without attribution.
[23]Henry Kamm, *Cambodia: Report from a Stricken Land* (New York: Arcade Publishing, 1998), 135.

terms such as "bourgeois" to political enemies, regardless of their genuine social class; thereby the Cham people were categorized as "bourgeois," regardless of occupation or social status. One party document defined class as a "level of people with distinctive political tendencies."[24] And unlike the Russian and Chinese parties, the KR made no pretense of basing their "socialism" on an allegiance or identification with the working class.[25]

The KR espoused and practiced other ideas similar to Maoist China's brand of "socialism": a fervent but formulaic romanticization of the peasantry; the conviction that huge social transformation could be carried out by acts of will; and the belief that the nation was beset by external and, even more menacingly, internal enemies. In its racism as well as its fierce advocacy of national self-reliance, the KR bore striking similarities to North Korea's ruling Communist Party. And the Khmer Rouge shared a cult of death with reactionary and fascist movements, which is alien to any form of pre-Stalinist or pre-Maoist socialism.[26] In characteristic language, the KR transmitted this message over the radio in April 1977: "Respected brothers and comrades-in-arms: Your blood, red and fresh, flows swiftly like streams and rivers wetting the hallowed soil of our beloved Cambodian motherland."[27] A party anthem, "The Red Flag," began with this startling image: "Glittering red blood blankets the earth—blood given up to liberate the people."[28]

REMAKING CAMBODIAN SOCIETY

During the bitter war against Lon Nol, the Khmer Rouge had proven itself capable of horrendous abuses and shown that ethnic minorities would suffer under a KR government. But few could have imagined that, in less than four years, the new regime would single out multiple groups for destruction—ultimately turning upon the Khmer people themselves—and that more than one-fifth of the nation's population would perish.

The new rulers renamed their country "Democratic Kampuchea" (DK) after taking power. Before the 1975 takeover, a "Party Center," later known to Cambodians and

---

[24]David Chandler, *The Tragedy of Cambodian History* (New Haven, CT: Yale University Press, 1993), 208.
[25]The industrial working class was miniscule in the 1960s and 1970s, it should be noted—probably no more than 10,000 people.
[26]A prominent characteristic of all fascist movements was the glorification of war and violence, beginning with the Italian Fascist Party under Benito Mussolini and including the Nazis under Hitler and the Falangists in Spain. The Iron Guard, for example, a fascist party in Romania that briefly came to power during World War II, glorified violence and death through songs proclaiming, "Death [for the cause of the party] is a gladsome wedding for us." Larsen, Hagtvet, and Mykleburst, eds., *Who Were the Fascists: Social Roots of European Fascism* (New York: Oxford University Press, 1985), 389. Likewise, fascist parties in Hungary, Croatia, and elsewhere extolled violence, bloodshed, and self-sacrifice.
[27]Kiernan, *Pol Pot Regime*, 352.
[28]Alexander Laban Hinton, *Why Did They Kill? Cambodia in the Shadow of Genocide* (Berkeley, CA: University of California Press, 2004), 84.

others simply as the Center or "Angkar Loeu" ("High Organization"), had emerged. It was led by Pol Pot, who after assuming power took the title of prime minister; his deputy Nuon Chea; his brother-in-law Ieng Sary and Son Sen, who were named deputy prime ministers; Khieu Samphan was appointed "head of state"; and some of the party's key military leaders, in particular army chiefs Mok and Ke Pauk. The Party Center ran the country at the national level and gradually turned on other communist veterans with regional bases of support, such as the CPK Eastern Zone leader So Phim, who committed suicide in June 1978 during a purge and murder of regional party leaders and their followers whom the Center considered too close to the Vietnamese Communists.

On its first day in power the KR ordered mass evacuations of the cities, most important Phnom Penh, which because of an influx of refugees was then home to roughly one-quarter of the nation's population of 8 million. Within one week, the KR had driven more than 2 million Cambodians into the countryside. The KR used various pretenses, some of which would have seemed feasible—for example, that the United States might unleash bombing raids upon the capital, and that Phnom Penh was dangerously short of food. The expelled peoples had little knowledge of their destination, and their travails were exacerbated by the severe heat. (April is the hottest month of the year in most of Cambodia.) The KR gave little attention to food, medicine, or other necessities. Tens of thousands of people died in the forced marches, some by summary executions and more from disease and starvation.

The evacuations were fueled by two intertwined ideological beliefs: the KR's idealization of agrarian life, and the party's anti-urban animus, which it shared with the German Nazis, Bosnian Serb militias that besieged Sarajevo in the 1990s, and other reactionary political movements of recent history. Such movements have seen the cities as centers of decadence, cosmopolitanism, and cultural mixing. For Pol Pot, the city—in particular, the capital, Phnom Penh—was also "impure" because of its large non-Khmer populations. In the 1950s and 1960s, roughly half of the city's populace was composed of ethnic Chinese merchants, Vietnamese civil servants and laborers, and smaller numbers of Thais, Malays, Indians, and others.[29]

Another expression of this worldview was the KR's division of the populace into "base people" (the peasantry) and "new people" (city dwellers), a term of denigration that would soon carry fatal consequences. The so-called new people were viewed as disloyal and of having "led corrupt lives," recalled Loung Ung, a young girl at the time, in her powerful memoir. The "new people" therefore "must be kept under an ever-watchful eye for signs of rebellion" and "must be trained to be productive workers," which in reality meant they were "given the hardest work and the longest hours."[30] The KR also wasted little time launching an assault on one of the most fundamental bases of the Cambodian culture and society: the family. The attack on the family was part of the new regime's imposition of an extensive

[29]Philip Short, *Pol Pot: Anatomy of a Nightmare* (New York: Holt Paperbacks, 2006), 24.
[30]Ung, *First They Killed*, 62.

system of forced labor, whereby most of the population—both "base people" and "new people," although the so-called new people suffered harsher conditions—was compelled to work in the fields for 12- to 16-hour shifts. Food was available only in the communal kitchens the KR set up, and any attempt to go outside this system, for example by foraging or bartering, would be deemed "sabotage" and duly punished. Family or personal networks were disrupted and broken up by these arrangements, and devotion to family was to be replaced by loyalty to the mysterious "Angkar"—the party, which had yet to reveal its name—and "Brother Number 1," Pol Pot. By undermining family and personal relationships, the KR further atomized society and minimized resistance. And as if intent on confirming the hoariest Cold War caricatures of "communism," the KR abolished currency and imposed other extreme policies that they proclaimed would rapidly propel the country to socialism. Stalin and Mao had nationalized industry, merged family farms and estates into collectives, and banned most small private enterprises; but no "communist" system went to the anti-property extremes of the KR, which collectivized household items, including pots, pans, and axes.[31]

Such experiments do not lead inexorably to genocide. But the regime's racist and xenophobic obsessions; its expansionist goals, which led to warfare with several neighboring countries; its drive to forge a homogenous society by ethnic cleansing; and its economic failures converged to plunge Cambodia into disaster. Whereas the Soviets had proclaimed a series of unrealistic "Five-Year Plans," and Mao had followed suit with his own such plans—the second of which culminated in the catastrophic "Great Leap Forward" that probably caused the deaths of tens of millions of Chinese—the Khmer Rouge decreed a "Four-Year Plan" in the summer of 1976, and a "Super Great Leap Forward" the following year. These plans set production goals that could not possibly be met. Political consciousness and willpower could achieve anything, the party declared; the people can become "masters of the earth and of water," and of "all vegetation . . . and of the yearly floods."[32]

The plans necessitated long workdays, which were carried out with minimal sustenance provided for the laborers; by 1977 malnutrition and starvation were rampant. What incentive or goal did the KR promise its people? The hope that, one day, everyone would have dessert after a meal.[33] During the harshest years of his reign, Joseph Stalin had insouciantly proclaimed that "life has become more joyous" for the Soviet people. Similarly indifferent to the disastrous results of its experiments, the KR claimed in 1977 that "the water is gushing forth. And when there is water the scenery is fresh, life is pleasant, humor is lively, culture is evergreen."[34]

---

[31] Eric Weitz, *Century of Genocide: Utopias of Race and Nation* (Princeton, NJ: Princeton University Press, 2005), 151.

[32] Ibid., 152.

[33] Chandler, *A History*, 263.

[34] Ben Kiernan, "External and Indigenous Sources of Khmer Rouge Ideology," in Odd Arne Westad and Sophie Quinn-Judge, eds., *The Third Indochina War: Conflict Between China, Vietnam and Cambodia, 1972–79* (New York: Routledge, 2006), 190.

TARGETING OF MINORITY GROUPS

Before the deadly persecutions and expulsions of the Lon Nol era, the Vietnamese were Cambodia's most numerous non-Khmer segment of the population, but only one of some twenty ethnic minorities, which together constituted 15 to 20 percent of the country's populace.[35] Entire ethnicities were linked in the KR's delusional, siege-mentality imagination to outside enemies, magnifying their presumed threat. This way of thinking was hardly unique to the Khmer Rouge; the Young Turks and the German Nazis had also linked the victims of their genocides to presumed external threats, and Joseph Stalin viewed multiple national minorities as internal "fifth columns" serving foreign powers. But the impetus for the KR's attacks on minorities came primarily from the party's racist and ultra-nationalist philosophy and its goal of creating a "pure" Khmer nation.

The Chams—a predominantly Muslim people who inhabit various parts of Indochina—suffered terribly, as the KR viewed their distinctive culture as an obstacle to a homogenized Khmer society. The Chams lost one-third to one-half of their population.[36] In a depressing parallel with the other episodes examined in this book, the perpetrators sometimes devised creative but cruel torments; for example, Chams were killed for the crime of not eating pork, which is proscribed by Islam. In some cases, Cham villagers avenged themselves upon their oppressors, killing KR soldiers; but such acts would simply invite massive reprisals.

The Cham were singled out for both ethnic and religious reasons (not easily separated in many cases in history). The KR also assaulted one of its country's central, defining traditions by attacking Buddhism. Monks were singled out for extermination: Of 60,000 Buddhist monks, only 3,000 survived Pol Pot's brief reign, and in less than two years the KR succeeded in closing or destroying virtually every monastery in the country.[37] In some cases, temples were turned into pigsties or otherwise desecrated.[38] The Thai population, which the KR had already targeted in regions it controlled before taking power, dropped from 20,000 to 8,000; the number of Laotian families declined from 1,800 to 800; and the small Kola minority, 2,000 or so people in western Cambodia, virtually disappeared.[39]

An eternal quest for enemies caused the party to split into mutually suspicious factions, as the dominant group was always on the alert for signs of dissent or political heresy. The disastrous policies of the first year had indeed generated dissent within the party, which radicalized the siege mentality that Pol Pot and his

---

[35]Weitz, *Century*, 170.

[36]Ibid., 172. Pre-1975 population statistics are unreliable, but most recent authorities have cited a pre-KR population of about 250,000. Chams in other parts of the region adhere to Hinduism and other faiths.

[37]Adam Jones, *Genocide: A Comprehensive Introduction* (New York: Routledge, 2011), 299.

[38]May Ebihara and Judy Ledgerwood, "Aftermaths of Genocide: Cambodian Villagers," in Alexander Laban Hinton, ed., *Annihilating Difference: The Anthropology of Genocide* (Berkeley, CA: University of California Press, 2002), 280.

[39]Jones, *Genocide*, 299.

coterie had long nurtured. This period, from the fall of 1976 onward, marked the most dangerous phase of the KR's rule, as well as its unraveling. A series of internal party purges cost thousands of lives but further destabilized the regime, as did its military conflicts with three of its neighbors: Thailand, Vietnam, and Laos. The conflict with Vietnam was particularly ill-advised and ultimately led to the KR's downfall. The two Communist regimes, which had come to power only two weeks apart, regarded each other with mutual suspicion and distrust. Border skirmishes occurred regularly in 1975 and 1976. The tension was exacerbated by the KR's stated desire to claim parts of Vietnam for Cambodia, and Pol Pot's alliance with China, which provided the KR with substantial military aid by 1977.[40] The skirmishes grew more serious in 1977. Through artillery fire and an incursion into southeast Vietnam, Cambodia killed several hundred Vietnamese villagers in April, and again in September, then in December Vietnam carried out a brief offensive into Cambodia.[41]

After Vietnam's withdrawal, Pol Pot launched an extensive purge of his party and army leaderships in Cambodia's Eastern Zone, one of seven administrative zones that the KR established, and where even before the 1975 victory over Lon Nol many KR leaders displayed independence from the KR leadership. In 1978, Pol Pot declared that the entire population of the Eastern Zone had "Khmer bodies with Vietnamese minds." The KR evacuated about one-third of the region's population, leading to mass death through killings and starvation. Of the Eastern Zone's 1.7 million people, between 100,000 and 250,000 perished by December 1978.[42] At about this same time, Pol Pot announced that the revolution was threatened by "microbes" that are "buried," and will "rot us from within" if not exposed and eradicated.[43] The ominous accusation against "Vietnamese in Khmer bodies" was applied to any Khmers who had married Vietnamese, had Vietnamese blood, or were simply suspected of pro-Vietnamese sympathies. The attacks on Vietnamese broadened to include their own KR comrades who had trained in Hanoi, of which there were about a thousand.[44]

Many purge victims met their fate in the torture center Tuol Sleng (also known as S-21). Much as Hitler's and Stalin's camp systems defined those systems, Tuol Sleng has—along with the "killing fields"—come to symbolize the KR's brief, catastrophic reign. Located in Phnom Penh, the prison housed roughly 14,000 prisoners between 1975 and 1979—fewer than a dozen of whom are

[40]Chandler, A History, 270.
[41]Stephen J. Morris, Why Vietnam Invaded Cambodia (Stanford, CA: Stanford University Press, 1999), 98–102.
[42]Ben Kiernan, Genocide and Resistance in Southeast Asia (Piscataway, NJ: Transaction Publishers, 2007), 59.
[43]David Chandler, Ben Kiernan, and Chantou Boua, eds., Pol Pot Plans the Future: Confidential Leadership Documents from Democratic Kampuchea, 1976–1977 (New Haven, CT: Yale University Southeast Asia Studies, 1988), 183, 207, 183–184, 189, 190.
[44]Weitz, Century, 172.

believed to have survived.[45] A large majority of Tuol Seng's jailers were young, between the ages of seventeen and twenty-one. Pliable and beholden to the KR leadership, these young men would torture and murder many veterans of the Communist movement.[46]

As the conflict with Vietnam intensified, KR propaganda grew ever more shrill and bloodthirsty. On May 10, 1978, the government radio station proclaimed: "So far, we have succeeded in implementing this slogan of one against 30: that is to say, we lose one against 30 Vietnamese killed . . . We need only 2 million troops to crush the 50 million Vietnamese—and we would still have 6 million people left."[47] After some diplomatic attempts to resolve the crisis, Vietnamese forces, accompanied by thousands of Cambodian rebels, invaded on December 25, 1978. The Vietnamese advance was greatly aided by the involvement of dissident former KR members and other Cambodians who fought alongside the Vietnamese troops.[48] In only two weeks, Vietnam defeated the KR, whose leaders fled into exile or to remote areas of western Cambodia.

A pro-Vietnamese government has remained in power, in various configurations, since 1979. Hun Sen has been prime minister through most of this period. He was born in 1952 and joined the KR in the 1970s, rising to the position of battalion commander in the Eastern Zone during the war against Lon Nol. After the KR took power, he served as a political commissar—also in the Eastern Zone, where many KR figures had had closer relationships with the Vietnamese Communists. In 1977, as the KR leadership was purging Eastern Zone cadre, Hun Sen fled to Vietnam.[49] Norodom Sihanouk managed to regain a prominent position in 1993, accruing more titles and only announcing his final resignation, as king, in 2004. Meanwhile, the Hun Sen government dropped the façade of democracy when it carried out a coup in 1997.

As for the Khmer Rouge, it waged a long, unsuccessful military and diplomatic campaign to regain power. Supported diplomatically by the United States and China, the KR presented itself at the UN as the legitimate Cambodian government until the early 1990s. After national elections in 1993, the Khmer Rouge finally disintegrated, but not peacefully. Pol Pot staged a final purge in 1997, murdering long-time comrade Son Sen and his family; but this finally turned other close allies, including long-time KR leader and army general Mok, against him. Pol Pot was convicted by a "people's tribunal" and sentenced to life imprisonment, and died a year later.[50] "My conscience is clear. Everything I have done and contributed

[45]Jones, *Genocide*, 298.
[46]Kiernan, *Pol Pot Regime*, 316.
[47]Ben Kiernan, "Myth, Nationalism and Genocide," *Journal of Genocide Research* 3, no. 2 (2001), 193.
[48]Kiernan, *Genocide and Resistance*, 62.
[49]Elizabeth Becker, *When the War Was Over: Cambodia and the Khmer Rouge Revolution* (New York: Public Affairs, 1998), 305–314.
[50]Like so much else surrounding the late despot's life, the circumstances of his death are unclear. His captors claimed that he died of heart failure; others suspect that he was poisoned. Pol Pot was cremated before an autopsy could be performed.

S-21

At least 14,000 people were executed at Tuol Sleng, usually after being charged with "espionage" or of supporting the ousted Lon Nol government. In its final months, the Khmer Rouge—in a fashion reminiscent of the Soviet Union in the late 1930s—purged thousands of party leaders, many of whom met their deaths here. The prison administration photographed the inmates upon arrival; typically an inmate would then suffer several weeks of appalling conditions and repeated torture before finally being killed in brutal and often grisly fashion.

is first for the nation and the people and the race of Cambodia," he explained to journalist Nate Thayer, who interviewed Pol Pot while he was being held prisoner by his former comrades.[51] The KR ceased to exist by the end of 1998, when Mok surrendered to the Hun Sen government.

HOW MANY WERE KILLED?

Precise numbers are elusive because of the disparities in pre-genocide population estimates as well as the generalized chaos of regional war and huge population shifts. The latest, most reliable estimates indicate a death toll under the Khmer Rouge of between 1.7 and 2.2 million people.[52] In addition, at least a half a million

---

[51]Hinton, *Why Did They Kill?*, 15.

[52]Ewa Tabeau and They Kheam, ECCC [Extraordinary Chambers in the Courts of Cambodia] document D140/1/1, 30 September 2009, "Demographic Expert Report: Khmer Rouge Deaths in Cambodia, April 1975–January 1979: A Critical Assessment of Major Estimates." This is the most recent and most reliable estimate. The report concludes that at least 1.7 million people perished, and that at the "high end" of credible estimates, Craig Etheson's figure of 2.2 million is "plausible and in line with the most serious attempts of estimating the excess deaths in Cambodia." Tabeau and Kheam, 139.

perished during the conflict of 1970–1975. Today's Cambodia carries the psychological and physical scars of its years of carnage. Like other war-torn countries, such as Afghanistan and Angola, it has a large percentage of amputees, and the countryside is littered with landmines and unexploded ordnance, which claim hundreds of lives and limbs each year.

For the targeted groups, statistics again vary widely. The Cham population was reduced by one-third, with roughly 85,000 victims of KR repression, starvation, and murder.[53] Half the Chinese population, more than 200,000, was wiped out, and most shockingly, as mentioned earlier, virtually all the country's Vietnamese (somewhere between 10,000 and 20,000) died. The Khmer Rouge had deported many more in the regime's first year, thus inadvertently sparing them. The Cambodian genocide is sometimes characterized inaccurately as an "autogenocide"—a genocide directed at the government's own people or nation—or as a genocide directed solely at "class enemies." While this is superficial—it does not account for the KR's targeting of ethnic minorities—it is not wholly inaccurate. As the country descended into a maelstrom of forced labor, starvation, purges, and the arbitrary singling out of people accused of sabotage or disloyalty, ethnic Khmers eventually constituted the majority of the victims.

The methods by which many murders transpired are grim to contemplate. A Tuol Sleng killer said that his colleagues took prisoners to a ditch, ordered them to kneel, then struck them on the back of the neck with a heavy iron bar, repeating this many times if necessary and dumping the bodies into a mass grave.[54] One survivor told of an incident in 1978 in which thousands of people, both Eastern Zone peasants and former Phnom Penh residents—all decreed to be "enemies"— were driven into her village. The KR then instructed on pain of death "some of us 1975 people"—those who had been deported to the village in the first weeks of the regime—to kill the new arrivals. "Ten 1975 evacuees would be given axes and told to kill one hundred Svay Rieng people [the recent arrivals], who had been told to undress . . . They didn't want to kill them but they had no choice. They even killed young children with a single blow of the ax."[55]

"GENOCIDE IS TOO HEAVY FOR THE SHOULDERS OF JUSTICE"

Each of this book's four genocides led to attempts to bring the perpetrators to justice and, to varying degrees, to produce momentum toward education and reconciliation.[56] In each case, trials as well as commemoration have been at the mercy

---

[53]Kiernan, *Genocide and Resistance*, 276.
[54]Hinton, *Why Did They Kill?*, 3.
[55]Weitz, *Century*, 177.
[56]The quotation, "Genocide is too heavy," is from human rights advocate and legal expert Zarir Merat, quoted in Janine Natalya Clark, "The 'Crime of Crimes': Genocide, Criminal Trials and Reconciliation," *Journal of Genocide Research* 14, no. 1 (March 2012), 55.

of political considerations, both domestic and international. In Cambodia, many leading politicians, including long-serving prime minister Hun Sen, are tainted by their past associations with the Khmer Rouge, and have an interest in limiting the scope of genocide-related investigations and trials.

Nonetheless, in the first few years of the new century several steps were taken by the Cambodian government and the UN that eventually led to the establishment of the "Extraordinary Chambers in the Courts of Cambodia" (ECCC) for crimes committed in the KR period.[57] Also known as the "Khmer Rouge Tribunal," it began its first trial in 2007. In the Tribunal's first case, "Comrade Duch," the notorious director of Tuol Seng, was convicted in 2010 of crimes against humanity and sentenced to thirty-five years in prison (later extended to life).[58] Nuon Chea, aka "Brother Number Two"—the highest-ranking surviving Khmer Rouge leader from the period of the genocide—was arrested in 2007. A few months later, Khieu Samphan and Ieng Sary—long-time KR leaders who were among the chief perpetrators of the genocide—were arrested, and all three were indicted in 2010. Ieng Sary died the following year, but in August 2014 Samphan and Nuon Chea were convicted of "crimes against humanity," including "extermination, political persecution, forced transfer, attacks against humanity, [and] enforced disappearances."[59] They were each sentenced to life in prison.

CONCLUSIONS

Upon taking power, the KR launched a fantastical attempt to propel Cambodia nearly overnight into a "communist" future, requiring enormous sacrifice and suffering, and involving the destruction of centuries-old social institutions. That led to tremendous turmoil and suffering, while undermining or destroying the social and economic networks that might have made survival more feasible. The regime's economic failures, massive repression, and foreign-policy miscalculations rapidly engendered discontent, propelling the regime to accelerate its course of action. Like Stalin and Mao, the state blamed its failures on "hidden enemies," as Pol Pot had exclaimed only a few months after taking power.

The genocide unfolded in the context of the Cold War conflict between the USSR and the United States. Alongside this global political competition, the major "communist" powers (the Soviet Union and China) competed for influence among smaller left-wing or national liberation movements. For both these

---

[57]David Crowe, *War Crimes, Genocide, and Justice: A Global History* (New York: Palgrave Macmillan, 2014), 360–366.

[58]Kang Kek Iew, aka "Comrade Duch," had been detained since 1999 and was transferred to the ECCC in July 2007.

[59]Eben Saling, "Trial Chamber Finds Nuon Chea and Khieu Samphan Guilty of Crimes Against Humanity, Issues Life Sentences," *Cambodia Tribunal Monitor*, August 7, 2014: http://www.cambodiatribunal.org/2014/08/07/trial-chamber-finds-nuon-chea-and-khieu-samphan-guilty-of-crimes-against-humanity-issues-life-sentences/ (accessed August 8, 2014).

Cambodian refugees, 1979
As the Khmer Rouge regime crumbled, tens of thousands of desperate refugees fled to camps in Thailand. This 1979 photograph was taken at a camp near the Thai town of Aranyaprathet—a camp that, like most, was poorly provisioned. The Thai government exacerbated the refugees' plight by treating them as "illegal immigrants" and declining international aid from the UN and other agencies.

competitions—capitalist-Communist as well as inter-Communist—Southeast Asia, from Indonesia to Vietnam, was a major theater. The US government fought a lengthy and very destructive war in Vietnam in order, ostensibly, to prevent the advance of Communism, and to the south the Americans were committed to the survival of Indonesia's military dictatorship, which came to power after a bloodbath against its left-wing rivals in 1965–1966 and was a bastion of anti-communism.

As part of its global struggle with the Soviet Union, the US government in the early 1970s sought a closer relationship with the Chinese government, which had split acrimoniously from the USSR some years earlier. Accordingly, US policy was indulgent of Chinese clients or allies in the region, such as the Khmer Rouge. After exiting Vietnam in defeat, the Americans also wanted to do anything in their power to punish Vietnam and to weaken its influence—goals that again indirectly benefitted the Khmer Rouge. US National Security Adviser Henry Kissinger explained to the Thai foreign minister in November 1975 that the US government would "prefer to have Laos and Cambodia aligned with China rather than North Vietnam," and then emphasized the desirability of Chinese (rather than Vietnamese) influence in Cambodia. At this point, Kissinger notoriously uttered, "You should also tell the Cambodians [the Khmer Rouge] that we will be friends with them. They are murderous thugs, but we won't let that stand in the way."[60] For many

---

[60]"Memorandum of Conversation: Secretary's Meeting with Foreign Minister Chatchai of Thailand," November 26, 1975, available at The National Security Archive: http://www.gwu.edu/~nsarchiv/NSAEBB/NSAEBB193/HAK-11-26-75.pdf (accessed June 23, 2013).

years after its overthrow, the KR enjoyed the indirect diplomatic support of the American government.[61]

This context is important to consider, but the rise of the Khmer Rouge and the genocide were produced above all by local circumstances and traditions and by the regime's ability to implement its xenophobic and fantastical worldview. It is commonplace to describe the Khmer Rouge—as well as Stalin's party and state—as the polar opposite of fascism or as inhabiting the "far left" of the political spectrum. But in ideology, methods, values, and attitudes, a movement like the Khmer Rouge is much closer to modern right-wing ideologies. In many cases it is best to reject a simple left-right dichotomy, as if the KR and the German Nazis, as two examples, inhabit polar ends of an ideological spectrum. And ironically, the KR was shaped largely by the very forces it most abhorred: Western imperialism, in the form of European racial ideologies, and Vietnamese Communism, which played a leading role in the KR's origins, growth, and victory in the civil war of 1970–1975.

In summary, the CPK blended elements of Soviet and Chinese Communism with indigenous traditions to produce a distinctly xenophobic ideology, imbued not only with extreme nationalism and racism but also with a sense of urgency that legitimized massive violence and led the leadership far from reality. In March 1978, in one of many such examples, Pot Pot—having destroyed his country's educational system—proclaimed that his government had eliminated illiteracy. In the same speech, he optimistically but falsely declared, "We have eliminated malaria."[62] This sense of urgency was matched by the regime's wanton recklessness and disdain for human life: "Better to kill ten friends than to leave one enemy alive" went one party slogan.[63]

The end of the Cold War brought momentary hope that the world was entering a period of democratic progress and international unity. Optimism was quickly dispelled by a series of ruinous wars in Yugoslavia that killed at least 100,000, drove many more into flight, and introduced the ugly term "ethnic cleansing" to our lexicon. But that violence was eclipsed by a terrifying explosion of genocidal violence in central Africa that exceeded the Holocaust in murderous efficiency.

---

[61]Zbigniew Brzezinski, Jimmy Carter's national security adviser, later said, "I encouraged the Chinese to support Pol Pot. Pol Pot was an abomination. We could never support him, but China could." Elizabeth Becker, *When the War Was Over* (New York: Simon & Schuster, 1986), 440. Only a few years later, the US administration supported Saddam Hussein's Iraqi regime for similar reasons: it seemed to be a counterforce to a regional power (Iran) that was perceived as a more dire threat to US interests.
[62]Kamm, *Cambodia*, 134.
[63]Weitz, *Century*, 167.

PRIMARY SOURCES
AND STUDY QUESTIONS

Source 3.1: Two Khmer Rouge hymns

Like other political movements throughout the world, the Khmer Rouge composed or com-
missioned songs to celebrate its exploits and promote their worldview.

Like political or nationalist anthems from other parts of the world, these songs, in
form as well as content, reflect the country's culture and traditions. David Chandler, the
pioneering historian of Cambodia who collected these and other songs from the KR era,
noted that while the Khmer Rouge adapted existing folk tunes, their versions were to be
sung in unison (rather than by an individual), in accord with the songs' messages, "which
praise collective efforts at the expense of individual ones." Chandler added that these
songs were "used intensively by the regime . . . as part of its program of 'national culture'
and as weapons of the revolution." Survivors who later wrote memoirs, such as Loung Ung
(First They Killed My Father: A Daughter of Cambodia Remembers), *often recall the*
incessant singing of party anthems or chanting of slogans.

"The Beauty of Kampuchea"
O beautiful, beloved Kampuchea, our destiny has joined us
   together, uniting our forces so as not to disagree. Even
   young girls get up and join in the struggle.

Pity our friends who shoulder arms. Thorns pierce their feet;
   they do not complain; this is an accomplishment of Khmer
   children struggling until blood flows out to cover the ground.

They sacrifice themselves without regret, they chase the Lon Nol
   bandits, with swords and knives hacking at them, killing them,
   until the Lon Nol bandits are destroyed.

"Rainfall in Pisakh (April–May)"[64]
   The rain falls in pisakh. There's a cool breeze.
   Dear friends, the rain falls now and then.

SOURCE: From David Chandler, *The Early Phases of Liberation in Northwestern Cambodia: Con-*
versations with Peang Sophi (Melbourne: Monash University's Centre of Southeast Asian
Studies, 1977).
[64]Pisakh is a month on the lunar calendar that falls in April and/or May on the Gregorian
calendar. It is a time of greater rainfall in most of Cambodia, after the dry months of
January–March. Although not under the Khmer Rouge, a major festival ("Pisakh Bochea")
was conducted celebrating the Buddha's birthday and life.

We hear roosters crowing everywhere, and our brothers the peasants
Join together to increase production.

This is the sowing season: we toss corn and beans in front of us.
We strive to work, so as to supply the army,
Holding on and struggling at the front.

The Khmer are happy now, no longer feeling tired,
Striving to clear the road to peace.
All the Khmer children are happy,
For the revolution guides Khmer and Khmer toward solidarity.

Intertwined, as one, our angers shoots out at the imperialists—
The Americans, and their reactionary lackeys,
Killing them until they disappear.

Questions and Themes

1. Among the striking elements of Khmer Rouge songs are the transitions, which, with little if any warning, move from uplifting to violent imagery. But perhaps the Khmer Rouge did not detect these jarring shifts; maybe the extermination of enemies was a joyous activity.
2. These lyrics are calculated to foment violent, murderous rage against political enemies. Why would it be useful for the KR to fan the flames of such intense hatred?
3. Think about the absence of individuals in these two songs and the emphasis on the collective: self-sacrifice for the good of the revolution or nation.

Source 3.2: The Confession of Hu Nim

In the latter stages of its brief rule, the Khmer Rouge carried out large-scale purges, usually ending in the execution of party leaders deemed potential oppositionists. These purges replicated practices made notorious by Joseph Stalin in the Soviet Union. During "The Great Terror" of 1936–1938, tens of thousands of Soviet party and military officials were arrested on phony charges of economic sabotage, working on behalf of external enemies such as Nazi Germany, plotting Stalin's assassination, and so on. Many of these purge trials, which were later replicated in Eastern European countries after Communist parties took power following World War II, ended with unconvincing "confessions" and prompt executions. Some of the victims genuinely believed that their confessions might serve the larger cause (of building a "socialist" future), which they still believed in.

SOURCE: Courtesy of the Documentation Center of Cambodia.

After being implicated by another official who had been charged with "counterrevolutionary" activities, Hu Nim was arrested on April 10, 1977; while in custody he was tortured at the notorious Tuol Sleng (aka "S-21") prison; and he was executed on July 6. As you willl see in the reading, he "confesses" to working on behalf of American intelligence for many years; in fact, he never served the CIA in any capacity or even had contact with it.

Notes in brackets are my own; parentheses were inserted by the translators at the Documentation Center of Cambodia.

My father, Hou, died in 1936 when I was just six years old.[65] I then lived in the care of my mother, named Sorn, a poor peasant. . . . My [future] father-in-law's name was Va, and my mother-in-law's name was Leng. They were petty-bourgeois vendors at Tonle Bet Market, Tbaung Khmum District. My studies were made possible under [the] auspices of their elderly in-laws. After two years attendance, I passed Baccalaureate I and Baccalaureate II (French System). In 1952, I and Comrade Yeat entered into marriage, and then we moved to Phnom Penh.

1952: At Sisowath High School, I enrolled in the "People's Movement." . . . The movement served the CIA.

1957–1960: joined and served the CIA.

Eventually I prepared myself for being a representative.[66] As I told our Party earlier, to be a representative in Sangkum Reastr Niyum (Popular Socialist Community) I needed two sponsors. I met Phlek Phoeun, who I had known long before. He introduced me to Mao Say, who was a high CIA [agent]. They promised to support me in the election, on condition that "I accept their commands and accomplish missions given by the CIA." In the end I consented to their requirements. From that time I was a CIA agent. They promised to promote me, and my activities were carried out in connection with Mao Say's from then on.

Mao Say then assigned me to participate in two CIA newspapers: 1. Liberal People (Prachea Serei) headed by [the] contemptible Sim Va, a CIA. 2. Réalité Cambodgien managed by [the] contemptible Bare (CIA). These two newspapers were against people, revolution, socialism, and communism. They were written in favor of the U.S. capitalism, and imperialism.

To hide my real undertakings at the National Assembly, I joined the left wing chaired by Khieu Samphan [who, nearly twenty years later, was officially the head of state after the KR took power].

1961–1967: "Leftist (progressive) activities were just pictures, but their core meaning and strategic goals were for CIA's sake!"

My leftist activities, as a cover, were that the more activities I engaged in with socialist countries' embassies, especially with China, North Korea and North Viet Nam's, the warmer I felt. From 1962–1963, Sihanouk invited me to write for the

[65]Other sources indicate that Nim was born in 1932.
[66]Usually known as "the Sangkum," this party was set up by Prince Sihanouk in 1955 and included leftists such as Hu Nim, who was elected to the National Assembly, as a representative of the Sangkum, in 1958.

Nationalist newspaper (Neak Cheat Niyum) in order to assist the feudal capitalists and American imperialists. . . .

In July 1967 Lon Nol led several military officers to meet with Sihanouk and suggest that he give the order to arrest the three of us. This was another technique used by Mao Say, in order that the party would not suspect me and that I could burrow within the revolutionary movement even deeper. . . .

1968–1977: Mingled with the party members to destroy the party to serve the CIA. Details of my activities in that period of time have already been reported to the Party.

[Signed by Hu Nim, May 3, 1977]

Questions

1. Why do you think Hu Nim spoke about the social and class backgrounds of his family?
2. Hu Nim's claims to have worked for the CIA are absurd and unfounded. Why would the Khmer Rouge want to invent this narrative of an all-powerful American empire that had such extraordinary influence in Cambodia, and that regarded the Khmer Rouge as a dire threat to its interests?
3. Hu Nim was arrested after being denounced by another party leader, who had been tortured and compelled to turn in other "agents" or traitors. This is a typical pattern, which can be seen in purges in the USSR and elsewhere: "suspects" come up with names of supposed co-conspirators, and a deadly momentum builds. Do you see evidence of Hu Nim succumbing to the same pressure—that is, to name others (who doubtlessly were, like himself, innocent)?

Source 3.3: Interview with survivor Prak Sinan, age 59, Kampot (southern Cambodia, near Thailand), April 2013

The Cambodian Women's Oral History Project interviewed survivor Prak Sinan. Here are the notes from the interview: "Today, the most senior leaders of the Khmer Rogue regime are on trial for war crimes and crimes against humanity in a UN-back tribunal. . . . Among the charges is forced marriage, whereby thousands of Cambodians—both men and women—were assigned spouses, often complete strangers, and forced to marry in group weddings of up to one hundred couples. Traditional Khmer weddings are elaborate affairs lasting for a week or longer, with family and friends gathered and a Buddhist monk from a nearby pagoda officiating. In contrast, weddings during the Khmer Rouge

SOURCE: Courtesy of Cambodian Women's Oral History Project. Khmer transcription and English translation provided by Thorn Sina and You Sotheary, with editing provided by Theresa de Langis.

period lasted only a few minutes, excluded family and friends, and couples pledged loyalty not to each other but to the revolution. On the wedding night, cadres spied to be sure the marriage was consummated—and those who refused faced punishment or death.

As sexual relations were state-enforced, some have considered forced marriage as a form of state-ordered rape, with both men and women as victims . . . . Prak Sinan tells the story of her forced marriage to a disabled soldier during the regime. Her story also reveals the subtle ways women resisted the rape inherent to this system of marriage. Whispering to each other during the communal meal following the marriage ceremony, the women decided to persuade their spouses to avoid having children (and therefore sexual relations) while under the terrible burdens of the Khmer Rouge rule. Considering the dire health risks to pregnant women at the time, the plan likely saved some of these women's lives. Prak Sinan's story also demonstrates the human desire to preserve dignity and self-determination under acutely adverse circumstances, where cultural norms dictated that women could not openly refuse a husband's sexual advances."

Brackets with notes were inserted by the Cambodian Women's Oral History Project.

Q: Were you working with the mobile unit at the time?

PS: At the time [of my marriage], I was with the mobile unit. I was working on building the dyke of the rice field. My pants were torn from my work, and one day they sewed the pants for me and at about 4 pm they called me and said my name was on a list. The list had the names of 38 couples, paring people from my unit with people from other units. I was the 30th couple on that list. When they called for me, I had no idea it was for my wedding; I thought it was just another meeting. So when I went to join the meeting, I came from the field, and I was carrying my hoe and wearing my old clothes. I joined the other women, and we sat under the mango tree, and we waited for some time. Then, they told the men to stand in one row and the women to stand in another row. They called the men one by one to stand next to a woman, one by one, until there were 38 pairs. There was no choosing. . . .

[After the ceremony, each couple was sent to a private hut to consummate the marriage]

Q: Can you tell us about the wedding night? You were strangers to each other, so what was the first thing you and your husband talked about?

PS: He didn't say anything at first, he was just quiet, so I was the first to speak. I said, "This day we come together as spouses, but you should forgive me as I don't have enough food to feed myself. What then for our children? Our children will not have food to eat, or schooling. How can we give birth to them, for what reason? We should forgive each other, and when the country is independent again, you can meet me at my parents' house to ask for our marriage in the traditional way. I will wait for you. . . ."

We already knew the trick of the *chhlop*[67] to spy on every room to make sure the couple was not arguing about the marriage, or they will kill us immediately.

---

[67]KR spies, usually teenagers.

They went to listen at every room to make sure the pair was getting along on their wedding night [and having sexual relations]. We knew this trick. While we ate the wedding dinner, the women had whispered to each other. We decided we should not argue or resist, or we will be killed. We had to be careful because we were already marked for killing because of our family connections.

Q: Do you mean the women decided to pretend to have sexual relations but to try to get out of it?

PS: We only talked among the women. We dared not talk to the husband until we got in the room they gave each pair. In that room, we could talk. I could talk to him, but I could not refuse my husband or ban [him from having sexual relations]. I talked about not having a baby, without food or education, or a bright future at all. I just told him very simply like that. [Like the other married couples, we did not live together], and he came to visit me for a night now and then, and he brought some daily things, like toothbrush, toothpaste, soap and more from his army supplies. And then the next morning he hurried to go back to work with his unit. He always honored our agreement that we should not have children, so I felt pity for him, seeing him go. But he understood me and what I was saying. He had been a student in his home village of Kampong Cham. He was also a kind person, and we promised to meet each other again when the country had peace.

Questions

1. What was the purpose in organizing large-scale forced marriages? How does this relate to the Khmer Rouge's aim of creating an utterly new society?
2. What are some of the ways in which Prak Sinan, and the others she alludes to, seek to assert their humanity, help one another, and resist the regime?
3. The Khmer Rouge sought to control and monitor the most intimate aspects of Cambodians' lives, including their sexuality. Think about the fact the KR often assigned young teenage men (or boys) to monitor and police the populace. What does all this tell us about the KR's obsessions, social attitudes, and methods?

4

THE RWANDAN GENOCIDE

The truth is that many Hutus could not bear the Tutsis anymore. Why? That stubborn question haunts the banana groves.

—Claudine Kayitesi, Tutsi survivor[1]

AS THE "CENTURY OF genocide" neared its conclusion, the Nazi Holocaust had become widely known and commemorated in much of the world and had helped attract attention to other genocides and atrocities. The US Holocaust Memorial Museum was opened in Washington, DC, in April 1993. While standing in line to visit the museum one year later, journalist Philip Gourevitch "tried to read a local newspaper" to pass the time. "But I couldn't get past a photograph on the front page: bodies swirling in the water, dead bodies, bloated and colorless, bodies so numerous that they jammed each other and clogged the stream." Looking up from the newspaper's ghastly image from the ongoing Rwandan genocide, Gourevitch "saw a group of museum staffers arriving for work. On their maroon blazers, several wore the lapel buttons that sold for a dollar each in the museum shop, inscribed with the words 'Remember' and 'Never Again.'"[2]

In "the most efficient mass killing since the atomic bombings of Hiroshima and Nagasaki," somewhere between 500,000 and 800,000 people were killed in barely one hundred days in this small east-central African nation.[3] Most victims were

---

[1]Jean Hatzfeld, *Life Laid Bare: The Survivors in Rwanda Speak* (New York: Other Press, 2006), 202.
[2]Philip Gourevitch, *We Wish to Inform You That Tomorrow We Will be Killed with Our Families* (New York: Farrar, Straus and Giroux, 1998), 151–152.
[3]Ibid., 3. Adam Jones points out that the Nazis' killing of Soviet POWs in 1941–1942 may have actually been the most murderously efficient, extensive, concentrated mass murder in history: 2.8 million killed in 8 months. Jones, *Genocide: A Comprehensive Introduction* (New York: Routledge, 2010), 271.

members of the Tutsi minority, a group that lost half its population. Nearly all surviving Tutsi "both witnessed a killing and lost at least one family member."[4]

Shocking and sudden as the bloodshed seemed to outsiders, during the previous three or four years there had been many warnings of the impending violence, and once it began it was quickly and widely reported. The phrase "never again," a well-meaning platitude often invoked when commemorating the Holocaust, proved utterly hollow.

RWANDAN HISTORY AND EUROPEAN RACIAL PHILOSOPHIES

The region conforming closely to present-day Rwanda is a small part of the "Great Lakes" region of central and eastern Africa. This area includes present-day Burundi, another small country whose history has been closely connected to Rwanda's. The much larger Congo, which was called Zaire when the events discussed in this chapter took place, dominates central Africa and was the object of European colonial intrigue and competition in the nineteenth century.

During the sixteenth century Rwanda had come under the control of a king from the Tutsi group. By the late 1800s, the Kingdom of Rwanda was a centralized, unified state and with a strong military under the leadership of the powerful Kigeli IV (reigned 1853–1895), the king or "mwami" in the Kinyarwanda language. After his death, Rwanda was not strong enough to avoid falling under the control of Germany, which took advantage of the disarray among Tutsi royal factions. The Germans established indirect rule over Rwanda and Burundi, incorporating them into German East Africa (most of which is now Tanzania). These decisions were made at a conference in Brussels in 1890, which, like a similar conference in Berlin a few years earlier (1884–1885), decided upon boundaries and colonial spheres of influence without the input of any African—and, in this case, before any German had set foot in the country.

After genocidal campaigns against Herero and Nama in Southwest Africa (1904–1907; see the Introduction) and the murderous suppression of a rebellion in East Africa, Germany's colonial army invaded Hutu regions of northern Rwanda.[5] The Germans were assisted by Tutsi royal forces, contributing to long memories among the Hutu of colonial favoritism toward the Tutsi. Germany lost control of

---

[4]David Simon, "Researching Genocide in Africa: Establishing Ethnological and Historical Context," in Adam Jones, ed., *New Directions in Genocide Research* (New York: Routledge, 2012), 257.

[5]In suppressing the "Maji Maji Rebellion" in present-day Tanzania of 1905–1907, German forces used tactics similar to those employed in the Herero genocide (see Introduction): massacres of civilians, deliberate destruction of wells and food supplies, and famine. At least 200,000 Africans died; in contrast, fifteen German soldiers and a few hundred African auxiliary troops are believed to have perished. Isabel V. Hull, "Military Culture and the Production of 'Final Solutions' in the Colonies: The Example of Wilhelminian Germany," in Robert Gellately and Ben Kiernan, eds., *The Specter of Genocide: Mass Murder in Historical Perspective* (New York: Cambridge University Press, 2003), 161.

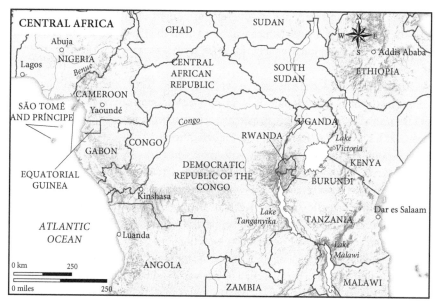

Contemporary Central Africa

its East African colonies during World War I, and after the war would be stripped of its remaining colonies in the west and southwest of the continent. Belgian troops occupied Rwanda in 1916, and after the war the League of Nations gave Belgium control of "Ruanda and Urundi"—Rwanda and the land to its immediate south, Burundi. The two were administered jointly until they split and gained independence between 1960 and 1962.

For centuries, Rwanda (as well as Burundi) has been populated almost entirely by three ethnic or social groups—the Hutu, Tutsi, and much smaller number of Twa—which originate and live in the same regions and share the same language (Kinyarwanda), clans, and religions, and have often intermarried.[6] Indeed, Hutu and Tutsi do not constitute "tribes," the term that was commonly used in the English-speaking news media when Rwanda came to its attention in the 1990s. While "tribe" can be interpreted in different ways, it usually refers to a micro-nation. Based on this definition, if tribes existed in Rwanda and Burundi, then a "Hutuland" and a "Tutsiland" would have existed in some form; but this was not the case.[7] "Tutsi" originally described social status, based on ownership of cattle, while "Hutu" implied a subordinate status. These ideas evolved into a perception of Tutsi as "pastoralists and power-holders" and Hutu as "cultivators and subjects." Before European colonization, though, these identities and perceptions varied in

---

[6]The Twa are a hunter-gather people, as opposed to the pastoralist Tutsi.
[7]Gérard Prunier, *The Rwanda Crisis: History of a Genocide* (New York: Columbia University Press, 1997), 5.

different regions and were not considered permanent or biologically determined: A Hutu could become a Tutsi (which was more desirable), perhaps by simply acquiring a few cows. "Caste" is probably the most accurate way to characterize the two groups.

The meaning and social implications of "Hutu" and "Tutsi" were drastically transformed by German and especially Belgian authorities. Upon taking control of Rwanda and Burundi, Belgium promptly dispatched scientists equipped with tools to measure noses, skull sizes, and so forth. Catholic Church officials also descended on the country in large numbers and worked closely with the colonialists, helping to determine and record ethnic designations. In 1933, Belgian authorities—in part because they were troubled by extensive intermarriage, which was making it harder to discern physical differences between the groups—began to require all Rwandans to carry identity cards designating their ethnicity.[8] (The population was determined to be 85 percent Hutu, 14 percent Tutsi, and 1 percent Twa—proportions that remained fairly constant until the genocide.) Because of these ID cards and Belgian records, it became much more difficult for Hutu to become Tutsi or vice versa. Additionally, the colonialists imposed strict segregation in religious, educational, and state institutions.

In brief, European colonialism not only exploited Africans: more dangerously, it "racialized" preexisting ethnic distinctions and social hierarchies. For their part, the Belgians created and then codified a rigid division between Hutu and Tutsi and invested it with European notions of race. For this they drew upon the work of an eccentric colonial adventurer of the previous century. A book by a British explorer, John Hanning Speke, was the source of many theories applied to Rwanda and Burundi. Speke made three trips to eastern Africa and, although he was nearly blind during his second and third expeditions, he published a lengthy collection of speculations in 1863, a few months before accidentally shooting and killing himself.

With little pretense of evidence or scientific precision, Speke's *Journal of the Discovery of the Source of the Nile* posited that the Tutsis' ancestors were "carriers of a superior civilization" who came from "the Galla of southern Ethiopia." Subsequent explorers would enhance this strange ethnography. Racially obsessed European authors rhapsodized about the relative physical beauty of the Tutsi, which they contrasted to the "inferior" Bantus. Speke and his successors also celebrated the "Hamitic" and even "Semitic" origins of the Tutsi, whose "love of money" and "capacity to adapt to any situation seem to indicate a Semitic-origin" according to another writer, invoking an anti-Jewish canard. Respected anthropologists took this race fixation even further, speculating that the Tutsi had "an absolutely distinct origin from the negroes." Some said they came from "a primordial red race," others that they hailed from India; a Dominican friar even suggested they originated in

---

[8] James Waller, *Becoming Evil: How Ordinary People Commit Genocide and Mass Killing* (New York: Oxford University Press, 2007), 222.

Racial identification card

Beginning in 1933 Belgian colonial administrators hardened the Hutu-Tutsi distinction by issuing identification cards that indicated the holder's "race" or "ethnicity" listed toward the top left in this image. (This card used the French word for "race"; others used the French word for "ethnicity"; the Kinyarwandan word, "ubwoke," means "tribe" or "ethnicity.") These cards were still used after decolonization, and during the genocide many Tutsi were identified and killed because of this. Some Hutu who presumably looked like Tutsi, and had lost their cards, were also killed.

the Garden of Eden, while a Belgian administrator, in 1926, contended that they were the last survivors of the mythical lost city of Atlantis.[9]

The Belgian colonizers believed that the Tutsi were destined to dominate—within the constraints of indirect European rule—because of their presumed racial superiority. The notion that the Tutsi originated in Egypt, Ethiopia, or elsewhere created the image that they were foreign invaders or interlopers: an image that would be skillfully invoked later and serve as a cornerstone of the genocidal philosophy that was implemented in 1994. Thus, the policies of German and especially Belgian authorities "inflat[ed] the Tutsi cultural ego inordinately and crush[ed] Hutu feelings until they coalesced into an aggressively resentful inferiority complex."[10] Exacerbating the division was the manner in which the groups

---

[9]Prunier, *Rwanda Crisis*, 7–8, and Elizabeth Neuffer, *The Key to My Neighbor's House: Seeking Justice in Bosnia and Rwanda* (New York: Picador, 2002), 87.
[10]Prunier, *Rwanda Crisis*, 9.

were defined as "opposing negatives: a Hutu was what a Tutsi was not, and vice versa."[11]

As in other lands in the colonial world, many of the Europeans' subjects eventually accepted and absorbed key elements of these constructions. In 1957, future president Grégoire Kayibanda and other Hutu nationalists composed the "Bahutu Manifesto," a major step in the creation of a Hutu political movement that would soon take power. The Manifesto was probably the first explicit example of the absorption and promotion of the colonizers' racial theories; it labeled the Tutsi as an "alien race" traceable to "Hamitic invaders from the north." These ideas have long outlived colonialism: "They come from Somalia. And then [they stole] that which exists in [our] country—the livestock, cows, chickens, domestic animals. . . . All the wealth of the country . . . was ours," declared a Hutu farmer after the 1994 disaster. "We were the natives of the country."[12] In 2013, I was startled to overhear a diatribe, delivered by an agitated Hutu businessman to a Tutsi restaurant worker, that repeated several of these notions in, of all places, Kigali's Hôtel des Mille Collines—a sanctuary for Tutsi during the genocide. The idea that the Hutu were the native, authentic Rwandans, while the Tutsi were foreign invaders, was particularly poisonous and, eventually, lethal. (In fact, if any group has a claim to "native" status in Rwanda, it is the Twa, who have historically been marginalized and discriminated against by both Tutsi and Hutu.) During the carnage of 1994, Hutu killers would sometimes dump their victims' corpses into tributaries of Lake Victoria, in order to carry them northward along the Nile to their supposed original homelands.

Fear and hatred toward one's neighbors did not come easily for everyone, even after generations of socialization about Tutsi-Hutu differences. "As far back as I can remember," wrote Rwandan sociologist Marie Béatrice Umutesi, who was born in 1959, "our house was full of Hutu and Tutsi children, neighbors and orphans that my mother took under her wing. I have no memory of preferences based on the ethnicity" of any of the children, and it was only later that she realized that she was designated Hutu. As with other racial inventions, the Hutu-Tutsi division defies scientific or sociological precision, and is further blurred by extensive marriage and other relations between members of the two groups. As Umutesi reported, during the genocide "Hutu with refined features were killed at the roadblocks, whereas Tutsi with Hutu features remained safe."[13]

Even if the more fanciful racial theories of Speke and others had subsided by the mid-twentieth century, Belgium continued to employ the classic colonialist strategy of divide and rule, favoring the Tutsi minority. In the late 1950s, 549 of 559

---

[11]Gourevitch, *We Wish to Inform*, 50.

[12]Liisa Malkki, *Purity and Exile: Violence, Memory, and National Cosmology among Hutu Refugees in Tanzania* (Chicago: University of Chicago Press, 1995), 67.

[13]Marie Béatrice Umutesi, *Surviving the Slaughter: The Ordeal of a Rwandan Refugee in Zaire* (Madison, WI: University of Wisconsin Press, 2000), 6–7. In the Rwandan language (Kinyarwanda), the plurals of "Hutu" and "Tutsi" are indicated by a prefix, rather than a final "s" (for example, "uMahutu" is singular for "Hutu" and "aMahutu" is the plural).

subchiefs were Tutsi.[14] This is only one of many examples of this favoritism, which further sowed the seeds for strife and violence in the post-independence era by deepening a sense of grievance and resentment that was keenly felt by many Hutu.

EMERGENCE OF HUTU PARTIES AND INDEPENDENCE

Independence movements gained strength throughout the continent after World War II, and most African nations won their self-determination between 1956 and 1964. In Rwanda, a series of events in the late 1950s and early 1960s laid the foundations for the terrible events of 1994. Belgium recognized it would have to relinquish its rule; the Tutsi elite and its political party, the Rwandan National Front, attempted to cling to power, resorting to violence against Hutu as well as Tutsi dissidents; Belgian administrators reversed their long-standing support for the Tutsi, and in November 1959 they backed the emerging Hutu movement and mounted a military operation on its behalf, helping to overthrow the monarchy; and a Hutu–dominated government was consolidated. Rwanda was transformed from a Belgian possession with a modicum of Tutsi elite control into a Hutu ethnocracy—a "one-party racial dictatorship," as a UN report termed it, under the veneer of a Hutu-majority democracy.[15]

The new government purged Tutsi from regional power structures and encouraged anti-Tutsi violence, which broke out in several deadly episodes between 1959 and 1964. The best-known incident occurred in Gikongoro in southern Rwanda, where government troops killed 5,000 to 10,000 Tutsi in January 1964.[16] In a pattern that would be reproduced more than once in the three decades before the genocide, the strife culminating in the Gikongoro killings began with a December 1963 invasion by a Tutsi-led guerilla band, in this case only a few hundred troops from a base in Burundi. The group was easily defeated, but the government nonetheless declared a national state of emergency and launched an extensive massacre, augmented by Hutu mob violence.[17] Periodic invasions of exile-based militias reinforced the image of Tutsi as foreign invaders and made it easier for the government to conflate Tutsi residing in Rwanda with Tutsi in exile. Ultimately, some 200,000 Tutsi fled or were driven into exile during those first five years of Hutu dominance and at least 50,000 were killed. The refugees settled primarily in Uganda, Burundi, Tanzania, and Zaire, and would provide the manpower for guerilla forces, called "inyenzi" ("cockroach" or "cockroaches") by the Hutu government and its propagandists.[18]

---

[14]Scott Straus, *The Order of Genocide: Race, Power, and War in Rwanda* (Cornell, NY: Cornell University Press, 2008), 181.

[15]Ibid., 182.

[16]Jacques Sémelin, *Purify and Destroy: The Political Uses of Massacre and Genocide* (New York: Columbia University Press, 2009), 67.

[17]Gourevitch, *We Wish to Inform*, 64–65.

[18]In the Kinyarwanda language, the singular and plural of "inyenzi" are the same.

HABYARIMANA'S "SECOND REPUBLIC"

Rwandan politics entered a new era with a July 1973 coup d'état led by Juvénal Habyarimana, who then proclaimed the Second Republic while instituting a one-party state.[19] To the south in Burundi in the summer of 1972, the Tutsi-led government and military carried out a genocidal campaign against Hutu, starting with educated elites, eventually killing between 100,000 and 200,000 people and sparking a mass exodus into Rwanda, one of several mass movements between the two countries between the late 1950s and the mid-1990s. Habyarimana and some other high-ranking army officers took power pledging to end anti-Tutsi violence that had broken out in response, and initially the new president announced his government's intention to end ethnic divisions and foster national unity. For much of the first fifteen years of his rule, Habyarimana's government presided over a period of economic growth and political stability. Yet his regime maintained a quota system to preserve Hutu privilege and encouraged or at least tolerated an extreme anti-Tutsi faction, the "akazu," which was led by his wife Agathe and other northern Hutu.

Several factors converged to destabilize the Habyarimana regime in the late 1980s and early 1990s: a severe economic crisis from 1985 onward, instigated by the precipitous fall in prices on the world market for coffee beans, the country's chief export; the resulting increase in poverty, fueling discontent among Hutu as well as Tutsi; and, in response, the emergence of a stronger Hutu political opposition, which criticized the government's inept handling of the deepening crisis and also exploited public dismay over the indiscreet displays of wealth by the president and his coterie. In characteristic fashion, the International Monetary Fund (IMF) imposed an "economic reform" package that forced the government to devalue its currency, which produced drastic inflation; to accept austerity measures; and to impose or increase user fees, which poor Rwandans were obliged to pay for education, health care, and "even access to water." As historian Catherine Newbury argued, these policies exacerbated poverty and "contributed significantly to social tensions and fear."[20]

The event that led most directly to the genocide was the October 1, 1990, invasion by the Rwandan Patriotic Front (RPF), an army composed and led largely by Tutsi who were a generation removed from the expulsion of their parents at the dawn of the Rwandan Republic thirty years earlier. The RPF was based in Uganda, where many Rwandan Tutsi exiles, including future RPF leaders such as Paul Kagame, had fought alongside Yoweri Museveni in a civil war that concluded with the victory of Museveni's National Resistance Army in 1986. (Museveni promised

---

[19]This party was the National Revolutionary Movement for Development (*Mouvement Révolutionnaire National pour le Développement*), known as the MRND.

[20]Catherine Newbury, "Background to Genocide: Rwanda," *Issue: A Journal of Opinion*, 23, no. 2 (1995), 14.

President Juvénal Habyarimana
President Juvénal Habyarimana visiting an Air Force base in Maryland, U.S., in 1980. The president, whose inner circle in later years included Hutu-power extremists—his wife Agathe Habyarimana prominent among them—enjoyed the support of many Western governments, principally France. Habyarimana's assassination—his airplane was shot down on April 6, 1994—served as the catalyst for the genocide: His wife and others immediately launched plans, already prepared, to kill important moderate politicians and exterminate the Tutsi.

to repay this service by helping these Rwandan Tutsi return to their country by force.) The RPF also drew upon Tutsi exiles in other nearby countries, but initially had little internal support and no organization within Rwanda. The RPF's 1990 offensive reinforced the long-held image of Tutsi as foreigners and aggressors. In its alarmist propaganda the Habyarimana government and the Hutu Power groups linked the RPF to domestic Tutsi—most of whom, remembering reprisals after earlier incursions by Tutsi-exile militias, were not enthusiastic about the RPF offensive.[21] The offensive provoked immediate, harsh reprisals against Rwandan Tutsi. On October 11, local authorities in the north-central town of Kibilira organized the killing of approximately 350 Tutsi civilians. This and other massacres over the next three years served as precursors of the genocide and involved a widening number of killers, who became adjusted to their duties and desensitized to

---

[21]In recent years, some scholars have pointed out—without shifting the responsibility for the genocide away from its Hutu architects—that RPF leader and future president Paul Kagame must have known that the offensive would provoke violence against Rwanda's Tutsi, but he was not overly concerned with these likely consequences. See Straus, *Order of Genocide*.

the suffering they were meting out. Meanwhile, the central government in Kigali began organizing civilian defense units after the RPF offensive, another significant step toward the eventual mass participation of civilians in carrying out anti-Tutsi pogroms and massacres. It must be noted that the RPF committed its own crimes against civilians during and after the war. As Gérard Prunier notes in his extensively researched history of the wars in Rwanda and Congo, "the whole life history of these men"—the "hard core" of the RPF, who "grew up as refugees in the violence of the Ugandan civil wars"—had been shaped by warfare "with its attendant atrocities and civilian massacres, committed against them, committed around them, or by them."[22] The RPF offensive also drove hundreds of thousands of Hutu civilians into internal exile, where some would later be recruited (often forcefully) by the genocidal killing squads.

The ever-worsening crisis prompted the akazu faction and other extremists to strengthen and expand a movement that by late 1993 would be called "Hutu Power" and that included members of assorted Hutu political and paramilitary groups. The magazine *Kangura*, founded in late 1990 with close connections to the government and military, served as a prominent mouthpiece for this more aggressive, racial Hutu nationalism. In December 1990, *Kangura* published "The Hutu Ten Commandments," which called for strict segregation, the maintenance of Hutu privilege in all spheres, and vigilance against the Tutsi and any Hutu "traitors." It included such alarming demands as "The Hutu should stop having mercy on the Tutsi."[23] This document's importance is sometimes exaggerated because of what we now know in hindsight. But at the least the "Ten Commandments" set down in writing certain key themes and paranoid delusions of Hutu-power advocates. The document is revealing in the emphasis it places upon women. It warns against the Tutsi woman who works "for the interest" of her group and seeks to infiltrate the Hutu populace by marrying, befriending, or being a "concubine" of a Hutu; any Hutu who allows this is a "traitor." The "Ten Commandments" simultaneously stresses the need to protect and celebrate Hutu women. "Are they not more beautiful, good secretaries and more honest?"[24] This obsession with protecting the purity of the women in the dominant population is reminiscent of other racist groups or societies, from the American South during the Jim Crow era (1877–1965) to Nazi Germany. Further, the "traitor" label was ominous; "traitors" as well as Tutsi would later be killed.

Throughout the early 1990s *Kangura*—which roughly translates as "wake others up"—kept up its drumbeat of alarmist, paranoid propaganda. A 1992 issue warned

---

[22]Gérard Prunier, *Africa's World War: Congo, the Rwandan Genocide, and the Making of a Continental Catastrophe* (New York: Oxford University Press, 2009), 13.

[23]The full text of the "Ten Commandments," as it appeared in *Kangura*, is available (translated to English for a post-genocide trial) at http://www.rwandafile.com/Kangura/k06 .html (accessed July 28, 2015). In Kinyarwanda: http://www.genocidearchiverwanda.org .rw/index.php?title=Kangura_Issue_06 (accessed May 8, 2013).

[24]*Kangura*, December 6, 1990, "The Ten Commandments": http://www.rwandafile.com/ Kangura/k06a.html (accessed March 3, 2014).

Anti-Tutsi Propaganda

A characteristic image from the Hutu-power newspaper *Kangura*. Published two months before the genocide ensued, this cartoon depicts a debauched General Dallaire—who had already made himself unpopular to the government and the Hutu-power fanatics—being manipulated by Tutsi seductresses. The text translates as "General Dallaire and his army have fallen into the trap of the [Tutsi] femme fatales." The obsession with Tutsi women and their presumed deviousness and haughtiness was also a common theme in Hutu-extremist propaganda.

its readers that "a proud and bloodthirsty minority mixed with you in order to dilute you, divide you, dominate you and massacre you."[25] A March 1993 issue is chillingly similar to other violent racist agitators: "a Tutsi stays always exactly the same . . . he has never changed," blaming the Tutsi for all the "malice" and "evil" that blighted Rwandan history.[26]

1993 STRIFE IN NEIGHBORING BURUNDI

Given their "parallel—and at times common—past histories" and "comparable social structures," Burundi and Rwanda have long been "two opposite ends of a political seesaw," as one expert phrased it—reflections of "each other's hopes, woes and transformations." Political turmoil or violence in one country often sparked counteractions in the other.[27] In June 1993 Melchior Ndadaye was elected president of Burundi. He was that nation's first Hutu president and garnered nearly two-thirds of the vote in an election deemed free and fair by international observers. His Tutsi rival in the election calmly accepted the results, and the handover of

---

[25]Ben Kiernan, *Blood and Soil: A World History of Genocide and Extermination from Sparta to Darfur* (New Haven, CT: Yale University Press, 2007), 558.
[26]Ibid., 559.
[27]Prunier, *Rwanda Crisis*, 198.

power appeared to be going smoothly. But on October 21, President Ndadaye was kidnapped and murdered by soldiers led by Tutsi extremists. The assassination sparked anti-Tutsi pogroms by Hutu organizations, which the Tutsi army responded to with excessive and often indiscriminate violence. Approximately 50,000 people were killed over the next few weeks, maybe 60 percent of them Tutsi. Three hundred thousand Hutu fled, most of them to Rwanda. They brought tales of the terror they had suffered at hands of Burundi's Tutsi army, which needed no exaggeration, but which provided valuable propaganda for Rwanda's radical Hutu groups. Many of these refugees would be recruited, a few months later, into the death squads that hunted down Tutsi.

DASHED HOPES FOR PEACE

In July 1993 Habyarimana's government began negotiations in Tanzania mediated by the Organization of African Unity (OAU) and diplomats from France and the United States. In August the parties announced the Arusha Accords, which stipulated power-sharing between the Habyarimana government and the RPF and the merger of government and RPF troops. The Accords also led to the establishment of the UN Assistance Mission for Rwanda (UNAMIR)—peace-keeping troops from the UN, to be composed of troops from Belgium, Canada, and Ghana and handful of other countries—as well as a peace-keeping contingent from the OAU to presumably enforce the Accords.

The possibility of peace threatened the Hutu Power extremists, who launched Radio-Télévision Libre des Mille Collines ("Free Radio-Television of One Thousand Hills," better known by its initials, RTLM)[28] just a few days before the talks in Tanzania began. In a country in which two-thirds of the population was illiterate, but nearly one-third owned a radio, this station had a larger audience and was more effective than *Kangura*.[29] The rebels were intent on reimposing Tutsi "feudal" rule, preached RTLM, which combined fear with hatred in its propaganda. Allison des Forges, a historian who in the early 1990s directed her full-time energies to human rights advocacy for central Africa, described this propaganda strategy as the "accusation in a mirror": to convince the public that "the enemy" will bring war, oppression, murder, and so on—in other words, to ascribe to the enemy what you yourselves are planning, thereby justifying preventive, "defensive" action.[30]

---

[28]A reference to the nickname bestowed upon Rwanda for its hilly, verdant landscape: the "Land of a Thousand Hills."

[29]Robert Melson, "Modern Genocide in Rwanda," in Gellately and Kiernan, eds., *The Specter of Genocide*, 333.

[30]Allison Des Forges, *Leave None to Tell the Story: Genocide in Rwanda* (New York: Human Rights Watch, 1999), 65–66. Before her tragic death in an airplane crash in 2009, Des Forges testified several times at the international tribunal that was established to try genocide suspects; she also served for many years as a "senior advisor" for African affairs for Human Rights Watch.

Des Forges summed up the period between the RPF invasion and the geno-cide (October 1990–April 1994) thus: A core group of hardliners within the ruling party radicalized in the face of the threat from the RPF as well as from domestic Hutu opposition; in order to keep power, they formed paramilitaries, funded racist media propaganda, and prepared to do whatever was necessary to retain power; as these threats worsened, the ruling party elite opted for genocide.[31]

ASSASSINATION OF HABYARIMANA AND THE DESCENT INTO GENOCIDE

The temporary hope raised by the Arusha Accords was destroyed by the assas-sination of President Habyarimana on the evening of April 6, 1994. Accompa-nied by Burundian president Cyprien Ntaryamira, Habyarimana was killed when his plane was shot down by a missile as it approached the airport of the Rwandan capital, Kigali. Hutu hardliners had incentive to get the president out of their way and to create a pretext for the well-planned massacres; yet the plane accident also killed some important figures among the Hutu-power ex-tremists, and it occurred at a time that was not propitious for that faction (because some high-ranking government officials were out of the country).[32] A 2004 French inquiry, which could be easily dismissed by the Kagame govern-ment because of France's earlier relationship with Habyarimana and its ongo-ing diplomatic feuds with the post-genocide government, asserted that the RPF was responsible. Yet a second French inquiry, concluded in 2012, that the missile was shot from an area that "was held by the Rwandan army—a unit of elite presidential troops."[33] Further clouding these issues, several former RPF leaders have claimed that Kagame ordered the missile attack. Rose Kabuye, a long-time RPF military and political leader, was arrested in Germany in 2008 on charges related to the assassination; she was eventually released and returned to a government post in Kigali but was fired by Kagame in 2010. Another former Kagame ally, Abdul Ruzibiza, wrote a book in 2005 in which he "confessed" to involvement in the assassination on behalf of the RPF, but he later recanted significant parts of his book.[34] Among scholars and other experts, a solid consensus on the question of responsibility has not yet taken

---

[31]Des Forges, *Leave None*, 522–524.
[32]Strauss, *Order of Genocide*, 45.
[33]"Rwanda genocide: Kagame 'cleared of Habyarimana crash,'" BBC, February 10, 2012 (http://www.bbc.com/news/world-africa-16472013, accessed April 14, 2014).
[34]Lieutenant Abdul Joshua Ruzibiza, *Rwanda: L'histoire secrète* (Paris: Éditions du Panama, 2005); Patrick de Saint-Exupéry, "Key witness in Kabuye trial retracts testi-mony," Radio France, November 19, 2008: http://www1.rfi.fr/actuen/articles/107/arti-cle_2190.asp (accessed April 15, 2014). Ruzibiza died in 2010 at the age of forty; no foul play was suspected.

shape. For an event with such momentous consequences, the assassination remains under-investigated.[35]

The identity of the culprits is less significant than the pretext it offered to unscrupulous politicians and Hutu Power advocates. Colonel Théoneste Bagosora, who at the time of the president's death was Cabinet Director in the Ministry of Defense, led a group of zealots that formed a Provisional Government, set up by military leaders the day after the airplane crash. There were initially some divisions in the party and army elite over the plan, initiated within hours, to annihilate the Tutsi population. These divisions were quickly overcome, and within hours Bagosora and his accomplices began the elimination of Hutu oppositionists, many of whom had been selected beforehand, and the initiation of mass murder of Tutsi.[36] The Hutu prime minister, Agathe Uwilingiyimana, was murdered in a grisly fashion the morning after the president's assassination, as were the ten Belgian peace-keeping troops who were supposed to protect her—despite the fact that they had already laid down their arms. Other prominent figures who were viewed with suspicion by Hutu-power radicals were also murdered: the president of the Constitutional Court, the Minister of Information, various liberal politicians and civil rights activists, the editor of a newspaper that had argued against the extremists, a former foreign minister who had negotiated the Arusha Accords, and so on.[37] These murders were instrumental in solidifying the takeover of power by the Provisional Government, composed principally of remnants of the Habyarimana regime.

On its first full day in power, this new government and allied groups launched the systematic murder of the country's Tutsi population. Much of the killing was done by the Interahamwe ("those who stand together," sometimes translated as "those who attack together"). The Interahamwe originated in the youth wing of the MRND over the two years prior to the genocide. "Hardliners within the military and MRND party hierarchy siphoned off some youth," explained Scott Straus in his penetrating analysis of the genocide, "and trained them militarily."[38] The groups, augmented by other militias such as the Impuzamugambi ("Those with a Single Purpose"), only had about 50,000 members when the genocide started, but they quickly "recruited," often coercively, tens of thousands of additional members once the killing began. The majority came from the vast pool of Hutu internally

---

[35]In a 2008 article, Tiphaine Dickson termed it "what is arguably history's least-investigated political assassination." Dickson, "Rwanda's Deadliest Secret: Who Shot Down President Habyarimana's Plane?," Global Research, November 24, 2008.

[36]It has become standard to use the term "moderate Hutu" to designate Hutu victims of the genocide. That term, though, is imprecise, implying that all Hutu victims were more or less within the same political camp. Some were politically moderate; some were immoderate; and many were apolitical. These terms are admittedly wordy but would more accurately describe the categories to which Hutu victims belonged: "Real or potential opponents of the genocidal regime"; "Hutu civilians who opposed the killing"; "Hutu who had close Tutsi relatives"—and also "Hutu who were misidentified as Tutsi."

[37]Prunier, *Rwanda Crisis*, 230, 242–243.

[38]Straus, *Order of Genocide*, 26.

displaced persons (IDPs), driven from their homes by the advance of RPF in the north. By early April, there were about 1 million IDPs scattered across forty camps.

Interahamwe gangs armed principally with machetes hunted down and slaughtered Tutsi in their houses; at improvised checkpoints; in large gathering places such as churches and schools; and in the marshes and swamps where survivors had sought refuge, or where some Tutsi had fled immediately upon hearing of the president's death. "We'd never gone near" the marshes before "because of the mosquitos and snakes and the boundless mistrust they inspired" said Claudine Kayitesi, a twenty-one-year-old mother at the time. But upon hearing news of the president's death, "I joined other fugitives in the forest" near her town of Kanzenze in central Rwanda. "Without slowing down for a second, we dove on our bellies into the mire," and then led a highly precarious and desperate existence in order to survive.[39] Roughly 80 percent of the killings took place between April 7 and the third week of April.[40] More than 90 percent of the victims were Tutsis, but Hutu who opposed the slaughter, or were misidentified as Tutsi, were also killed. The largest-scale massacres took place in churches and mission compounds in such towns as Nyamata, Musha, and Karubamba.[41] In the midst of social and political disintegration, many of the victims succumbed not to the Interahamwe but to cholera, dysentery, famine, or exhaustion.

The Western news media explicitly described the violence as the result of eternal tribal conflict, exacerbated by the weakness or collapse of the state. Warfare in Yugoslavia at that very time was similarly described as resulting from age-old conflicts within a failing nation; this was later "corrected" by inaccurately ascribing virtually all the blame to the Serbians. The perception of anarchy and chaos also fit into an image of other parts of Africa, in particular Somalia, which had no central government and had fallen into widely reported chaos and warfare in the previous few years. But the "failed state" argument image did not apply to Rwanda, where the violence was orchestrated by a highly organized, modern state. Rwanda was a model of hierarchical, efficient order—a "top-down network of control rooted in the pre-colonial kingdom, codified by colonizers, and preserved after independence."[42] As the genocide began, the central government delivered orders to prefects who forwarded them to mayors, who then organized local meetings in which they transmitted the orders to their communities.[43]

The chief culprits and organizers included Colonel Bagosora, who created the Provisional Government, and Defense Minister Augustin Bizimana, who had many organizational responsibilities. And perhaps not shockingly, given the imprecision

---

[39]Hatzfeld, *Life Laid Bare*, 198.
[40]Jones, *Genocide*, 346.
[41]Over 90 percent of the Rwandan populace identified themselves as Christian—the largest percentage in Africa at the time. Waller, *Becoming Evil*, 223.
[42]Bill Berkeley, *The Graves Are Not Yet Full: Race, Tribe and Power in the Heart of Africa* (New York: Basic Books, 2001), 260.
[43]Des Forges, *Leave None*, 24.

of ethnic lines, a Tutsi, Robert Kajuka, was one of the leaders of the Interahamwe and thus one of the chief *génocidaires* (genocidal killers).[44] An essential factor was the strength of the Rwandan state and its ability to swiftly mobilize masses of citizens, roughly 200,000 of whom are estimated to have participated in the killing of their neighbors.[45]

RAPE AS A WEAPON OF WAR AND GENOCIDE

The strife in Rwanda as well as in Yugoslavia, which was torn apart by warfare between 1991 and 1995, drew attention to a common feature of war: sexual violence. In both countries, regular military forces as well as militias raped large numbers of women, and smaller numbers of men. The use of rape was usually systematic, rather than instances of undisciplined soldiers running amok, although that was certainly not uncommon. And, as in Bosnia, rape was intended to undermine and demoralize the targeted community. While the Serb perpetrators in Bosnia viewed their victims with contempt, the Hutu rapists were motivated in part by a desire to not only degrade but to socially demote Tutsi women, whom they viewed as haughty and elitist.

Human Rights Watch compiled a powerful report in 1996 entitled "Shattered Lives," which merits a lengthy excerpt, as it raises some points that are applicable to many other cases:

> *Rape in conflict is also used as a weapon to terrorize and degrade a particular community and to achieve a specific political end. In these situations, gender intersects with other aspects of a woman's identity such as ethnicity, religion, social class or political affiliation. The humiliation, pain and terror inflicted by the rapist is meant to degrade not just the individual woman but also to strip the humanity from the larger group of which she is a part. The rape of one person is translated into an assault upon the community through the emphasis placed in every culture on women's sexual virtue: the shame of the rape humiliates the family and all those associated with the survivor. Combatants who rape in war often explicitly link their acts of sexual violence to this broader social degradation. In the aftermath of such abuse, the harm done to the individual woman is often obscured or even compounded by the perceived harm to the community.[46]*

---

[44]Prunier, *Rwanda Crisis*, 240–241.

[45]In his authoritative 2008 book *The Order of Genocide*, Scott Straus estimates that there were 175,000 to 210,000 perpetrators. Straus, *Order of Genocide*, 117.

[46]Human Rights Watch, "Shattered Lives: Sexual Violence During the Rwandan Genocide and Its Aftermath," September 1996. The report was written by Binaifer Nowrojee with the research assistance of Janet Fleischman. http://www.hrw.org/sites/default/files/reports/1996_Rwanda_%20Shattered%20Lives.pdf (accessed January 30, 2014).

It is always difficult to estimate the number of women (and men) subjected to sexual violence; as the HRW report noted, "victims of rape are stigmatized and made to feel shame for the crime committed against them. As a result, rape is one of the most under-reported crimes." A Rwanda rape survivor said, "after rape, you don't have value in the community." And in Rwanda, as in Yugoslavia and elsewhere, most perpetrators were never punished. "Women here are scared to talk because it was their neighbors who raped them," stated Bernadette Muhimakazi, a women's rights activist.[47] At least a quarter-million Tutsi women, and perhaps closer to twice that number, were raped during the genocide.[48] Studies by Amnesty International and other organizations have concluded that roughly two-thirds of the survivors were infected with HIV.[49]

The trauma has been carried into the next generation. As a 2004 report noted, "The children of the genocide themselves can face severe discrimination, belittled as offspring of *Interahamwe*, and are sometimes called the '*enfants mauvais souvenir*' or children of bad memories, even by their mothers. The mothers have often been humiliated and marginalized by their communities."[50]

DOWNFALL OF THE HUTU REGIME

Once the genocide began, the RPF no longer felt bound by the terms of the Arusha Accords and resumed its offensive, mobilizing units in Uganda and Tanzania. Displaying greater discipline and sense of purpose than the Rwandan army, the RPF accelerated its offensive. It was aided by the disarray of the army and of the Interahamwe and allied militias, which were composed largely of young boys and men hastily recruited after the president's assassination and which "crumbled into armed banditry . . . as the administrative structure which had recruited and supported them fell apart."[51]

On July 4, not quite three months after Habyarimana's death and the power grab by Hutu extremists, the RPF marched into Kigali, and over the next two weeks the RPF consolidated its power and put an end to the genocide. Some 500,000 Hutu civilians as well as tens of thousands of Interahamwe militants and government soldiers fled to Zaire; their numbers would eventually swell to 1.5 to 2 million.

---

[47]Ibid.

[48]Catrien Bijleveld, Aafke Morssinkhof, and Alette Smeulers, "Counting the Countless: Rape Victimization During the Rwandan Genocide," *International Criminal Justice Review* 19, no. 2 (June 2009), 208.

[49]"'Marked for Death': Rape Survivors Living with HIV/AIDS in Rwanda," Amnesty International 2004 report, http://www.amnesty.org/en/library/asset/AFR47/007/2004/en/53d74ceb-d5f7-11dd-bb24-1fb85fe8fa05/afr470072004en.pdf (accessed April 14, 2014).

[50]Ibid., 5.

[51]Prunier, *Rwanda Crisis*, 244.

FAILURE OF THE "INTERNATIONAL COMMUNITY"

Within seventy-two hours of the beginning of the genocide, American diplomats in Rwanda had informed their government that "well-armed extremists were intent on eliminating the Tutsi. And the American press spoke of the door-to-door hunting of unarmed civilians. By the end of the second week informed nongovernmental groups had already begun to call on the [Clinton] Administration to use the term 'genocide,'" reported Samantha Power in a powerful exposé in 2003, "causing diplomats and lawyers at the State Department to begin debating the word's applicability soon thereafter."[52] A secret but later unclassified "discussion paper" produced by several US agencies and officials candidly stated: "Be Careful. Legal at State was worried about this yesterday—Genocide finding could commit USG [the United States government] to 'do something.'"[53] Only in late May did US officials begin to invoke the term "genocide," by which time most of the victims were already dead. Only eight months earlier the United States had gotten entangled in Somalia, where eighteen American soldiers were killed and several of their bodies then dragged through the streets of the capital. So soon after this widely televised debacle, the Clinton Administration had little interest in finding itself embroiled in another conflict in an African country in which it had minimal strategic or economic interests.

The US government and other powerful institutions were later accused of "inaction" in Rwanda, but this term is inadequate. As Samantha Power wrote:

> In reality the United States did much more than fail to send troops. It led a successful effort to remove most of the UN peacekeepers who were already in Rwanda. It aggressively worked to block the subsequent authorization of UN reinforcements. It refused to use its technology to jam radio broadcasts that were a crucial instrument in the coordination and perpetuation of the genocide. And even as, on average, 8,000 Rwandans were being butchered each day, U.S. officials shunned the term "genocide," for fear of being obliged to act. The United States in fact did virtually nothing "to try to limit what occurred." Indeed, staying out of Rwanda was an explicit U.S. policy objective.[54]

While the United States was the world's remaining superpower after the demise of the Soviet Union, other countries share the blame for the abandonment of the Rwandan victims. UN troops, already stationed in the country, took positions

---

[52]Samantha Power, "Bystanders to Genocide: Why the United States Let the Rwandan Tragedy Happen," *The Atlantic Monthly*, September 2001: http://www.theatlantic.com/issues/2001/09/power.htm (accessed May 9, 2013).

[53]Quotation marks in original; "Discussion Paper Rwanda," May 1, 1994, p. 1. http://www.gwu.edu/~nsarchiv/NSAEBB/NSAEBB53/rw050194.pdf (accessed May 2, 2013). On the same page, the unsigned author(s) expressed caution about any other language that might lead to the "danger of signing up to troop contributions."

[54]Power, "Bystanders to Genocide."

Roméo Dallaire

Senator Roméo Dallaire (R) and Hassan Jallow, prosecutor for the International Criminal Tribunal for Rwanda, at an event in Ottawa, Canada in December 2013. Virtually alone among Western officials, Dallaire dedicated himself to preventing or at least halting the killing. He later wrote a riveting, unsparing account of the abysmal "failure of humanity" in 1994 as well as a book on the plight of children forced into service in militias and armies, an issue that his Roméo Dallaire Child Soldiers Initiative is trying to ameliorate.

around the capital and some other towns in the first week of the killing, briefly raising the hopes of the beleaguered Tutsi. But they came not to help the African victims but to evacuate white Europeans—and, in some cases, *their pets*.[55] Some Tutsi were removed from trucks and killed in front of French or Belgian soldiers who were under orders to not react. "I passed an assembly point where French soldiers were loading expatriates into vehicles" recalled Roméo Dallaire, commander of UN forces. "Hundreds of Rwandans had gathered to watch all these white entrepreneurs, NGO staff and their families making their fearful exits," yet "I saw how aggressively the French were pushing black Rwandans seeking asylum out of the way."[56] The French embassy meanwhile welcomed Hutu extremists while turning away potential victims; after a few days, the embassy was closed and the ambassador was on a flight back to Paris. Within one week of the Habyarimana assassination, "the whites [Europeans] were in full flight," with the exception of "a handful of missionaries and devoted secular humanitarian workers," according to journalist and Africa specialist Gérard Prunier. France refused to grant asylum to the five

---

[55] Jones, *Genocide*, 353.
[56] Roméo Dallaire, *Shake Hands with the Devil: The Failure of Humanity in Rwanda* (Toronto: Vintage Canada, 2003), 286.

children of Agathe Uwilingiyimana, the prime minister who was murdered in the early hours of the takeover of power by the extremists. (A private French citizen managed to sneak the children onto a flight to Paris in order to save them.)[57]

When the Western powers finally decided to take action, they were able to quickly mobilize humanitarian and even military assistance. In mid-June, France presented a plan for intervention to the UN Security Council, and within a week French troops arrived from neighboring Zaire and established a protection zone in southwest Rwanda. This probably saved thousands of would-be victims; it also aided in the evacuation and resettling of hundreds of thousands of Hutu, including many thousands of perpetrators, into camps in Zaire, where Interahamwe units promptly reconstituted themselves.

RESCUE AND RESISTANCE

In contrast to this dismaying indifference of the world's powers, there were those within the country who took enormous risks, and sometimes paid the ultimate price, to oppose the mass murder and rescue beleaguered Tutsi. The 2004 film *Hotel Rwanda* brought attention to the remarkable story of Paul Rusesabagina, manager of a luxury hotel in Kigali, the Hôtel des Mille Collines, which he transformed into a refugee shelter. Using the guile and charisma that had served him well in his business, Rusesabagina—a Hutu who was married to a Tutsi—bribed army officers and neutralized besieging troops by serving drinks and engaging in subterfuge ("Beer saved many lives" at the hotel, one journalist wrote).[58] Although the hotel was constantly threatened, and sometimes besieged, by hostile forces, Rusesabagina was able to use an old fax machine and other means to contact European foreign ministries and beseech them for assistance. He often stayed busy nearly until dawn "sending faxes, calling, ringing the whole world" he told Philip Gourevitch, whose 1998 book on Rwanda first brought attention to the drama at the Hôtel des Mille Collines. The wily and courageous hotel manager ultimately saved more than one thousand would-be victims.

One of the people who tried his best to help Rusesabagina was General Roméo Dallaire. As commander of the chronically underfunded UN force (UNAMIR), in January 1994 the Canadian general sent the "genocide fax," as it became known, to high-ranking UN officials warning of arms shipments to Hutu forces and well-documented plans to kill Tutsi as well as political opponents.[59] Through many other creative and often dangerous means, Dallaire attempted to force the UN to take action. Humbled as well as bitter and distraught by the "failure" of

---

[57]Ibid., 235–236.
[58]Quotation from Gourevitch, *We Wish to Inform*, 127.
[59]The text of the "genocide fax" which was addressed to the military adviser to Secretary General Boutros Boutros-Ghali and Kofi Annan, the Under Secretary General for Peace-Keeping Operations and later the UN Secretary General: http://www.gwu.edu/~n-sarchiv/NSAEBB/NSAEBB53/index.html (accessed June 2, 2013).

his mission, as he termed it, Dallaire did little to draw attention to the fact that, despite all the institutional and political obstacles he faced, he skillfully deployed his dwindling forces—the UN actually cut his forces in the midst of the genocide—to prevent killings and rescue targeted peoples; his actions saved many thousands of people.[60]

Ironically and sadly, Dallaire has probably suffered far more than those who argued against action. "My soul is in Rwanda," he later said. "It has never, ever come back, and I'm not sure it ever will." Samantha Power, who reported this in a powerful critique of US and European policy in Rwanda, wrote, "He carries the guilt of the genocide with him, and he feels that the eyes and the spirits of those killed are constantly watching him. He says he can barely stand living and has attempted suicide." In the years since, he has spoken and written extensively about posttraumatic stress syndrome; the need for international action to prevent or halt crimes against humanity; and the widespread use and exploitation of child soldiers, the topic of a book he published in 2011.[61]

While most Europeans quickly fled once the killing started, Dallaire was not completely alone in his dedication to the Rwandan people; some missionaries and humanitarian workers remained. Frenchman Marc Vaiter operated a Kigali orphanage and sheltered Tutsi as well as Hutu, "always managing to fend off the demands of the militiamen for ethnic lists."[62]

Based on her own interviews, political scientist Lee Ann Fujii told the stories of several people who confronted the killers and saved Tutsi and others. Sula, an elderly woman who was unusually poor even by Rwandan standards, sheltered and fed about twenty people. She devised a clever system of alerting Tutsi hiding nearby when they could come out of the bush to come to her house, where she fed them. Sula cleverly manipulated the militiamen, telling them that "evil spirits would harm them" if they violated her home; on another occasion, she refused a substantial financial offer (for turning in Tutsi).[63]

Although many church leaders were complicit in the genocide, others courageously opposed the killing and hid potential victims. Fujii uncovered the story of one parish in the north whose pastor and his colleagues placed themselves between the mass murderers and their targets, "warning the killers that they would have to

---

[60]For a more comprehensive account of UN decision making during this time, see Michael Barnett, *Eyewitness to a Genocide: The United Nations and Rwanda* (Cornell, NY: Cornell University Press, 2003) and his article "The UN Security Council, Indifference, and Genocide in Rwanda," *Cultural Anthropology* 12, no. 4 (1997), 551–578.

[61]Dallaire's book is titled *They Fight Like Soldiers, They Die Like Children: The Global Quest to Eradicate the Use of Child Soldiers* (New York: Walker & Company, 2011). Dallaire's account of his experience in Rwanda is cited earlier: *Shake Hands with the Devil: The Failure of Humanity in Rwanda* (2004).

[62]Prunier, *Rwanda Crisis*, 236.

[63]Lee Ann Fujii, "Rescuers and Killer-Rescuers During the Rwandan Genocide," in Jacques Sémelin, Claire Andrieu, and Sarah Gensburger, eds., *Resisting Genocide: The Multiple Forms of Rescue* (New York: Columbia University Press, 2011), 149–150.

kill the pastors first" if they were to succeed. This sort of courageous statement would not have always succeeded, but in this case numerous Tutsi were saved.[64]

African Rights, a London-based advocacy group, compiled a pamphlet to relate other instances of rescue. Father Célestin Hakizimana gave refuge to hundreds of people in his church in Kigali. "Hakizimana intervened at every attempt by the militia to abduct or murder [the refugees]," reported African Rights, using "persuasion and bribes" and other means to save the large majority of the refugees. "Father Hakizimana took care of the refugees' physical needs at a time when all resources were in short supply," continues the account. "He brought them food and water, although on one occasion he was shot at as he went to fetch [water]."[65]

Despite the exhaustion and trauma of seeing their loved ones die; and the wearying daily struggle for survival, some Tutsi undertook collective resistance. A survivor related the saga of a brave stand against *génocidaires* in Bisesero, a mountainside in the country's southwest: "We did everything possible to kill any of them who stood in our way. Sometimes, we even managed to wrest soldiers and policeman. We killed many of these aggressors."[66] Faced with a tenacious, well-organized resistance that developed its own command structure, the Hutu militias were obliged to call for reinforcements; the rebellion held out for five weeks.[67] Here and elsewhere, the hunted peoples adopted a tactic they called "merging": "lying down and waiting until assailants had moved in among the intended victims, then rising up to face them in close combat."[68]

There were numerous less-known rescuers and of Hutu officials or civilians who attempted, sometimes successfully, to resist the pressure to conform and to join or profit from the killing frenzy.[69] Some rescuers surprised themselves as well as their beneficiaries: An Interahamwe leader outside Kigali saved most of the people "on his hill by telling authorities that 'there was no need to send any men, I have already killed the enemies.'" For his efforts he was nearly arrested anyway by the RPF after it came to power.[70] Other examples are even more ambiguous and startling: Some individuals could be perpetrators one day and rescuers another. An admitted murderer from the Ngali prefect of the capital city tried to hide several Tutsi neighbors on one occasion while on other occasions, as he freely admitted, he participated in killings.[71] This should not surprise us: In all cases this book ex-

---

[64]Ibid., 148.
[65]African Rights, *"Rwanda: Tribute to Courage"* (London: African Rights, 2002), available online: http://aristotle.oneonta.edu/41_reconciliation_in_rwanda-stories_of_rescue/archive/293_stories_from_tribute_to_courage_african_rights_publication.html (accessed May 27, 2013).
[66]African Rights, *Rwanda: Death, Despair and Defiance* (London: African Rights, 1994), 665, quoted in Jones, 357.
[67]Des Forges, *Leave None*, 218–220.
[68]Ibid., 217.
[69]Scott Straus, "From 'Rescue' to Violence: Overcoming Local Opposition to Genocide in Rwanda," in Sémelin et al., *Resisting Genocide*, 331–343.
[70]Prunier, *Rwanda Crisis*, 257.
[71]Fujii, "Rescuers," 153–155.

amines, many individuals acted inconsistently, pulled in one direction or another by their consciences, by coercion and social pressure, and by other factors from day to day. "Compassion and brutality can coexist in the same individual," even "in the same moment," observed Holocaust survivor Primo Levi.[72]

These anecdotes provide some relief from this grim saga and serve as necessary reminders that, in the extraordinary circumstances of war and genocide, humans of all social groups respond in a variety of ways. Cases of opposition and rescue serve as a reminder that the killing did not stem from an inexorable pattern in Rwandan history. Peace, or at least the absence of ethnic violence, was more common than murderous strife in the preceding decades.

POST-GENOCIDE RWANDA

Like Cambodia, Guatemala, and other countries ravaged by warfare and genocide, Rwanda has attempted with mixed results to confront this terrible chapter of its history. The United Nations helped to establish an "International Criminal Tribunal for Rwanda" (ICTR) at the end of 1994. Progress toward justice has been limited, and it is complicated by the existence of several legal and court systems. For years the jails and prisons were overcrowded with tens of thousands of suspects who cannot possibly be processed in the near future, and many of whom were picked up on highly specious grounds (e.g., denounced by neighbors harboring a grudge). The individual cases are often tragic as well as absurd, and indicative of the nature of Kagame's Rwanda:

> A Tutsi RPF soldier falls in love with a Hutu girl. Relative[s] try to stop the marriage by saying she was involved in the genocide and get her arrested. The young soldier frantically begs anybody who can help him save his beloved. Through the agency of one of his officers he gets the girl freed. He then gets arrested for "interfering with justice" and spends eighteen months in jail.[73]

Periodic amnesties have ameliorated but not solved this problem. The ICTR has nonetheless made some important contributions to international human rights law. A 1998 trial deemed systematic rape a crime against humanity, a valuable legal precedent; in 2003 two former officials of RTML (the Hutu Power radio station) were convicted of using the news media to foment genocide. Jean Kambanda, the prime minister of the Provisional Government during the mass murder, was convicted of "aiding and abetting" as well as "inciting" genocide—the first and, until April 2012, only former "head of state" to be convicted by an international court since the Nuremberg trials for war crimes and crimes against

---

[72]Primo Levi, "The Gray Zone," in Levi, *The Drowned and the Saved* (New York: Vintage, 1989), 56.
[73]Prunier, *Africa's World War*, 2.

humanity.[74] The ruling RPF party, though, has exerted control over the ICTR, blocking it from investigating RPF war crimes and thereby taking the character of "a de facto 'victor's court,'" according to Victor Peskin, an expert on international human rights law.[75] And with time we have learned more about RPF atrocities during its 1994 offensive and in the months after overturning the genocidal regime. According to an investigation commissioned by the UN High Commission for Refugees, the RPF killed 25,000 to 45,000 people between April and mid-September 1994—mostly Hutu, often lured to "peace and reconciliation" meetings and then murdered.[76]

In the first two years after the genocide, many tens of thousands of Hutu were arrested in Rwanda. The numbers swelled to 70,000 per month by early 1996, producing squalid and fatal conditions: In Gitarama, for example, 6,750 prisoners were held in a jail built to accommodate less than one-tenth that number, and roughly 1,000 people perished there between October 1994 and June 1995.[77] And those arrested included not only genuine killers but "hapless hangers-on, victims of property quarrels, cuckolded husbands, and common criminals."[78] The country's criminal justice system was in a shambles after the war and genocide, and there was no possibility of processing such a large number of prisoners through traditional forms of trials. After a series of meetings among government leaders at the end of the decade, the National Assembly, in October 2000, established a system of local courts called "Gacaca": an adaption of "an indigenous dispute resolution mechanism" whose name means "small grass," as political scientist Timothy Longman explained, "after the lawns where community elders would gather to consider disputes within families or between community members." Initially the purpose of Gacaca was to accelerate "the prosecution of the tens of thousands of individuals languishing in prison, but people also quickly perceived that Gacaca could serve other useful purposes in helping to rebuild Rwandan society. Like South Africa's Truth and Reconciliation Commission, Gacaca courts would allow

---

[74]It should be noted, though, that while this case is often cited as the first such case (in which a former head of state was convicted of such charges), despite his title Kambanda was less powerful than others in the short-lived genocidal regime. In subsequent developments in international law: In April 2012, a special court at The Hague convicted Charles Taylor, former president of Liberia (1997–2003), of "aiding and abetting" a range of severe war crimes including rape; use of child warriors; "unlawful killings"; and slavery during a civil war in neighboring Sierra Leone. He was sentenced to fifty years imprisonment. Slobodan Milošević, former president of the Serbian republic (1989–1997) and Yugoslavia (1997–2000), faced charges of mass crimes (including genocide and forced deportations) at another special tribunal at The Hague. The trial began in 2002, but before the trial's conclusion Milošević died in prison (in March 2006).

[75]Victor Peskin, *International Justice in Rwanda and the Balkans: Virtual Trials and the Struggle for State Cooperation* (New York: Cambridge University Press, 2008), quoted in David Crowe, *War Crimes, Genocide, and Justice: A Global History* (New York: Palgrave Macmillan, 2014), 350.

[76]Prunier, *Africa's World War*, 16.

[77]Ibid., 11.

[78]Ibid., 11.

Genocide memorial in church
Memorial in Nyamata, in southern Rwanda. The scraps of wallets and other artifacts belonged to victims. The memorial includes this text: "When the Genocide began in April of 1994, many residents of the region gathered in Nyamata and sought protection at the local Catholic Church. The church compound . . . provided a haven for the frightened masses that flocked to the compound, hoping to escape death. The church was thought of as a place of refuge and of sanctuary where the militia would not dare to attack. Unfortunately, this was not the case. According to testimonies given by survivors and evidence gathered, approximately 10,000 civilians were killed in and around the Catholic Church compound on April 10, 1994."

communities to confront the past and develop a collective account of the violence that had occurred."[79] A few *Gacaca* courts opened in June 2002, and by early 2005 they were functioning nationwide.

Judges, chosen by the village, would gather the community, "hear testimony and investigate charges," as Elizabeth Neuffer explained in her excellent study of postwar justice in Bosnia and Rwanda. "Drawing on the moral force of an assembled village, they would be more successful than a panel of judges in getting the guilty to confess," and "sentences would reward confession and participation, offering a blend of jail time and community service."[80] Yet "the trials have few legal safeguards," Neuffer continued, and "no defense lawyers" and untrained judges. Longman noted similar possibilities as well as pitfalls: it "encouraged public participation in the judicial process in an unprecedented way and thus greatly expanded the impact that trials could have on communities, encouraging dialogue about the past and allowing victims and perpetrators to enter into conversation." But he also arrived at pessimistic conclusions: "Subtle government intimidation compromised the integrity of the courts, leading to the convictions of thousands

---

[79]Timothy Longman, "An Assessment of Rwanda's Gacaca Courts," *Peace Review: A Journal of Social Justice*, 21, no. 3 (2009), 306. Also see Peter Harrell, *Rwanda's Gamble: Gacaca and a New Model of Transitional Justice* (New York: Writers Club Press, 2003). *Gacaca* is pronounced "ga-cha-cha."
[80]Neuffer, *Keys*, 398–399.

of individuals on erroneous charges and limited evidence." And worrisome for the future, "*Gacaca* served not so much to bridge the gap between perpetrators and victims as to reinforce the very ethnic divisions that were at the heart of the genocide" through its exclusive prosecutions of Hutu and its unsubtle narrative of collective guilt of the Hutu population.[81] Many other experts and researchers have share this critical or ambivalent appraisal of the process.[82]

These courts concluded their work in May 2012, having tried approximately 1.2 million people. Roughly two-thirds of them were convicted, but even those found guilty of murder—if they confessed and were "repentant and sought reconciliation with the community"—were usually sentenced to community service.[83] *Gacaca* initially appeared to be a boldly creative alternative, but "legal systems," even a relatively decentralized one, "inescapably embody prevailing constellations of power."[84] Yet there is much to learn from this attempt at a "popular/informal justice" model, despite its uneven record.[85] And it should be said that no other examples or experiments in postwar or post-genocide justice have been truly successful in balancing justice with reconciliation as well as compassion.

Perhaps the most formidable obstacle to genuine reconciliation and justice is the sheer extent and depth of the cruelties of 1994. And, after all, "genocide goes beyond human laws," as survivor and school teacher Édith Uwanyiligira wisely observed.[86] Confronting the legacies of such monumental crimes would be a daunting task, even for a more democratic and honest government. Deep fear, distrust, and bitterness linger. "You're always asking us to forgive and forget. Well, why should I? None of the men who raped me have ever shown the slightest sign of remorse," a survivor stated. "In fact, when I look out my window in the morning, I see the men who raped me freely walking on their way to work. I will never forgive and forget."[87] According to one report, 97 percent of child survivors "witnessed killing and death."[88]

---

[81]Longman, "An Assessment," 304–312. Susan Thomson and Rosemary Nagy, who conducted dozens of interviews with Tutsi as well as Hutu in 2006, also arrived at negative conclusions, arguing that the process left "the average Rwandan citizen largely powerless over individual processes of reconciliation while serving to maintain a climate of fear and insecurity in their everyday lives." Susan Thomson and Rosemary Nagy, "Law, Power and Justice: What Legalism Fails to Address in the Functioning of Rwanda's *Gacaca* Courts," *International Journal of Transitional Justice* 5, no. 1 (2011), 12.

[82]It will be several years before the lasting impact of *Gacaca* on Rwandan society can analyzed more closely; in the short term, the success of *Gacaca* has varied substantially from community to community.

[83]The Outreach Programme on the Rwanda Genocide and the United Nations, "Background Information on the Justice and Reconciliation Process in Rwanda": http://www.un.org/en/preventgenocide/rwanda/about/bgjustice.shtml (accessed April 19, 2014).

[84]Thomson and Nagy, "Law, Power and Justice," 11.

[85]Kasaija Phillip Apuuli, "Due Process and Prosecution of Genocide Suspects," *Journal of Genocide Research* 11, no. 1 (2009), 14–15.

[86]Hatzfeld, *Life Laid Bare*, 174

[87]From Anne-Marie de Brouwer and Sandra Ka Hon Chu, eds., *The Men Who Killed Me: Rwandan Survivors of Sexual Violence* (Vancouver: Douglas & McIntyre, 2009), 2.

[88]Waller, *Becoming Evil*, 225.

Gacaca hearing
After the victory of the RPF in July 1994, Rwanda faced a nearly impossible task: how to balance justice with reconciliation in a country where the Hutu remain a large majority, and where many tens of thousands of people participated in the genocide? Introduced in 2001, the Gacaca system was a creative if imperfect alternative to traditional criminal justice. Above, a Gacaca court in Kivu, in southern Rwanda, tries an accused perpetrator in 2005.

AUTHORITARIANISM AND WAR UNDER KAGAME

Another impediment to genuine, lasting peace, justice, and reconciliation has been the nature of the new government. The political and military force that put an end to the genocide, Paul Kagame's RPF, transformed itself into the ruling party. Following the pattern of many postcolonial regimes in Africa and elsewhere, it has parlayed the authority it gained through the war against the genocidal regime into justification for an authoritarian state. The RPF has created a rigid official ideology that, rather than confront the nation's complex history, denies that ethnic divisions exist. One is only to speak of the Banyarwanda—the people of Rwanda—and not of Hutu or Tutsi. Unsurprisingly, the state's top-down attempt to "de-ethnicize" Rwanda is not working. By rendering the Hutu-Tutsi divide taboo for public discussion, the "result has been to emphasize rather than de-emphasize ethnicity and reproduce the 'ethnic' logic that underpinned the genocide," reported a British scholar who interviewed numerous young Rwandans ten to fifteen years after the killings. In her interviews, most Rwandans, despite the fact that they had grown up after the RPF took power and sought to suppress discussion of ethnicity, "referred to well-worn stereotypes" about physical differences, down to "position of

the hairline" and "shape of the heel."[89] Yet the government invokes "Hutu" when it
serves it purposes, for example by on occasion referring derisively to the respected,
nonpartisan Human Rights Watch as "Hutu Rights Watch."[90] That has been characteristic of the Kagame government—to link opponents to previous oppressors
or outside interests. Although some other parties are allowed, they function under
many constraints. Kagame won the 2003 presidential elections with the suspicious figure of 95.5 percent of the popular vote, the sort of lopsided result seen in
one-party dictatorships.

Since 1996 the Rwandan government and army have been heavily involved in
the devastating wars in Congo. Fought by several African governments and roughly
two dozen armed forces, the wars have killed more than 6 million people. This has
been the deadliest conflict to afflict humanity since World War II, and it merits
much more attention that I can give it here or that it has received in the world's
news media. The "First Congo War" (1996–1997) began with an invasion by Rwanda
and its close ally, Uganda, ostensibly to capture or disperse Interahamwe fighters
who had taken refuge there. They then assisted the overthrow of Zairean dictator
Mobutu Sese Seko, who since 1965 had presided over one of the world's most corrupt, despotic regimes, and the installation of long-time guerilla fighter Laurent-
Désiré Kabila. During the Second Congo War (1998–2003) Rwanda allied with
anti-Kabila forces and may have orchestrated the president's assassination in
2001.[91] Complex political and tribal rivalries and competition for Congo's tremendous mineral wealth have, among other factors, prevented a genuine or lasting
peace. The Second Congo War and subsequent conflict have not only cost millions of
lives but have been marked by widespread sexual violence against women, men (perhaps 10 percent of the rape victims, who number in the hundreds of thousands),
and children.[92] Rwandan forces and their allies have committed well-documented
atrocities, further diminishing any moral legitimacy that the Kagame regime initially enjoyed.[93]

[89]Lyndsay McLean Hilker, "Everyday Ethnicities: Identity and Reconciliation Among Rwandan
Youth," *Journal of Genocide Research* 11, no. 1 (March 2009), 96, 87.
[90]Waller, *Becoming Evil*, 229. The Kagame government also explicitly commemorates "the
genocide of the Tutsi" each year in April.
[91]Arnaud Zajtman, "Murder in Kinshasa: Who really killed DR Congo's President Laurent-
Desire Kabila and is the world ignoring a major miscarriage of justice?," *Al-Jazeera*, October
28, 2011.
[92]See and Paula Drummond, "Invisible Males: A Critical Assessment of UN Gender Main-
streaming Policies in the Congolese Genocide," in Adam Jones, ed., *New Directions in Genocide
Research* (New York: Routledge, 2012), 96–111; and Kirsten Johnson, Jennifer Scott, et al.,
"Association of Sexual Violence and Human Rights Violations with Physical and Mental
Health in Territories of the Eastern Democratic Republic of the Congo," *JAMA* (Journal of the
American Medical Association) 304, no. 5 (2010), 553–562.
[93]"Six foreign armies have been involved in the theft of the DRC's resources over the past
ten years" and the accompanying bloodletting, mass rape, and other atrocities, "but Rwanda's was singled out by the UN's report on the catastrophe there for the 'institutional'
nature of its piracy." George Monbiot, "Victim's Licence," *The Guardian*, April 13, 2004:
http://www.monbiot.com/2004/04/13/victims-licence/ (accessed May 25, 2013).

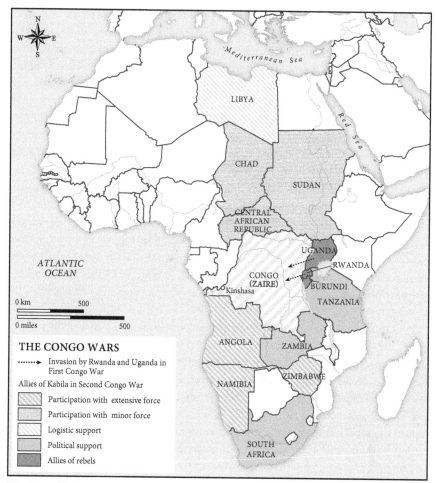

The Congo Wars

CONCLUSIONS: HOW WAS IT POSSIBLE?

Like all genocides, this case leaves us with profoundly troubling questions. And like other such cases, the Rwandan cataclysm has its distinctive features, none more troubling than the participation of many tens of thousands of ordinary Hutu civilians, few of whom had previously demonstrated the potential for such wanton cruelty. This feature of the genocide—the relatively high degree of popular participation—distinguishes this genocide from all others, in my view. As Gérard Prunier argues, the Rwandan genocide is incomparable "because its massive horror had been carried out within the confines of a small, tightly knit community," while other genocides consisted in larger measure of "strangers killing other strangers," usually "in the wider violence of large international wars and revolutions."[94]

---

[94]Prunier, *Africa's World War*, 1.

In his classic work *The Roots of Evil: The Origins of Genocide and Other Group Violence*, Irvin Staub identified a "progression along a continuum of destruction. People learn and change by doing, by participation."[95] This idea of a continuum, and of unnoticeable but rapid transformations, is evident in the testimony of numerous Hutu killers. "At the time of those murders I didn't even notice the tiny thing that would change me into a killer," a Hutu perpetrator told French journalist Jean Hatzfeld, who interviewed a group of prisoners for his 2005 *Machete Season*, a masterpiece of journalism and scholarship.[96] While serving a prison sentence for his enthusiastic leadership in the hunting down and slaughter of Tutsi in 1994, Léopord Twagirayezu told Hatzfeld: "we forgot our torments as farmers." A friend and fellow perpetrator in the same prison stated, "worries let go of us" about the trials and tribulations of eking out an existence as a farmer: "We overflowed with life for this new job."[97] This "job," which was organized like a workday—starting at the break of day and concluding in the evening, followed by roasted goats and other meats, washed down with copious quantities of beer—also engendered a sort of solidarity among the murderers. "Suddenly Hutus of every kind were patriotic brothers," said one man while serving a prison sentence for his involvement, "without any partisan discord."[98]

Economic factors contributed to the turmoil and bloodshed, although by themselves poverty and hopelessness can lead to many behaviors other than ethnic violence. The economy disintegrated as the war intensified, driving larger numbers of people into desperate straits. Per capita income was US $320 per year in 1989, making it the nineteenth poorest country in the world; by 1993, income had dropped to $200.[99] To compound this, Rwanda like other underdeveloped countries was trapped in global international economic arrangements that forced it to accept austerity programs and other policies that deepened the country's extreme poverty. The prospect of economic gain was one of many factors that induced ordinary people to commit terrible crimes. Peter Uvin has investigated this and argued persuasively that "continuous structural violence" against the poor—and the "inequality of life chances" they possessed while observing the "corruption, arbitrariness, and impunity" of the wealthy and also of foreigners—"provokes frustration, anger, ignorance, despair, and cynicism," increasing the potential for mass violence.[100] In 1994 most Rwandans were young, yet lacked realistic hope of acquiring land or otherwise improving their socioeconomic status. Added to this was an element of "social envy." In Kigali, Tutsi were more likely to be better off and to occupy better professions;

[95]Irvin Staub, *The Roots of Evil: The Origins of Genocide and Other Group Violence* (New York: Cambridge University Press, 1989), 17.
[96]Jean Hatzfeld, *Machete Season: The Killers in Rwanda Speak* (New York: Picador, 2006), 27.
[97]Ibid., 61–62.
[98]Ibid., 16.
[99]Jones, *Genocide*, 351.
[100]Peter Uvin, *Aiding Violence: The Development Enterprise in Rwanda* (West Hartford, CT: Kumarian Press, 1998), 107.

and in that same city, the Interahamwe recruited from the poorest of the poor, some of whom now saw an opportunity to avenge themselves upon those they had envied.[101] It is important, however, not to overstate these socioeconomic factors, which could produce misguided generalizations and would fail to explain the zealous participation of professionals and other educated, middle-class Hutu.

Some scholars have pointed to the premium put on obedience to authority within Rwandan culture, dating back many generations.[102] This has been explained in varying ways, and it is also apt to be exaggerated or simplified. It is true, though, that the government was highly authoritarian in nature and had to some degree molded the 1994 generation; further, its ability to enforce strict discipline was well known. During times of war and crisis most people are more likely to conform and less likely to resist the tide and draw attention to themselves. To a higher degree than in Nazi Germany, the consequences for disobedience were severe. It was not uncommon for Hutu to be killed on the spot for refusing to join in the killing or for suspicion of protecting Tutsi; insufficient enthusiasm was enough to invite harsh punishment. Balancing the coercion was the promise of reward: "when you receive firm orders, promises of long-term benefits, and you feel well backed up by colleagues, the wickedness of killing" is forgotten, observed Jean Hatzfeld.[103]

The nation's geography also aided the killers and hindered the victims. Rwanda is one of the most densely populated countries on earth; therefore, the Tutsi population was more visible as well as vulnerable. The victims also had the misfortune of residing in a strife-torn, often mountainous region of central Africa that offered few exits or escape routes. Many Burundian Tutsi who sought to escape their nation's violence in late 1993 actually fled *into* Rwanda, unable to foresee the disaster that awaited them only a few months later.

As in the other genocides this book examines, the state of war was an essential precondition for the terrible slaughter. In Rwanda the war provided a key rationale, skillfully deployed by the interim government: security. There was reason to fear the advancing rebel units, and Hutu had been the victims of mass, even genocidal violence in Burundi at different times in the recent past, most notably in 1972. These recurring massacres, argued the leaders of the 1994 genocide, "proved" that *all* Tutsi desired the elimination of the Hutu. Thus, to kill one's "fellow man [was] no longer a crime," but became "a duty or mission."[104]

---

[101]Prunier, *Rwanda Crisis*, 231–232.
[102]Prunier, *Africa's World War*, 23. See also Danielle de Lame, *A Hill Among a Thousand: Transformations and Ruptures in Rural Rwanda* (Madison, WI: University of Wisconsin Press, 2005). Scott Straus added, "obedience [during the genocide] stemmed from in-group coercion and social pressure." Strauss, *Order of Genocide*, 140.
[103]Hatzfeld, *Machete Season*, 233.
[104]Sémelin, *Purify and Destroy*, 145. The quotation is from Jacques Sémelin, who was referring more broadly to the manner in which warfare transforms human behavior and radicalizes hatred of the enemy. Sémelin's arguments are based on his study of Rwanda as well as Nazi Germany and Yugoslavia.

Memorial ceremony marking the twentieth anniversary of the Rwandan genocide
Memorial ceremony in Kagali's large Amoharo stadium on the twentieth anniversary of the start of
the genocide (April 7, 2014). This stadium's history reflects Rwanda's complex, tortured recent history:
It served briefly as a UN "safe haven" for Tutsi during the first days of the genocide; later, but before
taking power, the RPF gained entry to stadium and scoured the crowds for suspected "killers," many
of whom then disappeared.

We must kill them before they kill us, suggested the organizers and propagandists; this would be a "preventive genocide."[105] The regime skillfully combined
security concerns with the decades-old image of the Tutsi as eternal invaders,
aliens, and aggressors. The mass killing would finally cleanse the land of the
"cockroaches," the ugly but ubiquitous epithet applied to Tutsi at the time that
evoked images of a swarming, all-conquering horde—one that would never disappear unless exterminated.

Murderers commonly referred to the victim group as one, no longer recognizing
the individuality of the victims: "Umwanzi ni umwe ni umutusi" [The enemy is
one, it is the Tutsi]; to kill Tutsi was thus to fight an indivisible enemy.[106] The humanity of their individual victims completely evaporated. "It came to me only afterward" that "I had taken the life of a neighbor," said another imprisoned Hutu
génocidaire. "At the fatal instant . . . I struck someone . . . who wasn't exactly ordinary" or recognizable any longer.[107]

---

[105]The term "preventive genocide" was used by Gérard Prunier. Prunier, *Rwanda Crisis*,
199–200.
[106]Straus, *Order of Genocide*, 173.
[107]Hatzfeld, *Machete Season*, 24.

PRIMARY SOURCES
AND STUDY QUESTIONS

Source 4.1: November 22, 1992, speech by Leon Mugesera

Mugesera was a high-ranking official of the governing Hutu party, the MRND (National Revolutionary Movement for Development), and was part of the party's extremist faction. He delivered this speech at a large MRND gathering in the western province of Gisenyi. Before the genocide erupted, Mugesera moved to Canada. After a lengthy legal battle, he was deported to Rwanda in January 2012 to face genocide-related charges.[108] The first witness at his trial emphasized the powerful, murderous effect of the 1992 speech. "Immediately after the speech, three families who were Tutsis were killed." The Hutu-power radio station RTML frequently played the speech before and during the genocide.

In the full transcript of the speech, Mugesera used the term "inyenzi" ("cockroaches," to refer to Tutsi) more than two dozen times; he employed forms of the word "invade" roughly fourteen times. The speech is an early—perhaps the earliest—public expression of genocidal ambitions by the hardline elements of the government.

This text was submitted by the Canadian Minister of Citizenship and Immigration for Mugesera's 2003 deportation hearing in Quebec, one of several trials he underwent in Canada over the course of seventeen years. From the office of the Minister's introduction to the speech text: "For a full understanding of the issue, it seems necessary to set out in full the text of the speech made by Mr. Mugesera on November 22, 1992. The speech was made in the Kinyarwanda language.

It was neither broadcast nor televised. A transcription was made from a cassette recording to which we listened. Various translations of greater or lesser quality have been made. The speech was improvised. The translation finally accepted in the Appeal Division by Guy Bertrand, counsel for Mr. Mugesera, was that made by Thomas Kamanzi. I reproduce it as such, without any improvement in the style or grammar, as several of the words used are central to the issue. I have only added numbering of the paragraphs for ease of reference, and I have indicated by double square brackets ([[ ]]) the text amended by Mr. Kamanzi himself in his cross-examination."

Some have quoted the following saying: "Those who seek peace always make ready for war." . . . It says in the Gospel that if someone strikes you on one cheek, you

SOURCE: Léon Mugesera, et al., Appellants and The Minister of Citizenship and Immigration, Canada; Dockets A-316-01 and A-317-01; 9 August 2003. Full text of case made available by the University of Toronto Faculty of Law: http://www.law.utoronto.ca/documents/Mackin/mugesera.pdf (accessed June 30, 2015). Transcript and translation of the speech, pages 17–25.
[108]As this book goes to press in late 2015, the trial has not yet concluded.

should turn the other cheek. I tell you that the Gospel has changed in our movement: if someone strikes you on one cheek, you hit them twice on one cheek and they collapse on the ground and will never be able to recover!

Something else which may be called "not allowing ourselves to be invaded" in the country, you know people they call "Inyenzis" [cockroaches], no longer call them "Inkotanyi" [tough fighters], as they are actually "Inyenzis." These people called Inyenzis are now on their way to attack us. Why do they not arrest these parents who have sent away their children and why do they not exterminate them? Why do they not arrest the people taking them away and why do they not exterminate all of them? Are we really waiting till they come to exterminate us?

As to what they are going to say in Arusha, it is exactly what these "Inyenzi" accomplices living here went to Brussels to say.[109] They are going to work in Arusha so everything would be attributed to Rwanda, while there was nothing not from Brussels that happened there! Even what came from Rwanda did not entirely come from our government: it was a Brussels affair which they put on their heads to take with them to Arusha![110] So it was one "Inyenzi" dealing with another! As for what they call "discussions," we are not against discussions. I have to tell you that they do not come from Rwanda: they are "Inyenzis" who conduct discussions with "Inyenzis," and you must know that once and for all! In any case, we will never accept these things which come from there!

One important thing which I am asking all those who are working and are in the M.R.N.D.: "Unite!" People in charge of finances, like the others working in that area, let them bring money so we can use it. The same applies to persons working on their own account. The M.N.R.D. have given them money to help them and support them so they can live as men. As they intend to cut our necks, let them bring [money] so [we can defend ourselves by cutting their necks]! Remember that the basis of our Movement is the cell, that the basis of our Movement is the sector and the Commune. He [the President] told you that a tree which has branches and leaves but no roots dies. Our roots are fundamentally there. Unite again, of course you are no longer paid, members of our cells, come together. If anyone penetrates a cell, watch him and crush him: if he is an accomplice do not let him get away! Yes, he must no longer get away! Recently, I told someone [a Tutsi], "The mistake we made in 1959, when I was still a child, is to let you leave." I asked him if he had not heard of the story of the Falashas, who returned home to

---

[109]The Arusha negotiations . . . began four months before this speech and concluded the following summer (August 1993). Extremists such as Mugesera opposed the talks, believing there should be no compromise with the "Tutsi invaders and traitors." Their opposition became more intransigent after the Arusha Accords were signed. See the "Dashed Hopes for Peace"; sub: section, pages 162–163.

[110]Mugesera is implying, although in a rather confused manner, that the former colonial power, Belgium, was strongly influencing the talks.

Israel from Ethiopia?[111] He replied that he knew nothing about it! I told him, "So don't you know how to listen or read? I am telling you that your home is in Ethiopia, that we will send you by the Nyabarongo so you can get there quickly."[112]

Questions

1. Consider the implications of his denunciations of "Inyenzi accomplices," which refers to Hutu politicians, including President Habyarimana, who were willing to negotiate with the RPF.
2. Look for other sections of this speech and connect them to the specific sections of this chapter that they illustrate. What themes does the speech touch on?
3. Why do you think that this speech would be effective in mobilizing Hutu during the genocide and stirring them to violence?

Source 4.2: Interview with Roméo Dallaire, 2008

Roméo Dallaire served as Force Commander of the UN forces (UNAMIR) that were deployed to Rwanda in early October 1993, two months after the signing of the Arusha Accords. He attempted valiantly, but ultimately in vain, to protect the Tutsi communities from the violence that he foresaw. See the sections of this chapter under the subheads "Failure of the 'International Community'" and "Rescue and Resistance" for more. These excerpts are from an October 2008 interview conducted by the prominent psychiatrist, physician, and humanitarian David A. Hamburg. This book's author (John Cox) inserted the notes that appear in brackets.

[The interviewer asked a question about requests that Dallaire had submitted for "5,000 troops properly trained" with a "mandate," requests that were "turned down flat," Dallaire stated.]

DALLAIRE: I had asked for reinforcements previous to that but there was absolutely no will by anyone in the world to provide me with more troops. In my own country they were up to their ears in [the 1992–1995 war in] Yugoslavia.

---

[111]The Falasha are Ethiopian Jews who retained their Jewish faith after most people in the region converted to Christianity in the fourth century. In the previous twelve years (before this speech) a majority of the Falasha, suffering from worsening discrimination as well as famine in Ethiopia, migrated to Israel.
[112]He refers here to the Nyabarongo River, which flows northwest through central Rwanda, eventually joining Lake Victoria, whence the Nile flows to Ethiopia. And indeed, this threat or prophecy came to pass: In 1994, thousands of murdered Tutsi were tossed into the Nyabarongo, symbolically returning them to their presumed homeland of Ethiopia.
SOURCE: Courtesy of Stanford University Digital Collections. Full text here: https://lib.stanford.edu/preventing-genocide/transcript-interview-romeo-dallaire (accessed May 15, 2015).

Before we move on I would like to raise one element—the disconnect that can exist between those in the field and those in the big headquarters. It is my impression that more often than not they will question significantly the value of the opinion that is coming in from the field at the higher headquarters. It is done not maliciously—it's [based on] the perspective that they see the big picture, also have more experience. And also, they do question the competencies of the people in the field. Now because there is no set methodology of choosing special representatives—it's very politically fiddled [i.e., compromised by political considerations]. Force commanders are chosen that don't necessarily have the skill sets to do peacekeeping. There's no specific instrument by which you can evaluate the quality of force commanders, and headquarters will tend to question, water down, lose confidence in, information they get from the field.

I think that was one of the significant factors as we were getting closer to the January, February, March time frame. Although the information that I'm giving them seems to me to be more solid it's getting less traction, as if [I am] overstating the case, crying wolf, or simply wanting more resources because of power building. It's rather interesting that if the Secretary-General wasn't having full confidence in us in the field . . . the nation states that make up the UN, who had hard data because of their ambassadors, because of their military attaches, never provided that information to either me . . . or to the UN Secretary-General. The nations that had a lot of information were not exchanging it with those who had the responsibility in the field to be able to do something about it.

I am not credible enough [in the view of such diplomats]. . . . All these nations have outside people. As an example, the French and the Belgians had officers throughout the [Rwandan] military, gendarmes, and police structures. They had been there for years training these guys—they knew them personally; they knew exactly what they were up to. When I asked the French and Belgian senior officers who were attached to the Rwandan gendarmes and army what was going on at a meeting in February the answer I got was, "We cannot serve two masters at the same time."

HAMBURG: So preventing genocide hinged upon former colonial powers and other member states that were unwilling to cooperate. Just one question: the Carnegie Commission on Preventing Deadly Conflict did a study with senior level military officers on your request for that force, and verified that had you received a positive response, you could have prevented the genocide or at least most of it. I wanted to ask you: you weren't anticipating fighting a war with Rwanda, you were more or less anticipating that you would separate the adversaries to make space for mediation?

DALLAIRE: I wasn't even going to go that far. I needed the 5,000 troops to be behind the lines of particularly one of the warring factions to stop the slaughtering. Then the rebels would have no more argument to continue the fighting and it would be brought to a peace process. The primary argument for why peace negotiations never went anywhere was that the dominant condition the rebels set for going into a peace process was stopping the massacres.

The government said, "We can't stop the massacre because all our troops are fighting you [the rebels]." No matter how much we said to the RPF to stop, they would say, "There's slaughtering, and we have to stop this by defeating this army." If I was able to stop the slaughtering, then there was no reason for the fighting anymore; and that's why I needed the 5,000 troops. I felt that with 5,000 troops if I gained control of the capital and then spread out to some of the major areas, essentially to prove to the Rwandans that it was more risky for them to be on those barriers killing Tutsis than it was staying home, we would have stymied massively the entity that was actually doing the slaughtering.

HAMBURG: The prevention opportunities were there and were missed in the most heartbreaking way.

Questions and Themes

1. Dallaire and his interviewer do not excuse the lack of support his mission received. Yet what are some genuine obstacles that help explain—in addition to indifference and other less excusable factors—the difficulty that any such UN mission would confront?
2. We now have the benefit of hindsight and know what occurred between April and July 1994. Yet the international community *did* know, from the start of the genocide, that Hutu extremists were systematically massacring Tutsi, even if the scale was not known. What are some measures that outside powers, such as the UN, could have taken to prevent, halt, or at least reduce the mass murders?
3. Dallaire stated that France and Belgium "had officers throughout the [Rwandan] military, gendarmes, and police structures. They had been there for years training these guys—they knew them personally; they knew exactly what they were up to." Consider the ways that former colonial powers, decades after independence, still pay strong (and often harmful) roles in their former colonies.

Source 4.3: Testimony of survivor Agathe (last name withheld), 2012

This testimony requires little introduction, other than to acknowledge its source: the Survivors Fund (SURF), established in London in 1995 to "work with survivor's organizations to develop, manage, monitor, evaluate, fundraise and advocate for restorative justice programs to rebuild the lives and empower survivors of the Rwandan genocide." Readers may want to review this chapter's section subtitled "Rape as a Weapon of War and Genocide," pages 166–167.

SOURCE: Courtesy of the SURF (Supporting Survivors of the Rwandan Genocide): Survivors Fund. Full text here: http://www.un.org/en/preventgenocide/rwanda/education/survivor-testimonies.shtml (accessed May 15, 2015).

I have only one child. He is a permanent reminder of the 1994 genocide.

On April 6, 1994, I was visiting my sister. The next morning as I tried to return home, I was stopped at a roadblock. The only thought I had, was that if the killings had started, which I doubted, then I wished to die with my parents.

My sister had a Hutu husband. He went to hide her with his relatives and this is when the situation became worse for me. I was chased away from his house, and he took me to hide in another place. Being away from my sister, he took the opportunity to rape me. Wherever he took me I was chased away, so he brought me back to his home. He made me his wife, and I fell pregnant.

The man told me that my sister had been killed. I was sad but I thought he was lying to me. After the war, I found that she had really died. I learnt that she had been killed by her inlaws: the very people who were supposed to protect her.

When I confronted my captor after the genocide about the death of my sister, he denied everything. Fearing that I may implicate him in court, because his relatives had killed my sister, he disappeared.

I was rescued in July 1994. I was taken to an orphanage where I stayed until I gave birth in December 1994. The orphanage asked me to leave, and to take the child to its father. I was only 15 years old. I went to my cousin instead, but he chased me away as well, saying he could not look after a child of an Interahamwe.

The Government gave me a house. I now live with my son and four other orphans from my family. I decided to have an AIDS test, and I found that I am HIV positive. I discovered this organisation that brings people like me to together with one another in order to comfort us and help us where possible in our daily lives.

I don't have love to give to my son because he is a bad reminder of what happened to me during the genocide. Since I began attending meetings of this organization, I have learnt to stop insulting him. Before, I hated him so much. I used to tell him he was his father's child when he did something wrong. I'm now slowly learning to love him. I also know what it means to be alone and isolated. I try to compensate for all the time I have mistreated him. He is now 9 years old and helps me when I am not well. Being HIV positive, he is the only carer I have. Sometimes I worry that when I die, people will shut him out like I once did.

Questions and Themes

1. How would you explain—and one can try to explain or understand without endorsing—Agathe's feelings toward her son? And the attitudes of some other Tutsi toward her son?
2. What can we learn or deduce about Hutu attitudes toward Tutsi during the genocide, and about Tutsi attitudes toward Hutu following the genocide?
3. There is no single, easy answer to this: What sorts of measures might help to bring about reconciliation, understanding, and healing between Rwandan Hutu and Tutsi?

CONCLUSIONS: WHAT HAVE WE LEARNED AND WHAT REMAINS TO BE LEARNED?

A victim . . . has a name, a face, a past, hopes and aspirations for the future. In an amorphous mass, however, the victims become nameless and faceless statistics. The humanity of the victims is lost in the vastness of the crime. . . . We must strive to remember the human dimensions of these crimes, and not forget that these numbers . . . represent human lives brutally and tragically cut short.

—Alex Alvarez[1]

IN DECIDING WHICH GENOCIDAL atrocities to focus upon for this book, there were far too many to choose from. Genocide is not an aberration but an integral part of history and, more specifically, the modern world.

This book has been guided by the belief that we should not draw rigid boundaries between genocide(s), crimes against humanity, and war crimes. The borders between these categories are very thin and open to interpretation; so it is more accurate to see them as points on a spectrum of extreme violence. There are, however, academic, political, and legal reasons to differentiate genocide from other abominations. It is enduringly destructive: The annihilation, partly or wholly, of a group diminishes the diversity and richness of the human race. When a people is eradicated or dispersed and its traditions and culture erased, all of human civilization loses much that can never be regained. In Germany, a Jewish community has reemerged in recent years, yet it is disconnected from the vibrant pre-1933 traditions of German Jewry, which can never be rebuilt or resurrected. The Jewish people not only suffered an irreparable tragedy in the Holocaust: Europe and the world lost something irreplaceable as well, as we did through the disappearances of hundreds of indigenous groups in the Americas and the decimation of so many

---

[1]From Alex Alvarez, *Governments, Citizens, and Genocide: A Comparative and Interdisciplinary Approach* (Bloomington, IN: Indiana University Press, 2001), 18.

other peoples, only a minority of whom this book could even mention. We can never imagine or calculate "the sum of thoughts unthought, of unfelt feelings, of works never accomplished, of lives unlived to their natural end."[2]

AN INTEGRATED APPROACH
TO THE STUDY OF GENOCIDE

The Holocaust is often considered to be history's defining genocide and example of evil.[3] There are compelling reasons for this, principally the scale, organization, and geographic ambitions of Nazi genocide. The Holocaust first drew our attention to the problem of genocide and sparked inquiry and activism, and thus will continue to be for many people the foremost case of genocide. The preeminent place of the Holocaust can, though, generate a competition for victimhood—both within the Holocaust (among the groups that were targeted by the Nazis) and among assorted genocides— and can serve to detract from other horrors, for example when the Holocaust is upheld as an unapproachable standard. Conversely, the Nazis' massive crimes can be trivialized by the automatic, casual invocation of the Holocaust, which has become routine when an atrocity occurs or police-state tactics are exposed.

The prominence of the Holocaust can also lead to assertions of its utter "uniqueness." This argument points us in the direction of obscurity rather than clarification—after all, *everything* is "unique," and therefore the word has no analytic value—and is sometimes employed to belittle or disregard other genocides out of a misguided fear that the Holocaust will decline in public attention. Assertions of Holocaust "uniqueness" often rest upon the conviction that the Nazis betrayed and overturned the values of Western civilization. As the book's Introduction suggests, the belief that the Holocaust is incomparable would be difficult to sustain from the perspective of peoples in the colonial and postcolonial worlds. The noble values espoused and unevenly practiced in North America and Europe were never exported to the colonies; quite the contrary. Historian Enzo Traverso summarized some of the thoughts and practices that influenced the Nazis: "The natural supremacy of the white race and its corollary, Europe's civilising mission in Africa and Asia; the view of the world beyond Europe as a vast area to be colonised; the idea of colonial wars as conflicts in which the enemy was the civilian population of the countries to be conquered, rather than an army; the

---

[2] Jan Gross, *Neighbors: The Destruction of the Jewish Community in Jedwabne, Poland* (New York: Penguin, 2002), xv.
[3] We should be aware that, outside Europe and North America and perhaps Australia, the Holocaust does not possess this centrality in the public consciousness. It is "not a unique event for the Japanese or for most other Asians," as philosopher Richard Rubinstein noted; while in countries with strong Christian traditions, its importance is linked to the centuries-long struggle over "the matrix of meanings concerning Jews and Judaism." Richard Rubinstein, "Religion and the Uniqueness of the Holocaust," in Alan S. Rosenbaum, ed., *Is the Holocaust Unique? Perspectives on Comparative Genocide* (Boulder, CO: Westview Press, 1996), 15.

theory that the extinction of the inferior races was an inevitable consequence of progress: these central tenets of Nazi ideology were commonplaces of 19th-century European culture."[4]

Other ideological and logistical elements often considered unique to the Holocaust can be found in varying degrees elsewhere. The Holocaust was not the only genocide in which ideological goals took precedence over pragmatic aims, as is widely believed by those who have yet to look more closely at other examples; and the Rwandan genocide rivaled the Holocaust in its lethal efficiency, claiming as many lives per day as the deadliest months of Nazi genocide. The Holocaust remains a sobering example of the marshaling of the institutions and technologies of the modern state and its bureaucracy for genocide. This feature is misinterpreted, though, when we view the Holocaust through the iconic imagery of the Auschwitz-Birkenau death camp, the final destination for nearly 1 million Jews. Most of the Jewish victims had already been killed before Auschwitz-Birkenau expanded its gassing operations in the summer of 1943.[5] They and hundreds of thousands of the Nazis' other victims had been killed through less impersonal, industrialized means—and the death camps were not as antiseptic or depersonalized as implied by the adjective "industrial," which is often deployed to characterize the Nazis' killing process. Millions of Jews and other victims of Nazism were shot at close range and dumped into mass graves; starved to death; or succumbed to disease or starvation. In his riveting, deeply disquieting Neighbors, Jan Gross told of the murder of hundreds of Jews by their fellow villagers in the Polish town of Jedwabne by "primitive, ancient methods and murder weapons . . . stones, wooden clubs, iron bars, fire, and water."[6]

Much more can be (and has been) written about the Holocaust in relation to other genocides, but in recent years scholars have strayed away from old, fruitless debates over the utter "uniqueness" of the Holocaust, searching instead for common patterns, dynamics, and origins. Indeed, "distinctive" is a more useful and precise term than "unique." Many of the Nazis' Jewish victims had the added, special misfortune of suffering many months and even years of degradation, abuse, and physical and emotional violence. Another distinguishing characteristic of the Holocaust is that, once committed to a genocidal "final solution," the Nazis pursued their aims with an ambition and thoroughness that have probably not been matched elsewhere. The Nazi leadership genuinely believed that they were not only waging, but had no choice but to wage, a worldwide war against the Jews, a delusion that Hitler continued to rant about until his death. The nature of this obsession is also distinctive and finds few if any parallels: In other genocides, the

---

[4] Enzo Traverso, "Nazism's Roots in European Culture: Production Line of Murder," Le monde diplomatique, February 2005: http://mondediplo.com/2005/02/15civildiso (accessed July 23, 2015). Traverso expands upon these themes in his book The Origins of Nazi Violence (New York: New Press, 2003).
[5] See Donald Bloxham and Tony Kushner, The Holocaust: Critical Historical Approaches (Manchester: Manchester University Press, 2005), 68–70.
[6] Gross, Neighbors, 80.

perpetrator could array some sort of evidence, no matter how thin or exaggerated, to demonstrate that its target(s) represented some sort of threat. But as Alon Confino avers in a revelatory book published in 2014, "the persecution and extermination" of the Jews "was built on fantasy," as the Nazis' "anti-Jewish beliefs had no basis in reality." Hitler "waged a war against an imaginary enemy that had no belligerent intentions toward Germany and that possessed no army, state, or government."[7]

Hitler and other Nazi leaders had global ambitions for their attempted destruction of the Jewish people.[8] Other genocidal regimes did not have the compulsion to track down their victims far beyond their own borders, although Khmer Rouge leaders declared unrealistically their desire to wipe out the entire population of Vietnam. "There is *nothing* [emphasis in the original] in the annals of genocide, before or since the Nazi anti-Jewish assault, which replicates its spatial dimension across sovereign state boundaries," concluded genocide expert Mark Levene. "Not just were entire communities in this or that village, town, or city consciously and systematically blotted out of existence, but this happened throughout entire regions."[9] Chapter 2 stressed that the Holocaust was not a purely German crime, either in its origins and precedents or in its perpetrators and accomplices. Here, too, is an unusual feature of the Jewish genocide: the numbers and varied nationalities of direct and indirect perpetrators. Once Nazi Germany had set the killing process in motion, it was aided and abetted by independent states such as Romania, Croatia, and Slovakia, sometimes acting with little if any prompting from Berlin; Ukrainians and members of Baltic nations often served as death camp guards, sometimes composing the majority of the guards at a particular camp (e.g., Sobibor, Treblinka); civilians conducted murderous pogroms against their Jewish neighbors in Poland, Belarus, and elsewhere; government functionaries from Vichy France (which also controlled parts of northern Africa and their Jewish populations) to Norway to the Balkans deported Jews to Nazi killing centers. The widespread participation of peoples outside the perpetrator's own group is not at all unusual, but in no other genocide do we find such a large and diverse assortment of accomplices.

This book has chronicled four episodes, each entailing its own set of horrors that, to most of us, are unimaginable. We have only recently begun to examine *other* genocides in relation to each other or to broader patterns. I do not fear for the future of Holocaust research and education—in Western Europe and North America, anyway—but I am unhappily surprised, on a daily basis, with lack of knowledge or

---

[7]Alon Confino, *A World without Jews: The Nazi Imagination from Persecution to Genocide* (New Haven, CT: Yale University Press, 2104), 6.

[8]Gerhard Weinberg, "A World Wide Holocaust Project," paper presented at the "Global Perspectives on the Holocaust" international conference, Middle Tennessee State University, October 21, 2011.

[9]Mark Levene, *The Crisis of Genocide*, Vol. 2, *Annihilation: The European Rimlands, 1939–1953* (Oxford: Oxford University Press, 2013), 76.

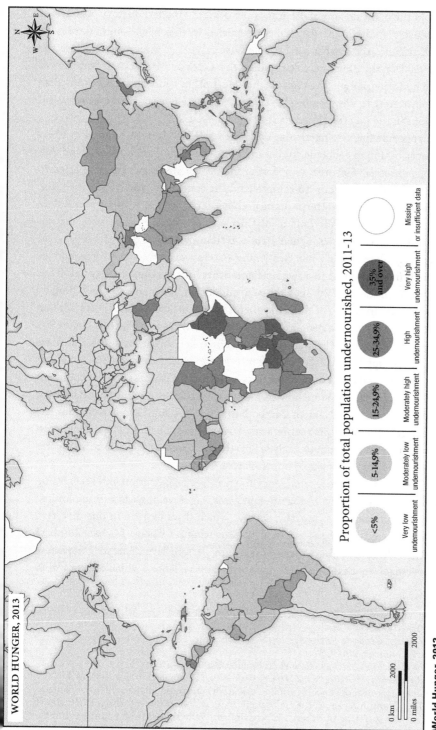

Proportion of total population undernourished, 2011-13

<5%	5-14.9%	15-24.9%	35% and over
Very low undernourishment	Moderately low undernourishment	Moderately high undernourishment	High undernourishment	Very high undernourishment	Missing or insufficient data

WORLD HUNGER, 2013

0 km   2000
0 miles   2000

World Hunger, 2013

Violence often arises out of competition for scarce resources. Terrible conflicts wrack virtually all the countries that are indicated here as having high rates of malnutrition. The state of hunger itself, caused by unequal global economic relations that are a legacy of colonialism and imperialism, constitutes massive violence and injustice. Tens of thousands of people die each day for lack of clean water, adequate sustenance, and medical care, and the UN Food and Agriculture Organization estimates that 800 million people in the underdeveloped world suffer chronic hunger.

interest in the many dozens of other mass atrocities in modern history. As I delved into intensive study of the genocides chronicled in this book—and admittedly, I started this project as above all a Holocaust expert—I came to appreciate the wisdom of Donald Bloxham's critique of the excessive Holocaust-centrism of Western historiography: "The truth is that most other genocides have been of insufficient interest to Western intellectuals for them to ponder their metaphysical dimensions in the way the Holocaust has been pondered."[10]

Each genocide has its "particular dynamic," as Mark Levene pointed out in a major contribution to genocide studies in 2008—its "peculiar, necessarily individual and *unrepeatable* features" (emphasis added).[11] By viewing them in relation to one another, we can attempt to comprehend the conditions and similarities that have produced genocide in the past and perhaps in the future. To analyze the ideological and political foundations of distinct episodes is not to compare the immense suffering that is wrought by such extreme violence. Seventeen-year-old Jeannette Ayinkamiye and her two young sisters watched as the Interahamwe found their mother hiding in a swamp; her mother "offered them money to kill her with a single machete blow." They refused, and instead dismembered her, limb by limb. "Mama lay in agony for three days before dying at last. . . . Now I often dream about her in a vivid scene deep in the marsh. I gaze at Mama's face . . . I give her something to drink but the water won't go down her throat anymore and flows away from her lips." Jeannette told her interviewer that the sorrow she feels "can never be fixed," and her manner bespeaks a permanent sadness.[12] Who could tell her that her suffering is somehow of a different order or quality than that of a victim of the Armenian, Nazi, or Cambodian genocides, or of some other murderous cataclysm? This story also confers upon us some responsibility to attempt with all due humility and realism to analyze how this occurred and to help build a world where such monstrosities would not transpire.

This book argues against a tendency to treat memorialization and recognition of humanitarian disasters as a "zero-sum game," as if we possess a finite, limited quantity of compassion, sympathy, sorrow, which if we expend in one direction must be subtracted elsewhere. In a thought-provoking 2009 book, Michael Rothberg asks, "Does collective memory really work like real-estate development?"[13] Rothberg argues persuasively that we should view "race and violence," which are central to

[10] Donald Bloxham, *The Final Solution: A Genocide* (Oxford: Oxford University Press, 2009), 318.

[11] Mark Levene, *Genocide in the Age of the Nation State*, Vol. 1: *The Meaning of Genocide* (London: I.B. Taurus, 2008), 32.

[12] Jean Hatzfeld, *Life Laid Bare* (New York: Picador, 2006), 23–25, 29.

[13] Michael Rothberg, *Multidirectional Memory* (Palo Alto, CA: Stanford University Press, 2009), 2. Leo Kuper, a pioneer of genocide studies, asked why one could not believe in the "uniqueness of Jewish annihilation in the Holocaust" while simultaneously feeling "a heightened concern for the suffering of others." He continued, "Why should it be manifested in the form of an exclusive suffering elect?" Kuper, "An Agonizing Issue: The Alienation of the Unique," *Internet on the Holocaust and Genocide* 27 (June 1990).

this exploration of genocide, "in a comparative framework that allows those interested in the Holocaust to benefit from a relaxation of the border patrol that too often surrounds and isolates discussion of the Shoah."[14]

ISRAEL-PALESTINE AND HOLOCAUST MEMORY

Knowledge of the genocidal potential in modern civilizations has encouraged activism for human rights, a relatively modern concept and development. The term "human rights" was not widely used in any language until the end of the eighteenth century. [15] During the next century, powerful anti-slavery abolitionist movements developed in England, the United States, Brazil, and elsewhere in Latin America. By the end of the century, humanitarians exposed and combated colonial abuses in the Congo and elsewhere (see the Introduction), and highly visible, effective women's rights movements appeared not only in England, Germany, and the United States, but also in Turkey and Egypt.

Knowledge of Nazi crimes sparked a new era of human rights after World War II. It is highly significant that the Universal Declaration of Human Rights was adopted by the UN within twenty-four hours of the UN's Genocide Convention, in December 1948. Although the Holocaust helped bring about a renewed commitment to human rights, a gulf has unfortunately opened between human-rights organizations and many individual and organizations dedicated to advancing public education on the Holocaust. The source of this divergence, which also lurks in the background of disputes among Holocaust and genocide scholars: Israel's relations with its Arab citizens and neighbors, and more precisely its treatment of Palestinian subjects in the West Bank and the Gaza Strip, which Israel has controlled since capturing those territories in 1967. The issues are less intractable than would be assumed from the bitterness, emotion, and lack of reason that defines public discussion. The enforcement of international decisions to end the occupation and the colonizing (through the construction of Israeli settlements) of the West Bank would be a tremendous step in the right direction.

As any occupying power, or for that matter any state power of any size in modern history, Israel commits human-rights abuses: this simple fact should not be treated as a shock or a slander, nor should it be justified or dismissed. The culprits are a state and its political and military leaders—and violent right-wing settlers, insufficiently restrained (and often encouraged) by Israeli officials—not "the Jews," as asserted by reactionary regional figures. Israeli historians such as Tom Segev, Ilan Pappé, and Benny Morris have published evidence of well-orchestrated ethnic cleansings that drove 800,000 Palestinians from their villages and land

---

[14]Rothberg, *Multidirectional Memory*, 132.
[15]Peter Stearns, *Human Rights in World History* (New York: Routledge, 2012), 1. Also see Lynn Hunt, *Inventing Human Rights: A History* (New York: Norton, 2008), and Samuel Moyn, *The Last Utopia: Human Rights in History* (Cambridge, MA: Harvard University Press, 2010).

in 1947–1948.[16] Brave Israeli journalists like Amira Hass and Gideon Levy, and intrepid human-rights groups such as B'Tselem and the Israeli Coalition against House Demolitions, have amply documented ongoing abuses against Palestinians.[17] The existence of these journalists and activist groups should suffice to counter charges of "antisemitism" that are sometimes recklessly hurled at critics, usually as a (highly effective) means to discredit the wide humanitarian opposition to the Israeli government's dispossession and collective punishment of the Palestinian people.

There is ample room for differing interpretations of the facts and for their extent, as well as for justifications based on security concerns. What one chooses to stress or to ignore is another contentious matter. Israel is hardly the worst offender of human rights in the world; like all human creations, it is an imperfect state and society. The Israeli people are beset by genuine dangers: Israel faced the combined forces of Arab armies in 1948, 1967, and 1973; over the years several Palestinian organizations have systematically targeted non-combatants in terrorist attacks; and, since the early 2000s, crude missiles have been indiscriminately launched from the Gaza Strip into northern Israeli towns, often with the approval of the governing Hamas party, killing roughly three dozen Israelis while injuring and traumatizing many more.[18] These dangers do not compare to the plight of European Jewry in the 1930s, which had no state or army, nor powerful friends or allies in the world. But in view of Jewish history, threats and attacks on Israel elicit deep distress and conjure images of pogroms and catastrophes of the past.

Misperceptions and misunderstandings abound, and present huge obstacles to peace. Former diplomat Vamik Volkan told of a meeting between Egyptian and Israeli representatives in 1980 that serves as an unfortunate example of other attempts at Arab-Israeli dialogue. "They began by reciting past injuries inflicted by the other group, as if competing to see who had suffered more." This contest quickly became so absurd that they "interrupted one another, refusing even to

---

[16]These scholars and others are often termed Israel's "New historians." Major works include Tom Segev's *The Seventh Million: The Israelis and the Holocaust* (published in Hebrew in 1991 and English in 1993) and *One Palestine, Complete: Jews and Arabs Under the British Mandate* (2000); Ilan Pappé, *The Making of the Arab-Israeli Conflict, 1947–1951* (New York: I.B. Tauris, 1992); and Benny Morris, *The Birth of the Palestinian Refugee Problem, 1947–1949* (Cambridge University Press, 1987; published in Hebrew in 1991).

[17]The websites of these two groups: http://www.btselem.org/; http://www.icahd.org/. Hass and Levy write for the English-language daily *Ha'aretz* (http://www.haaretz.com/). More on Hass, whose parents both survived the Holocaust: *Reporting from Ramallah: An Israeli Journalist in An Occupied Land* (Los Angeles: Semiotext(e), 2003). For a sampling of Levy's journalism: *The Punishment of Gaza* (New York: Verso, 2010).

[18]These statistics are compiled from Human Rights Watch's "World Reports" on "Israel/Occupied Palestinian Territories" from 2001 to 2011. Official Israeli government statistics also report the deaths of between twenty-four to twenty-five Israelis from 2001 to 2011; according to other reports, an additional six were killed in 2012 and six more in 2014, some of them during the July-August war in Gaza that killed roughly 1,500 Palestinian civilians.

listen to the other side," while drawing upon centuries-old incidents to buttress their cases.[19] Volkan detected that Israelis as well as Arabs were afraid to acknowledge that the person on the other side of the table had suffered in any way, as if such acknowledgment would undermine their own claim to victimhood. Speaking to the Israeli parliament (Knesset) in 1977, Egyptian president Anwar Sadat pointed to a "psychological barrier" that divided their peoples, "a barrier of distorted and eroded interpretation of very event and statement."[20] These patterns continue to be played out on a larger scale every day.

This chapter confronts these matters because of their connection to the historical memory of the Nazi genocide, and the politicized manipulation of that memory. It is not helpful to invoke the Holocaust in connection with Israeli-Arab tensions, but unfortunately this has become commonplace by various parties. This is invariably done to manipulate emotions and score political points, certainly not for historical clarity. Israeli politicians often invoke the specter of the Holocaust to justify aggressive policies and even to denounce one another. Expansion into Palestinian territory (the West Bank in particular) is sometimes justified by asserting that Israel's pre-1967 borders are the "borders of Auschwitz"—that is, that to end the occupation would evince vulnerability and invite another genocide.[21] In arguing for the impending 1982 invasion of Lebanon, Prime Minister Menachem Begin asserted in a cabinet meeting that "the alternative is Treblinka, and we have decided that there will be no more Treblinkas."[22] The state and army and their actions, civilian and military leaders often argue, are the natural and legitimate extension and protector of all Jewish history. In a 1976 speech at Yad Vashem, Israel's memorial to the Jewish victims of the Holocaust, Chief of Staff Mordechai Gur stated that his army (the Israeli Defense Force or IDF) draws its "power and

---

[19]Vamik Volkan, *Blood Lines: From Ethnic Pride to Ethnic Terrorism* (New York: Basic Books, 1998), 32–34.

[20]Volkan, *Blood Lines*, 30.

[21]Robert Mackey's blog, "The Lede," collected several further examples of the term "Auschwitz borders" in a May 19, 2011 entry co-authored by Elizabeth A. Harris, "Israeli Settlers Reject the 'Auschwitz Borders' of 1967": http://thelede.blogs.nytimes.com/2011/05/19/israeli-settlers-reject-the-auschwitz-borders/ (accessed August 3, 2012). In May 2011 President Barack Obama expressed his hope that peace talks resume based on "1967 lines" with "mutually agreed upon land swaps," which in earlier years would have been uncontroversial but that was promptly and firmly rejected by Israeli Prime Minister Benjamin Netanyahu. The Zionist Organization of America promptly accused the Obama Administration of "promoting and supporting the establishment of a Hamas/Fatah/Iran terrorist state"—run by the "Nazi-like" Hamas—"on the Auschwitz 1967 indefensible armistice lines." The Simon Wiesenthal Center also referred to 1967 "Auschwitz" borders in a press release. "Both statements are morally and intellectually repugnant" argued American liberal journalist Eric Alterman. "Millions of European Jews did not die at the hands of Hitler's henchmen for the honor of becoming political footballs." Eric Alterman, "The Republicans Heart Netanyahu," *Jewish Daily Forward*, June 17, 2011: http://forward.com/articles/138463/the-republicans-heart-netanyahu/#ixzz25odJBeir (accessed August 3, 2012).

[22]Tom Segev, *The Seventh Million: The Israelis and the Holocaust* (New York: Hill and Wang, 1993), 399.

strength" from the "holy martyrs of the Holocaust," which is "the root and legiti-mation of our enterprise."[23]

It is also commonplace for Israeli leaders to link current Arab leaders or movements to Nazism, another form of trivialization and political misuse of the Holocaust. As the 1982 Lebanese war dragged on; produced dreadful atrocities; and polarized public opinion, the famed Israeli writer Amos Oz criticized Begin's persistent misuse of Holocaust analogies: "Tens of thousands of dead Arabs will not heal the wound" of the Holocaust. "Adolf Hitler died thirty-seven years ago," Oz continued, and "is not in hiding" in Beirut or elsewhere in Lebanon. After thirty years, Oz's critique is still relevant: "Again and again, Mr. Begin, you reveal . . . a strange urge to resuscitate Hitler in order to kill him every day anew in the guise of terrorists."[24] Much more recently, Avraham Burg, former Chair of the World Zionist Congress, lamented that "we have displaced our anger and revenge from one people to another . . . We will never forgive the Arabs, for they are allegedly just like the Nazis."[25]

Historian Tom Segev, an Israeli liberal who has been at the fore of a movement to confront the nation's founding with greater honesty, asserted that "The 'heri-tage of the Holocaust,' as it is taught in the schools and fostered in national me-morial ceremonies, often encourages insular chauvinism and a sense that the Nazi extermination of the Jews justifies any act that seems to contribute to Israel's security, including the oppression of the population" in the West Bank and Gaza. Segev countered that the Holocaust should lead to "different conclusions. The Holocaust summons all to preserve democracy, to fight racism, and to defend human rights."[26]

Undoubtedly, antisemitism motivates some of Israel's critics. It is suspicious when supporters of the Palestinians rail fiercely against Israeli abuses but evince no indignation over any other issue in the world, or when they invoke antisemitic canards related to the supposed power and wiliness of world Jewry. In the Middle East especially, political and religious leaders are often explicit in their antisemi-tism. Demagogic and cynical politicians regularly denounce Israel in order to deflect attention from their own misdeeds, while posturing as champions of the cause of the Palestinians. Some, like former Iranian president Mahmoud Ahmadinejad, promote Holocaust denial, usually as part of a political agenda based on the deeply misguided belief that to acknowledge the Holocaust would be to legitimate Israeli actions. This is the "anti-Zionism of fools," as Lebanese-born scholar Gilbert

---

[23]Arno Mayer, "History and Memory: On the Poverty and Remembering and Forgetting the Judeocide," *Radical History Review* 56 (1993), 13.

[24]Segev, *The Seventh Million,* 400. In response, the editor of the leading daily newspaper *Yediot Aharonot* argued that the Palestinian leader Yasir Arafat, "were he only to get enough power, would do to us things that even Hitler never imagined." Hitler exercised "a certain restraint," he continued, which Arafat would eschew. Ibid., 400.

[25]Avraham Burg, *The Holocaust is Over, We Must Rise From Its Ashes* (New York: Palgrave Macmillan, 2008), 79.

[26]Segev, *The Seventh Million,* 517.

Achcar points out—a pathetic, reactionary substitute for genuine solidarity with the Palestinian people.[27]

The only path toward peace and justice is for the two "sides" to listen to one another's histories, perceptions, and fears, and to try to understand them.[28] Fortunately, there are many people in Israel and the Palestinian territories who are working toward a just solution. An inspiring example is "Parents Circle—Families Forum," consisting of Palestinian and Israelis who have lost family members in the conflict. "Our most important ongoing work on the ground is conducting dialogue meetings in schools," explained Robi Damelin, whose son was killed while serving for the IDF in the Occupied Territories. These "dialogue meetings . . . allow us to reach more than 25,000 students every year. We speak to 16- and 17-year-old Palestinian and Israeli students who, for the most part, have not met" their counterparts. The group aims to "open the eyes" of the young people "to the humanity and narrative of the other side."[29]

The history of Jewish-Arab and Jewish-Muslim relation teaches us that there is nothing inevitable about these disputes. Edward Said (1932–2003) was a well-known and prolific scholar, and also an effective spokesperson for the Palestinian cause. With the famed Israeli conductor Daniel Barenboim, Said started the "West-Eastern Divan Orchestra," which brings together Palestinian and Israeli children. "We must [try to understand] our histories together," Said wrote in 1997, "in order for there to be a common future. And that future must include Arabs and Jews together, free of any exclusionary, denial-based schemes for shutting out one side by the other, either theoretically or politically. That is the real challenge. The rest is much easier."[30]

THE PSYCHES OF GENOCIDE PERPETRATORS

One is never in another's place. Each individual is so complex that there is no point in trying to foresee his behavior, all the more in extreme situations; nor is it possible to foresee one's own behavior.[31]

—Primo Levi

The architects and organizers of genocides—men like Hitler and Pol Pot—exhibited numerous signs of psychopathy and cruelty earlier in life. We cannot fully

---

[27]Gilbert Achcar, "Assessing Holocaust Denial in Western and Arab Contexts," *Journal of Palestine Studies* 41: 1 (Autumn 2011), 92–93.
[28]Jeff Halper, a prominent Israeli human-rights activist, told me in 2002: Rather than viewing the Israelis and the Palestinians as the two "sides," we should view one "side" as those of both populations who support and work toward peace with justice, and the other "side" as those Israelis and Palestinians opposed to peace and justice.
[29]Robi Damelin, "Israeli and Palestinian Victims Break Cycle of Violence": http://www.commongroundnews.orgma/article.php?id=29486&lan=en&sp=0 (accessed September 12, 2012).
[30]Edward Said, *The End of the Peace Process: Oslo and After* (New York: Vintage, 2001), 209.
[31]Primo Levi, "The Gray Zone," in Levi, *The Drowned and the Saved* (New York: Vintage, 1989), 60.

Survivors of a Nazi concentration camp cheer their liberators
American tanks entering Mauthausen, one of the Nazis' most brutal
concentration camps, on May 6, 1945. Thousands of Spanish socialists
and communists, who had fought to defend their republic from Hitler's
ally Francisco Franco, ended up in Mauthausen a few years after Franco's
victory. The banner reads "Antifascist Spaniards greet the forces of
liberation." The concept of "genocide" should expand to include the
wholesale murder of peoples who are targeted for membership in
political groups. Large-scale examples include Spain during its Civil War
(1936–39) and under the subsequent Franco dictatorship; the massacres
of "communists" in Indonesia in 1965–66; and the torture and murder
of political dissidents by the Argentine military dictatorship (1976–83).

understand their fanaticism and their deeply warped personalities and world-
views, although there is some consistency and internal logic to their brutish decisions. Yet how to explain the acts of not only the officers and functionaries who
carried out murderous orders, but the soldiers and even civilians without whom
this book would have no subject? Jean-Baptiste Munyankore survived the Rwandan massacres and witnessed Hutu neighbors, some of whom he had known for
years, being swept into the killing frenzy. Munyankore said their crimes were "the
abnormal actions of perfectly normal people."[32] This chilling insight is shared by
experts who have scoured records, testimonies, and interviews in search of clues.

In a book that helped to establish the study of genocide as an academic field,
Frank Chalk and Kurt Jonassohn identified four collective motives for genocidal

---

[32]Hatzfeld, *Life Laid Bare*, 73.

violence: elimination of a real or imagined threat; spreading terror among real or potential enemies; acquiring economic wealth; and implementing a belief, theory, or ideology.[33] Michael Mann categorized the profiles or impulses of individuals who participate in murderous ethnic cleansing and genocide as "ideological killers," who genuinely believe in the ideology guiding their actions; "bigoted killers"; "violent killers," who are drawn to murder for its own sake; "fearful killers," who, usually with some justification (as in the Rwandan militias), fear the consequences "if they do not kill"; "careerist killers" and "bureaucratic killers," functionaries in bureaucratic machines whose career ambitions and compulsion to "do their job" override any moral obstacles; "materialist" perpetrators, who are "lured by the prospect of direct economic gain"; and "disciplined" or "comradely" participants, who are "caged into conformity by peer group pressure."[34] Psychologist James Waller's work on perpetrator motivation has exerted a profound influence on genocide studies. Among other factors, Waller pointed to "collectivistic values" that emphasize differences, rather than similarities, with other groups; self-esteem that is rooted in feelings of collective superiority; and "social dominance," which is shared by other animals and fosters "aggressive-submissive relations."[35] Waller also points to the tendency to dehumanize other peoples, or the "psychological construction of the 'Other,'" which makes "victims' lives—and deaths—meaningless."[36] This is related to "Us-them thinking," a powerful instigator of violence and as "one of the few true human universals."[37] Like many human impulses, this instinct can be channeled in positive directions—the longing to create a sense of community, for example—or in negative directions, when "us" is defined in opposition to an exaggerated threat posed by "them." As Yugoslavia disintegrated, Serb nationalists rallied around the slogan "Only Unity Saves the Serb"—a unity that was defined in opposition to Serbia's presumed eternal enemies. In a notorious speech in 1989—on a date (June 28) of great significance for Serb mythology—Slobodan Milošević made clear that unity or harmony meant "the unity of Serb against Albanian, and by extension, against all others."[38]

The annals of history are replete with vivid examples of the consequences of the devaluation of the humanity and dignity of "the Other"—those outside a group, who are deemed culturally alien and vaguely threatening. British officers serving in colonial India sometimes invented maliciously "comical" torments, which they

---

[33]Frank Chalk and Kurt Jonassohn, *The History and Sociology of Genocide: Analyses and Case Studies* (New Haven, CT: Yale University Press, 1990), 29.
[34]Michael Mann, *The Dark Side of Democracy: Explaining Ethnic Cleansing* (New York: Cambridge University Press, 2004), 27–29.
[35]James Waller, *Becoming Evil: How Ordinary People Commit Genocide and Mass Killing* (New York: Oxford University Press, 2007), 178–183.
[36]Ibid., 297.
[37]Ibid., 199.
[38]Michael Sells, *The Bridge Betrayed: Religion and Genocide in Bosnia* (Berkeley, CA: University of California Press, 1998), 86–87. June 28, 1389, was the date of the Serbian defeat at the Battle of Kosovo, the significance of which is explained later in this chapter.

inflicted at random or for minor offenses. In 1919 General Reginald Dyer issued a "crawling order": All Indians going along a particular lane had to "squirm along on their stomachs," much to the mirth of the British. By systematically devaluing the humanity and dignity of their Indian subjects, it became easier for the British troops to commit much larger atrocities, such as the infamous massacre at Amritsar— ordered by Dyer himself a few days earlier.[39] A US Army lieutenant in Vietnam described his unit's desecration of enemy corpses, which were placed in "amusing" poses and arrangements. He was dimly aware, as he explained later, that he should have felt "outrage," but "inside I was . . . laughing. [Pause in original.] I laughed."[40] An American corporal who served a tour in 1969–1970 testified, "I never had a specific hatred for the Vietnamese, I just tended to ignore them. They didn't figure in any calculations as to being human. They either got in the way or they weren't there."[41] During the long decades when lynching was commonplace in the United States, photographs captured images of gleeful white men, and some women and children, posing or simply socializing alongside the charred bodies of the victims.[42] So acceptable were these practices that perpetrators often fashioned postcards out of the photos, unabashedly celebrating their acts of racist terrorism.[43] A witness to

[39]Jonathan Glover, *Humanity: A Moral History of the Twentieth Century* (New Haven, CT: Yale University Press, 2001), 23–24. On April 13, 1919, British troops fired on a peaceful demonstration in Amritsar in northern India, killing several hundred people. See also Vinay Lal, "The Incident of the Crawling Lane: Women in the Punjab Disturbances of 1919," *Genders* 16 (Spring 1993).

[40]Glover, *Humanity*, 56.

[41]Corporal William Hatton, who was twenty-three years old while serving in Vietnam, gave this testimony at the "Winter Soldier Investigations," organized in January–February 1971 by Vietnam Veterans Against the War. With other testimonies, it was later read into the Congressional Record later that year during war-crimes hearings. It is available here: http://www.wintersoldier.com/staticpages/index.php?page=20040315221813511 (accessed May 12, 2014). He continued, "And also, we had this habit, when we'd leave the combat base—I frequently traveled between Quang Tri and Dong Ha and contact teams and we'd take C ration crackers and put peanut butter on it and stick a trioxylene heat tab in the middle and put peanut butter around it and let the kid munch on it. Now they're always looking for 'Chop, Chop' and the effect more or less of trioxylene is to eat the membranes out of your throat and if swallowed, would probably eat holes through your stomach." Ibid.

[42]For roughly eighty years, from the early 1880s to the mid-1930s, an average of more than 1.5 people per week were lynched (that is, murdered extra-legally by a mob, often by hanging). This frightful practice peaked in the 1880s and 1890s. Most victims were black; Mexicans, Mexican Americans, Italians, and other ethnic minorities and immigrants were sometimes targeted as well, in addition to labor leaders like Frank Little, who was murdered in Butte, Montana, in 1917. During the Civil Rights Movement some well-known lynching cases involved white civil rights activists. Lynching was not confined to the Jim Crow South, although it was much more prevalent there; an infamous photo depicts a smiling crowd at a lynching in Indiana in 1930. Lynching declined steeply after 1935 but racist terrorism did not disappear. Statistics from the Tuskegee Institute, available at this website maintained by the University of Missouri Law School: http://law2.umkc.edu/faculty/projects/ftrials/shipp/lynchingyear.html (accessed July 23, 2012).

[43]For an excellent, contextualized collection of such horrifying images, see James Allen, ed., *Without Sanctuary: Lynching Photography in America* (Santa Fe, NM: Twin Palms Publishers,

a lynching in Tennessee in 1915 reported that "Hundreds of kodaks clicked all morning at the scene of the lynching. . . . Picture card photographers installed a portable printing plant at the bridge" where Thomas Brooks was murdered; they did a thriving business. At several nearby schools "the day's routine was delayed until boy and girl pupils could get back from viewing the lynched man."[44]

With good reason, scholars who approach this topic—the motives and instincts that drive individual behavior in genocides and ethnic or racial mass murder—often refer to two famous psychological studies conducted in the early 1960s and early 1970s, respectively: the Milgram and Zimbardo (aka Stanford Prison) experiments. Stanley Milgram sought to understand the behavior of such Nazi criminals as Adolf Eichmann, whose widely publicized trial had recently ended in Jerusalem. For his experiment Milgram chose forty male volunteers, representing a range of professions, experiences, and ages, from his community (New Haven, Connecticut). They were divided at random into "teachers" and "learners," told that the experiment would measure the effect of punishment upon the learning process, and placed in separate rooms. The "teachers" were instructed by an administrator to deliver electric shocks of intensifying degrees to the other subjects, punishing them for wrong answers. The "teachers" were unaware that the electrodes were not really wired. Nearly two-thirds of the "teachers"—despite labels on the generator's switches that read "extreme intensity shock" and "Danger: Severe Shock"—"obeyed the orders of the experimenter to the end," Milgram reported, "proceeding to punish the victim until they reached the most potent shock available on the generator."[45]

Philip Zimbardo assigned two dozen Stanford University students to act as prisoners or guards in a fake jail, in order to see how quickly and thoroughly they adapted to their roles. Through extensive screenings, Zimbardo had excluded anyone who exhibited unusually strong predilections for obedience or servility. Yet with little delay, the "jailers" began to revel in their authority and the power they wielded over others, upon whom they inflicted brutal and humiliating treatment. "Most dramatic and distressing to us was the observation of the ease with which sadistic behavior could be elicited" from people "who were not 'sadistic types.'"[46] Several "prisoners," meanwhile, passively accepted their

2000). This book helped inspire a traveling exhibit of the same name: http://www .freedomcenter.org/without-sanctuary/ (accessed October 14, 2012).

[44]Unsigned, "Lynching," *The Crisis* 10, no. 2 (June 1915), 71. The article added several other disturbing details, which again were typical of these events, revealing the extent of racialized dehumanization: Brooks's lifeless body hung from a railroad bridge, dangling "over the public highway . . . low enough for travelers along the road today to reach up and spin the corpse around." Ibid., 71.

[45]Stanley Milgram, *Obedience to Authority: An Experimental View* (New York: Harper Perennial, 1995), 33. Milgram's original 1963 journal article about this study, "Behavioral Study of Obedience," is available here: http://www.wadsworth.com/psychology_d/templates/student_ resources/0155060678_rathus/ps/ps01.html (accessed September 7, 2012).

[46]Philip Zimbardo and Banks Haney, "The Stanford Prison Experiment: Slide Show and Audio Cassette," quoted in Christopher Browning, *Ordinary Men: Reserve Police Battalion 101 and the Final Solution in Poland* (New York: Harper, 1992), 168.

unjustified suffering or turned on their fellow inmates. Both the Milgram and Zimbardo experiments produced deeply troubling revelations. The rapid, easy transformation "of likeable and decent American boys into near monsters of the kind allegedly to be found only in places like Auschwitz or Treblinka" received widespread media attention.[47]

The motives and impulses referred to earlier, and uncovered with disturbing ease by Milgram and Zimbardo, are encapsulated in the principal source of genocide: war.

WARFARE AND GENOCIDE

All wars generate savage temptations that are more or less murderous. The bloodthirsty madness of combatants, the craving for vengeance, the distress, fear, paranoia, and feelings of abandonment, the euphoria of victories and anguish of defeats, and above all a sense of damnation after crimes have been committed—these things provoke genocidal behavior and actions.

—Jean Hatzfeld, *Machete Season: The Killers in Rwanda Speak*[48]

In the most fundamental sense, war upends moral norms by legitimizing killing. As Vietnam veteran and author Mark Marlantes observed in a 2011 book, warfare demands of soldiers that they forsake "the most fundamental rule of moral conduct we've been taught—do unto others as you would have them do unto you. When called upon to fight, we violate many codes of civilized behavior."[49] Moral teachings and precepts common to most societies do not simply evaporate; they can be replaced by a new moral code that decrees that it is not only necessary but just and laudable to kill the enemy, a category that expands to include noncombatants.[50]

Warfare also deepens "'us versus them' mentalities, creating a sharply divided world in which 'the enemy' is easily objectified and removed from the community of human obligation," concluded Christopher Browning in his classic 1992 *Ordinary Men*, among the most perceptive analyses of perpetrator behavior.[51] War-makers and their propagandists often endeavor to conflate internal and external enemies, and to associate civilians with those threats. This is a key ingredient factor in

---

[47]Zygmunt Baumann, *Modernity and the Holocaust* (Ithaca, NY: Cornell University Press, 2001), 167.

[48]Jean Hatzfeld, *Machete Season: The Killers in Rwanda Speak* (New York: Picador, 2006), 105.

[49]Mark Marlantes, *What It Is Like to Go to War* (New York: Atlantic Monthly Press, 2011), 48.

[50]By the end of the twentieth century, roughly nine of ten war victims were civilians; in the US-Vietnam war, the ratio was roughly thirteen to one. Jacques Sémelin, *Purify and Destroy: The Political Uses of Massacre and Genocide* (New York: Columbia University Press, 2007), 133; Levene, *The Meaning of Genocide*, 53.

[51]Browning, *Ordinary Men*, 162. Browning alluded to a phrase introduce by Helen Fein in a path-breaking 1979 book. Fein wrote that the "universe of obligation" consisted of individuals or groups "toward whom obligations are owed; to whom rules apply, and whose injuries call for amends." Fein, *Accounting for Genocide: National Responses and Jewish Victimization During the Holocaust* (New York: Free Press, 1979), 4.

modern genocides: a propaganda offensive to convince the nation that it is facing a grave and even mortal threat, and that the external enemy is closely linked to an internal population that has been targeted.

In some cases, such as the Nazi belief that they faced an existential enemy in the form of a worldwide Jewish conspiracy, such fears are purely fantastical, yet the *perceptions* were real and powerful.[52] In other examples, perpetrator regimes could seize upon (and often exaggerate) the participation of members of the targeted group in oppositional or revolutionary political movements or rebel armies. A self-fulfilling prophecy is often at work: Members of harshly oppressed minorities can be expected to support or join revolutionary movements, especially when other means of political redress are foreclosed. Victims of harsh and systematic racist oppression—large numbers of Guatemalan Mayans, for example—did indeed support rebel groups that fought the military dictatorship; many East Timorese supported the guerilla struggle against Indonesian occupiers.[53] This pattern can be found in many cases of counterinsurgency: A population sees no alternative to forcible resistance; this resistance then provokes harsher measures, creating a dynamic that spirals into ever greater, more indiscriminate violence as a repressive government seeks to suppress an uprising or rebellion and wipe out its base of support among civilians. In addition to many more recent examples, this dynamic also fueled the genocide of the Tasmanian people, who from 1824 forcefully resisted the land theft and other offenses against their community. Their resistance engendered harsher measures, leading quickly to destruction of the group.

A perception of vulnerability can heighten the sense of crisis and urgency among the perpetrators and the society that condones (or at least allows) their actions. A Hutu murderer told an interviewer that his militia determined, "we are going to kill them before being killed *by* them."[54] Serbian massacres in Bosnia often occurred "immediately after the local news announced that the Croats and Muslims were about to exterminate Serbs."[55] Ben Kiernan notes that even before the Khmer Rouge took power, Cambodian elites and many common people firmly believed, despite a dearth of evidence, that, in a will written shortly before his death in 1969, Vietnamese Communist leader Ho Chi Minh, "had called upon his fellow Vietnamese to take over Cambodia."[56] This myth tapped into long-standing

---

[52]In the famed theorem of sociologist William I. Thomas, "If men define situations as real, they are real in their consequences." William Isaac Thomas and Dorothy Swaine Thomas, *The Child in America: Behavior Problems and Programs* (New York: Knopf, 1928), 572.
[53]For more on the relation of counterinsurgency to genocidal violence, especially during the Cold War, see Christian Gerlach, *Extremely Violent Societies: Mass Violence in the Twentieth Century* (New York: Cambridge University Press, 2010), Chapter Five.
[54]Scott Straus, *The Order of Genocide: Race, Power, and War in Rwanda* (Cornell, NY: Cornell University Press, 2008), 74. Emphasis added.
[55]Sells, *Bridge Betrayed*, 66.
[56]Ben Kiernan, "Myth, Nationalism and Genocide," *Journal of Genocide Research* 3, no. 2 (June 2001), 188.

Otto Dix "War" etchings
The famed German artist Otto Dix marched off to war, in 1914, as a patriot; he returned as a bitter, unsparing critic of war and militarism. In 1924 he completed a series of fifty-one etchings called "Der Krieg" ("War"). Alongside the works of Goya, these are among the strongest artistic statements against war. Note that the soldiers—the artist and his comrades—no longer appear human. In an interview many years later, Dix said, "As a young man you don't notice at all that you were, after all, badly affected. For years afterwards, at least ten years, I kept getting these dreams, in which I had to crawl through ruined houses, along passages I could hardly get through."

anti-Vietnamese fears and resentments, and was skillfully deployed by the Khmer Rouge to justify the extermination of Cambodia's ethnic Vietnamese population (see Chapter 3).

War also promotes genocide by allowing "specialists in violence"—military leaders and soldiers, as well as gang leaders, criminals, mercenaries, and so on—to "enter domestic arenas."[57] In the Ottoman Empire during World War I and during the genocides in East Pakistan, Guatemala, and Cambodia, there was little if any separation between the political and military leaderships. In other cases, such as Yugoslavia and Rwanda, war pushed military or paramilitary leaders (or ultra-nationalist politicians closely linked to them) to the fore and undermined the authority of civilian leaders. And while buttressing the power and influence of military leaders, war increases the state's autonomy from internal social forces,

[57]Straus, *Order of Genocide*, 234.

including public opinion and political opposition. Additionally, governments often become more centralized and secretive during times of crisis and conflict.[58]

Wars and occupations with pronounced colonial and racist characteristics are especially liable to generate genocidal violence. Young soldiers finding themselves in an "alien environment . . . can easily come to feel that rules of civilized behavior no longer need to apply."[59] In his illuminating essay about a 2009 Chinese film about the "Rape of Nanjing," Ian Buruma referred to "the tenuous borderline between ritualized violence and the real thing" and "the danger of putting young men, locked in the cocoon of their own culture, in an alien environment, where they can easily come to feel that rules of civilized behavior no longer need to apply."[60] In November 2011, US Staff Sergeant Calvin Gibbs was convicted of organizing an Army unit that "killed Afghan civilians for sport." Gibbs also mutilated his victims' corpses and kept body parts as gruesome trophies. What enabled Sgt. Gibbs, who had no history of violent or cruel behavior in civilian life, to commit such depravities? He told the court "that he had 'disassociated' the bodies from being human, that taking the fingers" and a tooth "was like removing antlers from a deer."[61] In his classic memoir of the Pacific theater of World War II, veteran E. B. Sledge reflected on the atrocities committed by each side against enemy troops: "The fierce struggle for survival . . . eroded the veneer of civilization and made savages of us all. We existed in an environment totally incomprehensible to men behind the lines." Sledge added, "Time had no meaning, life had no meaning."[62]

In his classic study of German murderers on the Eastern Front, Christopher Browning determined that "brutalization was not the cause but the effect of these men's behavior." After their initiation into genocidal mass murder, the "horrors . . . eventually became routine, and the killing became progressively easier."[63] Varnado Simpson killed twenty-five people, by his count, during the My Lai Massacre of 1968. Simpson admitted not only to the killings but to "cutting off their hands and cutting out their tongue" and scalping them. "The part that's hard is to kill,"

---

[58]Robert Melson, "Modern Genocide in Rwanda," in Robert Gellately and Ben Kiernan, eds., *The Specter of Genocide: Mass Murder in Historical Perspective* (New York: Cambridge University Press, 2003), 337.

[59]Ian Buruma, "From Tenderness to Savagery in Seconds" (Review of "City of Life and Death"), *New York Review of Books*, October 13, 2011.

[60]John W. Dower, *War without Mercy: Race and Power in the Pacific War* (New York: Pantheon, 1986), 36.

[61]William Yardley, "Soldier Is Convicted of Killing Afghan Civilians for Sport," *New York Times*, November 10, 2011: http://www.nytimes.com/2011/11/11/us/calvin-gibbs-convicted-of-killing-civilians-in-afghanistan.html?_r=1&hp (accessed December 2, 2012).

[62]E. B. Sledge, *With the Old Breed* (New York: Oxford University Press, 1990), 121. Sledge also wrote of the moral corruption of "decent men . . . when reduced to a brutish existence in their fight for survival." Ibid., 120.

[63]Browning, *Ordinary Men*, 161.

he reminisced, "but once you kill, it becomes easier." He found himself with "no feelings or no emotions or no nothing."[64]

Warfare can also produce random, extreme violence through the emotions it stirs in combatants. "The least acknowledged aspect of war," according to a US veteran of the Vietnam War, is "how exhilarating it is."[65] "Life's not the same anymore," said a Soviet veteran after returning from his country's war in Afghanistan in the 1980s. "I actually want to go on killing."[66] Widespread targeted mass killing (against Jews and national minorities) and deportations afflicted large parts of Europe before and during World War I. This created terrible precedents, and many European veterans— as well as civilians in some places—participated in later atrocities. Many of them spent the interwar years trying to revive the "spirit of annihilation" they had imbibed.[67] An Italian socialist of that era opined that World War I "accustomed the youngsters as well as the grown-ups to the daily use of usual and unusual weapons," and glorified "individual and collective murder, blackmail, arrest" and summary executions, creating a postwar political climate favorable to the growth of fascism.[68] Rightist paramilitaries in Germany were composed of young men who sought to recreate the camaraderie, excitement, and adventure of the war experience. For them, life away from the front was mundane and strangely stressful.

Warfare also obscures or hides terrible atrocities. Even in relatively democratic societies, governments tend to be spared sufficient scrutiny by the news media during wartime. If journalists are not "embedded" and thereby come to identify (more than usual) with their nation's troops, then they are far from the sites of atrocities. When news *does* emerge—in recent years, the proliferation of web-based sources of news and commentary has made it much harder to conceal the realities of war—domestic populations, conditioned to support the war effort, are often unreceptive or disbelieving.

Warfare has provided a cover for the radical goals and actions of violent regimes. Henry Morgenthau—the US ambassador to the Ottoman Empire, whose reports would provide substantial firsthand documentation of the Armenian genocide of 1915–1916—wrote: "The conditions of war gave to the Turkish Government its longed-for opportunity to lay hold of the Armenians."[69] Joseph Goebbels effused

---

[64]Glover, *Humanity*, 61–62. I have chosen a number of examples from US wars not because Americans are *more* prone to such conduct than peoples of other societies: Like other humans placed into extreme, inhumane circumstances, they are *equally* susceptible to war's brutalizing effects, despite training and instruction that is supposed to minimize violations of international laws of warfare. As the United States descends further into a permanent state of war and militarism, its citizens should challenge themselves to think more deeply about war's realities and consequences.

[65]Marlantes, *What It Is Like*, 62.

[66]Glover, *Humanity*, 55.

[67]Cathie Carmichael, *Genocide before the Holocaust* (New Haven, CT: Yale University Press, 2009), 26.

[68]Michael Mann, *Fascists* (New York: Cambridge University Press, 2004), 104.

[69]Quoted in Taner Akçam, *A Shameful Act: The Armenian Genocide and the Question of Turkish Responsibility* (New York: Metropolitan Books, 2006), 120, and Vahakn Dadrian, *The History of the Armenian Genocide* (New York: Berghahn, 2003), 207.

Indonesian dictator Suharto with President Richard M. Nixon
Indonesian head of state General Suharto (left) with Richard Nixon in Washington in May 1970. With the exception of the Sudanese government of Omar al-Bashir, which took power in 1989, the Indonesian military regime (1965–1999) is the only genocidal "repeat offender." Suharto's regime came to power by slaughtering 500,000 Indonesians for their presumed political allegiances, one of the foremost examples of genocide of a political group. Suharto's regime later conducted a protracted genocide in East Timor, killing one-fourth of the population. Documents that were unclassified in 2001 reveal that Suharto had the support of the U.S. administration for his invasion of East Timor in 1976.[1]

in his diary in March 1942, "Thank God, during the war we now have a whole series of possibilities which were barred to us in peacetime. We must exploit them."[70] The descent into warfare against Vietnam and other neighboring countries in 1977–1978, alongside other factors, pushed the Khmer Rouge to greater violence and an expanding search for disloyal or traitorous elements that finally encompassed hundreds of thousands of ethnic Khmers.[71]

The impersonal, bureaucratized nature of modern warfare creates various forms of emotional and physical distancing that make it easier to escape responsibility or feelings of personal guilt for one's role in terrible violence—or even to witness

---

[70]Elke Fröhlich, ed., *Die Tagebücher von Joseph Goebbels*, Part 2, Vol. 3 (Munich: K.G. Saur: 1994), 561.

[71]"The Secretary's 8:00 a.m. Staff Meeting, Tuesday, August 12, 1975," National Archives, Record Group 59, Department of State Records, Transcripts of Staff Meetings of Secretary of State Henry Kissinger, 1973–77; available at website of The National Security Archives (http://www2.gwu.edu/~nsarchiv); see also The National Security Archives, press release entitled "Ford and Kissinger Gave Green Light to Indonesia's Invasion of East Timor, 1975: New Documents Detail Conversations with Suharto," December 6, 2001: http://www2.gwu.edu/~nsarchiv/NSAEBB/NSAEBB62/press.html (accessed May 20, 2014).

the results.[72] The language of bureaucratized warfare aids in this distancing effect. Between 1969 and 1973 the US government conducted a bombing campaign that killed hundreds of thousands of civilians in Cambodia; the campaign was called "Operation Menu," and target areas were given such mundane codenames as "Lunch," "Dinner," and "Snack." A few years later, a member of the staff of Henry Kissinger (National Security Advisor to President Nixon) described the untroubled manner in which his colleagues, including Nixon and Kissinger, bandied about euphemisms to shield themselves from the consequences. "Though they spoke of terrible human suffering," observed the official, Roger Morris, "reality was sealed off by their trite, lifeless vernacular: 'capabilities,' 'objectives,' 'our chips,' 'give-away.'" With indignation, Morris added, "They were immune to the bloodshed and suffering they administered to their stereotypes" and seemed to believe that their "cool, deliberate detachment" and "banishment of feeling" were laudable.[73] After the bombing of Dresden in February 1945—a bombing campaign specifically aimed at civilians that claimed roughly 30,000 lives—the deputy to the British commander, Arthur "Bomber" Harris, deftly sidestepped all responsibility, direct or indirect. "I was not in any way responsible," he wrote, "nor was my Commander-in-Chief," Sir Harris. Their job was merely "to carry out . . . the instructions we received from the Air Ministry." And remarkably, the Air Ministry was also not responsible: It was "merely passing on instructions" from "those responsible for the higher direction of the war," whoever that may have been.[74]

Further reducing or masking human agency and individual responsibility, the US military has since 2004 launched thousands of unmanned "drone" bomber attacks in Pakistan, killing hundreds of civilians while terrorizing entire communities.[75] The drones, which have killed hundreds of civilians and terrorize large numbers of communities, are operated by military personnel stationed many

---

[72]Levene, *The Meaning of Genocide*, 53.
[73]John Pilger, *Heroes* (London: Vintage, 2001), 387.
[74]Glover, *Humanity*, 82–83.
[75]Regions of Pakistan have been the main targets, but "drones" (unmanned combat aerial vehicles) have also been deployed in Yemen and elsewhere under the justification of the "War on Terror." A comprehensive September 2012 report by an institute at Stanford University (with the collaboration of the Law Schools of Stanford as well as New York University) concludes that "from June 2004 through mid-September 2012, available data indicate that drone strikes killed 2,562–3,325 people in Pakistan, of whom 474–881 were civilians, including 176 children. The number of 'high-level' targets killed as a percentage of total casualties" is estimated at only 2 percent. Stanford International Human Rights & Conflict Resolution Clinic, "Living Under Drones: Death, Injury, and Trauma to Civilians from US Drone Practices in Pakistan," September 2012: http://livingunderdrones.org/wp-content/uploads/2012/10/Stanford-NYU-LIVING-UNDER-DRONES.pdf (accessed July 31, 2014). The Stanford report also chronicled the devastating emotional effects and the wide-spread disruption of daily life: "Drones hover twenty-four hours a day over communities in northwest Pakistan, striking homes, vehicles, and public spaces without warning. Their presence terrorizes men, women, and children, giving rise to anxiety and psychological trauma among civilian communities. . . . The US practice of striking one area multiple times, and evidence that it has killed rescuers, makes both community members and humanitarian workers afraid or unwilling to assist injured victims. Some community members shy away from gathering in groups, including important tribal dispute-resolution bodies, out of fear

thousands of miles away. In 2012 *The New York Times* and other sources reported that the Obama Administration commissioned a legal briefing that "embraced a disputed method for counting civilian casualties" that "in effect counts all military-age males in a strike zone as combatants . . . unless there is explicit intelligence posthumously proving them innocent."[76] This follows a long, dishonorable tradition whereby civilian victims of military aggression are categorized as belligerents, terrorists, or partisans. It is a "general characteristic of violence in war," argue Sönke Neitzel and Harald Welzer in a profoundly insightful inquiry into mentalities and motives of German soldiers on the Eastern Front, that "the behavior of those defined as 'enemies' confirms the legitimacy of that designation." Neitzel and Welzer also examined interviews and transcripts from American soldiers in Vietnam and Iraq who, like other occupying forces, came to see threats or enemies where they did not necessarily exist: "The only characteristic of 'target persons' that counts is that they pose a threat," and "any indication to that effect"—attempting to flee the occupiers, for example—"provides sufficient reason to kill."[77]

NATIONALISM, VULNERABILITY, PERCEPTIONS OF GRIEVANCE, AND HUMILIATION

The Introduction went into some detail concerning the place of racism and nationalism in fomenting aggression and violence. Each of our four case studies illustrated the lethal potential of delusional racial beliefs and aggressive ethnic nationalism. The CUP (the "Young Turks"), the German Nazis, the Khmer Rouge, and the Hutu-power extremists all employed the ugly concepts and terminology of "cleansing," stemming from obsessions with racial purity. The "Young Turk" architects of the Armenian genocide, steeped in the rhetoric and philosophy of racial science, spoke of Armenians as "tubercular microbes" infecting the national body or race. "Isn't it the duty of a doctor to destroy these microbes?" rhetorically asked a government leader who was also a doctor—and who, like Nazi doctors, happily lent his talents to genocide, believing it served the cause of progress.[78]

---

that they may attract the attention of drone operators. Some parents choose to keep their children home, and children injured or traumatized by strikes have dropped out of school."
[76]Jo Becker and Scott Shane, "Secret 'Kill List' Proves a Test of Obama's Principles and Will," *The New York Times*, March 29, 2012: http://www.nytimes.com/2012/05/29/world/obamas-leadership-in-war-on-al-qaeda.html?pagewanted=all (accessed July 13, 2012); see also Conor Friedersdorf, "What Bush's Iraq War and Obama's Drone Strikes Have in Common," *The Atlantic*, June 16, 2012: http://www.theatlantic.com/international/archive/2012/06/what-bushs-iraq-war-and-obamas-drone-strikes-have-in-common/258533/ (accessed July 13, 2012).
[77]Sönke Neitzel and Harald Welzer, *Soldaten: On Fighting, Killing and Dying: The Secret WWII Transcripts of German POWs* (New York: Knopf, 2012), 327–329.
[78]Balakian, *Burning Tigris*, 164. This was Behaeddin Shakir, a CUP leader and death-squad organizer. He exceeded his colleagues in sadistic cruelty against the Armenians, "nailing horseshoes to their feet and marching them through the streets." Balakian, 164. In 1922 he was assassinated by an Armenian group that killed several of the genocide's organizers.

A comparative study of genocide reveals many other common threads. In each of these four episodes and many similar ones, perpetrators felt aggrieved or humiliated by perceived injustices in the recent or distant past. Genocide requires a "great vision to justify a great wrong," in the words of Peter Uvin, who wrote about Rwanda. "Once a serious episode of violent conflict occurs, it leaves a permanent residue in people's memories and attitudes" and can be invoked by political leaders for many years.[79]

Serb nationalism was driven by a long-standing cultural tradition that depicted Bosnian Muslims, who are themselves a Slavic people, as traitors to the Slavs: They were allegedly "*bajile* or Turks, race traitors and killers of the Christ-Prince Lazar," a semimythical figure who holds a Christ-like place in Serbian religious-nationalist thought.[80] This myth derives from a 1389 battle against the Ottomans that is the cornerstone of Serb nationalism. The Serbian prince, Lazar, was killed, according to legend, defending his people from the Turks and hence from Islamic expansion and aggression. (In reality, Turkish soldiers fought on both sides, as did Serbs.) Lazar's martyrdom was adopted into a nationalist mythology with close similarities to Christianity's emphasis, for many centuries, on Jews as "Christ killers."[81]

How better to assert one's nationalism and redress perceived injustices than by aggressively expunging the source of weakness and subversion: the supposedly traitorous, alien peoples that you have allowed to settle in your midst? This was an impetus for the Bosnian genocide as well as for each of the four examples in the preceding chapters. Ziya Gökalp, chief ideologue for the CUP, argued that "Turkey could only be revitalized if it rid itself of its non-Muslim elements."[82] Like many other genocidal leaders and movements, the CUP promised national redemption and revival. A year or two before his government initiated its attacks on the Armenians, Gökalp wrote a poem in which he reflected upon his empire's recent disastrous defeats in the Balkan Wars (1912–1913): "We were defeated because we were backward," Gökalp lamented. "On progress we will set our heart / We shall skip five hundred years / And not stand still. Little time is left."[83]

In his stilted style—poetry is ill-suited to the cause of nationalist propaganda—Gökalp expressed a profound sense of urgency that often drove genocidal parties. The most murderous regimes of the last century, and therefore of human

[79]Peter Uvin, *Aiding Violence: The Development Enterprise in Rwanda* (West Hartford, CT: Kumarian Press, 1998), 219–220.
[80]Sells, *Bridge Betrayed*, 77.
[81]See Sells, *Bridge Betrayed*; Sells condensed his arguments for an essay, "Serbian Religious Mythology and the Genocide in Bosnia," in Omar Bartov and Phyllis Mack, eds., *In God's Name: Genocide and Religion in the Twentieth Century* (New York: Berghahn, 2001). Journalist and activist Chris Hedges pointed out that these types of nationalist myths "allow us to make sense of mayhem and violent death. It gives a justification to what is often nothing more than gross human cruelty and stupidity." Hedges, *War Is a Force That Gives Us Meaning* (New York: Anchor Books, 2003), 23.
[82]Balakian, *Burning Tigris*, 163–164.
[83]The poem is titled "Esnaf Destani." Levene, *The Meaning of Genocide*, 181.

Serbian nationalist propaganda
This 1916 poster exhorted Serbians to remember a battle in 1389 that forms the basis of a racist, nationalist mythology that contributed mightily to the atrocities of the 1990s. The 1389 "Battle of Kosovo," won by Turkish forces, fostered a myth that combined betrayal and martyrdom (a Serbian prince who died), racism (Muslims were a traitorous and malevolent "race"), and self-pity and humiliation (the notion that Serbia has always defended Europe from the "Turks," i.e., Muslims, but yet these sacrifices are not appreciated by the rest of Europe.) This myth did not always exert great force, but as Yugoslavia entered a profound crisis in the late 1980s, it was resurrected by politicians such as Slobodan Milosevic.

history, were the Hitler, Stalin, and Mao governments, all of which felt a burning, immediate need to remake their worlds. The similarities between these regimes, which ostensibly inhabited the far right and far left of the political spectrum, are stronger than their differences: a willingness to sacrifice large numbers of people, including their own citizens, in pursuit of abstract, unattainable ideological goals; fervent racial and nationalist philosophies; and the sheer depth and inflexibility of their respective ideologies. Huge numbers of people were killed not for utilitarian purposes—in order to clear them from a land that was desired, for example—but for political purposes. Alexander Solzhenitsyn, the Soviet dissident writer, observed: "Macbeth's self-justifications were feeble—and his conscience devoured him. Yes, even Iago was a little lamb too. The imagination and the spiritual strength of Shakespeare's evildoers stopped short at a dozen corpses. Because they had no *ideology*:"[84]

ANOTHER CENTURY OF WAR AND GENOCIDE?

If I am not for myself, then who will be for me? And if I am only for myself, then what am I? And if not now, when?

—Hillel the Elder, first century BCE

---

[84]From Solzhenitsyn's celebrated *The Gulag Archipelago* (published in English in 1974); quoted in Glover, *Humanity*, 252. Emphasis in original.

I was encouraged to end this book on a somewhat hopeful note, perhaps by re-
minding the readers that, even in the midst of the horrors chronicled in the preceding chapters, humans are capable of magnanimous acts of moral courage and
solidarity—of acting upon Hillel's injunction. Indeed, upon closer inspection of
any genocide, we find examples of not only the most barbarous but the most noble
impulses and acts. In the latter, we cannot easily discern the source of the motives;
like perpetrator behavior, brave and self-sacrificing defiance cannot be fully explained.[85] Anti-Nazi resisters Hans von Dohnanyi and Dietrich Bonhoeffer were
executed three weeks before the regime's downfall. "With apt simplicity," before
his death Dohnanyi explained their courageous efforts by saying they were "on the
path that a decent person inevitably takes."[86] Many other resisters and rescuers
were similarly disinclined to tout themselves as extraordinary or to seek praise.
I recently met a young woman from southern Rwanda whose family was decimated
during the genocide. She witnessed the deaths of her father and brothers but was
saved by a Hutu neighbor, who risked arrest and summary execution by the ram-
paging Interahamwe. When she spoke with her rescuer many years later, he was
embarrassed by her gratitude. "As a human being, what else could I have done?"
was his reply.

It would be misguided and false, though, to conclude this book by documenting
too many such hopeful anecdotes. Of course they exist, and the previous chapters
have uncovered, in appropriate proportion, examples of resistance, rescue, and
the full range of human responses in times of extreme crisis and moral chaos.
As this book goes to press, though, we see far too many examples of the failure of
the "international community" and of the human race to learn anything of value
from our shared history of war and genocide. Cynical diplomats and powerful
politicians exploit the Holocaust and the term "genocide" for political purposes—
either to deny that a genocide is unfolding or to invoke the Holocaust to generate
support for foreign-policy adventures. Saddam Hussein, an ally of the Americans
and the British while he committed his worst crimes, suddenly became "worse than
Hitler" when those same governments decided to invade Iraq for reasons having
nothing to do with human rights; the world dallies for years, debating whether
the term "genocide" applies to Darfur, rather than lifting a finger to alleviate the
suffering there. After a few years as a *cause célèbre*—a very easy way for Westerners
to lament the suffering and wring their hands—Darfur has disappeared from the

---

[85]I don't wish to overstate this point; like perpetrator behavior, we *do* have some highly
insightful analyses at our disposal: Pearl M. Oliner and Samuel M. Oliner, *The Altruistic
Personality: Rescuers of Jews in Nazi Europe* (New York: New Press, 1988); Eyal Press, *Beautiful
Souls: The Courage and Conscience of Ordinary People in Extraordinary Times* (New York: Farrar,
Straus and Giroux, 2012); Ervin Staub, *The Psychology of Good and Evil: Why Children, Adults,
and Groups Help and Harm Others* (New York: Cambridge University Press, 2003); and
Kristina E. Thalhammer, Paula L. O'Loughlin, et al., *Courageous Resistance: The Power of
Ordinary People* (New York: Palgrave Macmillan, 2007).
[86]Elisabeth Sifton and Fritz Stern, "The Tragedy of Dietrich Bonhoeffer and Hans von
Dohnanyi," New York Review of Books, October 25, 2012, 72.

headlines. Yet massive, government-directed violence continues, as reported by Radio Dabanga, "an extraordinary, collaborative effort by Darfuris in region and in the diaspora."[87] A murderous regime clings to power by raining bombs and poisonous chemicals on civilians in Syria; Muslims are sadistically killed by mobs and militias in the Central African Republic, while 3,000 miles to the south and west an army claiming the mantle of Islam (the "Boko Haram") abducts and enslaves teenage girls and commits other abominations. More lethal but less visible, thousands of people are condemned by an unjust global economic order to die in their childhood—more than 1,000, on average, every single hour. Throughout the globe, girls and women are oppressed and abused, and as one or two forms of bigotry recede in some places, others take their place. Millions of people are forced to flee their homelands because of war or economic devastation and are then treated as criminals, from Myanmar to southern Europe to South Africa to Arizona. We are all members of the same human family, and few of us have any emotional or material interest in economic exploitation, wars of aggression, or mass violence. But we allow all these evils, and time is running short. Humanity cannot survive another century like the last.

---

[87]"From these endless dispatches we learn that there is no security in the camps, most roads are too dangerous to travel, murders by marauding militia groups are a daily occurrence . . . and the epidemic of rape—often gang rape—of women and girls continues to have a distinct ethnic animus." Eric Reeves, "Failure to Prevent Genocide in Sudan and the Consequences of Impunity: Darfur as Precedent for Abyei, south Kordofan, and Blue Nile," *Genocide Studies International* 8, no. 1 (Spring 2014), 60.

BIBLIOGRAPHICAL ESSAY
AND SUGGESTED FILMS

"Why study genocide?," I am often asked, usually by students who despair of the subject a few weeks into a semester. In the preface to a book mentioned later in this chapter—the foremost textbook on the topic—Adam Jones remarks that by studying these patterns in human history we "study our historical inheritance"—an integral part of our existence for millennia, and one that is unlikely to disappear soon. He adds that by studying genocide we come into "contact with some of the most interesting and exciting debates in the social sciences and humanities":

> To what extent should genocide be understood as reflecting epic social transformations such as modernity, the rise of the state, and globalization? How has warfare been transformed in recent times, and how are the wars of the present age linked to genocide? How does gender shape genocidal experiences and genocidal strategies? How is history "produced," and what role do memories or denial of genocide play in that production[1]

And perhaps above all, Jones notes, for those of us concerned with "peace, human rights, and justice, there is a sense that with genocide you are confronting the 'Big One,' what Joseph Conrad called the 'heart of darkness.' . . . Whatever energy and commitment you invest in understanding genocide will be directed towards comprehending and confronting one of humanity's greatest scourges."[2]

Genocide studies originated in the study of the Holocaust in the 1960s and 1970s, which inevitably led to research that sought to understand the Holocaust in a longer lineage of targeted killing and mass atrocity. In the late 1970s and into the 1980s, pioneers such as Leo Kuper, Helen Fein, and Israel Charny began to stake out a territory now known as "genocide studies" or sometimes "comparative genocide" (a term subjected to compelling and thought-provoking scrutiny in Martin Shaw's "From Comparative to International Genocide Studies, *European Journal of International Relations* 18, no. 4, December 2012). The fact that genocide had hardly disappeared after 1945—the Cambodian catastrophe was prominently reported around the world—also forced these issues onto research and legal agendas. The Holocaust continues to attract far greater scholarly and

---

[1] Adam Jones, *Genocide: A Comprehensive Introduction* (New York: Routledge, 2010), xxiv–xxv.
[2] Ibid., xxiv–xxv.

public attention in the United States and Europe than other genocides, an imbalance reflected in this bibliography. I have attempted to point the reader to the most important works for each topic while balancing various subfields and subgenres within each; yet the Holocaust section is inevitably longer because several Holocaust books are published for each book on other genocides. I take note of this without making grand statements about the justice or injustice of this imbalance; it is simply a fact.

The following bibliographic summaries offer only English-language texts. Several websites provide more extensive (and occasionally annotated) bibliographies, in particular the University of Minnesota's Center for Holocaust & Genocide Studies (http://www .chgs.umn.edu/webbib/biblio/). Moreover, most of the recently published books listed in the next section include extensive bibliographies. Each issue of the quarterly journal *Holocaust and Genocide Studies*, which is published by the US Holocaust Memorial Museum in Washington, DC, includes an up-to-date list of new books in genocide studies and subfields.

GENOCIDE, WAR CRIMES, AND CRIMES AGAINST HUMANITY

Raphael Lemkin introduced the concept and terminology of "genocide" in his 1944 *Axis Rule in Occupied Europe: Laws of Occupation, Analysis of Government, Proposals for Redress* (latest edition: The Lawbook Exchange, Ltd., 2012). We still have much to learn from Lemkin's attention to the interplay between imperialism and genocide, his subtle understanding of cultural genocide, and many other issues. The 2012 edition includes excellent introductory essays by William Schabas and Samantha Power. Lemkin's unfinished autobiography, *Totally Unofficial*, was edited by Donna-Lee Frieze and published by Yale University Press in 2013. It is a deeply engaging book, and one completes reading it with great admiration for the author.

A full generation or so passed before others picked up Lemkin's mantle. Several pioneering works appeared at the end of the 1970s and early 1980s, marking the emergence of a distinctive field of studies. Helen Fein's *Accounting for Genocide: National Responses and Jewish Responses During the Holocaust* (New York: Free Press, 1979), ranges beyond Nazi atrocities in its concerns and in its nimble approach to the ever-vexing question of defining genocide. Leo Kuper's *Genocide: Its Political Use in the Twentieth Century* (New Haven, CT: Yale University Press, 1981) was another milestone—probably the most thorough analysis, to that point, since Lemkin. Kuper's book looks at the common features and dynamics of atrocities that do not always fit into a "genocide" definition, helping to broaden the field of vision of his successors.

First published in 1976 with a slightly different title, Irving Louis Horowitz's *Taking Lives: Genocide and State Power* (Piscataway, NJ: Transaction Publishers, 1981) was an important part of this emerging oeuvre. Israel Charny's work was also groundbreaking in creating and extending the genre. A psychotherapist, his *How Can We Commit the Unthinkable? Genocide, the Human Cancer* (Boulder, CO: Westview Press, 1982) identified historical and political stages and psychological processes that can lead to mass killing. Later in the decade Charny embarked on several path-breaking initiatives, such the creation of an international network, which produced the newsletter "Internet on the Holocaust and Genocide" from 1985 to 1995; and the two-volume *Encyclopedia of Genocide*, which he edited (Santa Barbara, CA: ABC-CLIO, 1999) and which possesses enormous scope. Frank Chalk and Kurt Jonassohn's *The History and Sociology of Genocide* (New Haven, CT: Yale University Press, 1990) was another milestone of enduring value. It includes short selections from dozens of experts, and to this day few single-volume books feature its geographic and chronological breadth.

There are several outstanding overviews available today. Best among the single-author volumes is Adam Jones's *Genocide: A Comprehensive Introduction* (New York: Routledge, 2010; a third edition will be published in 2016). Adam Jones is among today's leading—and most prolific—scholars of genocide. *Genocide* is truly comprehensive, ranging from antiquity to numerous episodes that straddle the porous borders between "genocide" and "mere" crimes against humanity. The book also ventures to offer strong passages on the psychology of perpetrators; genocide denial; international law; and artistic representations. It is perfectly suited for classroom purposes, while challenging scholars with its numerous striking insights regarding gender and other issues. Having long established himself as the English-speaking world's leading expert on the Khmer Rouge genocide, Ben Kiernan embarked on an ambitious synthesis of the latest research on multiple cases: *Blood and Soil: A History of Genocide from Sparta to Rwanda* (New Haven, CT: Yale University Press, 2007). As its name indicates, this is a sweeping history, successfully integrating such episodes as English involvement in Ireland in the sixteenth century; the genocide of the Aboriginal people of Australia; and "settler genocides" in nineteenth-century Africa, in addition to depressingly familiar episodes from the last one hundred years. If the book sometimes suffers from its author's compulsion to apply his central thesis—that genocide stems from "cults of agriculture" and "antiquity" as well as from expansionism and racism—to each episode, this is nonetheless the most successful attempt at a world history of genocide. With Robert Gellately, Kiernan coedited *The Specter of Genocide: Mass Murder in Historical Perspective* (New York: Cambridge University Press, now in its fourth printing, 2006), which contains essays by leading scholars on topics ranging from Stalin's atrocities to East Timor and Ethiopia, with an emphasis on the twentieth century. Some essays are devoted to more complex theoretical and historical issues (e.g., "the modernity of genocides"), and most chapters delve into relevant theoretical considerations (modernity, total war, ideology) that are highly illuminating. For a well-written, accessible introduction to the topic of genocide by one of today's top experts: Martin Shaw, *What Is Genocide?* (Cambridge, UK: Polity, 2007; second edition, 2015). Shaw has made several notable contributions to the field, including his *War and Genocide: Organized Killing in Modern Society* (Cambridge, UK: Polity, 2003), and his website is an excellent resource (http://martinshaw.org/).

One of the finest genocide-themed collections currently in print is *Centuries of Genocide: Eyewitness Accounts and Critical Views* (New York: Routledge, 2013), edited by Samuel Totten and William S. Parsons. Now in its fourth edition (Israel Charny coedited the first two editions), this book is quite useful for the college classroom because of its emphasis on primary readings; each of the fifteen chapters is accompanied by a handful of eyewitness accounts. Aimed at advanced students and fellow scholars, Donald Bloxham and A. Dirk Moses edited *The Oxford Handbook of Genocide Studies* (New York: Oxford University Press, 2010), with chapters on theory (gender, memory), practical matters (law), and disciplinary approaches (anthropology, political science, sociology). The series of chapters that confronts the connections with colonialism and imperialism are particularly cogent, and anything by Bloxham or Moses demands attention. For *Defining the Horrific: Readings on Genocide and Holocaust in the Twentieth Century* (Pearson Prentice Hall, 2003), William L. Hewitt compiled primary and secondary readings on more than a dozen genocides. He includes other cases of human rights abuses and atrocities (Argentina's dictatorship of 1976–1983; famines in Soviet Ukraine, Maoist China, North Korea, and Sudan) that not all scholars would characterize as genocidal, but that warrant inclusion in an overview of state-sponsored criminality. Following a similar format, but much more extensive, is Jens Meierhenrich, editor, *Genocide: A Reader* (New York: Oxford University Press, 2014). This book would be well worth its price for the editor's introductory essay alone ("The Study and History of Genocide"), and Meierhenrich exercised great skill and wise judgment in assembling and editing the readings. His book is truly a marvelous accomplishment, surpassing in its scope other comparable works.

There are many other single-author books that are more narrowly focused, addressing several cases in a comparative framework: Eric Weitz's *A Century of Genocide: Utopias of Race and Nation* (Princeton, NJ: Princeton University Press, 2005) ties together the atrocities of the Soviet Union, Nazism, Cambodia, and the Bosnian War by uncovering their common origins in the utopian (or dystopian) passions unleashed by racism and nationalism. Michael Mann's *The Dark Side of Democracy: Explaining Ethnic Cleansing* (New York: Cambridge University Press, 2004) explores the violent logic of demographic obsessions and schemes from the "Young Turks" and the Nazis to Yugoslavia and Rwanda. Donald Bloxham furthers this line of enquiry in a collection of his essays, *The World Wars and the Unweaving of Europe* (London: Vallentine Mitchell, 2008), focusing on the Armenian and Nazi genocides.

Compelling, persuasive recent inquiries into the origins of targeted mass killing include Mark Levene, *Genocide in the Age of the Nation State*. Vol. 1: *The Meaning of Genocide* (London: I.B. Taurus, 2005), which systematically traces the role of key elements of the modern experience, arguing that genocide is part and parcel of these processes. Levene's Vol. 2: *The Rise of the West and the Coming of Genocide* (London: I.B. Taurus, 2005) traces genocidal belief systems to late the eighteenth century and the age of European expansionism. One of the more influential as well as prolific authors in this field, Levene has recently completed a massive two-volume work that is already inducing us to reconsider many categories and concepts: *Devastation*: Volume I: *The European Rimlands 1912–1938* and *Annihilation*: Volume II: *The European Rimlands, 1939–1953* (both published by Oxford University Press in 2014).

Other important recent books and articles that have sparked discussion and debate about the origins and dynamics of genocidal violence in the modern world include the following: Jacques Sémelin, *Purify and Destroy: The Political Uses of Massacre and Genocide* (New York: Columbia University Press, 2009); Christopher Powell, *Barbaric Civilization: A Critical Sociology of Genocide* (Montreal and London: McGill-Queen's University Press, 2011), which includes a succinct account of the genocides of Australian Aboriginals as well as Tasmanians; and Christian Gerlach, *Extremely Violent Societies: Mass Violence in the Twentieth-Century World* (New York: Cambridge University Press, 2010), which breaks out of definitional debates by taking a new approach and, as Dirk Moses wrote in a promotional blurb, "convincingly argues that complex processes during transitional crises enlist all social groups in producing these terrible outcomes." Ernesto Verdeja, "On Situating the Study of Genocide Within Political Violence" (*Genocide Studies and Prevention* 7, no. 1, Spring 2012) also adroitly transcends the boundaries that we sometimes erect between various expressions of mass violence. Michael Rothberg, who is a professor of literature and language, published *Multidirectional Memory: Remembering the Holocaust in the Age of Decolonization* (Redwood City, CA: Stanford University Press, 2009), an elegant inquiry into postcolonial and post-Holocaust memory in Europe and the United States, drawing upon the experience of France's ruthless war to maintain colonial rule in Algeria.

In addition to the book mentioned earlier, Adam Jones has written or edited many substantive and valuable works, such as *New Directions in Genocide Research* (New York: Routledge, 2012), which has chapters on reconciliation (in Rwanda), structural violence, and "genocidal masculinity" (and another chapter titled "Invisible Males," about the sexual violence against men in Congo). *Genocide, War Crimes, and the West* (London: Zed Books, 2004), also edited by Jones, includes short essays and longer articles that put a spotlight on numerous deplorable crimes committed in the name of "democracy," anti-Communism and counterinsurgency, or the opening of "free markets." It is a much-needed corrective to mainstream scholarship and journalism. Paul Bartrop is editor or coeditor of several significant works in our field. See in particular *The Genocide Studies Reader*, with excellent chapters on sexual violence and many other under-researched topics, coedited with Samuel Totten (New York: Routledge, 2009), and *Fifty Key Thinkers on the Holocaust and Genocide*, coedited with Steven L. Jacobs (New York: Routledge, 2010), an astute analysis of the main thinkers and issues in genocide studies. Totten's name adorns the covers of many important collections, including *Genocide of Indigenous Peoples: A Critical Bibliographic Review* (Piscataway, NJ: Transaction Publishers, 2010), which he coedited with Robert K. Hitchcock. The world's powers can no longer claim ignorance of atrocities in far-flung corners of the globe. Samantha Power's *"A Problem from Hell": America and the Age of Genocide* (Harper, 2002) offers a penetrating analysis of the unhelpful (at best) role of the world's powers, concentrating on US policy in the late twentieth century with lengthy chapters on Cambodia, Iraq under Hussein, Bosnia, and Rwanda. The book would be well worth reading simply for Power's poignant description of Lemkin's life and work in the first chapters.

Readers of this essay may have deduced that for many years Lemkin's 1944 book occupied a lonely place on library shelves. In 1951, long before genocide attracted serious attention in the worlds of academia or law, the Civil Rights Congress, an organization of prominent African American activists, presented to the UN a lengthy petition entitled *We Charge Genocide: The Crime of Government Against the Negro People*. It was then published in book form (New York: International Publishers, 1951). The principal author was William L. Patterson, and Paul Robeson, W. E .B. Du Bois, and Claudia Jones were among his colleagues in this endeavor, which represented a significant early attempt to take seriously the Genocide Convention of 1948 and to apply it to events beyond the Holocaust. *We Charge Genocide* consists largely of accounts of racist violence in the United States, which it relates to specific articles in the Genocide Convention. Not everyone will agree fully with its application of the term "genocide," but this document forces the reader to confront the scale and implications of institutionalized, violent racism over a very long stretch of American history. This pioneering effort of Patterson, Robeson, et al. merits greater recognition; unfortunately, it has often been ignored or denigrated. The Dan Stone book mentioned at the end of this section contains an excellent discussion, by Ann Curthoys and John Docker, of *We Charge Genocide*.

Colonialism and imperialism have often produced genocidal violence, as most observers since Lemkin have detected. But precisely how should we understand the relations between these phenomena and go beyond superficial observations about "parallels" and "precedents"? These questions have been skillfully elucidated in a collection edited by A. Dirk Moses, *Empire, Colony, Genocide: Conquest, Occupation, and Subaltern Resistance in World History* (New York: Berghahn, 2009). Moses's earlier *Genocide and Settler Society: Frontier Violence and Stolen Indigenous Children in Australian History* (New York: Berghahn, 2004) is among the most incisive texts on this topic.

Because racism is an essential element of virtually all modern genocides, I will also list some important, influential works on the construction and history of "race": Stephen Jay Gould's classic 1981 *The Mismeasure of Man*, re-published in an expanded edition in 1996 (New York: Norton); William H. Tucker, *The Science and Politics of Racial Research* (Champaign, IL: University of Illinois Press, 1994); Theodore Allen's two-volume *The Invention of the White Race* (1994, 1997; republished in 2012); Charles W. Mills, *The Racial Contract.* (Ithaca, NY: Cornell University Press, 1997); several books by George M. Fredrickson over his long career (d. 2008), including *Racism: A Short History* (Princeton, NJ: Princeton University Press, 2003), which distills many of his pioneering arguments; Patrick Brantlinger, *Dark Vanishings: Discourse on the Extinction of Primitive Races* (Ithaca, NY: Cornell University Press, 2003); *Race in North America: Origin and Evolution of a Worldview* (4th edition published in 2011) by anthropologist Audrey Smedley, who has written other valuable books and articles on this topic; and Nell Irvin Painter's *The History of White People* (New York: Norton, 2011). By searching online for "PBS 'race: power of an illusion'" you will find an exceptionally useful website that complements a 2003 televised series of that title. It includes videos, other resources, and short articles—perfect for classroom use—by such authorities as Fredrickson and Smedley.[3]

Racism is the "original sin," so to speak, of the United States, and if it were within my power I would mandate the reading of these recent books in all US high schools and colleges so that more white Americans could begin to understand the depth, viciousness, and persistence of racist oppression: Timothy Tyson, *Blood Done Sign My Name: A True Story* (New York: Broadway Books, 2005); James A. Loewen, *Sundown Towns: A Hidden Dimension of American Racism* (New York: Touchstone, 2006); Harriet A. Washington, *Medical Apartheid: The Dark History of Medical Experimentation on Black Americans from Colonial Times to the Present* (New York: Anchor, 2008); Douglas A. Blackmon, *Slavery by Another Name: The Re-Enslavement of Black Americans from the Civil War to World War II* (New York: Anchor, 2009); Danielle L. McGuire, *At the Dark End of the Street: Black Women, Rape, and Resistance—A New History of the Civil Rights Movement from Rosa Parks to the Rise of Black Power* (New York: Vintage, 2011) ; Michelle Alexander, *The New Jim Crow: Mass Incarceration in the Age of Colorblindness* (New York: The New Press, 2012) ; Bryan Stevenson, *Just Mercy: A Story of Justice and Redemption* (Spiegel & Grau, 2014); and Ta-Nehisi Coates's 2014 essay for *The Atlantic*, "The Case for Reparations," which is easily found on the author's excellent blog at www.theatlantic.com, as well as Coates's 2015 *Between the World and Me* (New York: Spiegel & Grau).

Scholars and activists have recently turned their attention to sexual violence in relation to genocide. In 2012 John Roth, editor of an important early collection on gender in the Holocaust, coedited (with Carol Rittner) *Rape: Weapon of War and Genocide* (St. Paul, MN: Paragon House, 2012), with chapters on Guatemala and other less-known examples of rape as an element of genocidal destruction. This book also possesses perhaps the most thorough, updated bibliography on related issues. *Sites of Violence: Gender and Conflict Zones* (Berkeley, CA: University of California Press, 2004), edited by Wenona Giles and Jennifer Hyndman, features essays on Iraqi Kurdistan and other cases; Elizabeth D. Heineman, who helped pave the way for greater research into gender issues in Nazi Germany, recently edited a valuable collection on gender issues in other contexts: *Sexual Violence in Conflict Zones: From the Ancient World to the Era of Human Rights* (Philadelphia: University of Pennsylvania Press, 2011). Jane L. Leatherman's *Sexual Violence and Armed Conflict* (Cambridge, UK and Malden, MA: Polity, 2011) is a slimmer volume that makes links to other economic and cultural processes and is another strong addition to this ever-growing field of study. The Japanese empire's systematic use of sexual slavery and violence in China, Korea, the Philippines, and elsewhere—many thousands of Japanese women were also abused and exploited by these practices—in the 1930s and 1940s has prompted scholarly attention; see Yuki Tanaka (2009), Sarah C. Soh (2009), and George Hicks (1995). Cynthia Enloe has contributed powerfully to our understanding of warfare, militarism, and gender; see especially *Maneuvers: International Politics of Militarizing Women's Lives* (Berkeley, CA: University of California Press, 2000) and *Globalization and Militarism: Feminists Make the Link* (New York: Rowman & Littlefield Publishers, 2007). In 2004 Tara Gingerich and Jennifer Leaning produced a report entitled *The Use of Rape as a Weapon of War in the Conflict in Darfur, Sudan* (available online through the

---

[3]While completing this book I discovered that my rather humble friend Chuck Barger helped design this site.

Physicians for Human Rights), which again offers broader insights into gender relations and dynamics during war and conflict. Amnesty International has produced numerous well-researched studies of sexual violence in Rwanda, Yugoslavia, and elsewhere.

Norman Naimark's *Stalin's Genocides* (Princeton, NJ: Princeton University Press, 2010) catalogs the long list of crimes against a vast range of ethnic, social, and political groups during Stalin's reign, arguing forcefully for the "genocide" designation. Naimark had earlier written *Fires of Hatred: Ethnic Cleansing in the Twentieth Century* (Cambridge, MA: Harvard University Press, 2002), which is particularly useful for its insightful chapters on the Armenian genocide and the Yugoslav wars of the 1990s. *Fires of Hatred* also includes a chapter on the mass expulsions of ethnic Germans in the aftermath of World War II. For more extensive treatments of this topic, also see, most recently: R. M. Douglas, *Orderly and Humane: The Expulsion of the Germans After the Second World War* (New Haven, CT: Yale University Press, 2012) and Keith Lowe, *Savage Continent: Europe in the Aftermath of World War II* (New York: St. Martin's Press, 2012).

"How can human beings commit such deplorable, cruel acts?" is the question that haunts genocide studies. Christopher Browning (see the Holocaust bibliography later in this chapter) wrote a book in 1993, *Ordinary Men,* that exerts a lasting influence on all subsequent investigations of perpetrator motivations. Ervin Staub's *The Roots of Evil: The Origins of Genocide and Other Group Violence* (New York: Cambridge University Press, 1989) has retained its value for a new generation; he examined the torturers of Argentina's military dictatorship (1976–1983), among other perpetrators. Staub contributed an essay that opens *Understanding Genocide: The Social Psychology of the Holocaust* (New York: Oxford University Press, 2002), edited by Leonard S. Newman and Ralph Erber, a book that provides insights of relevance far beyond the Nazi experience. In recent years, any discussion of perpetrator behavior will refer to psychologist James Waller's *Becoming Evil: How Ordinary People Commit Genocide and Mass Killing* (New York: Oxford University Press, 2007). I hasten to add that "perpetrator" is an inadequate term. Like "collaborator" or "bystander"—or even "resister"—the term implies rigid boundaries between the myriad of human responses in times of extreme crisis, tyranny, and warfare; yet there is not a simple and well-understood alternative to "perpetrator." Each genocide has also uncovered moral heroism in addition to opportunism and compliance. Jacques Sémelin, Claire Andrieu, and Sarah Gensburger coedited *Resisting Genocide: The Multiple Forms of Rescue* (New York: Columbia University Press, 2011).

Dan Stone edited a major collection in 2008 that sums up and also enhances this field of study: *The Historiography of Genocide* (Basingstoke, UK: Palgrave Macmillan, 2008). Each issue of the *Journal of Genocide Research* should be read carefully by researchers and students who are interested in these issues. Other journals in the field include *Genocide Studies & Prevention* and *Holocaust and Genocide Studies*. Reflecting the strong health and steady expansion of genocide studies, with each passing year at least one or two major multiauthor volumes appear. Among the stronger such collections in recent years: Joyce Apsel and Ernesto Vardeja, editors, *Genocide Matters: Ongoing Issues and Emerging Perspectives* (New York: Routledge, 2013). Graduate students looking for an original research topic would profit from consulting the editors' introductory essay; other contributors include established and emerging authorities. Finally, for those with access to a good university library: The three-volume *Encyclopedia of Genocide and Crimes Against Humanity* (Dinah L. Shelton, editor in chief; Thomson Gale, 2005) is the most comprehensive such collection, and the entries are written by experts in their respective fields. The *Online Encyclopedia of Mass Violence* (http://www.massviolence.org/) is extremely useful and is regularly updated with intriguing, scholarly articles. As examples: As I write this, the last two articles posted were "Bombs Bursting in Air: State and Citizen Responses to the US Firebombing and Atomic Bombing of Japan" and "Aid Offered Jews in Nazi Germany: Research Approaches, Methods, and Problems."

In his 2009 book *The Final Solution: A Genocide*, Donald Bloxham remarked that while *all* genocides should demand us to contemplate their philosophical implications, "most other genocides have not been of sufficient interest to western intellectuals for them to ponder their metaphysical dimensions in the way the Holocaust has been pondered."[4] This helps explain the imbalances in the following sections of this essay: The section on Holocaust literature is considerably longer than the sections devoted to the Armenian, Cambodian, and Rwandan genocides for the simple fact that the Holocaust has been the subject of much more extensive research and writing in the English language, as statistics from WorldCat database, the Library of Congress catalog, and other such sources indicate.

THE ARMENIAN GENOCIDE

As Donald Bloxham and Fatma Müge Göçek noted in an essay for Dan Stone's *The Historiography of Genocide*, there exist two "mutually exclusive historiographies": one that encompasses the worldwide scholarly community and "the other assembled by the proponents of the Turkish state," which is a historiography that does not merit inclusion here.[5] The Turkish government continues to deny the systematic murder of Armenians, and therefore Turkish historians who argue that there *was* an Armenian genocide perpetrated by Turkish authorities risk persecution and even prosecution. Taner Akçam ran afoul of Turkey's right-wing government for his political activism and fled prison, and the country, in 1977. Settling in Germany, he has written several of the most important, probing works on the genocide, including his recently updated *The Young Turks' Crime Against Humanity: The Armenian Genocide and Ethnic Cleansing in the Ottoman Empire* (Princeton, NJ: Princeton University Press, 2012). Akçam has written, cowritten, or edited numerous other texts in various languages.

Vahakn Dadrian's *The History of the Armenian Genocide* (New York: Berghahn, 2004) is also highly recommended as an introduction and analysis of Ottoman genocide. Without sacrificing academic rigor, Peter Balakian's *The Burning Tigris: The Armenian Genocide and the American Response* (New York: Harper Perennial, 2004) aimed at (and reached) a much larger audience than the aforementioned works. After establishing himself as a well-regarded writer and poet, Balakian turned his attention to the disaster that had claimed a large part of his grandmother's family. Despite its daunting size (1,000 pages including notes and other materials), Raymond Kévorkian's *The Armenian Genocide: A Complete History* (London: I.B. Tauris, 2011) is a significant new addition to the growing literature. *A Question of Genocide* (New York: Oxford University Press, 2011), edited by Ronald Grigor Suny, Fatma Müge Göçek, and Norman Naimark, collects several insightful essays that delve into such topics as the role of present-day Turkish nationalism in promoting genocide denial; the emergence and activities of Armenian political organizations prior to the genocide; and the Assyrian genocide.

With his *Massacres, Resistance, Protectors: Muslim-Christian Relations in Eastern Anatolia During World War I* (Piscataway, NJ: Gorgias Press, 2006), David Gaunt provided the most lucid account of a dimension that is sometimes neglected: the attacks on Assyrians, Greeks, and other Christian populations in addition to the Armenians. For a longer look at Armenian history, Ronald Grigor Suny, *Looking Toward Ararat: Armenia in Modern History*

---

[4]Donald Bloxham, *The Final Solution: A Genocide* (Oxford: Oxford University Press, 2009), 318.
[5]Dan Stone, *The Historiography of Genocide* (Basingstoke, UK : Palgrave Macmillan, 2008), 344.

(Bloomington, IN: Indiana University Press, 1994) is an earlier work by a historian who has made many profound contributions to our understanding of the histories of Russia and elsewhere in the region. US Ambassador Henry Morgenthau struggled in vain to halt the massacres, and his *Ambassador Morgenthau's Story* (New York: Doubleday, 1919) is still available (via new editions from small publishers, as well as on Kindle) and still of substantial value for its contemporaneous accounts.

Each genocide in this book was shaped by regional relations and conflicts. In *Shattering Empires: The Clash and Collapse of the Ottoman and Russian Empires 1908–1918* (Cambridge, UK: Cambridge University Press, 2011), Michael A. Reynolds presents a well-researched account of these larger contexts. Donald Bloxham's *The Great Game of Genocide: Imperialism, Nationalism, and the Destruction of the Ottoman Armenians* (New York: Oxford University Press, 2007) also skillfully integrates this sad tale into broader developments in that era, and is characteristically well-researched and sharply written.

Akçam and Dadrian cowrote a captivating history of the trials that took place shortly after World War I and that left mixed, unsatisfactory conclusions: *Judgment at Istanbul: The Armenian Genocide Trials* (New York: Berghahn, 2011). Michael Bobelian's *Children of Armenia: A Forgotten Genocide and the Century-Long Struggle for Justice* (New York: Simon & Schuster, 2009) takes a longer, albeit succinct and engaging, view of legal and political issues and with justified indignation traces the long history of denial and acquiescence in that denial. *The Armenian Genocide: Cultural and Ethical Legacies* (Piscataway, NJ: Transaction Publishers, 2007) by Richard G. Hovannisian is another solid contribution to this subgenre. Donald Miller and Lorna Touryan Miller edited an effective collection of testimonies: *Survivors: An Oral History of the Armenian Genocide* (Berkeley: University of California Press, 1999). Several historical studies appeared in 2015 to mark the genocide's centennial, the strongest of which appear to be Ronald Grigor Suny, *"They Can Live in the Desert but Nowhere Else": A History of the Armenian Genocide* (Princeton, NJ: Princeton University Press) and Thomas de Waal, *Great Catastrophe: Armenians and Turks in the Shadow of Genocide* (New York: Oxford University Press).

Several memorable autobiographical accounts and novels have appeared in English in the last two decades. Peter Balakian's *Black Dog of Fate: A Memoir* (New York: Basic Books, 2009) is essential reading for students of this topic. In some ways *Black Dog* is similar to a film mentioned later in this bibliography, *Ararat*, that confronts complex issues of individual and collective memory two or three generations after a terrible trauma. Balakian helped uncover and publish a memoir that his great-uncle had written as events unfolded around him: Grigoris Balakian, *Armenian Golgotha: A Memoir of the Armenian Genocide, 1915–1918* (New York: Vintage, 2010). Both books have earned high praise from experts in history and literature. Greek and Assyrian Christians were also massively targeted in the genocide. Thea Halo wrote movingly about the experiences of her Pontian Greek family's arduous flight and, by extension, that of many others: *Not Even My Name: A True Story* (New York: Picador, 2001).

THE NAZI HOLOCAUST

Raul Hilberg is largely responsible for the inception of Holocaust studies with his three-volume *The Destruction of the European Jews* (3rd edition, New Haven, CT: Yale University Press, 2003). A condensed version is also available ("Student One-Volume Edition," Boulder, CO: Holmes & Meier, 1985). Surprising though this sounds today, in the 1950s there was little scholarly or popular interest in the study of the Holocaust. Hilberg's doctoral adviser pled with him—in vain, fortunately—to choose another topic, and after completing his 2,000-page dissertation Hilberg waged a long, lonely struggle to find a publisher.

The Destruction of the European Jews appeared without fanfare in 1961, published by the now-defunct Quadrangle Books (Chicago). Hilberg seems to have been driven into this practically nonexistent field of study by both his abhorrence of Nazism and his conclusion that previous book-length studies—all two of them!—were inadequate. We have benefited enormously from Hilberg's tome, for which the overused adjective "magisterial" is entirely suited. After fifty years it continues to inspire and challenge our field of study. Another pioneering work that, because it was ahead of its time, lurked in obscurity and was later overshadowed by Hilberg's work, is Leon Poliakov, *Harvest of Hate: The Nazi Program for the Destruction of the Jews of Europe* (Syracuse University Press, 1954; paperback edition, Talman Co., 1979). Poliakov situated the Holocaust within the long history of anti-Jewish persecutions, and also within the context of Nazi expansionism and racism. The work of Filip (aka Philip) Friedman has also sadly become obscure to nonspecialists and even many specialists. The Polish-Jewish Holocaust survivor wrote a Polish-language history of Auschwitz in 1946, and after emigrating to the United States Friedman wrote other works on the Holocaust that are among the very first scholarly examinations of the Shoah. A posthumous collection published by his wife in 1980, *Roads to Extinction: Essays on the Holocaust* (Philadelphia: Jewish Publication Society of America) shows the range and detail of his work.[6]

There are several excellent Holocaust overviews that are aimed at college and larger audiences. At the forefront of the latest generation of Holocaust historians, Doris Bergen is the author of the most useful short text: *War & Genocide: A Concise History of the Holocaust* (Rowman & Littlefield, 2009). Bergen's judgment on key issues is impeccable, and this book is perfectly suited to the college classroom. David Crowe takes full advantage of additional space—his book is roughly twice the length of Bergen's—to delve deeper into the background and aftermath of the genocide in *The Holocaust: Roots, History, and Aftermath* (New York: Westview, 2008). The book profits greatly from Crowe's expertise in Eastern European history, the history of the Romanies, and international law. Other well-researched and highly regarded assessments include Leni Yahil's classic *The Holocaust: The Fate of European Jewry, 1932–1945* (New York: Oxford University Press, 1991) and Deborah Dwork and Robert Jan Van Pelt, *The Holocaust* (New York: Norton, 2003). Virtually anything by Yehuda Bauer deserves to be read and reread. For introductions and assessments on key debates within Holocaust studies, Donald Niewyk has edited and updated the widely assigned *The Holocaust: Problems and Perspectives of Interpretation* (4th edition: Stamford, CT: Wadsworth Publishing, 2010).

Christopher Browning's *Ordinary Men: Reserve Police Battalion 101 and the Final Solution in Poland* (New York: Perennial, 1993) is widely considered a classic of modern historical literature. Through its examination of the most disturbing question raised by the study of genocide—the factors that induce seemingly normal people to commit such acts—*Ordinary Men* has exerted a powerful influence far beyond the realm of Holocaust studies. On other central questions, such as the debate between "functionalists" and "intentionalists" (regarding the decision-making process and ideological origins of the Holocaust), Browning has often led the way. Two important collections of his essays are *Fateful Months: Essays on the Emergence of the Final Solution* (New York: Holmes & Meier, 1985) and *The Path to Genocide: Essays on Launching the Final Solution* (New York:

---

[6]For an assessment of Friedman's work and its influence, see Laurence Weinbaum, "Remembering a Forgotten Hero of Holocaust Historiography," *Jewish Political Studies Review* 24, no. 3–4 (Fall 2012); and Roni Stauber, "Philip Friedman and the Beginning of Holocaust Historiography," in David Bankier and Dan Michman, eds., *Holocaust Historiography in Context: Emergence, Challenges, Polemics and Achievements* (Jerusalem: Yad Vashem Publications, 2009), 83–102.

Cambridge University Press, 1992). More recently, Browning's *The Origins of the Final Solution: The Evolution of Nazi Jewish Policy, September 1939–March 1942* (Lincoln, NE: University of Nebraska Press, 2004) earned lofty and justified praise from Hilberg and others, while *Remembering Survival: Inside a Nazi Slave Labor Camp* (New York: W.W. Norton & Co., 2010) deepens our understanding of the multiple types of traumatic memory and the value, when used judiciously, of survivor testimony.

Nazi victimization of the Roma and Sinti has still not received adequate scholarly or public attention. Ian Hancock, an energetic advocate for the Romani people, has written many articles that can be found online quickly, in addition to contributions he has made to edited volumes such as the one listed earlier. An excellent and easily accessible source is this collection of essays: *Roma and Sinti: Under-Studied Victims of Nazism (Symposium Proceedings)*, available on the website of the US Holocaust Memorial Museum (http://www.ushmm.org/research/center/publications/occasional/2002-06/paper.pdf). Two general histories of the Roma and Sinti peoples that have strong chapters on their persecution by the Nazis: Isabel Fonseca, *Bury Me Standing: The Gypsies and Their Journey* (New York: Vintage, 1996) and David Crowe, *A History of the Gypsies of Eastern Europe and Russia* (Basingstoke, UK: Palgrave Macmillan, 2007). Crowe is also the author of the most thorough biography of Oskar Schindler. On the murder of disabled Germans and others: Henry Friedlander's *The Origins of Nazi Genocide: From Euthanasia to the Final Solution* (Chapel Hill, NC: University of North Carolina Press, 1997) is still considered the classic study, and Friedlander showed the continuity from the T-4 program to the wartime mass murder of Jews and other "racial" targets.

Other significant books that have helped broaden and deepen our understanding of Nazi genocide: Timothy Snyder's widely discussed *Bloodlands: Europe Between Hitler and Stalin* (New York: Basic Books, 2010; Snyder regularly contributes erudite essays to the *New York Review of Books*), and two books that vividly demonstrate the value of military history when combined with other concerns: Richard G. Fritz, *Ostkrieg: Hitler's War of Extermination in the East* (Lexington, KY: University Press of Kentucky, 2011) and Antony Beevor, *The Second World War* (New York: Little, Brown and Company, 2012).

More than 3 million Soviet POWs—close to the combined death tolls of the Armenian, Cambodian, and Rwandan genocides—perished in miserable circumstances during the Nazi invasion and occupation of their country. Snyder, Fritz, Beevor, and others have helped tell their story, but we await an adequate English-language treatment of this terrible crime. Among the attempts to analyze Nazism within longer lineages of German and European imperialism, these are at the fore: Wendy Lower, *Nazi Empire-Building and the Holocaust in Ukraine* (Chapel Hill, NC: University of North Carolina Press, 2005); Volker Langbehn and Mohammad Salama, editors, *German Colonialism: Race, the Holocaust, and Postwar Germany* (New York: Columbia University Press, 2011); and Mark Mazower's *Hitler's Empire: How the Nazis Ruled Europe* (New York: Penguin, 2008), which is written with a sharp eye for memorable details and anecdotes and is based on extensive research in multiple languages. *Empire, Colony, Genocide: Conquest, Occupation, and Subaltern Resistance in World History* (New York: Berghahn, 2008), edited by A. Dirk Moses, extends far beyond Nazi imperialism and includes two particularly strong chapters on Nazism's relation to pre-1933 imperialism. Harald Welzer, a German social psychologist, and Sönke Neitzel recently published a fascinating, sharply researched and contextualized book: *Soldaten: On Fighting, Killing, and Dying: The Secret WWII Transcripts of German POWs* (New York: Knopf, 2012). This book is essential for anyone seeking to understand the relationship between warfare and genocidal violence.

Gilbert Achcar's *The Arabs and the Holocaust: The Arab-Israeli War of Narratives* (New York: Henry Holt and Company, 2009) is, to date, the best overview of the Holocaust's connection to Arab-speaking lands. Achcar also provides thought-provoking insights into the postwar uses and misuses of the Holocaust in Israel as well as in Arab societies, and the book confronts the nettlesome issue of Holocaust denial, which is more prominent today in the Middle East than in Western Europe or the United States, albeit with somewhat different origins and content. His key arguments are condensed for a 2011 article in the *Journal of Palestine Studies* (41, no. 1, Autumn 2011). Robert Satloff's *Among the Righteous: Lost Stories from the Holocaust's Long Reach into Arab Lands* (New York: PublicAffairs, 2006) is an engagingly written work that, while lacking Achcar's academic rigor, conveys the complexities of these issues and highlights some striking examples of Arab and Muslim solidarity with the beleaguered Jews. (Satloff's chapter on this topic, Chapter 5, can be found easily at http://www.ushmm.org or by searching for "Satloff among the Arabs chapter 5"). For more on the place of the Holocaust in Israeli life and politics, I highly recommend these three books: Tom Segev's *The Seventh Million: The Israelis and the Holocaust* (published in Hebrew in 1991 and English in 1993; most recent edition is Picador's 2000 paperback); Idith Zertal, *Israel's Holocaust and the Politics of Nationhood* (Cambridge, UK: Cambridge University Press, 2005); and Avraham Burg, *The Holocaust Is Over, We Must Rise from Its Ashes* (New York: Palgrave Macmillan, 2008). Among many other important arguments that Segev advanced (in *Seventh Million* and elsewhere), he criticized the misuse within Israel of the "heritage of the Holocaust" to justify or deflect attention from human rights abuses. Zertal and Burg also pursue these themes, which Segev was among the first to raise in a scholarly context.

Dalia Ofer and Lenore J. Weitzman helped open a new field of inquiry with their coedited *Women in the Holocaust* (New Haven, CT: Yale University Press, 1998). Wendy Lower's *Hitler's Furies: German Women in the Nazi Killing Fields* (Boston: Houghton Mifflin Harcourt, 2013) received well-deserved attention far beyond the academic world, and after reading this book it is impossible to uphold any simplistic views of gender roles and women's potential for violence. See also *Experience and Expression: Women, the Nazis, and the Holocaust* (Detroit: Wayne State University Press, 2003), edited by Elizabeth R. Baer and Myrna Goldenberg, who has written or edited many other path-breaking articles and books. Sociologist Nechama Tec has also helped to make gender more central to Holocaust research; her *Courage and Resilience: Women, Men, and the Holocaust* (New Haven, CT: Yale University Press, 2003) looks at gender relations in German-occupied lands in Eastern Europe. Tec is also a pioneer in the study of Jewish resistance; she wrote, for example, the best-researched study of the Bielski Brothers: *Defiance* (New York: Oxford University Press, 2008). For several decades the study of anti-Nazi resistance focused too exclusively on the July 1944 plot to assassinate Hitler; less visible forms of resistance were neglected. At present, the books I would recommend most heartily were written many years ago, and never reached large audiences: Henri Michel, *The Shadow War: European Resistance, 1939–1945* (New York: Harper & Row, 1972) and Werner Rings, *Life with the Enemy: Collaboration and Resistance in Hitler's Europe, 1939–1945* (New York: Doubleday, 1982). More recently, Bob Moore has written or edited two valuable works: *Resistance in Western Europe* (Oxford: Berg, 2000), which he edited, and his own monograph, *Survivors: Jewish Self-Help and Rescue in Nazi-Occupied Western Europe* (New York: Oxford University Press, 2010). For more on this topic and on the relevant literature, see my own essay: John Cox, "Jewish Resistance Against Nazism," in *The Routledge History of the Holocaust*, edited by Jonathan C. Friedman (New York: Routledge, 2011).

For studies of Jewish life under Hitler in all its travails as well as resilience: Saul Friedländer has long been in the front ranks of Holocaust historians, and his life's work is summed up in these two magnificent books: *Nazi Germany and the Jews: The Years of Persecution 1933–1939* (New York: Harper, 1998) and *Nazi Germany and the Jews: The Years of Extermination: Nazi Germany and the Jews, 1939–1945* (New York: Harper, 2008). Harper has also condensed the two massive books into one volume. Marion Kaplan's

From Dignity to Despair: Jewish Life in Nazi Germany (New York: Oxford University Press, 1998) will retain its influence for many years and is full of illuminating as well as heartbreaking stories that she uncovered through extensive use of diaries, letters, and other such primary sources. Victor Klemperer's two volumes of diaries, *I Shall Bear Witness*, are a fascinating and indispensable resource for their descriptions and reflections on living as a Jew while Germany descended into madness.

Among the most common questions from students and others: "What did the German people know; how could they allow this to happen?" Ian Kershaw pioneered the study of German public opinion with his 1983 *Popular Opinion and Political Dissent in the Third Reich* (2nd edition published by New York: Oxford University Press, 2002). Kershaw has also written the strongest biography of Adolf Hitler, convincingly placing the dictator within his historical context (*Hitler*, two volumes, New York: Norton, 1998 and 2000). We are beginning to venture into territory, though, that could easily consume another large section: literature related less to the Holocaust than to life in Nazi Germany. Suffice it to say that Ian Kershaw's *The Nazi Dictatorship: Problems and Perspectives of Interpretation* (New York: Bloomsbury, 2000) is an excellent summary and critique of the principal historical questions, and it is perceptive and wise in its appraisals. A newer edition does not appear to be forthcoming, but any of Kershaw's work can be read with great profit. Robert Gellately has written two books that delved into the complexities of the willingness to adapt and to assist Nazi repression: *The Gestapo and German Society: Enforcing Racial Policy 1933–1945* (New York: Oxford University Press, 1992) and *Backing Hitler: Consent and Coercion in Nazi Germany* (New York: Oxford University Press, 2001). Eric Johnson and Karl-Heinz Reuband's *What We Knew: Terror, Mass Murder, and Everyday Life in Nazi Germany* (New York: Basic Books, 2006) is another important work, making effective use of testimonies and interviews. Alon Confino, whose work has for many years helped open new paths of inquiry, published an exceptionally thought-provoking book in 2014: *A World without Jews: The Nazi Imagination from Persecution to Genocide* (New Haven, CT: Yale University Press). This book will surely challenge us to think more deeply about the strength of religious nostrums and sensibilities, for better or worse (in this case, far worse), in the popular imagination in modern societies.

My editor will justly rebel at my use of "innumerable," a term that should only rarely be employed; yet the numbers of Holocaust-themed novels and memoirs published (often by small or vanity presses) can barely be counted. As in other sections of this bibliography, many worthy books cannot be mentioned, but these are among the enduring classics: Primo Levi's *Survival in Auschwitz* (New York: Touchstone, 1995) could never be adequately praised in a few sentences. Levi was arrested for his involvement in a small partisan group in German-occupied northern Italy; he was sent to Auschwitz, where he endured the camp's final twelve months. With profound philosophical insight and great eloquence, *Survival in Auschwitz* dissects the camp experience and ponders its implications for humanity. The book's original (Italian) title, *Se questo è un uomo* (*If This Is a Man*) conveys its themes far better than the English title foisted upon him by his publisher. Levi's final collection of essays, *The Drowned and the Saved* (New York: Vintage, 1989), contains an essay that, like much of his work, resists comparison to other literature and is full of moral and philosophical challenges to its readers: "The Gray Zone." Elie Wiesel's *Night* was written from a much different perspective: While Levi was urban, secular, and ten years older, Wiesel wrote from his vantage point as a youngster from a religious family for whom his experience in Auschwitz raised deep theological questions; he also writes movingly of his attitudes toward his father's pitiable suffering (they endured the camp together, and his father died on the "death march" back into Germany). *Night* has been and will continue to be published in various editions; an inexpensive trilogy (including two other important books by Wiesel: *Dawn* and *Day*) was published in 2008

(New York: Hill and Wang). Ruth Kluger wrote a much different sort of memoir, in which she advances numerous strong observations about gender, survival, the complexities of personal relationships under such extreme duress, and much else: *Still Alive: A Holocaust Girlhood Remembered* (New York: The Feminist Press, 2003).

Władysław Szpilman survived the long German occupation of Warsaw and recorded his ordeal in a text of elegance and clarity suffused with a pervasive sense of melancholy and loss: *The Pianist: The Extraordinary True Story of One Man's Survival in Warsaw, 1939–1945* (New York: Picador, 2000). Published in Polish in 1946 under a much different title (*Death of a City*) and in English and other languages in the late 1990s and beyond. Szpilman's book attracted wider attention after the 2002 Roman Polanski film, *The Pianist*. On its own merits, it belongs in the front ranks of Holocaust literature. Szpilman witnessed and survived two uprisings and the destruction first of the Jewish Ghetto and then of nearly the entire city; he poignantly renders to the story of daily life in such degrading circumstances. The book would be a classic merely for its brief, heartbreaking portrait of schoolteacher and orphanage director Janusz Korczak leading his 200 children to the deportation site, whence they were transported to their deaths at Treblinka. In 2013, historian Otto Dov Kulka published a book he had tried to avoid for six decades: *Landscapes of the Metropolis of Death: Reflections on Memory and Imagination* (Cambridge, MA: The Belknap Press of Harvard University Press). It has received high acclaim, drawing comparisons to Levi's work, astonishing and almost heretical as that sounds. "Primo Levi's testimony, it is often said, is that of a chemist: clear, cool, precise, distant," wrote one reviewer. "So with Kulka's work: this is the product of a master historian—ironic, probing, present in the past, able to connect the particular with the cosmic."[7]

The US Holocaust Memorial Museum offers the best online bibliography on the Holocaust: http://www.ushmm.org/research/library/bibliography/.

See also "A Teacher's Guide to the Holocaust," a wonderful resource for many purposes: http://fcit.usf.edu/holocaust/default.htm.

CAMBODIA

Before the Khmer Rouge was driven from power, journalistic accounts and serious academic studies brought their crimes to worldwide attention. Much of the early work has stood the test of time, in particular the research of Ben Kiernan, the leading expert on this period and the founder of Yale's Cambodian Genocide Project and Genocide Studies Program. Originally published in 1985, *The Pol Pot Regime: Race, Power, and Genocide in Cambodia Under the Khmer Rouge, 1975–79* (New Haven, CT: Yale University Press, 2008) is Kiernan's most comprehensive, exhaustively detailed account. Other major works by Kiernan include *How Pol Pot Came to Power: Colonialism, Nationalism, and Communism in Cambodia, 1930–1975* (New Haven, CT: Yale University Press, 2004) and a book with a somewhat different focus, *Genocide and Resistance in Southeast Asia* (Piscataway, NJ: Transaction Publishers, 2007). Elizabeth Becker's *When the War Was Over: Cambodia and the Khmer Rouge Revolution* (New York: PublicAffairs, 1998) is a more compact and approachable book, perhaps the best concise summary of the Khmer Rouge's reign of terror.

In the 1970s David Chandler, an expert on the region for the US foreign service earlier in his career, became a well-known expert on earlier periods of Cambodian history. (He also served as Kiernan's dissertation advisor.) He subsequently wrote a biography of Pol Pot that uncovered many clues to the dictator's virulent racism and psychopathic personality: *Brother Number One: A Political Biography of Pol Pot* (Boulder, CO: Westview

---

[7]Thomas W. Laqueur, "*Landscapes of the Metropolis of Death* by Otto Dov Kulka—review," *The Guardian*, January 25, 2013.

Press, 1992). Chandler also produced the harrowing but revealing *Voices from S-21: Terror and History in Pol Pot's Secret Prison* (Berkeley, CA: University of California Press, 2000). With his former student Kiernan and Chantou Boua, Chandler coedited a startling collection of primary documents that sheds light on the twisted, often inconsistent philosophy and goals of the party: *Pol Pot Plans the Future: Confidential Leadership Documents from Democratic Kampuchea, 1976–1977* (New Haven, CT: Yale University Southeast Asia Studies, 1988). Soon after the ousting of the regime, Kiernan and Boua published an edited collection, *Peasants and Politics in Kampuchea, 1942–1981* (London: Zed Press, 1982), and Boua has worked and written on Cambodian women during and since the genocide. Anthropologist Alexander Laban Hinton has made several key contributions to Cambodian and genocide studies. His most influential book on this genocide is *Why Did They Kill? Cambodia in the Shadow of Genocide* (Berkeley, CA: University of California Press, 2004), a book of wide relevance for its uncovering of the cultural and psychological processes that foment mass violence.

Genocidal violence invariably leaves numerous difficult social, political, and legal legacies. Craig Etcheson's *After the Killing Fields: Lessons from the Cambodian Genocide* (Westport, CT: Praeger, 2005) confronts some of those that plague Cambodia. Both Tom Fawthrop and Helen Jarvis have intimate knowledge of modern Cambodian history, and their *Getting Away With Genocide: Cambodia's Long Struggle Against the Khmer Rouge* (London: Pluto Press, 2004) details the Pol Pot years and the partially successful efforts since 1979 to achieve some modicum of legal justice. (Greater progress has been made since the book's publication.) *Genocide in Cambodia and Rwanda: New Perspectives* (Piscataway, NJ: Transaction Publishers, 2005), edited by Susan E. Cook, is an often thought-provoking collection of essays by scholars from Yale and elsewhere. Most chapters confront one or another of these genocides, while some offer comparative insights.

Born in 1970 in Phnom Penh, Loung Ung wrote a justly popular memoir that is engaging yet full of disturbing, harrowing details: *First They Killed My Father: A Daughter of Cambodia Remembers* (New York: Harper, 2000). Her memoir is frequently assigned to college classes, and the author is an energetic human rights advocate. Another powerful memoir is *Haing Ngor: A Cambodian Odyssey*, later amended and republished as *Survival in the Killing Fields* by Haing S. Ngor, a survivor and untrained actor who starred in the movie *The Killing Fields* (New York: Basic Books, 2003; epilogue by Roger Warner. Originally published in 1988 by Macmillan Publishers of London). A meditation on cultural distance as well as on personal loss, Kim Echlin's *The Disappeared* is a compact and emotionally engaging novel that deserves the acclaim it has received (New York: Grove Press/ Black Cat, 2009).

RWANDA

Although the most recent of these four cases, Rwanda has received considerable attention in English-language publications—more than other genocides, with the exception of the Holocaust. Unlike the post–World War II era, little time elapsed before the first works appeared, foremost among them Gérard Prunier's *The Rwanda Crisis: History of a Genocide* (New York: Columbia University Press, 1997) and Allison des Forges's massive, exhaustively researched *Leave None to Tell the Story: Genocide in Rwanda* (New York: Human Rights Watch, 1999). Less than a year after the genocide's inception, the human rights organization African Rights had published the first version of *Rwanda: Death, Despair and Defiance* (London: African Rights, 1995), compiling eyewitness testimonies and delving into great deal from each region. Another early work is journalist Philip Gourevitch's gripping *We Wish to Inform You That Tomorrow We Will Be Killed with Our Families* (New York: Farrar, Straus and Giroux, 1998). Lacking Prunier and des Forges's depth of knowledge, Gourevitch's appraisal of Kagame and the RPF is far too rosy; yet the book contains many strong personal anecdotes and some key insights, and it is useful in undergraduate courses.

The best of the books on this genocide have also made profound contributions to more universal questions. Scott Straus's *The Order of Genocide: Race, Power, and War in Rwanda* (Cornell, NY: Cornell University Press, 2008) advances a forceful argument about the linkages between war, security, and genocide, and Straus has emerged as one of the world's leading experts on this frightful episode. Linda Melvern's *Conspiracy to Murder: The Rwandan Genocide*, updated in 2006 (New York: Verso) is another important and influential text. Any adequate study of Rwanda must concern itself with the invention and evolution of ethnic identities in that country. Mahmood Mamdani's *When Victims Become Killers: Colonialism, Nativism, and the Genocide in Rwanda* (Princeton, NJ: Princeton University Press, 2002) helped pave the way with its dissection of the "Hamitic Hypothesis" and the malignant, lingering influence of European racial obsessions.

Rwanda raised anew the problem of worldwide indifference and incompetence in the face of terrible slaughter. Roméo Dallaire, the Canadian general who fought a lonely battle to rattle the conscience of the world's powers, distilled his experiences into the riveting *Shake Hands with the Devil: The Failure of Humanity in Rwanda* (Toronto: Vintage Canada, 2003). In addition to his justified condemnation of American and NATO inaction and interference, Dallaire's book paints indelible portraits of some of the genocide's architects, such as Théoneste Bagosora. Samantha Power's *A Problem from Hell* (listed earlier, under "Genocide, War Crimes, and Crimes Against Humanity") devotes a large section to the unhelpful, often obstructionist role of the Clinton Administration. Power wrote an article on this theme for *The Atlantic*, which is readily available online: "Bystanders to Genocide" (September 2001). Linda Melvern's *A People Betrayed: The Role of the West in Rwanda's Genocide* (New York: Zed Books, 2000) is a devastating book-length treatment of these abysmal moral and political failures. Nigel Eltringham's *Accounting for Horror: Post-Genocide Debates in Rwanda* (London: Pluto Press, 2004) sums up very well the genocide's psychological and political legacies, which have evolved further—and in some cases ominously—since its publication. See also Elizabeth Neuffer, *The Key to My Neighbor's House: Seeking Justice in Bosnia and Rwanda* (New York: Picador, 2001).

The Yugoslav wars were still raging as Rwanda descended into genocide between April and July 1994. These two cases attracted greater legal and scholarly attention to sexual violence and the systematic use of rape. *The Men Who Killed Me: Rwandan Survivors of Sexual Violence* (Vancouver: Douglas & McIntyre, 2009), edited by Anne-Marie De Brouwer and Sandra Ka Hon Chu, collects several survivor testimonies that the book ably contextualizes. See also Human Rights Watch, "Shattered Lives: Sexual Violence During the Rwandan Genocide and Its Aftermath," initially published as a short paperback in 1996 and still easily accessible (the full text) online; Catrien Bijleveld, Aafke Morssinkhof, and Alette Smeulers, "Counting the Countless: Rape Victimization During the Rwandan Genocide," *International Criminal Justice Review* 19, no. 2 (June 2009); and an extensive 2004 report by Amnesty International, "'Marked for Death': Rape Survivors Living with HIV/AIDS in Rwanda." (See the footnotes to Chapter 4 for URLs; these articles can be quickly found through an Internet search.)

With enormous humanity and sensitivity, French journalist Jean Hatzfeld has written two masterful explorations of the mysteries of perpetrator behavior as well as survival and resilience: *Machete Season: The Killers in Rwanda Speak* (New York: Picador, 2006; originally published in French and English in 2003) and *Life Laid Bare: The Survivors in Rwanda Speak* (New York: Other Press, 2007). A product of sophisticated research and extensive reflection, Lee Ann Fujii's *Killing Neighbors: Webs of Violence in Rwanda* (Ithaca, NY: Cornell University Press, 2009) deepens our ability to comprehend this genocide by helping uncover long-standing social and community dynamics. As their titles or subtitles indicate, the following three books tackle specific factors that enabled or, in the last case, resulted from the genocide: Peter Uvin, *Aiding Violence: The Development Enterprise in Rwanda* (West Hartford, CT: Kumarian Press, 1998); Daniela Kroslak, *The Role of France in the Rwandan Genocide* (London: Hurst Publishers, 2007); and Sarah Kenyon Lischer, *Dangerous Sanctuaries: Refugee Camps, Civil War, and the Dilemmas of Humanitarian Aid* (Ithaca, NY: Cornell University Press, 2005).

Since 1994 this region—primarily Rwanda's huge neighbor, Congo—has continued to suffer some of the most extensive, deadly violence seen anywhere in the world since World War II. There are two excellent books on this issue, by authors whose names have already been introduced: René Lemarchand's *The Dynamics of Violence in Central Africa* (Philadelphia: University of Pennsylvania Press, 2009) and Gérard Prunier's *Africa's World War: Congo, the Rwandan Genocide, and the Making of a Continental Catastrophe* (New York: Oxford University Press, 2011). Bill Berkeley's *The Graves Are Not Yet Full: Race, Tribe and Power in the Heart of Africa* (New York: Basic Books, 2001) looks at conflict in West Africa as well. He wrote this book with verve and accessibility, and individual chapters stand on their own as memorable vignettes; taken together, *The Graves Are Not Yet Full* is a sobering assessment of Western neglect and support for corrupt despots, tempered by a harsh critique of certain African political and military figures.

A handful of memoirs have received critical acclaim and help lead to a deeper understanding of the terrible events of 1994, their origins, and their aftermath—although, to date, there is room on the bookshelves for many more. (For better or worse, most of the memoirs available in English have been published by Christian publishers and are explicitly faith-oriented.) Louise Mushiwabo's *Rwanda Means the Universe: A Native's Memoir of Blood and Bloodlines* (with Jack Kramer; New York: St. Martin's, 2006) weaves personal experiences (much of her family was killed) with sharp historical insights. Tracy Kidder's *Strength in What Remains* (New York: Random House, 2010) straddles various literary genres; it is the beautifully wrought story of a young man, Deo, who survives the bloodshed in his homeland of Burundi as well as Rwanda; eventually finds refuge in New York; and ultimately returns to his Burundian village to build and operate a medical clinic. I can attest to this book's value in the classroom. The story that Kidder relates in his wonderful *Mountains Beyond Mountains: The Quest of Dr. Paul Farmer, a Man Who Would Cure the World* (New York: Random House, 2003) intersects in some ways with Deo's tale. Also highly recommended is a collection coedited by Samuel Totten and Rafiki Ubaldo, *We Cannot Forget: Interviews with Survivors of the 1994 Genocide* (Rutgers, NJ: Rutgers University Press, 2011).

SUGGESTED FILMS

Novels, memorials, music, and other artistic creations have all helped illuminate the many dark questions arising from genocides and other atrocities, their human consequences, and their many complex legacies.[8] This final section concentrates on the cinema, where as well as in most other genres of art the Holocaust has predominated. I have only listed a small, representative sampling of some of the best films for each. *Film and Genocide*, edited by Kristi M. Wilson and Tomás F. Crowder-Taraborrelli (Madison, WI: University of Wisconsin Press, 2012) includes a helpful if not comprehensive list; Adam Jones has posted his own filmography as an accompaniment to his *Genocide* text at http://www.genocidetext.net/gaci_filmography.html. Wikipedia will continue to provoke howls of

---

[8]The University of Minnesota's Genocide Studies Center maintains an excellent collection of relevant artwork: http://chgs.umn.edu/.

protest from many professors, but at the moment it contains the best lists of genocide-themed films that can be quickly accessed. Simply search within Wikipedia for "film" or "popular culture" in addition to "Rwanda," "Cambodia," and so on. There are few narrative or documentary films related specifically to the Armenian genocide, and thus the list that immediately follows is much shorter than I would like; the tragedies in Cambodia and Rwanda have each inspired at least 100 narrative and documentary films that have reached audiences in much of the world; while several hundred movies related to the Holocaust and Nazi Germany have been produced since the 1940s, the best of them originating in the United States, Germany, and France. Annette Insdorf and Lawrence Baron, among others, have written excellent books about Holocaust-related film.[9]

Ottoman Genocide

Ararat. Directed by Atom Egoyan, France-Canada, 2002. Challenging, intelligent exploration of the genocide's complex emotional and psychological effects on the survivors and descendants. Highly recommended, although not the easiest or most accessible film for a wide audience.

The Armenian Genocide. Directed by Andrew Goldberg, United States, 2006. This documentary was broadcast on PBS. In the space of one hour, it effectively makes the case for greater recognition of the tragedy and for an end to acquiescence in the Turkish government's denial. Interview subjects include Peter Balakian, author of *The Burning Tigris.*

Screamers. Directed by Carla Garapedian, United States, 2006. Featuring commentary by genocide experts Samantha Power, Taner Akçam, and Hrant Dink, the Turkish journalist who was assassinated by ultra-nationalists (see Chapter 1). A well-made, compelling documentary that draws connections to other genocides.

The Holocaust

Defiance. Directed by Edward Zwick, United States, 2008. Pleasantly surprising for a big-budget Hollywood movie, *Defiance* is nuanced as well as compelling; it relates the story of the Bielski Brothers, who organized a rescue and resistance operation in Poland.

Judgment at Nuremberg. Directed by Stanley Kramer, United States, 1961. Interesting in retrospect for what it *doesn't* explicitly confront (that is, the targeting of Jews, which had not yet emerged from a general public knowledge of Nazi crimes). The film made a strong impact at the time and has aged well in most regards. Certain story lines, especially those featuring Judy Garland's and Montgomery's Clift's characters, retain their poignancy and incisiveness.

Korczak. Directed by Andrezj Wajda, Poland, 1990. Wajda has been among the world's finest filmmakers since his startling entrance with a World War II trilogy in the 1950s. He also produced a rare but starkly moving, experimental cinematic treatment of the experiences of the talented Polish writer Tadeusz Borowski, who survived Auschwitz but committed suicide six years later (*Landscape After Battle*, Poland, 1970); and a grimly effective depiction of the Soviet massacre of Polish officers, *Katyn* (Poland, 2007).

Night and Fog. Directed by Alain Resnais, France, 1955. Haunting, philosophical exploration of Nazi crimes. Holocaust survivor and poetic Jean Cayrol provided the narration, and the score is by celebrated Austrian-Jewish composer Hanns Eisler. See the excellent article on this film (and on several new books about it) by Stuart Lieberman in the Winter 2012 *Cineaste*, a quarterly magazine on politics, film, and history.

---

[9]Annette Insdorf, *Indelible Shadows: Film and the Holocaust* (New York: Cambridge University Press, 2002); Lawrence Baron, *Projecting the Holocaust into the Present: The Changing Focus of Contemporary Holocaust Cinema* (New York: Rowman & Littlefield, 2005).

The Pianist. Directed by Roman Polanski, France/Germany/Poland/United Kingdom, 2002. Remarkably faithful to its source—the memoir by Władysław Szpilman, survivor of Warsaw—this movie was justly praised (winning several Academy Awards) for its evocation of daily struggles within the Ghetto and, in the film's second half, its harrowing depiction of Szpilman's lonely struggle for survival. The director's own experience—Polanski survived the Krakow Ghetto but lost several close relatives—is evident.

Schindler's List. Directed by Steven Spielberg, United States, 1993. Not above reproach on either aesthetic or historical grounds, yet this will probably remain, for many years, *the* Holocaust film. Told through the story of Oskar Schindler, an unlikely rescuer, the film contains many powerful, indelible scenes.

Shoah. Directed by Claude Lanzmann, France, 1985. An artistic masterpiece, this nine-hour film is composed almost entirely of interviews conducted by the film-maker. Considered at the top of the list of films on the subject.

The Sorrow and the Pity. Directed by Marcel Ophuls, France, 1969. Initially suppressed by the French government, Marcel Ophuls's four-hour-long documentary helped debunk France's postwar mythology of widespread resistance. Ophuls makes clever, often entertaining use of interviews to highlight the wartime realities of conformity and willing, enthusiastic collaboration.

The Specialist. Directed by Eyal Sivan, Israel, 1999. Sivan is a dissident Israeli film-maker and has made several films, sometimes in collaboration with Palestinian artists, which are critical of his country's policies. For this film Sivan remastered videos of the 1961 Adolf Eichmann trial and, inspired by Hannah Arendt's book on the trial (*Eichmann in Jerusalem: A Report on the Banality of Evil*, 1963), he forces the viewer to contemplate the logic and potential of conformism, bureaucracy, and moral cowardice.

Uprising. Directed by Jon Avnet, United States, 2001. A gripping made-for-television movie about the Warsaw Ghetto. More intelligent and well-researched than one would expect.

Unzere Kinder (Our Children). Directed by Nathan Gross, Poland, 1948. Recently uncovered and restored, this Yiddish-language film is the last feature film in that language to be produced in Poland, at least for now. You will not find it on most lists of Holocaust-themed movies, but for teachers and students of the Holocaust this short film, told from the perspective of the children of an orphanage (whose parents were killed in the Holocaust), this is a fascinating, evocative blend of humor (based on traditions that were disappearing), traumatic memory, and the possibility of resilience. Recently uncovered and restored.

Cambodia

The Killing Fields. Directed by Roland Joffé, United Kingdom, 1986. This film received numerous awards and raised awareness of the catastrophe. It also introduced an evocative term (the movie's title), which now is applied to many other crimes against humanity. Through the experiences of journalist Dith Pran and a colleague from the *New York Times*, *The Killing Fields* effectively humanizes the disaster and also provides crucial background information (for example, concerning the American bombing of Cambodia in the early 1970s).

Rice People. Directed by Rithy Panh, Cambodia, 1994. This Khmer-language feature film was first shown at the 1994 Cannes Film Festival. Panh escaped the genocide, which claimed much of his family, and studied film in France. In addition to the two films listed here, he has made others that confront, directly or indirectly, the Khmer Rouge period, including *One Evening After the War* (1998), *The Land of the Wandering Souls* (documentary, 2000), and *The Missing Picture* (2013), a highly original, haunting, and award-winning production.

The Secrets of S-21: Legacy of a Cambodian Prison. Directed by Rithy Panh, Cambodia/ France, 2003. This short documentary provides insight into a question that haunts all genocides: the participation of seemingly ordinary people. Panh brought former inmates together with their jailers, who find ways to deflect responsibility in a fashion reminiscent of the mantra of former Nazi officials, "I was only following orders." For more on Panh's life and work, see Richard Bernstein, "The Insoluble Questions," in *New York Review of Books,* April 3, 2014.

Year Zero: The Silent Death of Cambodia. Directed by David Munro, United Kingdom, 1979. Written and produced by John Pilger, an outstanding, politically engaged Australian and British journalist who later made three additional documentaries about Cambodia during and after the genocide. These are available on his website (http://www. johnpilger .com), where you will find dozens of other documentaries on topics ranging from the human toll of US policy in Iraq; to the plight of Australia's Aborigines; to Indonesia's genocide in East Timor.

Rwanda

Flower in the Gun Barrel. Directed by Gabriel Cowan, United States, 2008. This documentary consists largely of interviews with survivors, with some commentary by experts; it is narrated by Martin Sheen.

Ghosts of Rwanda. Directed by Greg Barker, United States, 2004. Produced for PBS, and the full 110 minutes as well as supplemental materials can be found on its site (http:// www.pbs.org/wgbh/pages/frontline/shows/ghosts/). This documentary contains interview excerpts from Roméo Dallaire and highlights the disgraceful inaction of the world's powers. While the film focuses on the world's abandonment of Rwanda, it sheds light on other elements of the genocide as well. Highly recommended.

Hotel Rwanda. Directed by Terry George, United States, 2004. This film has received well-earned critical praise and found a large audience. *Hotel Rwanda* tells the story of Paul Rusesabagina, played by Don Cheadle, the manager of an upscale Kigali hotel that provided sanctuary to hundreds of desperate refugees, despite constant threats from Interahamwe troops. The film scrutinizes the constructed, flexible (but lethal) nature of the Hutu-Tutsi divide and the scandalous abandonment of Rwanda by the "international community." This intelligent, thought-provoking film leaves you with many strong images and humanizes the genocide through nuanced portrayals of its characters (most characters, that is; the central figure in the film is admirable but less saint-like than Cheadle's character).

Munyurangabo. Directed by Lee Isaac Chung, Rwanda/United States, 2007. The first feature-length film on the genocide in the Rwandan language and produced in that country, it premiered at the 2007 Cannes festival, where it was highly acclaimed. A. O. Scott of *The New York Times* praised its use of neorealism "to illuminate the psychological and emotional landscape of a still-traumatized place."

Shake Hands with the Devil. Directed by Roger Spottiswoode, Canada, 2007. Well-made, captivating feature film based on the book of the same title by Roméo Dallaire. Like the book, the movie offers detailed, astute criticism of the UN's role during the disaster.

Sometimes in April. Directed by Raoul Peck, France/United States, 2005. Starring Idris Elba, who soon became famous for American television roles, Peck's film explores the breakdown (but sometimes the resilience) of family and community ties and other emotionally complex issues. Peck also directed the 2000 film *Lumumba,* which focuses on the Belgian- and American-inspired overthrow of the popular Congolese prime minister in 1961 and suggests continuity from the time of King Leopold II to the era of decolonization.

Others

This book has dealt with a broad range of human rights issues and crimes against humanity as well as the long histories of colonialism, racism, and mass repression and murder. Of the many hundreds if not thousands of films from around the world that are relevant, it would be impossible to suggest a short list. I will, however, conclude with a brief list of films related to the Yugoslav wars of the 1990s, which inspired a large number of outstanding movies that are available to English-speaking audiences.

Before the Rain. Directed by Milčo Mančevski, Macedonia, 1994. A sorrowful film that depicts the descent into meaningless, wasteful hatreds and divisions; beautifully shot and acted, this is an artistic masterpiece.

In the Land of Blood and Honey. Directed by Angelina Jolie. United States, 2011. Jolie surprised many critics with her directing debut, an unsparing look at sexual violence during the Bosnian genocide. Among the film's virtues: it employs the correct languages, rather than asking its actors to speak accented English, a practice that mars *Schindler's List* and is common in the American cinema. For experts and those more intimately familiar with the cultures and peoples of the former Yugoslavia, some inaccuracies will be evident. Jasmila Žbanić's *Grbavica* (Bosnia and Herzegovina, 2006) confronts similar issues—that is, systematic rape—in a more lucid and accurate fashion. Unfortunately, *Grbavica* is difficult to access in the United States.

No Man's Land. Directed by Danis Tanović, Bosnia (coproduced by companies in Belgium, France, Italy, Slovenia, and the United Kingdom), 2001. By showing the common humanity of a Bosniak (Bosnian Muslim) and a Bosnian Serb soldier, who find themselves trapped in a landmine-rigged trench with another soldier, this tense, gripping film unmasks the absurdity and destructiveness of the artificial divisions that destroyed the country of Yugoslavia.

Vukovar (aka *Vukovar: The Way Home*). Directed by Branko Schmidt, Yugoslavia, 1994. Dramatizes the destruction of the Croatian city and the simultaneous destruction of personal relationships. The final scene is devastating.

TIMELINE OF GENOCIDE AND GENOCIDAL CRIMES AGAINST HUMANITY, 1900 TO PRESENT

Location/ Perpetrator	Victims	Dates	Approximate No. of Victims
Congo Free State	Congolese civilians	1885–1908	10 million
German South-West Africa	Herero and Nama	1904–1908	65,000–75,000
Putumayo region, Andes (Peru-Ecuador-Colombia)	Indigenous peoples	ca. 1900–1914	100,000
Ottoman Empire	Armenians, Greeks, Assyrian Christians	1915–1923	1.5 million
Soviet famines	Ukrainians, Kazakhs, others	1930–1933	5–7 million
Soviet political repression, terror, expulsions	"Kulaks," other political groups and perceived enemies; ethnic minorities	ca. 1930–ca. 1950	4–6 million
Dominican Republic	Haitians	1937	12,000–20,000
Turkey (eastern Anatolia)	Kurds of Dersim/Tunceli province	1937–1945	15,000–30,000
Japanese war and occupation in Asia	Chinese, Indochinese, Koreans, Malays, Filipinos, other Asian peoples	1937–1945	10–20 million
Nazi empire	Jews, Russians, Poles, Romanies, others	1939–1945	14–17 million

Location/ Perpetrator	Victims	Dates	Approximate No. of Victims
Croatian Ustaša regime	Serbs, Jews, Romanies	1941–1945	350,000–400,000
French war in Algeria	Algerians	1954–1962	400,000–700,000 civilians
China's "Great Leap Forward"	Peasantry, others	1959–1961	30–45 million
Indonesia	Leftists, other political enemies; ethnic minorities	1965–1966	500,000
US war in Vietnam	South and North Vietnamese	1964–1973	2–2.5 million civilians
Nigeria	Igbos	1966–1969	1–2 million
East Pakistan (Bangladesh)	Hindus, Bengalis	1971	1–3 million
Burundi	Hutus	1972	200,000
Cambodia	Ethnic minorities, political and social groups	1975–1979	1.7–2.2 million
Indonesian occupation of East Timor	East Timorese	1976–1999	150,000–180,000
Soviet war in Afghanistan	Afghan civilians	1979–1989	1.5–2.0 million
Guatemala	Maya Indians	1981–1983	100,000–200,000
Iraqi Kurdistan	Kurds	1987–1989	100,000
Rwanda	Tutsi	1994	500,000–800,000
Bosnia	Bosnian Muslims	1992–1995	50,000
Sudan, Darfur region	Fur, Masalit, other indigenous peoples	2003–	300,000–400,000
Sudan, South Kordofan and Blue Nile regions	Nuba peoples	2011–	Hundreds of thousands forcibly displaced; casualties are extremely difficult to estimate

These figures are based on the latest, most reliable estimates. Genocide scholars and human rights activists often settle upon the highest possible estimates in a misguided effort to maximize public attention and indignation (for example, deaths in the Wars of Yugoslav Succession of the 1990s are often doubled, to 200,000). I have tried my best to avoid this temptation.

Invariably many of these numbers are imprecise, as indicated by the ranges I have offered in most cases. This imprecision is not only because of the unreliability of census figures from many places; in addition, it is often difficult to assign blame or determine why certain people were displaced or killed—civilians in a wartime siege, for example, or victims of political or racial hysteria, which can sweep up people who are not in the targeted groups. Also, as merely one example of the difficulty in determining why some victims are killed: Ukrainians and others perished under Stalin as consequences of both famine and of political repression aimed at their nationality (and therefore there is some overlap between those two entries). In addition, we all have multiple identities, and the perpetrators are often unsure exactly who it is that they are killing (for example: a Nazi killer might wonder, if given to such thoughts, "Are these people I'm killing Jews, Poles, partisans, or maybe all three?").

This timeline was designed to complement the themes and case studies of the book, and therefore it lists examples of genocidal violence that conform to its definition (see Introduction). This is not a comprehensive accounting of politically motivated atrocities or crimes against humanity, which would include these egregious crimes, among many others:

- The Italian invasion and occupation of Libya and Ethiopia and the use of concentration camps in the former and poison gas in the latter in the 1920s and 1930s, during Benito Mussolini's inept but destructive attempt to build an empire.

- The India-Pakistan Partition (1947), during which roughly 1 million people, and probably many more, were killed because of their identity as either Hindus or Muslims. The Partition was also marked by the largest population displacement of all history (15 million displaced), surpassing the population upheavals and transfers at the end of World War II in Europe.

- Wars, military dictatorships, and revolutions and counterinsurgencies killed hundreds of thousands in Central America in the 1980s, and tens of thousands more in Chile, Argentina, and elsewhere in Latin America during the Cold War. Right-wing governments and militaries were primarily responsible.

- The Second Congo War of 1998–2003 was the most devastating conflict anywhere in the world since 1945: more than 5 million people were killed. Subsequent conflict, often genocidal in nature (i.e., targeting a specific group) has taken the lives of at least 1 million more. See Chapter 4, under "Authoritarianism and War Under Kagame," for further discussion.

- A more comprehensive list would also include more instances of the decimation of indigenous peoples, beyond those listed, in Asia, Africa, and the Americas (e.g., the Ache in eastern Paraguay in the 1960s–1970s) through violence, starvation, slave-like labor conditions, disease, forced assimilation, and forms of cultural genocide throughout the last century and up to the present. See Samuel Totten and Robert K. Hitchcock, eds., *Genocide of Indigenous Peoples: A Critical Bibliographic Review* (Piscataway, NJ: Transaction, 2010).

NOTES ON SELECTED ENTRIES

Congo Free State: See the Introduction. This is included because it stretched into the early twentieth century, and its enormity merits its acknowledgment whenever possible. The dates (1885–1908) are for the duration of Leopold II's personal rule; abuses and mass deaths persisted for a few years beyond 1908, when the Belgian government seized direct control. Adam Hochschild has popularized the figure of 10 million, and no one has offered a persuasive alternative. The actual numbers may have been somewhat lower or higher (e.g., Congolese historian Ndaywel e Nziem suggested 13 million, the highest scholarly estimate).

Dersim Kurds: Kurdish people in a province of eastern Anatolia (in eastern Turkey) known as "Dersim" in Kurdish and "Tunceli" in Turkish. Somewhere between 15,000 and 30,000 people were killed by the Turkish government of Mustafa Kemal Atatürk in its drive to consolidate its dominance in the region. This operation had a distinctly genocidal character, as it was aimed against specific ethnic and political groups. Some historians have used the term "ethnocide" in addition to (or rather than) genocide because it was also a campaign of forced assimilation.

Nazi war and genocide: These figures include victims of Nazi allies and accomplices. The Croatian and Romanian regimes killed hundreds of thousands of Jews, and both murdered large numbers of Roma and Sinti.

Croatian Ustaša regime: The fascist Ustaša party controlled large parts of Bosnia as well as all of Croatia. It is listed separately because of its genocidal campaign against Serbs, at least 300,000 of whom were murdered. Roughly 50,000 Serbs perished in the infamous Jasenovac camp complex.

Soviet Union, China: See the Introduction.

The Dominican Republic's genocide of Haitians: Known as "El Corte" (the cutting) or the "Parsley Massacre," this took place in October 1937. Haiti occupies the western side of the island of Hispaniola, and many Haitians lived across the eastern border in the neighboring Dominican Republic. Dominican dictator Rafael Trujillo orchestrated the killings of the darker-skinned Haitians, whom he demonized as racially inferior, as "cattle thieves," and so on.

Japanese atrocities in Asia: For Japan's genocidal mass killing in China, the largest of the Japanese Empire's crimes, estimates of casualties vary widely. Before its larger-scale 1937 invasion of China and subsequent aggressions against other Asian nations, Japan had invaded Manchuria in 1931 and employed the methods of indiscriminate killing, mass rape, and other atrocities that were later visited upon many other peoples. More in the Introduction.

Indonesia: The military dictatorship, which took power at this time, also targeted ethnic minorities (e.g., Chinese), but the violence was aimed primarily at Communist Party members or suspected members.

US-Vietnam War: South Vietnamese and North Vietnamese troops and their allies (i.e., for South Vietnam: South Korean regular forces; for North Vietnam: the NLF or

"Viet Cong" guerillas) also committed atrocities, but not nearly to the extent or with the technology and firepower of US forces. More in the Introduction.

Nigeria: A military government took power in 1966 and waged a harsh war to suppress the attempted secession of the "Republic of Biafra" in a southern region populated by ethnic minorities, primarily the Igbo (sometimes spelled "Ibo") people.

Guatemala: The small Central American nation was wracked by civil war and harsh repression from 1962 to 1996; the worst years of targeted genocidal violence were 1981–1983 (see the Introduction), which is why that period is indicated.

Bosnia: Croats and Serbs also suffered ethnic cleansing and other atrocities during the Yugoslav wars, which killed roughly 100,000 people. Half those victims were Bosnian Muslims, aka Bosniaks, who were singled out for genocidal destruction by Serbian and Bosnian-Serb forces and, in relation to the other nationalities, suffered a much higher proportion of civilian casualties. See the Introduction. In 1998–1999, the Milošević government conducted another wave of ethnic cleansings and massacres against the Muslim peoples (ethnic Albanians) of Serbia's Kosovo region, which subsequently gained independence.

Sudan: In southern Sudan (as of July 2011, the independent "Republic of South Sudan"), civil war accompanied by severe government violence killed as many as 2 million people between 1983 and 2005. The Sudanese government of Omar al-Bashir and the National Islamic Front/National Congress Party, which took power in 1989, used many of the same tactics that would later attract worldwide attention in Darfur.

Darfur: As this book goes to press, the violence in Darfur has not ended despite ceasefires and peace treaties in 2010 and 2011. The first two years of the conflict, which began in February 2003, marked the most intense period of government-sponsored crimes against humanity. Since 2011, the Nuba people—who endured ethnic cleansing and other forms of genocidal violence under the same regime between 1992 and the early 2000's—have again been targeted. The government has also expelled tens of thousands of Dinka Ngok from the Abyei region since seizing that area in May 2011. See the Spring 2014 special issue of *Genocide Studies International*.

CREDITS

INTRODUCTION

Image Credits

p. 3: picture-alliance/dpa/AP Images; p. 5: UN Photo/MB; p. 10: Album/quintlox/Album/Superstock; p. 13: United States Library of Congress's Prints and Photographs division under the digital ID cph.3b45499; p. 19: Monument à Léopold II, Wikimedia; p. 21: Universal Images Group/Universal Images Group/Superstock; p. 25: Library of Congress Prints and Photographs Division, LC-DIG-ppmsca-28668; p. 27: © Trocaire, Wikimedia Commons; p. 31: Marka/Marka/Superstock.

CHAPTER 1

Image Credits

p. 49: Abdulhamid celebrates the Turkish victory in 1897, Wikimedia; p. 51: Ismail Enver, Wikimedia; p. 54: © Armenian National Institute, Inc., courtesy of Sybil Stevens (daughter of Armin T. Wegner). Wegner Collection, Deutches Literaturarchiv, Marbach & United States Holocaust Memorial Museum; p. 57: © Armenian National Institute, Inc., courtesy of Sybil Stevens (daughter of Armin T. Wegner). Wegner Collection, Deutches Literaturarchiv, Marbach & United States Holocaust Memorial Museum; p. 59: The defense of Van, Wikimedia; p. 62: New-York tribune., June 04, 1921, Wikimedia; p. 64: © fulyaatalay/iStock.

Text Credits

p. 67: UK National Archives; p. 68: UK National Archives; p. 70: http://www.armenianhouse.org.

CHAPTER 2

Image Credits

p. 81: Le Peril Juif; p. 86: bpk, Berlin/Bildarchiv Preußischer Kulturbesitz/Heinrich Hoffmann/Art Resource, NY; p. 89: © United States Holocaust Memorial Museum, Washington, DC; p. 96: United States Holocaust Memorial Museum, courtesy of Marion Davy; p. 99: Frankreich, Paris.- Propaganda-Ausstellung gegen die Juden in Frankreich ("Le juif et la France"), September 1941. Bild 146-1975-041-07; p. 102: Saxon Memorial Foundation, © Gedenkstätte Ehrenhain Zeithain; p. 107: Photo Archives/United States Holocaust Memorial Museum; p. 111: © Berliner Verlag/Archiv/dpa/Corbis.

Text Credits

p. 113: Yad Vashem; p. 115: Document on the Holocaust: Selected Sources on the Destruction of the Jews of Germany and Austria, Poland, and the Soviet Union, Yitzhak Arad, Israel Gutman, Abraham Margaliot (eds.), published by Yad Vashem and the University of Nebraska Press, 1999, p. 459; p. 117: http://www.nizkor.org/hweb/people/h/himmler-heinrich/posen/oct-04-43/

ausrottung-transl-nizkor.html; p. 118: Oxford University Press gratefully acknowledges the USC Shoah Foundation for allowing us to use transcripts of the following testimonies: [Julia Lentini]. For more information: http://sfi.usc.edu/.

CHAPTER 3

Image Credits

p. 123: Marco Brivio/age fotostock/Super-stock; p. 128: © Bettmann/CORBIS; p. 130: Online communism photo collection Photo #AA344; p. 140: Marco Brivio/age fotostock/Superstock; p. 143: ASSOCIATED PRESS.

Text Credits

p. 145: "The Early Phases of Liberation in Northwestern Cambodia: Conversations with Peang Sophi" By David Chandler (pioneering Cambodia expert, who collected and trans-lated these song lyrics). Published by the Centre of Southeast Asian Studies, Monash University (Melbourne), 1977. Number 10 in the Centre's "Working Papers"; p. 146: The Confession of Hu Nim. The Documentation Center of Cambodia, aka DC-Cam http://www.d.dccam.org/Archives/Documents/Confessions/Confessions_Hu_Nim.htm; p. 148: Theresa de Langis, Transcript of Interview with Prak Sinan on April 6, 2012, Cambodian Women's Oral History

Project, Phnom Penh, Cambodia. http://cambodianwomensoralhistory.com.

CHAPTER 4

Image Credits

p. 155: www.genocidearchiverwanda.org; p. 159: Andrews Air Force Base, Maryland, USA - 1980, Wikimedia; p. 161: http://www.rwandafile.com/Kangura/k56c1.html; p. 175: Adam Jones. Flickr.com; p. 170: ASSOCIATED PRESS; p. 177: ASSOCIATED PRESS; p. 182: ASSOCIATED PRESS.

Text Credits

p. 183: Transcript from University of Toronto Law; p. 185: https://lib.stanford.edu/preventing-genocide/transcript-interview-romeo-dallaire; p. 187: Survivors Fund (SURF).

CONCLUSION

Image Credits

p. 200: Donald R. Ornitz - USHMM, courtesy of National Archives and Records Administration, College Park; p. 206: Fine Art Images/Fine Art Images/Superstock; p. 209: Everett Collection/Everett Collection/Superstock; p. 213: WWI poster – "Kossovo Day" 28 June 1916. Solidarity with the Serb allies, Wikipedia.

INDEX

Note: page numbers in italics refer to figures.

Printed in the USA/Agawam, MA
February 9, 2023

805534.195